Scientific Collaboration on the Internet

Acting with Technology
Bonnie Nardi, Victor Kaptelinin, and Kirsten Foot, editors

Scientific Collaboration on the Internet

edited by Gary M. Olson, Ann Zimmerman, and Nathan Bos

The MIT Press
Cambridge, Massachusetts
London, England

For information about special quantity discounts, please e-mail ⟨special_sales@mitpress.mit.edu⟩

This book was set in Stone Serif and Stone Sans on 3B2 by Asco Typesetters, Hong Kong.
Printed on recycled paper and bound in the United States of America.

Library of Congress Cataloging-in-Publication Data

Scientific collaboration on the Internet / edited by Gary M. Olson, Ann Zimmerman, and Nathan Bos ; foreword by William A. Wulf.
    p.   cm. — (Acting with technology)
Includes bibliographical references and index.
ISBN 978-0-262-15120-7 (hardcover : alk. paper)
1. Science—Computer network resources. 2. Internet. I. Olson, Gary M. II. Zimmerman, Ann, 1962– III. Bos, Nathan.
Q182.7.S36   2008
507.2—dc22   2008007300

10 9 8 7 6 5 4 3 2 1

Contents

Foreword

In 1988, I was offered the extraordinary opportunity to serve as an assistant director of the National Science Foundation (NSF), and be in charge of the Directorate of Computer and Information Science and Engineering (CISE). At the time, CISE was responsible for funding computer science and engineering research, but it also ran the National Supercomputer Centers and NSFnet.[1]

Several months elapsed between the time when I was offered the job and when I was able to actually assume it—months that afforded me the chance to think about what I should try to accomplish in the two years I expected to hold the job. It was then that the notion of leveraging the entire scientific enterprise with networking came to me. The idea was that we could both expand and improve research in all fields by providing remote access to colleagues, instrumentation, data, and computation. In 1989, Josh Lederberg, Nobelist and president of Rockefeller University, hosted a small workshop where we both tested and fleshed out the initial idea, and then wrote the report that was the guiding road map for subsequent work. The word *collaboratory* (an amalgam of *collaboration* and *laboratory*) was invented later, and not by me, but the concept it describes has changed remarkably little from the initial one of 1988–1999. I was completely naive, however, about how hard achieving the vision would be—as is shown by the successes and difficulties documented in the present volume.

In addition to the specifics of the various collaboratories depicted here, I am intrigued by the final chapter's question: Is there a "science of collaboratories"? Perhaps there is a reason why it has been hard to consistently achieve the original simple vision, and perhaps understanding that reason can be discovered using the scientific method. I hope so. I have a deep conviction that the goal of that vision is worthy of pursuit!

My thanks to the authors and editors of this volume for succinctly capturing the state of the art and science of collaboratories, and especially for doing so in an honest and balanced way.

William A. Wulf
Professor, University of Virginia
President emeritus, National Academy of Engineering

Note

1. NSFnet was the expansion of the old ARPAnet and the immediate predecessor of the current Internet. It was only accessible by researchers and not the general public.

Preface

As described in the introduction, the work included in this volume was in one way or another associated with the Science of Collaboratories (SOC) project headquartered at the University of Michigan's School of Information. We review some of the history of this project in the introduction. But here we'd like to give credit to a number of people who played important roles in the project.

A key organizing activity of this project was a series of workshops held during the study. To plan these workshops and the early directions of the project, we convened a group of expert advisers that included Jim Myers, Jim Herbsleb, Diane Sonnenwald, Mark Ellisman, and Nestor Zaluzec. This group met in February 2001 at Chicago's O'Hare Airport with Gary Olson, Tom Finholt, Joseph Hardin, and Ann Verhey-Henke from the University of Michigan.

At this O'Hare meeting, a series of workshops were planned to help define the focus of the project and engage a broader audience in its activities. Over the next couple of years five workshops were held. The first two, held in summer 2001, focused on the social and technical underpinnings of collaboratories, respectively. Two subsequent workshops, held in 2002 and 2003, presented preliminary analyses and case studies, which represented early versions of much of the Michigan-based material in this volume. Another workshop, held at the NSF in November 2002, took a broad look at knowledge environments for science and engineering.

In June 2005, many of the authors of material in this book gathered in Ann Arbor, Michigan, to present preliminary versions of their chapters. The give-and-take at this meeting generated a lot of cross-fertilization, which is hopefully reflected in the volume. We are grateful to all the contributing authors for their participation and patience throughout every aspect of this volume's preparation.

Many of the principals in the SOC project are authors of chapters in this book, so that can serve as their acknowledgment. But some others who have not written for this volume played crucial roles at various points in the project, including Dan Atkins, Bob Clauer, Michael Cohen, George Furnas, Margaret Hedstrom, Homer Neal, Jason Owen-Smith, Atul Prakash, Chuck Severance, and Beth Yakel from Michigan, and Deb

Agarwal, Prasun Dewan, Jamie Drew, Deron Estes, Bob Greenes, Jonathan Grudin, Jim Herbsleb, Paul Hubbard, Jorge Jovicich, Gillian Kerr, Jason Leigh, Gloria Mark, Laura Perlman, Vimla Patel, Steve Poltrock, Brian Saunders, Umesh Thakkar, John Trimble, Jessica Turner, John Walsh, Daniel Weber, Mike Wilde, and Steve Wolinsky from outside Michigan. Students and staff involved in the project who have not ended up as coauthors include Kristen Arbutiski, Julie Bailin, Vipul Bansal, David Chmura, Ingrid Erickson, Susannah Hoch, Larry Jacobs, Alex Kerfoot, John Lockard, Greg Peters, Abigail Potter, and Matthew Radey.

We are grateful to Bonnie Nardi, Victor Kaptelinin, and Kirsten Foot, editors of The MIT Press Acting with Technology series, for their support and feedback on our book proposal. Bonnie in particular worked closely with us during the early phases of the book's conception. Three anonymous reviewers provided constructive comments that helped to shape the volume's contents. Anne Pfaelzer de Ortiz assisted considerably with editorial work, including the preparation of figures. Susan Harris also gave us editorial support. Finally, we acknowledge the encouragement and expertise of The MIT Press staff who worked closely with us on all stages of the volume's preparation. Robert Prior, executive editor, offered the right combination of patient prompting and urgent solicitation that was required to bring the book to completion. Valerie Geary, former acquisitions assistant, worked with us in the early phases of the project, and later, Alyssa Larose handled many of the important details associated with getting the manuscript to press.

Financial support for the SOC project has come primarily from the NSF (IIS 0085951). Special thanks are extended to Suzi Iacono, who provided initial and ongoing encouragement for the project. More recently, funding from the Army Research Institute (W74V8H-06-P-0518) has allowed us to continue some of the threads launched during the SOC project.

Introduction

Gary M. Olson, Nathan Bos, and Ann Zimmerman

Modern science is increasingly collaborative. The rise in scientific collaboration reveals itself in many ways, but one established way is through coauthorship patterns over time. While there are clear differences among fields in the absolute numbers of co-authored articles, all fields show a similar pattern. Coauthored papers are becoming more common (e.g., Cronin, Shaw, and La Barre 2003; Katz and Martin 1997; Wray 2002; Glanzel 2002; Wuchty, Jones, and Uzzi 2007). A similar trend holds true for international collaborations: worldwide the proportion of scientific papers with international coauthors grew from 7 to 17 percent from 1986 to 1999 (National Science Foundation 2002). Another indicator of the growth in collaboration is an increase in multi-investigator grant proposals. An example of this can be found in the steady climb in the number of awards made by the National Science Foundation (NSF) in the time period from 1982 to 2001 that included more than one principal investigator (National Research Council 2004, 118). Several key factors lie behind these patterns. The urgency, complexity, and scope of unsolved scientific problems; the need for access to new, and often expensive, research instruments and technologies; pressure from funding agencies; and information and communication technologies (ICTs) that facilitate interaction and sharing all play a role in prompting scientists to cooperate with individuals both within and outside their disciplines and institutions. We briefly examine each of these factors in the paragraphs below, and discuss how the challenges and opportunities they present formed the basis for the research and case studies reported in this book.

Historically, colocated scientists carried out most of the collaborations, often under the auspices of a physically established laboratory (Finholt and Olson 1997). An example of the apex of a complex, physically colocated collaborative project was the Manhattan Project (Hales 1997). In this project, literally thousands of scientists converged on a remote plateau in Los Alamos, New Mexico. Physical location makes it easier to align goals and build trust, lowers communication costs, reduces coordination costs, and facilitates the sharing of resources. But Manhattan Project–scale relocation is not practical for all projects. Scientists may participate in many large collaborative projects over the course of their careers, sometimes simultaneously, and they cannot be expected to relocate to each one. Modern science needs to be able to take advantage of specialized talent available regardless of location.

One force driving collaboration is the fact that many of today's most complex scientific problems are beyond the realm of a single discipline or scientist to solve (National Research Council 2004). This situation is exacerbated by the increasing specialization of scientists due to the growth of scientific knowledge. Collaborative research makes it possible to tackle research questions that would otherwise not be feasible to address (Thagard 1997; Wray 2002). Researchers work together because there are questions they want to investigate that they cannot undertake alone. In addition, funding agencies, which must respond to the needs of society and the political environment, have encouraged collaborative research.

Fortunately, cost-effective and reliable ICTs have made it possible for scientists to put together more long-distance collaborations than ever before. Whereas in the past it would have been deemed necessary to bring colleagues together in a single laboratory, more such partnerships are now conducted at a distance thanks to technologies such as e-mail, videoconferencing, shared whiteboards, and centralized databases. Indeed, such technologies have enabled the emergence of modern distributed organizations (Chandler 1962; Yates 1989). Besides making long-distance collaborations feasible, new technologies make it possible to gather and share large amounts of data with increasingly specialized, sophisticated, and often expensive instrumentation. Powerful computational resources provide the muscle with which to analyze these data. In summary, important research continues to be conducted by a single scientist, but collaboration has become a critical feature of science. There is evidence that collaboration increases the quality of research, contributes to the rapid growth of scientific knowledge, and plays an important role in the training of new scientists (Wray 2002).

On the other hand, collaboration also presents social and organizational challenges. A recent editorial in the journal *Nature* asked: "Who'd want to work in a team?" (2003). This article acknowledged what existing research has shown over and over again to be the case: collaboration is difficult. In particular, collaborations that involve geographically dispersed participants have a higher likelihood of failure or underperformance (Olson and Olson 2000; Cummings and Kiesler 2005; 2007; chapter 5, this volume). In these situations it is more difficult to align goals and incentives, establish common ground, engender and maintain trust, allow for the costs of coordination and communication, and determine an appropriate division of labor and resources (e.g., Grudin 1988; Hesse et al. 1993; Orlikowski 1992). In sum, we have learned that even when advanced technologies are available, distance still matters (Olson and Olson 2000).

The challenges and rewards of collaboration that take place over space and time, approaches for overcoming the difficulties and evaluating the outcomes of such collaborative work, and conceptual frameworks for exploring and analyzing distributed scientific collaboration are the topics that are explored in detail throughout this book. In the remainder of this introduction, we describe the history and development of this volume as well as provide a road map to its contents.

The Concept of Collaboratories

In 1989, a distinguished group of senior scientists and engineers gathered at Rockefeller University to consider the then-new concept of a collaboratory. This term was defined as "center[s] without walls in which researchers can work together regardless of physical location" (Wulf 1993). The vision of this group was that networking and the associated information technologies had gotten to the point where it was feasible to think of the routine activities of science and engineering taking place across the emerging Internet. This group met several more times in the next few years to produce the influential National Research Council (1993) report on collaboratories. Much of the early focus of this group was on employing the Internet to exchange large amounts of data, access high-end computational resources, and use remote or expensive instruments. But over time the vision has grown to include the entire scope of activities required to do science and engineering, including all of the myriad human interactions that are an element of scientific collaboration. The sizes of the collaborations have also grown in scale to include both more individuals and more organizational complexity.

The concept of a collaboratory has thus been considerably expanded from these earliest workshops. The following definition was developed at a 2001 workshop that we organized with some other colleagues at the University of Michigan:

A collaboratory is an organizational entity that spans distance, supports rich and recurring human interaction oriented to a common research area, and provides access to data sources, artifacts and tools required to accomplish research tasks.

Over time, words such as *e-Science*, which is used in much of Europe, and *cyberinfrastructure*, which is the current term in the United States (Atkins et al. 2003), developed to refer to the same or related ideas communicated by the word collaboratories, except often on a larger scale. For example, Tony Hey and Anne Trefethen open this book with a chapter on e-Science, which they define as the "next generation of scientific problems, and the collaborative tools and technologies that will be required to solve them." In the second chapter, Michael Nentwich refers to *cyberscience*, which he describes as "all scholarly and scientific research activities in the virtual space generated by networked computers and advanced ICT." We argue that the concepts embodied in these newer terms were heavily influenced by the collaboratory vision and the lessons learned from the distributed scientific projects analyzed in this volume. Further, we contend that many of the issues raised by collaboratories—and addressed in this book—are as relevant today as they were in the mid-1990s.

In any new area of study, the terminology takes time to resolve, and the discussions that ensue are an important part of defining an emerging field. We chose to use the word collaboratory most frequently in this book because it has been in existence for almost twenty years, and continues to capture the social, technical, and organizational aspects of these collaborations (e.g., Finholt 2002, 2003). In addition, we use the term in the broader sense entailed by the definition above. As we will see later when we discuss the types of collaboratories (chapter 3, this volume), not all collaboratories implement all elements of the definition. Like any concept meant to describe naturally occurring things, there are, in addition to prototypes, a wide variety of instances that only partially satisfy the core definition.

The Science of Collaboratories Project

By the turn of the century, the collaboratory concept had spread to many science and engineering domains. It was quickly apparent that just because a collaboratory was organized and funded, there was no guarantee that it would succeed. Indeed, a number of early projects were informed by good concepts, but were ultimately not successful. At least on casual investigation it was not immediately apparent what factors differentiated successful from unsuccessful collaboratories. This dilemma prompted a group of us at the University of Michigan with experience in long-distance collaborations in science, engineering, business, and education to apply for funding under the NSF's Information and Technology Research program (Malakoff 2000). We were successful in obtaining support for a period of five years, and in 2000 we established the Science of Collaboratories (SOC) project. The goals of this project were to define, abstract, and codify the underlying technical and social mechanisms that lead to successful collaboratories. We also aimed to provide the vocabulary, associated principles, and design methods for propagating and sustaining collaboratories across a wide range of circumstances. These goals were pursued through three coordinated activities:

• The qualitative and quantitative study of *collaboratory design and usage*, examining both the technical and social aspects of performance
• The creation and maintenance of a *Collaboratory Knowledge Base*, a Web-accessible archive of primary source material, summaries and abstracts, relevant generalizations and principles, a database of collaboratory resources, and other related material
• The abstraction and codification of *principles, heuristics, and frameworks* to guide the rapid creation and deployment of successful collaboratories, including *principles of design or customization*

With guidance from an outside advisory committee, the SOC project convened a series of workshops to help define the social and technical issues, and later in the project, discuss specific case studies and preliminary findings from the research. Reports from these workshops as well as data from the project, a bibliography, and other material are available at the SOC Web site.[1]

A primary task has been to identify and describe a large sample of collaboratories. At the start of the study, the principal investigators compiled data on the collaboratories they were already aware of, and through a snowball process they worked from these initial examples to a collection of more than two hundred collaboratories as of the time of this writing.

A problem we faced in assembling this collection was that few of the collaboratories were well documented. For many of them we could find a Web site or some preliminary published description of the goals of the collaboration, but nothing about what actually happened over the course of the project. Only a few collaboratories were publicly documented, particularly with respect to the issues that interested us most. Thus, we faced the daunting task of creating a record for many of the projects we located.

Our documentation strategy took two forms. First, for all of the collaboratories that we found, we created a minimal-level record that included information such the project goals, funding source(s) and participants, collaboration technologies used, and if possible, outcomes and results. Many of these summaries are viewable at the SOC Web site, in the "Collaboratories at a Glance" database. The second strategy was to pursue a smaller number of collaboratories in greater depth. These constitute in-depth case studies, and the chapters in this volume cover many of these. For these projects, we conducted interviews with multiple project participants, and in some cases visited the sites of participants, to document the internal processes, challenges, and successes of these complex projects.

Unifying Questions

In this volume, we have brought together a series of chapters both from the SOC project and a variety of related projects from around the world. The result is a collection of chapters that gives both a broad and in-depth view of the use of the Internet to enable science and engineering. The volume begins with several overarching chapters and from there the content is organized by scientific discipline. We considered other, more thematic organizing frameworks, but in the end clustering by discipline seemed to make the material most approachable to readers. There are many threads running through these chapters that are independent of discipline; these are explored in the opening chapters and the conclusion. One reason for the common themes that emerge across the chapters is that the authors were encouraged to address the following questions and topics, particularly in those chapters that are case studies of specific collaboratories:

• Successes: What success stories are related to the collaboratory? What has been accomplished in terms of science, technology, and improving the human infrastructure, and what evidence exists for these accomplishments? What was this project like on the "inside"?

• Failures and challenges: We encouraged authors to be frank about their problems—both ones that have been overcome and those that have not. We also asked them to describe in a usable level of detail what their approaches have been to overcoming these challenges, and whether or not these methods were successful.

• The role of technology: How were new or not-so-new collaboration technologies used in the project? What technologies were important and which did not perform as anticipated? What is needed for the future? Although not all of the chapters emphasize technology, the project case studies probably would not have been attempted, and certainly would have been much more difficult to do, without the Internet infrastructure that did not exist even a few decades ago.

• Management practices: What new management practices were needed to enable long-distance collaborative science? The chapters in this book discuss management challenges at all levels, from person-to-person collaboration up to high-level decision making on funding entire programs. Many authors in this book had firsthand experience as managers of the projects they are describing, and the book contains numerous insights as to these authors' strategies and perceptions.

The book is divided into six parts, and we will overview each in turn.

Part I: The Contemporary Collaboratory Vision

As we noted earlier, the contemporary vision of distributed, scientific collaboration is of ever-larger scales. The volume opens with two chapters that reflect the influence of collaboratories on current initiatives and ideas of ICT-enabled scientific work. The authors of chapter 1, Tony Hey and Anne Trefethen, write about the implications of e-Science technologies for open access and scholarly communication on the construction of a *global research repository*. These two individuals are well positioned to address this topic. Hey is the former director of the United Kingdom's e-Science program and the current corporate vice president of external research at Microsoft, and his coauthor, Trefethen, is the director of the Oxford e-Research Centre at the University of Oxford. Their review discusses the challenges of acquiring, storing, searching, and mining huge volumes of digital data as well as the effects of this *data deluge* on all aspects of scientific practice. Case study chapters that appear in other parts of the book provide substance to the scenario offered by Hey and Trefethen.

The author of chapter 2, Michael Nentwich, is the director of the Institute of Technology Assessment of the Austrian Academy of Sciences. His study of European scientists detailed the changes in daily practices brought about by online conferencing, digital libraries, and other current innovations (Nentwich 2003). In this chapter, he draws from these findings and anticipates a future where collaboration is increasingly common, while both physical proximity and physical objects become less important to scientists.

Part II: Perspectives on Distributed, Collaborative Science

The large-scale projects described in the rest of this book have consumed many millions of dollars and thousands of hours by researchers from numerous fields. Has cumulative wisdom emerged from all of this effort? Will future collaborations benefit not just from the technology developed but from the mistakes, lessons learned, and best practices of prior efforts? Every chapter in this book addresses these issues in some way, but the three chapters in this part are the most direct attempts to build theory in the area of distributed, collaborative science. This issue will be revisited again in the book's conclusion, when we ask the question: Is there a science of collaboratories?

The taxonomy chapter by Bos and his coauthors describes work done in the first two years of the SOC study, where researchers were actively trying to go beyond previous technology-centric definitions of collaboratories and take a broader, truer measure of the landscape of large-scale scientific collaborations. In chapter 3, a seven-category taxonomy of collaboratory types that has guided subsequent research is presented.

Chapter 4 resulted from an attempt to distill basic theoretical issues from the host of best practices and lessons learned over the course of the SOC project. Judith Olson and her colleagues propose a broad set of success measures and analyze factors that affect those measures. The chapter also goes beyond research in collaboratories to draw from literature on computer-mediated communication, organizational behavior, management information systems, and science and technology studies. Thus, this chapter is our best attempt to date to define a science of collaboratories.

To conclude this part, chapter 5 describes contemporaneous work that was done by Jonathon Cummings and Sara Kiesler using a data set of all projects funded by one of the NSF's large-scale experiments in collaborative research—the Knowledge and Distributed Intelligence initiative. Taking the opportunity to study this diverse set of projects with a common set of measures, this research had some unique findings, especially related to the interaction of organizational and distance barriers.

Part III: Physical Sciences

The chapters in this part are focused on the physical sciences domain. These chapters are also some of the richest sources on emerging technology and technological innovation. There are several reasons for this. First, the physical sciences are fundamentally physical, and thus often require expensive devices. Making these devices more widely available, shareable, and functional at a distance have been the primary goals of early physical science collaboratories. Second, these projects represent some of the earliest collaboratories, and were therefore obliged to solve hardware and software challenges that later projects could take for granted.

An interesting thread that goes through two of these chapters—chapter 6 by James Myers, and chapter 9 by Gary Olson, Timothy Killeen, and Thomas Finholt—is how the projects dealt with the onset of new technologies that threatened to render discipline-specific alternatives obsolete. Another organizing thread also presents itself: chapters 7 through 10 could be ordered by grain size. For example, in chapter 10, Diane Sonnenwald takes a close look at a single tool, the nanoManipulator, while other chapters describe increasingly large organizational units. In chapter 8, for instance, Erik Hofer and his colleagues analyze the way an entire field, high-energy physics, has transformed itself to do large-scale collaborative science.

Part IV: Biological and Health Sciences

The next part covers topics in the biomedical domain. Currently, many of the most ambitious and exciting collaborative projects are in this area. This is due to both need and opportunity. The need is that progress in many research areas now requires tackling complex and data-intensive problems in areas such as genetics, proteomics, and neurobiology. The opportunity is in the high levels of public support for biomedical research, highlighted by Congress' doubling of the National Institutes of Health's (NIH) budget between the years of 1999 and 2003. One of the institutes, the National Institute of General Medical Sciences (NIGMS), held a workshop in 1998 to discuss how best to use this increase. Biomedical researchers have a reputation (deserved or not) for being competitive and individualistic, so it was somewhat of a surprise when workshop attendees recommended that the NIGMS *not* simply fund twice as many single-laboratory projects. Instead, as Michael Rogers, director of NIGMS's Pharmacology, Physiology, and Biological Chemistry Division, and his colleague James Onken explain in chapter 11:

A common theme that emerged from the meetings was a desire of already-funded investigators to work together on the solution of complex biomedical problems. This represented a major shift: established scientists with NIGMS-supported individual investigator-initiated basic research ("R01 research") were asking for a mechanism to provide support for them to work together in a team-like fashion.

The result of this was the NIGMS glue grant program, which so far has funded five major multilaboratory projects along with some smaller ones. This grand experiment has necessitated many new developments in organizational design and technology infrastructure as well as biomedical research practice. Rogers and Onken's chapter, written just as the first glue grants were coming up for their five-year review, is a snapshot of this initiative. Some of the NIH's more recent initiatives, such as the NIH Roadmap, the Clinical and Translational Science Award program, and the National Centers for Biomedical Computing, suggest that collaboration in biomedical research is even more urgent and essential today than when the glue grants program was established.

Is technological innovation also important for medical collaboratories? The next two chapters in this part focus on the technology infrastructure as well as organizational arrangements of large-scale collaboratories in the biomedical domain.

The Biomedical Research Information Network (BIRN), another major NIH initiative, is composed of a collection of three collaboratories centered on brain imaging and the genetics of human neurological disorders and the associated animal models. In chapter 12, the authors analyze BIRN in light of the emerging theory of remote scientific collaboration.

The case study by Stephanie Teasley and her colleagues in chapter 13 compares three NIH-sponsored distributed centers: the Great Lakes Regional Center for AIDS Research, New York University's Oral Cancer Research for Adolescent and Adult Health Promotion Center, and the Great Lakes Regional Center of Excellence in Biodefense and Emerging Infectious Diseases. The chapter provides important insights into the dynamics of biomedical research collaborations from the individual, cultural, social, and technical perspectives.

The final chapter in this part examines a specific issue that recurs in many collaboratories: how to motivate and sustain contributions from members. Using game-theoretical research on public goods as a background, chapter 14 looks at contributor recruitment strategies employed by a new organizational form called Community Data Systems. Together, these chapters paint a rich picture of how biomedical research is reinventing itself to take advantage of "the collaboratory opportunity."

Part V: Earth and Environmental Sciences

The fifth part covers four projects in the earth and environmental sciences. As with biomedicine, this field faces a clear need to scale up the level of analysis, from single investigator-size studies to collaborative efforts to tackle complex systems. Earth and environmental sciences have different funding structures, varying scientific cultures (or as David Ribes and Geoffrey Bowker describe in chapter 17, multiple scientific cultures), and different associated technologies than biomedicine. Each chapter in this part is a rich depiction of a project that evolved over time, confronted and overcame challenges, and had its share of successes. An interesting take on this collection is to think of each one as extending previous science along a particular dimension. The National Center for Ecological Analysis and Synthesis, as Edward Hackett and his colleagues depict it in chapter 15, extended ecology beyond single principal investigator efforts by bringing them together within the same institution. Chapter 16 looks at the Long Term Ecological Research program, which as the name implies was focused on extending the science over time. The Geosciences Network (GEON), as Ribes and Bowker describe it, is focused on extending the science across multiple subdisciplines, and also working closely with computer scientists. Finally, chapter 18 by B. F. Spencer Jr. and his coauthors relates the experiences and lessons learned from the NEESgrid project, an interdisciplinary effort to develop and deploy cyberinfrastructure across the experts who comprise the field of earthquake engineering. A key challenge for NEESgrid included bridging the gap between modelers and experimentalists, and like GEON, between computer scientists and domain specialists.

Part VI: The Developing World

Globalization has arguably proceeded more slowly in science than in industry. This might be surprising, because compared to other peer groups scientific communities are often egalitarian and broadly international. But as pointed out by Bos and his colleagues in the chapter on collaboratory taxonomy, science is harder to partition and subcontract than other types of work because of the importance of tacit knowledge along with a deep understanding of the topics. It is relatively easy to outsource a manufactured commodity; it is a dicier proposition to outsource analysis and insight. The last two chapters in this book document efforts to bridge this formidable gap.

In chapter 19, Matthew Bietz, Marsha Naidoo, and Gary Olson describe a partnership between AIDS researchers in the United States and South Africa. Both sides stood to benefit from this cooperation: the U.S. researchers needed access to the untreated subject population, and the South Africans wanted to improve their infrastructure as well as make progress on the AIDS epidemic. The barriers to a productive collaboration, however, were substantial. The chapter examines the technical, institutional, and cultural barriers, and accompanying solutions, that collaborations between developed and developing worlds can expect to face.

Airong Luo and Judith Olson continue this area of inquiry in chapter 20. Luo interviewed more than thirty scientists from China, Korea, Morocco, New Zealand, South Africa, and Taiwan who have participated in collaboratories with developed countries. She documents both the benefits, such as learning about data quality standards, and the challenges of trying to participate as equals in a collaboration centered thousands of miles away.

This book attempts to strike a balance between the real stories of scientific collaboratories, and the need for a deeper understanding of and scientific approach to conceiving, designing, implementing, and evaluating collaboratories. A science of collaboratories lies at the intersection of many different scientific fields, including computer science and science and technology studies, and is thus in itself a research domain that must be approached collaboratively. The conclusion to this book takes a more in-depth look at the way forward toward a true science of collaboratories that builds on aspects from multiple disciplines.

Note

1. See ⟨http://www.scienceofcollaboratories.org⟩.

References

Atkins, D. E., K. Droegemeier, S. Feldman, H. Garcia-Molina, M. L. Klein, D. G. Messerschmitt et al. 2003. *Revolutionizing science and engineering through cyberinfrastructure: Report of the National Science Foundation Blue-Ribbon Advisory Panel on Cyberinfrastructure.* Arlington, VA: National Science Foundation.

Chandler, A. D. 1962. *Strategy and structure: Chapters in the history of the American industrial enterprise.* Cambridge, MA: MIT Press.

Cronin, B., D. Shaw, and K. La Barre. 2003. A cast of thousands: Coauthorship and subauthorship collaboration in the 20th century as manifested in the scholarly journal literature of psychology and philosophy. *Journal of the American Society for Information Science and Technology* 54 (9): 855–871.

Cummings, J. N., and S. Kiesler. 2005. Collaborative research across disciplinary and institutional boundaries. *Social Studies of Science* 35 (5): 703–722.

Cummings, J. N., and S. Kiesler. 2007. Coordination costs and project outcomes in multi-university collaborations. *Research Policy* 36 (10): 1620–1634.

Finholt, T. A. 2002. Collaboratories. In *Annual Review of Information Science and Technology*, ed. B. Cronin, 74–107. Washington, DC: American Society for Information Science.

Finholt, T. A. 2003. Collaboratories as a new form of scientific organization. *Economics of Innovation and New Technology* 12:5–25.

Finholt, T. A., and G. M. Olson. 1997. From laboratories to collaboratories: A new organizational form for scientific collaboration. *Psychological Science* 8:28–36.

Glanzel, W. 2002. Coauthorship patterns and trends in the sciences (1980–1998): A bibliometric study with implications for database indexing and search strategies. *Library Trends* 50:461–475.

Grudin, J. 1988. Why CSCW applications fail: Problems in the design and evaluation of organizational interfaces. In *Proceedings of the 1988 ACM Conference on Computer-Supported Cooperative Work*, ed. I. Grief and L. Suchman, 85–93. New York: ACM Press.

Hales, P. B. 1997. *Atomic spaces: Living on the Manhattan Project.* Urbana: University of Illinois Press.

Hesse, B. W., L. S. Sproull, S. B. Kiesler, and J. P. Walsh. 1993. Returns to science: Computer networks in oceanography. *Communications of the ACM* 36 (8): 90–101.

Katz, J. S., and B. R. Martin. 1997. What is research collaboration? *Research Policy* 26 (1): 1–18.

Malakoff, D. 2000. National Science Foundation: Information technology takes a different tack. *Science* 288 (5466): 600–601.

National Research Council, Committee on a National Collaboratory. 1993. *National collaboratories: Applying information technology for scientific research.* Washington, DC: National Academies Press.

National Research Council, Committee on Facilitating Interdisciplinary Research. 2004. *Facilitating interdisciplinary research.* Washington, DC: National Academies Press.

National Science Foundation. 2002. *Science and engineering indicators, 2002.* Washington, DC: National Science Foundation.

Nentwich, M. 2003. *Cyberscience: Research in the age of the Internet.* Vienna: Austrian Academy of Sciences Press.

Olson, G. M., and J. S. Olson. 2000. Distance matters. *Human Computer Interaction* 15:139–179.

Orlikowski, W. 1992. Learning from Notes: Organizational issues in groupware implementation. In *Proceedings of the 1992 ACM Conference on Computer-Supported Cooperative Work*, ed. J. Turner and R. Kraut, 362–369. New York: ACM Press.

Thagard, P. 1997. Collaborative knowledge. *Nous* 31:242–261.

Who'd want to work in a team? 2003. *Nature* 424 (6944): 1.

Wray, K. B. 2002. The epistemic significance of collaborative research. *Philosophy of Science* 69:150–168.

Wuchty, S., B. F. Jones, and B. Uzzi. 2007. The increasing dominance of teams in production of knowledge. *Science* 316:1036–1039.

Wulf, W. A. 1993. The collaboratory opportunity. *Science* 261 (5123): 854–855.

Yates, J. 1989. *Control through communication: The rise of system in American management.* Baltimore, MD: Johns Hopkins University Press.

I The Contemporary Collaboratory Vision

1 E-Science, Cyberinfrastructure, and Scholarly Communication

Tony Hey and Anne Trefethen

In the last few decades, computational science has evolved to become a scientific methodology in its own right, standing alongside the traditional pillars of experimental and theoretical science. In the next few decades it is likely we will see the emergence of a fourth paradigm: "e-Science" or datacentric science. The development of this new mode of scientific research is being driven by an imminent "data deluge" (Hey and Trefethen 2003). In almost every field of science, researchers will soon be facing the problems of acquiring, storing, searching, and mining huge volumes of digital data. Typically, these data sources will be distributed across several sites and require researchers to access resources outside their own laboratories. In addition, in many cases the scale and complexity of the scientific problems now being addressed will require the efforts of distributed, collaborative, and often multidisciplinary teams, and are beyond the capabilities of the traditional isolated scientist or research group. Faced with these demands, the computer science research community now has a clear opportunity to develop powerful new software tools and assist in building a new research infrastructure on top of the global research network (Emmott 2006). Such a new "cyberinfrastructure"—called "e-Infrastructure" in Europe—would raise the level of abstraction for scientists, and allow them to focus on their science rather than be enmeshed in the problems of moving, managing, and manipulating hundreds of terabytes of data (Atkins et al. 2003).

We use the term *e-Science* to represent this next generation of scientific problems, and the collaborative tools and technologies that will be required to solve them. These next-generation e-Science problems range from the simulation of complex engineering and biological systems to research in bioinformatics, proteomics, and pharmacogenetics. In many of these instances, researchers need to combine the expertise of other research groups and access specialized resources, often distributed across the globe. Although our focus is on e-Science, other research fields such as the social sciences, arts, and humanities will also require and benefit from this emerging cyberinfrastructure. In the classics, for example, many artifacts are now being made available in digital form, allowing researchers for the first time to bring together not only the disparate pieces of the actual artifact but also the knowledge around them. Similarly, in the social sciences, the data sets that need to be analyzed are frequently so large and distributed that both the memory storage as well as the computational power of individual workstations are inadequate, and the use of distributed computing resources will become the norm. The federation of data that might be "owned" by a particular party, with access restricted through perhaps a license or specific authorization policies, is a common theme in many areas of research.

In addition to this distributed, datacentric future, the traditional patterns of scholarly communication and publishing are about to undergo radical changes. The Internet and the Web are transforming the world of scholarly publishing. Increasingly, research papers will be live documents linked to RSS feeds and the primary data sources. While peer review will remain an important component of the scholarly publishing model, we will see the emergence of new, more informal, and more dynamic forms of peer review. Commentaries, such as those pioneered in print by Stevan Harnad during his editorship of the journal *Behavioral and Brain Sciences*, will become the norm, using Web 2.0 social networking tools like wikis and blogs. In some fields, the publication of an annotated database is now an accepted form of scholarly communication. Another significant trend is the move toward open access—the principle that the results of government-funded research should be accessible by the taxpayers who paid for the research. There are movements in many countries including the United States and within bodies such as the European Union to mandate open access to both the data and literature of publicly funded research.

To quote Michael Keller (2006), the librarian at Stanford University who has pioneered many groundbreaking developments for scholarly publishing, we are in the midst of the "perfect storm"—and it is certainly not possible to predict the precise shape of the future scholarly publishing landscape. Nevertheless, it is clear that a key part of the cyberinfrastructure of the future will be the ability to access and search distributed digital repositories of research material comprised not only of text but also data, images, and software.

In this chapter, we will focus primarily on the implications of these e-Science technologies and cyberinfrastructure for open access and scholarly communication, and the construction of a global research repository. The chapter is structured as follows. We begin with brief reviews of e-Science and cyberinfrastructure. Then we discuss the trends in silicon technology and give some examples of the data demands of the new generation of scientific experiments. We conclude this section with a summary of the present state of grid middleware. The next section introduces the issue of open access as applied to research publications and offers examples of subject research repositories—arXiv and PubMedCentral—and institutional research repositories—ePrints and TARDis. The section that follows is concerned with open access to data, and reviews the data-sharing policies of several funding agencies and highlights the data issues in several major grid projects. The next-to-last section discusses the growing trend of publications linking directly to the primary data on which the data analysis is based and utilizes examples from the UK e-Science Program. Finally, we conclude the chapter with remarks and speculations as to the future shape of scholarly communication.

E-Science and Cyberinfrastructure

Silicon Technology

The two key technological drivers of the information technology (IT) revolution over the past twenty years have been Moore's law—the exponential increase in computing power and solid-state memory—and the dramatic increase in communication bandwidth made possible by optical fiber networks using optical amplifiers and wave division multiplexing. In a very real sense, the actual cost of any given amount of computation and/or sending a given amount of data is falling to zero. While this statement is of course true for a fixed amount of computation and the transmission of a fixed amount of data, scientists are now attempting calculations that require many orders of magnitude more computing and communication than was possible even a few years ago. Moreover, in many currently planned and future experiments, scientists will generate several orders of magnitude more data than have been collected in the whole of human history up to now.

The highest-performance supercomputing systems of today consist of thousands of processors interconnected by a high-speed, low-latency network. On appropriate problems, it is possible to achieve a sustained performance of several teraflop/s—or several tens of trillions floating-point operations per second. Systems are now under construction that aim for petaflop/s performance within the next few years. Such extreme high-end systems are expensive and will always be relatively scarce resources located in a few sites. Most computational problems do not require such massively parallel processing, and can be satisfied by the widespread deployment of inexpensive clusters of computers at the university, department, and research group levels.

In addition to this race for the petaflop, there is another revolution on the horizon. Although the feature size of transistors on silicon will continue to shrink over the coming decade, this increase in transistor density will no longer be accompanied by an increase in clock-cycle speed. Because of heat and power constraints, although we can continue to fabricate smaller and smaller microprocessors, an individual central processing unit will not run faster than previous generations. The unavoidable conclusion is that the only way to improve performance is to exploit the parallelism of the application using multicore chips. This represents a serious challenge for the IT industry— as well as the scientific community. In the early 1980s, Geoffrey Fox and Chuck Seitz introduced us to the world of distributed memory parallel computing with their

Cosmic Cube parallel computer (Seitz 1992). This was the first successful distributed memory parallel computer to be used for parallel applications, and Fox and his group pioneered many of the techniques and algorithms that are now routinely used on present-day parallel supercomputers (Fox 1987; Fox, Williams, and Messina 1994). In the intervening twenty years, progress has been slow on making parallel computing easy and error free. Although most applications can benefit from parallelism, producing optimized parallel versions of the application is still largely an art practiced by a small community of experts. Intel predicts that there will be over a hundred processors on a chip within the next decade (Gruener 2006). The challenge for the IT industry and scientific community is clear.

Scientific Data

One of the crucial drivers for the emerging cyberinfrastructure is the imminent deluge of data from the new generations of scientific experiments and surveys (Hey and Trefethen 2003). One example will make the point. The Sloan Digital Sky Survey pioneered the ongoing transition from small-scale individual observations to detailed whole sky surveys with many tens of terabytes of data (Thakar et al. 2003). Now the astronomy community has plans for a new generation of astronomical surveys using new, large field-of-view telescopes dedicated to such survey work (chapter 7, this volume). One such instance is the proposal for the Large Synoptic Survey Telescope.[1] This will be an 8.2 m telescope with a 3.5-gigapixel camera that would survey the entire sky every five nights. The data requirements are breathtaking. Each image is about 6.5 gigabytes, and one image is taken every fifteen seconds. The processed data will be more than 100 terabytes per night, and the catalogs alone will take up more than 3 petabytes per year. The goal is to make these data immediately accessible to both the global astronomy community and the general public. To do this, the International Virtual Observatory Alliance will have to provide access to this content along with tools for data discovery, movement, analysis, and understanding.[2] Yet these fields have the advantage that the data, although large in volume, is essentially all of the same character. In other fields, such as bioinformatics, the data will come from many different sources such as genomic databases, 2-D microarray data, 3-D protein structures, and so on. The challenge here is how to analyze and combine data from these heterogeneous databases to extract useful information and knowledge. In both cases, it is clear that it will no longer be possible for researchers to mine and analyze such volumes of data using the present generation of tools.

In order to exploit and explore this flood of scientific data arising from these high-throughput experiments, supercomputer simulations, sensor networks, satellite surveys, and so forth, scientists will need specialized search engines, data-mining tools, and data-visualization tools that will make it easy to ask questions and understand the answers. To create such tools, the data will need to be annotated with relevant metadata giving information as to the provenance, content, experimental conditions, and so on, and the sheer volume of data will increasingly dictate that this metadata annotation process is automated. These vast distributed digital data repositories will also require content management services similar to those being explored in the more conventional digital library world in addition to more data-specific services. The ability to search, access, move, manipulate, and mine such data will be a central requirement for the new generation of collaborative e-Science applications. Technologies and tools to manage the entire data life cycle—from acquisition and provenance, to digital curation and long-term preservation—will be of critical importance.

Cyberinfrastructure

As we have discussed in the introduction, a component of the vision for a new cyberinfrastructure to support new forms of distributed collaborative science is concerned with providing technologies in the form of middleware and tools operating on top of the global research networks. Part of this cyberinfrastructure will be in the form of grid middleware that allows the setting up of secure virtual organizations consisting of distributed groups of researchers (Foster, Kesselman, and Tuecke 2001). These virtual organizations must not only allow easy and flexible resource sharing between the participants but also provide mechanisms for access control with robust authentication, authorization, and accounting services. The resources being shared are of many types—from research data and software, to remote specialized facilities such as telescopes, accelerators, or supercomputers. Particle physicists have constructed a global grid for accessing, moving, and analyzing data from the Large Hadron Collider (LHC) at CERN (chapter 8, this volume). This LHC Grid is an example of what is primarily a computational grid in which many sites contribute compute cycles to enable the data analysis of the vast data sets from each experiment.[3] By contrast, astronomers have constructed a working data grid; the International Virtual Observatory enables users to access and query data from over twenty different astronomy databases.

There are many other examples of grids, but at present it is probably fair to say that most, if not all, of these systems are still somewhat ad hoc and experimental. Nevertheless, with the merger of the Global Grid Forum and the Enterprise Grid Alliance to form one new organization, the Open Grid Forum, there is hope of rapid progress toward defining some core grid service standards based on a set of widely adopted Web services. Only by having some grid standards that are agreed on and accepted by both the IT industry and the research community, and that allow for competing implementations, can grid middleware mature toward the robust, reliable middleware for collaboration that is needed by both academia and industry.

In addition to this low-level grid middleware for setting up the collaborative virtual organization infrastructure, there is a need for powerful new tools and technologies to assist scientists in their research. Some of the potential for computer science technologies applied to these e-Science problems has been enumerated in the *2020 Science* vision sponsored by Microsoft Research and edited by Stephen Emmott (2006). Another strand is the evolution of grid middleware toward an "intelligent" middleware infrastructure such as that envisaged by ambient intelligence (Aarts and Encarnação 2006). In another work (De Roure, Hey, and Trefethen 2006), we have described how the application of semantic Web technologies is leading to a convergence of the Web and grid communities in the concept of the semantic grid. In this chapter, we focus on a third important component of cyberinfrastructure—namely, the transformation of scholarly communication by open access to digital data and information.

Open Access and Scholarly Communication

The *Berlin Declaration on Open Access to Knowledge in the Sciences and Humanities* (2003) was drafted "to promote the Internet as a functional instrument for a global scientific knowledge base and human reflection and to specify measures which research policy makers, research institutions, funding agencies, libraries, archives and museums need to consider." The signatories to the original declaration included research organizations such as the Frauenhofer and the Max Planck institutes in Germany, the Centre National de la Recherche Scientifique (CNRS) and the Institut National de Recherche en Informatique et en Automatique (INRIA) in France, the Royal Netherlands Academy of Arts and Sciences (KNAW) and the SURF Foundation in the Netherlands, the Joint Information Systems Committee (JISC) in the United Kingdom, and CERN and the Swiss Federal Institute of Technology (ETH) in Switzerland as well as many other international organizations and universities. The Berlin meeting followed in the footsteps of one convened in Budapest by the Open Society Institute on December 1–2, 2001, which led to the Budapest Open Archive Initiative (2002). The Berlin declaration is not just concerned with textual material. The declaration defines open-access contributions to include "original scientific research results, raw data and metadata, source materials, digital representations of pictorial and graphical materials and scholarly multimedia material."

In this section, we will consider the ways in which the research community is responding to the challenge of open access to textual data. Open access to data collections will be explored in the next section. Different research communities have responded in different ways to the availability of the World Wide Web as a medium for scholarly publishing. We will give three examples. The theoretical particle physics community has long had a tradition of circulating hard copy "preprints" of papers submitted to conventional journals, ahead of the completion of the formal peer review and publication process. In such a fast-moving field as particle physics, the community is used to discussing the latest ideas at informal seminars and workshops, and it makes no sense to delay the examination of new ideas and results until after the formal publication. With the coming of the Web, the production and circulation of multiple hard copies of the preprint became redundant. It was therefore a natural but significant step for Paul Ginsparg to establish an electronic archive at Los Alamos where "e-prints," electronic versions of preprints, could be displayed on a Web site supported by a machine in his office at the laboratory. From these small beginnings, Ginsparg has demonstrated the viability of a new mode of scholarly communication outside the traditional scholarly publishing route via refereed journal articles.[4] The e-print service is now called "arXiv" and has moved to Cornell University with Ginsparg (Sincell 2001). It is now managed by the Cornell University Library, and is the first port of call for scientists looking for the latest developments in particle physics as well as several other subfields of physics, mathematics, computer science, and quantitative biology.[5] This mode of publication leads to many headaches for librarians: the proliferation of versions—e-prints, preprints, postprints, and so on—along with the confusion about the precise date of "publication" are all areas of concern. From the scientific point of view, these issues may seem trivial—since there is no doubt that claims for priority would be determined by the date of the e-print—but they are not at all trivial from the perspective of librarians and archivists. It would of course be desirable if search engines were able to recognize that all these slightly different versions constituted the same research and for it to be able to group the search results under a single "opus." Such a facility is not yet practicable, but is clearly needed for both librarians and researchers. This type of open access to the research literature has not been mandated by any external body such as a funding agency, but is the spontaneous, collective "decision" of this particular scientific community that the results of its research should be collected in an open-access international digital "subject repository."

As a second example, we consider the U.S. National Library of Medicine (NLM).[6] The National Institutes of Health (NIH) in the United States has a mandate to make biomedical and health care resources publicly available through the NLM. The Entrez Life Sciences Search Engine gives access to PubMed—a service containing over sixteen million citations from the MEDLINE database and life science journals for biomedical articles going back to the 1950s—as well as a wide collection of other biological databases. In February 2005, the NIH announced a new policy designed to accelerate the public's access to published articles resulting from NIH-funded research. The policy calls on scientists to release to the public manuscripts from research supported by the NIH as soon as possible, and certainly within twelve months of final publication. These peer-reviewed, NIH-funded research publications would then be made available in PubMed Central (PMC), a Web-based archive managed by the National Center for Biotechnology Information for the NLM.[7] It is interesting that although the scientific journals have accepted this requirement for delayed open access, the research community has not been diligent in responding to the call to deposit electronic versions in PMC. For this reason, there are now calls to make such open-access deposits a mandatory condition of receiving an NIH or any other federally funded research grant. There is a bill before Congress—the Federal Research Public Access Act (2006), sponsored by John Cornyn (R-TX) and Joseph Lieberman (D-CT), that seeks to make open access mandatory.

With the addition of PMC, Entrez searches can now be directed to free full-text versions of the research article. Jim Gray and Jean Paoli from Microsoft have worked with David Lipman and his team at National Center for Biotechnology Information (NCBI) to develop a "portable" version of PMC, which is now being deployed in other countries around the world. The Wellcome Trust (2007) in the United Kingdom is now mandating that the research results from its funded research projects must be deposited in the UK version of PMC. It is likely that the NLM's archiving template for XML documents—the Document Type Definition—will become a de facto standard for such archives. In another initiative, the Wellcome Trust in partnership with the JISC and the NLM are working on a project to digitize the complete backfiles of a number of important and historically significant medical journals.[8] The digitized content will be made freely available via PMC and will augment the content already available. The Wellcome Library exists as a resource to provide access to the documentary record of medicine. This project is one way of translating that vision into the digital age as part of a global cyberinfrastructure.

The two repositories described above are examples of subject- specific repositories. In contrast, in our third example, Stevan Harnad has tirelessly been advocating author self-archiving in departmental or institutional repositories (Harnad and Hey 1995). The resulting open-access archives or repositories are digital collections of research articles that have been deposited by their authors and are freely accessible via the Web. In the case of journal articles, the deposition may be done either before publication, as a preprint or e-print, or after publication as a postprint. In order to allow searching across such repositories, "OAI-compliant" repositories are required to expose the metadata of each article (the title, authors, and other bibliographic details) in a format specified by the Open Archives Initiative Protocol for Metadata Harvesting (OAI-PMH) (Lagoze et al. 2004). OAI-compliant search engines can then harvest the metadata from each repository into large databases of worldwide research, which enables researchers to locate articles of interest. Such open-access repositories can be centralized and subject based, such as the examples of arXiv and PMC, or they may be distributed and multidisciplinary, located in universities or other research-based institutions. A list of open-access archives is maintained at the Registry of Open Access Repositories (ROAR) and the Directory of Open Access Repositories (OpenDOAR) sites.[9] There is now considerable evidence that publication in an open-access archive significantly increases the visibility and number of citations for research articles (Brody and Harnad 2004; Giles and Councill 2004).

There are several possible software solutions to building research repositories. Harnad and his colleagues at Southampton have developed the EPrints system, one of the leading software solutions, which has been used to build repositories around the world (Simpson and Hey 2005). These repositories can range from displaying the output of an individual research group to the research output of an entire department or institution. It is essential to emphasize that these research repositories can capture not only the formal research journal articles but also all sorts of research gray literature such as theses, technical reports, and presentations. One interesting investigation into the practical implications of creating an institutional research repository is the JISC-funded Targeting Academic Research for Deposit and Disclosure (TARDis) project at the University of Southampton.[10] The project began with a survey of the attitudes of the university's researchers, from senior management to individual academics, toward such a repository. The key feedback from this survey was the importance of not only integrating the repository into the process of serving the university's current research management needs but also integrating the deposit process into the researchers' work practice. In the case of Southampton, one of the crucial requirements for the institutional repository is the ability to record publications for use by the university, the department, the research group, and individuals at an early stage in the scholarly research cycle, rather than at some more remote time such as that corresponding to formal publication, which can be long after the initial production of a research output. The information capture can therefore take place either at the working paper stage, or the more final published paper and book chapter stage. A good summary of the goals of an institutional repository can be found in Lynch (2003) and Crow (2002).

The TARDis project was also able to feed information management requirements to the developers of the EPrints software at Southampton. In particular, they were able to influence the provision of fields and citation styles necessary to allow for the flexible reuse of the metadata. For instance, in an institutional context, setting up a separate database solely for papers available with full text would require a huge duplication of effort if implemented on a university scale. The TARDis model therefore simply requires that searches of the whole database should reflect all types of research output, and that searches for "full text only" items can be obtained from either the open-access archive—the subset of research outputs for which the full text is stored on the same server—or links to publishers' sites. With the increase in content in subject repositories such as arXiv and PMC as well as other subject or conference-based archives, it seems likely that the institutional research repository, as it grows in size and complexity, will be a pragmatic mix of links directly to the full text, where the process of deposition is either straightforward or there is a need to ensure the saving of a local copy, together with links to trusted repositories where necessary.

Open Access to Data

In 1991, the U.S. Global Change Research Program (1991) laid out what became known as the "Bromley Principles" for data management practices:

• The Global Change Research Program requires an early and continuing commitment to the establishment, maintenance, validation, description, accessibility, and distribution of high-quality, long-term data sets.
• Full and open sharing of the full suite of global data sets for all global change researchers is a fundamental objective.
• Preservation of all data needed for long-term global change research is required. For each and every global change data parameter, there should be at least one explicitly designated archive. Procedures and criteria for setting priorities for data acquisition, retention, and purging should be developed by participating agencies, both nationally and internationally. A clearinghouse process should be established to prevent the purging and loss of important data sets.
• Data archives must include easily accessible information about the data holdings, including quality assessments, supporting ancillary information, and guidance and aids for locating and obtaining the data.
• National and international standards should be used to the greatest extent possible for media and for processing and communication of global data sets.
• Data should be provided at the lowest possible cost to global change researchers in the interest of full and open access to data. This cost should, as a first principle, be no more than the marginal cost of filling a specific user request. Agencies should act to streamline administrative arrangements for exchanging data among researchers.
• For those programs in which selected principal investigators have initial periods of exclusive data use, data should be made openly available as soon as they become widely useful. In each case, the funding agency should explicitly define the duration of any exclusive use period.

Programs in the National Aeronautics and Space Administration (NASA) and the National Science Foundation (NSF) also put forward similarly forward-looking open-access policies during the 1990s. The NIH (2003) established a data-sharing policy stating that "data should be made as widely and freely available as possible while safeguarding the privacy of participants, and protecting confidential and proprietary data." It also identified five data-sharing methods: publishing in scientific journals; a researcher's CD or Web site; a data enclave that is secure and has controlled access; a data archive with policies and mechanisms for ingest, curation, and distribution; and a mixed mode enclave or archive that allows for multiple levels of access. More recently, the NIH has imposed the condition that all large NIH grant proposals must contain a data management plan to enable data sharing (Lynch and Lippincott 2005).

In 2004, there was progress on the international front with the Organisation for Economic Co-operation and Development's (OECD) *Declaration on Access to Research Data from Public Funding*. This resolution was supported by the governments of more than thirty countries and recognized that:

• Optimum international exchange of data, information and knowledge contributes decisively to the advancement of scientific research and innovation.
• Open access to, and unrestricted use of, data promotes scientific progress and facilitates the training of researchers.
• Open access will maximise the value derived from public investments in data collection efforts.
• Substantial benefits for science, the economy and society at large could be gained from the opportunities from expanded use of digital data resources.
• Undue restrictions on access to and use of research data from public funding could diminish the quality and efficiency of scientific research and innovation. (OECD 2004).

Given the intrinsically global nature of environmental science, it is not surprising that this research community is actively building grids to allow for the exchange and sharing of environmental data. In the United Kingdom, the Natural Environment Research Council (NERC) is funding the NERC DataGrid project to be the core of its long-term data management strategy.[11] The goals of the project are to build a grid that makes data discovery, delivery, and use much easier than it is now, and to facilitate better use of the existing investment in the curation and maintenance of quality data archives. It is also intended that the connection between data held in its managed archives and data held by individual research groups should be seamless in that the same tools can be used to compare and manipulate data from both sources. A partner project to the NERC DataGrid is the U.S. Earth Systems Grid.[12] When fully functional, the DataGrid will give environmental scientists the completely new ability to compare and contrast data from an extensive range of U.S. and European data sets from within one specific context.

Other global communities such as astronomers and particle physicists have advanced plans for data sharing. Both the proposed Large Synoptic Survey Telescope's International Virtual Observatory project and the LHC's particle physics grid are introducing detailed data management plans from the outset.[13] There is an interesting difference between these two communities as regards reusability. In astronomy, there is a large and active professional and amateur community that wants access to the data. By adding appropriate metadata it will be possible for scientists not involved in collecting the data to mine, combine, and analyze these data. For particle physicists, the situation is much more complicated. The LHC particle physics experiments are now hugely complex, and the ATLAS and CMS detectors require complex, compute-intensive Monte Carlo simulations to determine trigger rates, detector efficiencies, acceptance, and so on. Access to the raw data without a detailed understanding of the experimental apparatus would clearly be of no value. It is an interesting question as to whether some summary of the data and the detector that would allow other scientists to use the data to do physics is actually feasible.

Besides the data problems of these giant global projects, significant data challenges exist for the smaller, more local communities that typically need to aggregate and analyze a variety of heterogeneous data sources. The bioinformatics community is one such example, and the chemistry community is another. The UK Comb$e$Chem project explored data-access issues as well as some other important e-Science themes.[14] One theme concerned the use of a remote X-ray crystallography service for determining the structure of new compounds. By exposing it as a grid service, it can be combined in workflows with other grid services for computer simulations on clusters or searches through existing chemical databases. A second theme was explored in the associated Smart Tea Project, in which computer scientists studied the way chemists used their lab notebooks within the laboratory and were concerned with developing acceptable interfaces to handheld tablet technology.[15] This capability is important since it facilitates information capture in a digital form at the earliest stage of the experiment. Using tablet PCs the Smart Tea system has been successfully tested in a synthetic organic chemistry laboratory and linked to a flexible back-end storage system. A key usability finding, not surprisingly, was that users needed to feel in control of the technology and that a successful interface must be adapted to their preferred way of working. This necessitated a high degree of flexibility in the design of the lab book user interface.

Linking Publications to Data

The TARDis project was focused on research output, but it is possible to envision a more ambitious role for an institutional repository such as that of embracing the entire research output of an institution—publications, data, images, and software. In working toward such a goal, there is much still to be learned about the infrastructure required for a research library—both in recording research outputs, and in the management of publications and data. For example, the National Oceanography Centre at Southampton (NOC) is one of the world's leading centers for research and education in marine and earth sciences, the development of marine technology, and the provision of large-scale infrastructure and support for the marine research community. The National Oceanographic Library at NOC has long had the traditional role of recording research publications, but it has also played a major part in the TARDis project and the development of the University of Southampton Research Repository. It is now investigating the role of the library in the management and preservation of local data sources. Through the JISC-funded Citation, Location, and Deposition in Discipline and Institutional Repositories (CLADDIER) project, the National Oceanographic Library is exploring the linking of its publications in the institutional repository with environmental data holdings in the British Atmospheric Data Centre.[16] The result will be a step on the road to a situation where environmental scientists will be able to move seamlessly from information discovery, through acquisition, to the deposition of new material, with all the digital objects correctly identified and cited. The experience at Southampton shows that a partnership between librarians and researchers is likely to give the best results: an experienced information manager/librarian is helpful in creating good citations for data entities (now given unique Digital Object Identifiers—DOIs) in the repository.

Publishing biological data as part of, or the output of, research has been and continues to be a major topic of discussion (Bourne 2005; Robbins 1994). An important e-Science theme of the CombeChem project described above was the exploration of new forms of electronic publication—both of the data and research papers. This e-publication theme was examined in the companion eBank project funded by the JISC.[17] One of the key concepts of the CombeChem project was that of Publication@ Source, which aims to establish a complete end-to-end connection between the results obtained at the laboratory bench and the final published analyses. In this sister project, raw crystallographic data were annotated with metadata and "published" by being archived in the UK National Data Store as a Crystallographic e-print. Publications can then link back directly to the raw data for other researchers to access and analyze or verify. For example, the citation:

Coles, S. J., Hursthouse, M. B., Frey, J. G. and Rousay, E. (2004), Southampton, UK, University of Southampton, Crystal Structure Report Archive. (doi:10.1594/ecrystals.chem.soton.ac.uk/145)

links via the Digital Object Identifier (DOI) resolver, using the URL ⟨http://dx.doi.org/ 10.1594/ecrystals.chem.soton.ac.uk/145⟩, which resolves to the eBank Web page. This is another example of the need for links between the University of Southampton Research Repository and a data archive such as the eCrystals Crystal Structure Report Archive.[18] Complications arise in that Southampton is the home of the National Archive for Crystal Structures generated by both the University of Southampton's Chemical Crystallography Group and the Engineering and Physical Sciences Research Council's National Crystallography Service, located on the Southampton campus. This raises questions as to which organization owns the long-term responsibility for such a national archive. The lessons learned from these examples will be valuable in establishing clear relationships and responsibilities between discipline-based and institutional repositories.

Concluding Remarks

E-Science is enabling scientists to take different research approaches to answering scientific questions through the integration of distributed digital resources and facilities.

From the examples above, one sees that not only is the nature of scientific research changing but in concert so, too, is scholarly communication. Not only is publication on the Web, in one form or other, enabling access to a much wider range of research literature; we are also seeing the emergence of data archives as a complementary form of scholarly communication. In some fields, such as biology, databases are already one of the primary mechanisms of scholarly publishing. It is clear that links from research paper to research data will become a common feature of scholarly publications in the future. Moreover, since the data may change or more relevant data may become available subsequent to the original publication date, research papers will be linked to RSS feeds giving live updates of data. In addition, scholarly communication will become much more interactive. Social networking technologies such as those typified by the name Web 2.0 (O'Reilly 2005) will allow interested communities to develop through tagging and tools like del.icio.us, citeulike, and Connotea.[19] Wikis and blogs giving commentaries will also be commonplace, and alternatives to traditional peer review are likely to emerge. For instance, new services are being developed, such as those offered by the Faculty of 1000 Biology and Medicine.[20] For a subscription fee, these services highlight the most interesting new papers in biology and medicine, based on the recommendations of over one thousand leading scientists.

Not only is scholarly communication in the midst of drastic change, so too are libraries. The digitization of books and search services offered by Google, Microsoft, and others threaten to "disintermediate" libraries and usurp the traditional expert role of the librarian. Yet the digital revolution also offers new opportunities to libraries. Certainly, institutional research repositories are the natural evolution of a university library as the guardian of the intellectual output—almost all now "born digital"—of the institution. In order to compete with commercial search engines, however, librarians need to work with the research community to construct a global federation of interoperable research repositories. This distributed digital archive will constitute a key part of the research cyberinfrastructure containing traditional full-text research documents, research data, software, and images. By exposing their content as a Web service, the passive catalog of the past will be turned into a flexible component of more sophisticated services and workflows. The e-Science mashups will have arrived![21]

Notes

1. Large Synoptic Survey Telescope, available at ⟨http://www.lsst.org/lsst_home.shtml⟩.

2. "The International Virtual Observatory Alliance (IVOA) was formed in June 2002 with a mission to *facilitate the international coordination and collaboration necessary for the development and deployment of the tools, systems and organizational structures necessary to enable the international utilization of astronomical archives as an integrated and interoperating virtual observatory*" (⟨http://www.ivoa.net/pub/info/⟩).

3. LHCb Experiment, available at ⟨http://lhcb-public.web.cern.ch/lhcb-public/default.htm⟩.

4. Somewhat surprisingly, the system has no formal refereeing process to restrict "publication" on the site. Perhaps it is the mathematical nature of the field that prevents the site from being overwhelmed by the "noise" of low-quality material.

5. Cornell University Library arXiv project, available at ⟨http://arxiv.org/⟩.

6. National Library of Medicine, available at ⟨http://www.nlm.nih.gov/⟩.

7. PubMed Central, available at ⟨http://www.pubmedcentral.nih.gov⟩.

8. A description of the Medical Journals Backfiles Digitisation Project is available at ⟨http://library.wellcome.ac.uk/node280.html⟩.

9. Registry of Open Access Reprints, available at ⟨http://archives.eprints.org/⟩; Directory of Open Access Repositories, available at ⟨http://www.opendoar.org/⟩.

10. TARDis project, available at ⟨http://tardis.eprints.org/⟩.

11. NERC DataGrid, available at ⟨http://ndg.nerc.ac.uk⟩.

12. Earth Systems Grid, available at ⟨http://www.earthsystemgrid.org⟩.

13. For information on the International Virtual Observatory, see note 2 above. Information on the Worldwide LHC Computing Grid is available at ⟨http://lcg.web.cern.ch/LCG/⟩.

14. CombeChem, available at ⟨http://www.CombeChem.org⟩.

15. Smart Tea Project, available at ⟨http://www.SmartTea.org⟩.

16. For more information on the Citation, Location, and Deposition in Discipline and Institutional Repositories project, see ⟨http://claddier.badc.ac.uk⟩.

17. eBank UK, available at ⟨http://www.ukoln.ac.uk/projects/ebank-uk/⟩.

18. eCrystals, available at ⟨http://ecrystals.chem.soton.ac.uk/⟩.

19. See ⟨http://del.icio.us/⟩, ⟨http://www.citeulike.org/⟩, and ⟨http://www.connotea.org/⟩.

20. Faculty of 1000, available at ⟨http://www.facultyof1000.com/⟩.

21. "A mashup is a website or application that combines content from more than one source into an integrated experience" (Wikipedia).

References

Aarts, E. H. L., and J. L. Encarnação, eds. 2006. *True visions: The emergence of ambient intelligence.* Berlin: Springer-Verlag.

Atkins, D., K. Droegemeier, S. Feldman, H. Garcia-Molina, D. Messerschmitt, P. Messina et al. 2003. *Revolutionizing science and engineering through cyberinfrastructure: Report of the National Science Foundation Blue-Ribbon Advisory Panel on Cyberinfrastructure.* Washington, DC: National Science Foundation.

Berlin declaration on open access to knowledge in the sciences and humanities. 2003. October 22. Available at ⟨http://oa.mpg.de/openaccess-berlin/berlindeclaration.html⟩ (accessed April 23, 2007).

Bourne, P. 2005. In the future will a biological database really be different from a biological journal? *PLoS Computational Biology* 1 (3): e34. Available at ⟨http://compbiol.plosjournals.org/perlserv/?request=get-document&doi=10.1371%2Fjournal.pcbi.0010034⟩ (accessed April 24, 2007).

Brody, T., and S. Harnad. 2004. Comparing the impact of open access (OA) vs. non-OA articles in the same journals. *D-Lib Magazine* 10 (6). Available at ⟨http://www.dlib.org/dlib/june04/harnad/06harnad.html⟩ (accessed April 23, 2007).

Budapest open access initiative. 2002. February 14. Available at ⟨http://www.soros.org/openaccess/read.shtml⟩ (accessed April 23, 2007).

Crow, R. 2002. *The case for institutional repositories: A SPARC position paper.* Washington, DC: Scholarly Publishing and Academic Resources Coalition. Available at ⟨http://www.arl.org/sparc/bm~doc/ir_final_release_102.pdf⟩ (accessed April 23, 2007).

De Roure, D., T. Hey, and A. E. Trefethen. 2006. A global e-infrastructure for e-science: A step on the road to ambient intelligence. In *True visions: The emergence of ambient intelligence*, ed. E. H. L. Aarts and J. L. Encarnação. Berlin: Springer-Verlag.

Emmott, S., ed. 2006. *Towards 2020 science.* Cambridge, UK: Microsoft.

Foster, I., C. Kesselman, and S. Tuecke. 2001. The anatomy of the grid: Enabling scalable virtual organizations. *International Journal of High Performance Computing Applications* 15 (3): 200–222.

Fox, G. C. 1987. Questions and unexpected answers in concurrent computation. In *Experimental parallel computing architectures*, ed. J. J. Dongarra, 97–121. Amsterdam: Elsevier Science.

Fox, G. C., R. D. Williams, and P. C. Messina. 1994. *Parallel computing works!* San Francisco: Morgan Kaufmann.

Giles, C. L., and I. G. Councill. 2004. Who gets acknowledged: Measuring scientific contributions through automatic acknowledgment indexing. *Proceedings of the National Academy of Sciences of the United States of America* 101 (51): 17599–17604.

Gruener, W. 2006. Intel promises "100's of cores" per processor within 10 years. *Tom's Hardware Guide*, March 6. Available at ⟨http://tomshardware.co.uk/2006/03/06/idfspring2006_tera_scale/⟩ (accessed April 21, 2007).

Harnad, S., and J. M. N. Hey. 1995. Esoteric knowledge: The scholar and scholarly publishing on the Net. In *Networking and the future of libraries 2: Managing the intellectual record*, ed. L. Dempsey, D. Law, and I. Mowat, 110–116. London: Library Association Publishing.

Hey, T., and A. E. Trefethen. 2003. The data deluge. In *Grid computing: Making the global infrastructure a reality*, ed. F. Berman, G. Fox, and T. Hey, 809–824. Chichester, UK: Wiley.

Keller, M. A. 2006. Whither academic information services in the perfect storm of the early 21st-century? Paper presented at the eighth International Bielefeld Conference, Bielefeld, Germany, February. Available at ⟨http://conference.ub.uni-bielefeld.de/2006/docs/presentations/keller_biconf06_finalpaper.pdf⟩ (accessed April 21, 2007).

Lagoze, C., H. Van de Sompel, M. Nelson, and S. Warner, eds. 2004. *Open archives initiative protocol for metadata harvesting.* Open Archives Initiative. Available at ⟨http://www.openarchives.org/OAI/openarchivesprotocol.html⟩ (accessed April 23, 2007).

Lynch, C. A. 2003. Institutional repositories: Essential infrastructure for scholarship in the digital age. *ARL Bimonthly Report* 226. Available at ⟨http://www.arl.org/resources/pubs/br/br226/br226ir .shtml⟩ (accessed April 23, 2007).

Lynch, C. A., and J. K. Lippincott. 2005. Institutional repository deployment in the United States as of early 2005. *D-Lib Magazine* 11 (9). Available at ⟨http://www.dlib.org//dlib/september05/ lynch/09lynch.html⟩ (accessed April 24, 2007).

National Institutes of Health (NIH). 2003. *Final NIH statement on sharing research data.* February 26. Available at ⟨http://grants2.nih.gov/grants/guide/notice-files/NOT-OD-03-032.html⟩ (accessed April 24, 2007).

National Institutes of Health (NIH). 2005. *NIH calls on scientists to speed public release of research publications.* February 3. Available at ⟨http://www.nih.gov/news/pr/feb2005/od-03.htm⟩ (accessed April 23, 2007).

O'Reilly, T. 2005. *What is Web 2.0: Design patterns and business models for the next generation of software.* September 30. Available at ⟨http://www.oreillynet.com/pub/a/oreilly/tim/news/2005/09/30/ what-is-web-20.html?page=1⟩ (accessed April 24, 2007).

Organisation for Economic Co-operation and Development (OECD). 2004. *Science, technology, and innovation for the 21st century: Meeting of the OECD Committee for Scientific and Technological Policy at ministerial level, 29–30 January 2004—final communique.* Available at ⟨http://www.oecd.org/ document/15/0,2340,en_2649_34487_25998799_1_1_1_1,00.html⟩ (accessed April 24, 2007).

Robbins, R. J. 1994. Biological databases: A new scientific literature. *Publishing Research Quarterly* 10:3–27.

Seitz, C. 1992. Mosaic C: An experimental fine-grain multicomputer. In *Proceedings of the International Conference on Future Tendencies in Computer Science, Control and Applied Mathematics: Vol. 653, lecture notes in computer science,* ed. A. Bensoussan and J.-P. Verjus, 69–85. London: Springer.

Simpson, P., and J. M. N. Hey. 2005. Institutional e-print repositories for research visibility. In *Encyclopedia of library and information science,* ed. M. Drake, 2nd ed. New York: Marcel Dekker. Available at ⟨http://eprints.soton.ac.uk/9057/⟩ (accessed April 23, 2007).

Sincell, M. 2001. A man and his archive seek greener pastures. *Science* 293 (5529): 419–421.

Thakar, A. R., A. S. Szalay, P. S. Kunszt, and J. Gray. 2003. The Sloan Digital Sky Survey science archive: Migrating a multi-terabyte astronomical archive from object to relational DBMS. *Computing in Science and Engineering* 5 (5): 16–29.

U.S. Congress. 2006. *Federal research public access act of 2006.* S. 2695, 109th Congress, 2nd sess. Available at ⟨http://thomas.loc.gov/cgi-bin/query/z?c109:S.2695⟩ (accessed April 23, 2007).

U.S. Global Change Research Program. 1991. *Data management for global change research policy statements.* July. Available at ⟨http://www.gcrio.org/USGCRP/DataPolicy.html⟩ (accessed April 24, 2007).

Wellcome Trust. 2007. *Wellcome Trust position statement in support of open and unrestricted access to published research.* March 14. Available at ⟨http://www.wellcome.ac.uk/doc_wtd002766.html⟩ (accessed April 23, 2007).

2 Cyberscience: The Age of Digitized Collaboration?

Michael Nentwich

Since the early 1980s, the scholarly community has been witnessing a considerable increase in the use of information and communication technologies (ICTs). The networked personal computer, e-mail, the Internet, off- and online databases, the World Wide Web, electronic publications, discussion lists and newsgroups, electronic conferences, digital libraries, and "knowbots" are but a few of the trends that increasingly influence the daily work of the scientific community. As opposed to "traditional" science and research, which is done without networked computers, *cyberscience* designates the use of these ICT-based applications and services for scientific purposes. The increasing use of ICT in academia had, has, and will have manifold impacts on academic institutions, the daily work of researchers, the science publication system, and last but not least, the substance of research. This chapter, which examines many of these issues, is based on a major project on cyberscience that investigated how ICT affects the organization, practice, and products of science (Nentwich 2003; the study's conceptual framework is described in Nentwich 2005).

In this chapter, I first discuss the notion of cyberscience as opposed to related notions (such as e-Science). Following that, I present and examine in more detail the results of my research on collaboration among scholars and scientists in the age of cyberscience. This includes the following topics: results from a cross-disciplinary comparison; the impact of ICT on the spatial layout of research; the promises and limits of virtual conferencing; the increase of collaboration and the emergence of new collaboration patterns; and new infrastructure requirements. In my concluding remarks, I address the often-heard idea of the dematerialization of research.

What Is Cyberscience?

During the last decade, we have been flooded by various expressions with prefixes abbreviating "electronic," such as "e-" (e.g., e-mail or e-conferencing) or just a simple "e" immediately before the main word (eCommerce). Similarly, the prefix "i" or "i-"

as an abbreviation for "Internet" (iContent) or "intelligent" (iForms), "o" or "o-" for "online," and the use of the special character "@," originally defined to distinguish between the user name and the server in e-mail addresses, all became popular (br@ instorming). Wherever the new media and in particular the Internet is involved, a number of other letters such as "i" or "w" in a similar form—that is, with a thin line around it—are also used. Also "tele" can be seen quite frequently (like in "teleteaching"), meaning that the new word has to do with an activity performed from a distance. Finally, the prefix "cyber," as an abbreviation of "(related to) cyberspace," is similarly widespread (e.g., "cyberlaw"). While these prefixes are often used to make something old look more modern (especially in advertisements), their use can be justifiable in terms of writing economy—that is, with a view to abbreviate a whole concept. It is this latter purpose that allows me to elaborate on the notion of cyberscience. To the best of my knowledge, this term was first used in academic research by Paul Wouters (1996) as well as in a brief article by Uwe Jochum and Gerhard Wagner (1996), and then in a short chapter on "a day in the life of a cyberscientist" by Paul Thagard (2001), and since 1999, by this author. A session organized by Wouters at the joint conference of the Society for the Social Studies of Science and the European Association for the Study of Science and Technology held in Vienna in 2000 was also called Cyberscience. In addition, the term is frequently used on the Internet for a variety of purposes (thousands of hits resulted from a simple Google search), mainly by commercial enterprises to praise products such as software and publications. The word cyberscience is appearing in venues ranging from information gateways to e-magazines, and from school Web sites to sites containing complex, 3-D images of scientific research. The term has crept into journalism, although with a less precise meaning (see, e.g., Bernhofer 2001). With the publication of my book *Cyberscience: Research in the Age of the Internet* (Nentwich 2003), the notion seems to be used more widely in academic discourse.

I use the term *cyberscience* to designate the application as well as potential future development of ICTs and services in academia. As opposed to so-called traditional science, which does not use networked computers, I define cyberscience as all scholarly and scientific research activities in the virtual space generated by the networked computers and advanced ICT. Just as cyberspace means "the virtual space created by electronic networks" (Gresham 1994, 37), cyberscience is what researchers do in cyberspace. Thus, cyberscience comprises everything related to academia that takes place in this new type of space. Traditional academics traveled in either "thought spaces"—that is, in the world of thinking and ideas—or real places. Cyberscientists, by contrast, spend time not only in these places but also in new virtual spaces. For example, information rooms spread out before them via online databases; they meet and communicate electronically with fellow researchers in chat rooms or on discussion lists; they utilize digital libraries that deliver documents in bits and bytes; and they participate in virtual institutes that enable collaboration among researchers spread around the globe. Cyberscience technologies help to transcend real space.

It is the strong relationship between these technologies and space that makes it advisable not to use just the prefix "e" for electronic, as in "eScience" or "e-Science." These notions are used, among others, by the European Commission (2002, 6) in the context of the development of high-speed research networks and in a number of programs such as those in the United Kingdom and Germany that aim at financing grid technology. Similarly, "telescience" (as used by Carley and Wendt 1991; Lievrouw and Carley 1991; Walsh 1997) and "tele-communicative science" (Stichweh 1989; my translation) are too narrow, as my subject is not only about doing things from a distance but also about working with local people in a new mode. "E-mail science," a notion put forward by Bruce Lewenstein (1995), is also much too narrow, as is another recent addition to this babel of expressions, "digital academe," used by William Dutton and Brian Loader (2002). The latter phrase understands academe in a much narrower sense than I do here—namely, focusing on higher education and learning, and not on science and research. The point is that the new science is taking place in a new space, cyberspace, which can be reached via telecommunication. The connotations of cyber are more appropriate in these contexts, since cyberscience is about more than electronic ways of doing science.

The notion of cyberscience does not encompass all aspects having to do with the use of electronic means. In particular, it does not include the use of stand-alone computers as tools for modeling or computing, or other forms of nonnetworked data production and processing such as artificial intelligence. Furthermore, cyberscience is not the study of the cyberspace but of science and research *in* cyberspace, or termed differently, under cyberspace conditions. In other words, what I call cyberscience is mainly the use of computer-mediated communication (CMC) over computer networks (Walsh and Roselle 1999, 50).

If this chapter were written in German, a tricky problem with terminology would not have arisen. The English term *science*, when standing alone, primarily refers to the natural sciences. The study of cyberscience, however, encompasses all the various sciences, including the social sciences and humanities. English seems to have no straightforward, unambiguous shorthand to include all these fields. *Academia* normally refers to the world inside universities. *Scholarship* is mainly used with reference to the humanities. Perhaps the notion of *research* covers most aspects of my topic. Yet even the word *research* is often connected to the activities going on in laboratories (as in the notion of "research and development"). Whenever I use the term *science* (including cyberscience) and *scientific*, I refer not only to the natural sciences but also the broad panoply encompassed by the German meaning of the words.

Cybercollaboration

Cyberscience facilitates the establishment of networks at both the individual and macro level. In particular, ICT removes spatial barriers to the establishment and maintenance of social networks. Among the manifold issues of interest in the context of collaboration among scientists and academics in cyberspace are the following questions: Is cybercollaboration a cross-disciplinary phenomenon? What impact on the spatial layout of research can we expect to result from cyberscience? What are the promises and limits of virtual conferencing? Does cyberscience support the increase and development of new patterns of collaboration? How can we prepare the information infrastructure for cyberscience? This section examines specific results that relate to these questions. I begin with an overview of the study on which these findings are based.

Cybercollaboration across Academic Disciplines

My primary method of data collection was semistructured, in-depth interviews with fifty active junior- and senior-level researchers from thirteen disciplines who were located in Austria, Germany, and the Netherlands. The interviews, which were conducted during 2002, lasted from one to two hours, and focused on researchers' experiences with, among other cyberscience features, extended research groups and virtual institutes. While extended research groups work together on the basis of ICT e-conferencing, groupware, e-mail, and e-lists) for a single project or a series of them, virtual institutes go one step further by establishing some sort of institutional infrastructure stretching beyond projects, and collaboratories provide for remote access to laboratories. What all three forms—extended research groups, virtual institutes, and collaboratories—have in common is that they are (looser or denser) organizations without any, or only a small, home base in the real world, instead mainly existing as a network of researchers based in many different locations. In addition to the interviews with researchers, I collected cross-disciplinary data on the above topics through an extensive Internet search and in-depth investigation of the literature.[1] I also tested many e-tools (in particular e-conferencing) and conducted informal interviews with other experts, such as librarians, computer experts, and publishers.

At the time of the interviews, researchers in many fields were not aware of the concept of virtual institutes; nevertheless, there are a few genuine examples. So far, the best examples of virtual institutes in my sample of disciplines and subdisciplines are to be found in cultural studies and economics. There are also instances of collaboratories in the medical sector, such as in AIDS research (chapters 13 and 19, this volume). In five other areas—European studies, North American history, technology studies, applied linguistics, and information technology law—the experts reported the beginnings of such virtual entities. The funding agencies in particular, but not only the European Commission, are increasingly asking that project Web sites feature interim results and facilitate group communication. We may call these project networks, or extended work groups, an early stage of a virtual institute as they often carry over to successive projects and maintain a continued presence on the Internet, as is common, for instance, in high-energy physics. In the science disciplines under closer inspection here, I did not find any genuine example of a collaboratory in a narrow sense—that is, one that included collaboration in a remote virtual and/or physical laboratory space. Even the high-energy physicists do not work from a distance with the CERN facilities when they are at their home institutes (although they build stable project networks). Instead, they download files from the CERN servers in order to work with them in their home offices and travel in person to the experimental infrastructure. In sum, genuine virtual research organizations are not yet widespread, although there are a number of cases that come close (see also chapter 1, this volume).

By contrast, in many academic fields, working cooperatively from a distance is done on a daily basis. Specialized software, often called groupware, facilitates this. Yet with the exception of three subdisciplines in my sample, such tools are not used on a regular basis. The exceptions are in the fields of the social science studies of technology, molecular oncology, and high-energy physics. Even in these three fields, the experts' answer to how frequently groupware was used was "sometimes." Nonetheless, of the sample of fifty researchers, some of them reported at least limited experience with groupware. In addition to the fields listed above, those with experience came from regional economics, theoretical physics, applied linguistics, analytic philosophy, Pacific studies, information law, and tax law. Most interviewees, however, were unfamiliar with the term groupware.

The underlying reality probably differs from what interviewees reported. E-mail with attachments as well as shared access to dedicated directories on an institution's file server, which allows for the exchange of and access to common files, sometimes simultaneously, are quite common for many researchers. Hence, a lot of cooperation is actually going on in science and research with the help of electronic means. It is simply not known as groupware, and is less sophisticatedly organized. Furthermore, it seems that proper groupware is increasingly used in international and interdisciplinary projects, such as within the European Union research framework.

E-conferencing, with or without video transmissions, is still unusual in all disciplines. Except for some researchers from subfields in medicine, physics, sociology, and history, interviewees reported only experimenting with e-conferencing. High-energy physicists use videoconferencing, a telephone and satellite-based service, and North American historians use Internet-based e-conferencing on an almost-regular basis. In medicine, it was reported that conferences increasingly offer online access to parts of the event via live streaming. These conferences, sponsored by the pharmaceutical industry, have a physical venue. In most cases the online access is not synchronous and interactive, but the remote auditorium provides the opportunity by e-mail or through a Web form to post comments that will later be added to the respective page of the conference Web site. Asynchronicity and only partial interactivity seem to be the case in those other disciplines with at least some online events, too. Most personal experiences with Webcam-based communication took place in connection with teleteaching experiments or in the private domain.

The most frequent reason given by interviewees for this state of affairs is that they love to travel, and yet do not want to miss the opportunity for socializing, making new contacts, and so on. Furthermore, researchers often noted the (still) poor quality of Internet-based "Net meetings" coupled with the (still) high prices of both the infrastructure and the telecommunication fees for the available professional videoconferencing services. At the same time, the respondents pointed to decreasing travel budgets, and hence they saw some real potential for e-services' use in smaller workshop-type project meetings—while acknowledging that the use of the telephone, in most cases, is a good alternative to meeting in person.

All in all, collaboratories, virtual institutes, groupware, and e-conferencing are still the exception rather than the rule, but they are growing in importance. Therefore, in the following sections I consider the potential and possible consequences of these organizational forms and technologies.

The Impact of ICT on the Spatial Layout of Research

As I have defined cyberscience in relation to activities in a new kind of space, cyberspace, the use of networked computers obviously has the potential to affect spatiality in academia. Scholars may break free from spatial limitations to a considerable extent. Through telecommuting, the resources in the scholars' offices may be used even if the researcher is not present physically (telework). Online access to remote digital libraries with e-journals and access to various online databases may reduce the need to have a physical library close by. Extended research groups may cooperate in a virtual environment (e.g., in a collaboratory) while meeting only occasionally. Groupware applications may support this joint research, and virtual or e-conferences may take place on a larger scale, as I discuss in more detail later in this chapter.

By diminishing the importance of space, cyberscience may have a considerable impact on the way that research will be done in the not-so-distant future: multiauthorship may increase, oral scientific discourse might be replaced by written procedures, and scientific communities may be more fragmented (i.e., specialized but more interconnected worldwide). Further, research infrastructure requirements may shift, and this may alter the positioning of more peripheral research.

It can be shown that the spatial layout of academia is changing profoundly. An overall conclusion is that space—that is, the geographic distance between researchers, and between them and their facilities (offices, resources, libraries, etc.)—is diminishing in significance. Other dimensions are increasingly essential in shaping the circumstances in which research takes place. Among these dimensions are the reliability of the infra-structure, the conditions of access to specific resources, new organizational structures that slowly seize the new opportunities, and the possibilities presented by new cyber-tools. This is not to say that the traditional material basis will no longer play a role. By contrast, proximity to specific locales in the real world as well as the "core" researchers in a field will still be a key feature in many respects. When it comes to informal re-search activities in particular, the new media can only partially fulfill academics' needs. The café as a meeting place cannot be opened in cyberspace without losing much of its character. Furthermore, meetings in person will retain an important function when it comes to initial contact, "contracting"—that is, agreeing on the terms of a collabora-tive project—and conflict resolution. I nonetheless expect that CMC tools will soon become a regular part of all scholars' daily routine. Quick cybermeetings to discuss a research issue that arose in a collaborative project are likely to replace phone calls or lengthy e-mail exchanges. Asynchronous e-conferencing will be used to complement face-to-face meetings with a view to overcoming time restrictions and avoiding the loss of a crucial thread of argument. Distance cooperation based on e-mail will increas-ingly be enhanced by shared workspaces, such as file repositories and common data-bases. Access to written resources will largely shift to cyberspace, as specialized and near-comprehensive digital or virtual libraries will be available and accessible worldwide.

The Promises and Limits of Virtual Conferencing

Asynchronous e-mail lists are but one way of meeting virtually; there are various other ways to hold virtual seminars, workshops, or conferences, such as videoconferencing and/or audio conferencing, with or without desktop sharing, along with e-lists, multi-user object-oriented dialogues, and so forth. With a view to assessing the promises and limits of virtual conferencing, I propose to look at the functions of seminars and con-ferences, and ask whether these functions can be fulfilled in a virtual environment. The following functions of academic seminars, workshops, and conferences may be distinguished.

Quality Control   Here, the function involves quasi-experiments in the humanities and social sciences; a paper is tested against the arguments of an audience. This is probably the function most easily transferred to the electronic environment. In the context of e-journals, there is promising experience with this type of quality control. Philippe Hert reported that participants of the e-mail discussion he studied said their main goal was "to get their opinions across, to test the reactions elicited, and to get people used to these opinions" (1997, 352). He concluded that the "forum was used mostly by peo-ple to express, or at least to experiment with, their disagreement concerning some part of the heterogeneous [particular scientific] community" (355).

There is even potential for improvement in real seminars. The usual disadvantage of time constraints is less important in an electronic environment as there may be both a synchronous and an asynchronous part of the conference. Hence, lively debates do not have to be stopped because a coffee break is needed or the time is over—as they can continue in asynchronous mode in cyberspace. In addition, in an asynchronous virtual seminar, the advantages of a written "discourse memory" fully apply. A written record enables much more thorough analysis of the meat of arguments. If organized properly and supported by sophisticated software, another advantage applies: threading. The various related contributions (threads) may be separated more easily both during the debate and afterward. Whereas in the real world no particular argument can be pursued up to the point "where nothing is left to say," virtual seminars, as a matter of principle, are not restricted in this way.

Transmission   This function serves as an instrument to transmit knowledge and ideas to participants, a market for ideas, and an instruction for students. It is hotly debated whether knowledge can be transmitted as effectively in a virtual setting as in a physical one. The written format requires special skills, both on the part of the presenter and the receiver of the information. The virtual environment may offer the opportunity to follow a lecture in an asynchronous mode, thereby providing the choice to replay particular sections to enhance comprehension (Kling and Covi 1995).

Networking   This function is a node in the scientific network facilitating the renewal or establishment of relations, especially before and after seminars or during a conference. In principle, academics can "meet" in cyberspace and networking is possible. Renewing contacts in a virtual setting is certainly easier than establishing new contacts. There is the strong argument that first-time contacts are more promising if they occur face-to-face. Also, in the literature and among the interviewees for my study, there is a general sense that seminars and congresses are critical for sustaining academic networks (Fröhlich 1996, 22; Riggs 1998).

Yet virtual conferencing may play an important role in network building. Linton Freeman (1984) discusses in-depth how a (relatively primitive) e-mail-based conference system impacted the formation of a subdiscipline. He notes that the "whole of the scientific enterprise depends on effective communication among people working in an area" (203). As Freeman further states, "Particularly in the early stages of the emergence of a new specialty, progress requires communication in order to establish the sorts of norms and consenses that define both problem and approach" (203).

Social Management   The function here comprises instruments of institutional or associational social management: participants get socialized in the group; paper givers are being "initiated"; and seminars may even serve as a way for students to learn how to behave in the academic environment (e.g., when to talk and when to listen). Virtual seminars would certainly need some time to be able to become ritualized and fulfill the same function as face-to-face seminars. As long as they are something new and not a tradition, they cannot serve the same purpose. I hold, however, that there is no convincing reason why they should not do so in the long run. Many of the same social management functions can be enforced in the electronic environment.

Engendering Ideas and Discourse   Here, seminars and conferences help to generate new ideas and assertions by way of collective brainstorming and reflexive arguing. In the context of his look at a vivid e-mail discussion list debate, Hert observes that the properties and opportunities of the medium—that is, the possibility to compose one's message by "cutting and pasting" previous messages as well as marking and indenting original text—enabled the participants to use the discursive context. The "medium," explains Hert (1997, 345), "is then a resource for negotiating different interpretations of some messages." Hert speaks of the "collective appropriation" of the messages sent during an e-mail debate: "Unlike traditional written texts, these forms of writing show the process of constructing arguments in interaction with some of the recipients of those arguments. The debate is rewritten as it moves along, and one's texts are mixed with others' to become somehow the position emerging from the electronic discussion" (350). This is not to say that e-mail discussions will lead to consensus. Rather, they may contribute to dissension "more explicit to the general audience than is possible in a scholarly paper" (354), simply because an author cannot know all the points of dissent in advance. In addition, the asynchronous nature of e-lists allows participants to contribute ideas quickly without waiting for one's turn—as is necessary in a face-to-face situation. This might help to generate and record ideas.

To summarize, most of the functions of conferences and seminars may be met in a virtual setting. In some cases, it will take time until the results become satisfactory. It is, however, not yet clear whether the more socially oriented, informal functions can be fulfilled.

The Increase of Collaboration and the Emergence of New Collaboration Patterns
A number of studies show that collaboration has been increasing over the last decades. For instance, scientometric data document the increase in multiauthored papers, particularly in the natural sciences (see, e.g., Price 1986; Thagard 1997). One study found that the number of international collaboration papers approximately doubled, whereas at the same time there was a ninefold increase in the number of publications by large international collaborations (Walsh and Maloney 2002, 3). Furthermore, the percentage of papers published with authors from more than one country significantly increased (Walsh and Roselle 1999, 54). For instance, in theoretical physics, translocal cooperation is increasing (Merz 1997, 248–249; 1998). Physics projects that require

the resources and expertise of multiple teams of researchers have proliferated (Chompalov and Shrum 1999). Similar observations could certainly be made in other fields, too. Thus, scientific work is increasingly geographically distributed.

Cyberscience provides for a number of services essential for collaboration at a distance. In particular, fast communication, resource sharing, version control, and other groupware functions sustain cooperation without face-to-face meetings. In essence, CMC reduces the need for coworkers to be colocated. Arguably, multiauthorship and the increase of distant collaboration are not unilaterally caused by CMC, but the latter contributes to and favors the former to a large extent. Present-day research more often requires collaboration. There are a number of other reasons that favor the recent increase in transnational cooperation, among them funding policies, growing mobility, the increase of the overall number of researchers and their specialization, and last but not least, content-related reasons. There is, however, no doubt that many recent collaborative projects were started because the ICT infrastructure was at hand, and promised to secure their smooth and efficient operation. Had this new infrastructure not been available and had there not been another overwhelming reason to start the collaboration (e.g., tied funding), perhaps many would not have happened at all.

Collaboration is not only increasing; collaborative patterns themselves are changing. John Walsh and Ann Roselle (1999, 71) claim that the prior empirical work on the effects of the Internet on science suggest scientific work is changing in profound ways (see also Finholt and Olson 1997, 33; OECD 1998, 197). Whether the changes are profound is certainly open to debate. Nevertheless, at least the following significant novelties can be distinguished:

- *Increasing personal networks*: The number of individuals with whom a researcher can interact has expanded. This provides "greater access to potential collaborators and pathways for diffusing ideas" (Lewenstein 1995, 125).
- *Enabling larger groups of researchers to collaborate*: The new tools provide for an environment that potentially can be used to organize collaboration among a much larger group of researchers than ever before. A U.S. report on collaboratories rightly notes that "when too many human minds try to collaborate meaningfully, the requirements for communication become overwhelming" (Computer Science Technologies Board 1993, 7). Cyberscience attempts to facilitate the necessary robust communication among scientists. To be sure, it involves more than technical considerations such as access to useful computer facilities, networks, and data sets; social considerations also play an important role. For instance, the collaborative environment has to account for "differing academic traditions, approaches to and priorities in research, and budget constraints" (ibid.).
- *Increasing collaborative continuity*: Thanks to e-mail and other cybertools, two authors originally working together at one spot may more easily continue their collaboration

after one of them has moved to another job (Starbuck 1999, 189). This may also be true on a larger scale. E-lists are a perfect device to sustain the sense of community among a group of researchers between their rare face-to-face meetings.

• *Better match of competencies*: Collaboration patterns may become "more mediated by substantive fit, rather than geographic or personal linkages" (Walsh and Bayma 1996, 349). In other words, the composition of teams in terms of members' competencies may be optimized because of new opportunities to find researchers with highly specific matching or complementary skills. Also, due to increased communication, we may expect more attachment to the research group and the discipline (Walsh and Roselle 1999, 59). This might lead to overall better group performance in the research—as was supported by my interviewees. Although agreeing in principle, many respondents stated that personal acquaintance will remain as important as ever and that the Internet is only one factor pushing in this direction.

• *Specialization*: The possibility of becoming involved in worldwide collaborations may favor the trend to more specialization as specific skills and expertise can be used fruitfully despite the lack of local projects in need of them. When asked about this possible trend, the experts in my study indicated a potential specialization effect is only expected in political science and philosophy, and to some extent in law, language studies, and sociology, while in all other disciplines the answers were negative or split. Many pointed at a general "meandering" between specialization and generalization in their fields, and they were rather doubtful whether the former could be attributed to CMC. A number of my interviewees argued that specialization would increase due to the greater complexity and internationality of their fields as well as because of personal career path decisions. Further, they remarked that teaching obligations tend to discourage too much specialization.

• *New forms of collaboration*: Collaboration in the age of cyberscience may take the form of cooperative activities to build shared data or knowledge bases. In some fields, academics already contribute and have access to common databases, often managed by international networks (e.g., the Human Genome Project). Increasingly, filling and structuring e-archives and databases has become the content of whole research projects as well. Even more advanced would be what I call a "hyperbase" or "knowledge base" (Nentwich 2003, 270ff.), which as opposed to the multitude of articles in a field, is a dynamic database of manifold interlinked text modules that encompasses the knowledge of a given subject area. As already noted, researchers—like many others—tend to behave strategically and hence cooperatively when it comes to sharing information. The question is whether the Internet is about to create environments in which there are more incentives to cooperate than before.

• *Standardization of working habits*: Groupware may lead to the standardization of working habits (Scheidl 1999, 101). The idea is that the technology (groupware or database interfaces) would force different users to accept the same workflow—that is, to follow similar patterns, perform the same steps in the same order, search for the identical elements, and so forth. This may simply mean coordination of workflows or standard-ization. In some circumstances the latter could certainly have a positive impact on re-search; in others it may hamper creativity.

• *Intensification of communication*: While the traditional means of communication have been comparatively cumbersome (slow or needing simultaneity), the cybermeans are easy to use and may increase the frequency of communication among distant collaborators.

• *Different division of labor*: Further studies are needed to assess how researchers engaged in disembedded collaborations share, exchange, and divide problems and objects, and whether collaborators split up or parallel the work among them. "Are the rhythm and sequencing of these actions different when performed in an embedded or instead a disembedded locale?" (Merz 1998, 327).

Taken together, these nine changes lead me to the conclusion that the new tools indeed have the potential to create qualitatively different patterns of distant collabora-tion in cyberspace. They will accommodate the involvement of more researchers while allowing researchers to have larger networks of potential collaborators. Moreover, the competencies of coworkers may match better, and their workflows may be coordi-nated in a different way and perhaps become standardized.

New Information Infrastructure Requirements

The various elements of the new spatial layout also affect the academic infrastruc-ture as a whole. Looking at the totality of the cyberscience developments taking place at the moment, we may assume that the scientific infrastructure will become less characterized by well-equipped libraries with large archives, seminar rooms, and close proximity to an international airport. Rather, broadband and reliable access to the virtual information space via state-of-the-art multimedia desktop (or mobile) com-puters will be common. Here I will focus on only one aspect—the future information infrastructure—and leave aside such key issues as the infrastructure demands for uni-versities as teaching enterprises. For the emerging publishing infrastructure, see Nent-wich (2006).

The future information infrastructure will have various forms. Based on databases, archives, link collections, and full-text servers, digital and virtual libraries will probably spread. Traditional libraries aim at providing researchers with whatever is needed. Researchers have to go to the library to get what they want. Most research units have their own specialized library, which often parallels the holdings of similar collections elsewhere. In the case of university and other large libraries, these redundancies are particularly obvious. This multicenter spatial institutional model of the library may no longer persist in the networked world. Large domain-based libraries that serve all users within an entire nation (or even at the supranational level) or a specific discipline or subject domain (Owen 1997) are likely to emerge. A single center may succeed the multicenter model. While the parallel holding of identical items was useful and necessary in the predigital world, a single copy of a digital resource may serve a whole academic subdiscipline as long as the access rights are distributed widely.

As the World Wide Web with its typical hyperlink structure lends itself to distribution, the new "central" libraries and academic databases are, however, most likely to be of a decentralized nature; what is central is the access point (the "portal"), but the holdings may be distributed. Virtual libraries in general are of a distributed nature. Given the financial difficulties of many academic libraries, specialization and cooperation may be the key to overcoming the current crisis. MathNet, PhysNet, SocioNet, and the like are typical examples of this trend toward decentralized resource sharing and access. Similarly, projects like the Distributed Annotation System in biology are decentralized systems. In this case, there is a reference server with basic structural genome information, various other annotation servers around the world, and a Napsterlike browsing and exchange system (Rötzer 2001).

When it comes to digital resources provided by commercial publishers, however, the new global (virtual) library consortia will have to negotiate with the publishers to license the particular digital items for worldwide use. Different models are conceivable. For instance, it is possible that academic publishing will not be outsourced to the private sector any longer but taken care of by academia itself. In this case, a worldwide exchange system based on mutuality may be established (Nentwich 2001).

In sum, we observe a tendency toward central access to distributed resources, managed in a cooperative way. Traditional physical libraries will lose ground as more and more publications will be available in digital form. For some time, this will be parallel to print, but sooner or later central printing will cease for the majority of academic publications. The division of labor between libraries may be crucial as no single library can fulfill all the needs of local academics, but large consortia with each participating library having a unique specialization may be able to do so. Libraries may become virtual libraries for most of what they offer their users, yet stay a traditional and/or digital library for only a small fraction of the knowledge available. By becoming virtual or digital libraries, they transform themselves, but do not lose their traditional functions. Most important, their role as knowledge managers for researchers will be as important as ever. Librarians will become "cybrarians": information brokers and consultants (Nentwich 2003, 241).

The Dematerialization of Research?

While the above considerations support the conclusion that at least in the medium run, a completely virtual academia is not likely to emerge, the impact of this gradual shift to cyberspace activities on academia should not be underrated. We have to expect a further increase of distant collaborations. Furthermore, cybertools have the potential to create qualitatively different patterns of distant collaboration. For instance, more researchers will be involved, researchers' networks will be larger, collaborations may last longer, and workflows may change. While communication among remote collaborators will increase and perhaps be of a more instrumental character, the vision of isolated researchers in front of their computer screens seems unjustified. Cyberscience will be characterized, at least for a while, by an increase of written discourse. At the same time, academic writing is in part changing its character (e.g., through hypertext modularization or multimedia enhancements). Further important effects are to be observed with regard to the infrastructure of academia. In particular, there are many demands for a profound change as regards the traditional university. Equally, traditional physical libraries will lose ground, as discussed above. For researchers in the field, by contrast, mobile equipment with a good connection to the virtual infrastructure of their institutions becomes more attractive and essential. Peripheral institutes will profit from the diminishing significance of space. It is, however, uncertain if this will narrow down the gap between them and the top institutions (chapter 20, this volume). Especially in relation to the informal channels of research, it is rather unlikely that CMC will change much in favor of peripheral institutes, and hence there will be no "digital unity effect." The new media also both transform and reinforce the existing structure of communication within a community. The traditional invisible colleges will persist, but will increasingly communicate in cyberspace, and the emergence of such new colleges will be favored. Scientific communities will become increasingly worldwide with a highly improved communication infrastructure. In addition, the establishment of specialized—and thus tiny and yet worldwide—dynamic, and constantly shifting minicolleges whose members communicate much more among themselves than with outsiders is likely.

So where does all of this lead us? If we define as "material" the dedicated offices, books, libraries, and conference facilities, and as "immaterial" everything that flows among researchers in the form of bits and bytes, the notion of dematerialization surely depicts an overall trend. Yet the importance of physical locales will not disappear soon. Moreover, much of what researchers do is only marginally touched by these changes in the spatial layout, especially laboratory work and thinking itself. The future of academia is therefore by no means complete dematerialization, but will be characterized by a new balance of both material and immaterial elements.

Note

1. The results of the Internet search are in Cyberlinks, an online database, available at 〈http://www.oeaw.ac.at/ita/cyberlinks.htm〉.

References

Bernhofer, M. 2001. Cyberscience: Was macht die Wissenschaft im Internet? In *Gegenwort: Zeitschrift für den Disput über Wissen*. Vol. 8 of *Digitalisierung der Wissenschaften*, 27–31. Berlin: Berlin-Brandenburgische Akademie der Wissenschaften.

Carley, K., and K. Wendt. 1991. Electronic mail and scientific communication: A study of the Soar Extended Research Group. *Knowledge: Creation, Diffusion, Utilization* 12 (4): 406–440.

Chompalov, I., and W. Shrum. 1999. Institutional collaboration in science: A typology of technological practice. *Science, Technology, and Human Values* 24 (3): 338–372.

Computer Science and Technologies Board. 1993. *National collaboratories: Applying information technology for scientific research*. Washington DC: National Academies Press.

Dutton, W. H., and B. D. Loader, eds. 2002. *Digital academe: The new media and institutions of higher education and learning*. London: Routledge.

European Commission. 2002. *Research networking in Europe: Striving for global leadership*. Luxembourg: Office for Official Publications of the European Communities. Available at ⟨http://archive.dante.net/pubs/ECbrochure.html⟩ (accessed April 18, 2007).

Finholt, T. A., and G. M. Olson. 1997. From laboratories to collaboratories: A new organizational form for scientific collaboration. *Psychological Science* 8 (1): 28–36.

Freeman, L. C. 1984. The impact of computer based communication on the social structure of an emerging scientific specialty. *Social Networks* 6:201–221.

Fröhlich, G. 1996. Netz-Euphorien: Zur Kritik digitaler und sozialer Netz(werk-)metaphern. In *Philosophie in Österreich*, ed. A. Schramm. Vienna: Hoelder-Pichler-Tempsky. Available at ⟨http://www.iwp.uni-linz.ac.at/lxe/wt2k/pdf/Netz-Euphorien.pdf⟩ (accessed April 18, 2007).

Gresham, J. L. 1994. From invisible college to cyberspace college: Computer conferencing and the transformation of informal scholarly communication networks. *Interpersonal Computing and Technology* 2 (4): 37–52.

Hert, P. 1997. The dynamics of on-line interactions in a scholarly debate. *Information Society* 13 (4): 329–360.

Jochum, U., and G. Wagner. 1996. Cyberscience oder vom Nutzen und Nachteil der neuen Informationstechnologie für die Wissenschaft. *Zeitschrift für Bibliothekswesen und Bibliographie* 43:579–593.

Kling, R., and L. Covi. 1995. Electronic journals and legitimate media in the systems of scholarly communication. *Information Society* 11 (4): 261–271.

Lewenstein, B. V. 1995. Do public electronic bulletin boards help create scientific knowledge? The cold fusion case. *Science, Technology, and Human Values* 20 (2): 123–149.

Lievrouw, L. A., and K. Carley. 1991. Changing patterns of communication among scientists in an era of "telescience." *Technology in Society* 12:457–477.

Merz, M. 1997. Formen der Internetnutzung in der Wissenschaft. In *Modell Internet? Entwicklungsperspektiven neuer Kommunikationsnetze*, ed. R. Werle and C. Lang, 241–262. Frankfurt: Campus.

Merz, M. 1998. "Nobody can force you when you are across the ocean": Face to face and e-mail exchanges between theoretical physicists. In *Making space for science: Territorial themes in the shaping of knowledge*, ed. C. Smith and J. Agar, 313–329. London: Macmillan.

Nentwich, M. 2001. (Re-)de-commodification in academic knowledge distribution? *Science Studies* 14 (2): 21–42.

Nentwich, M. 2003. *Cyberscience: Research in the age of the Internet*. Vienna: Austrian Academy of Sciences Press.

Nentwich, M. 2005. Cyberscience: Modelling ICT-induced changes of the scholarly communication system. *Information, Communication, and Society* 8 (4): 542–560.

Nentwich, M. 2006. Cyberinfrastructure for next generation scholarly publishing. In *New infrastructures for knowledge production: Understanding e-science*, ed. C. Hine, 189–205. Hershey, PA: Information Science Publishing.

Organisation for Economic Co-operation and Development (OECD). 1998. The global research village: How information and communication technologies affect the science system. In *Science, technology, and industry outlook, 1998*, 189–238. Paris: Organisation for Economic Co-operation and Development.

Owen, J. M. 1997. The future role of libraries in the information age. Paper presented at the International Summer School on the Digital Library, Tilburg University, Netherlands. Available at ⟨http://eprints.rclis.org/archive/00002599/⟩ (accessed April 18, 2007).

Price, D. J. D. 1986. *Little science, big science—and beyond*. New York: Columbia University Press. (Orig. pub. 1963.)

Riggs, F. W. 1998. *Improving efficiency through better utilization of the Internet*. Available at ⟨http://www2.hawaii.edu/~fredr/WWWnotes.htm⟩ (accessed April 18, 2007).

Rötzer, F. 2001. Open source und offene Tauschbörsen für das postgenomische Zeitalter? *Telepolis*, February 16. Available at ⟨http://www.heise.de/tp/deutsch/special/leb/4926/1.html⟩ (accessed April 18, 2007).

Scheidl, R. 1999. Vor uns die Infoflut. *Das österreichische Industriemagazin* 9:100–102.

Starbuck, W. H. 1999. Our shrinking earth. *Academy of Management Review* 24 (2): 187–190.

Stichweh, R. 1989. *Computer, kommunikation und wissenschaft: Telekommunikative medien und strukturen der kommunikation im wissenschaftssystem (MPIfG discussion paper 89/11)*. Cologne: Max-Planck-Institut für Gesellschaftsforschung.

Thagard, P. 1997. Collaborative knowledge. *Noûs* 31 (2): 242–261.

Thagard, P. 2001. Internet epistemology: Contributions of new information technologies to scientific research. In *Designing for science: Implications from everyday, classroom, and professional settings*, ed. K. Crowley, T. Okada, and C. Schunn, 465–486. Mahwah, NJ: Lawrence Erlbaum.

Walsh, J. P. 1997. Telescience: The effects of computer networks on scientific work. Report to the OECD/STI/STP Information Technology and the Science System Project. Chicago: University of Illinois at Chicago.

Walsh, J. P., and T. Bayma. 1996. The virtual college: Computer-mediated communication and scientific work. *Information Society* 12 (4): 343–363.

Walsh, J. P., and N. G. Maloney. 2002. Computer network use, collaboration structures, and productivity. In *Distributed work*, ed. P. Hinds and S. Kiesler, 433–458. Cambridge, MA: MIT Press.

Walsh, J. P., and A. Roselle. 1999. Computer networks and the virtual college. *Science Technology Industry Review* 24:49–78.

Wouters, P. F. 1996. Cyberscience. *Kennis en Methode* 20 (2): 155–186.

II   Perspectives on Distributed, Collaborative Science

3 From Shared Databases to Communities of Practice: A Taxonomy of Collaboratories

Nathan Bos, Ann Zimmerman, Judith S. Olson, Jude Yew, Jason Yerkie, Erik Dahl, Daniel Cooney, and Gary M. Olson

Why are scientific collaborations so difficult to sustain? Inspired by the vision of William Wulf (1989, 1993) and others, researchers over the last twenty-five years have made a number of large-scale attempts to build computer-supported scientific collaboration environments, often called collaboratories (National Research Council 1993). Yet only a few of these efforts have succeeded in sustaining long-distance participation, solving larger-scale problems, and initiating breakthrough science.

Should we consider this surprising? Scientific progress is by nature uncertain, and long-distance collaboration always faces many barriers (Olson and Olson 2000). Still, the difficulties of sustaining large-scale collaboratories were unexpected to many scientists and funders, partially because modern studies of science have repeatedly emphasized the social nature of scientific communities. Pioneers in the social studies of science documented how the basic activities of scientists, such as deciding what counts as evidence, are fundamentally social undertakings (Collins 1998; Latour and Woolgar 1979). Thomas Kuhn (1963) showed how scientific peer groups determine what theories will be accepted as well as make more mundane judgments about what papers will be published and what grants will be funded. Diana Crane (1972) first described the loosely affiliated but highly interactive networks of scientists as "invisible colleges." Compared to other peer groups, scientific communities are often surprisingly egalitarian and broadly international. Mark Newman's (2001) social network analyses of scientific communities in biomedicine, physics, and computer science showed that each of these fields formed a well-interconnected or "small world" network (Watts and Strogatz 1998). Scientific users were early adopters and promoters of many of the technologies that long-distance collaboration now relies on, including e-mail, FTP servers, and the World Wide Web.

Given this context, it was natural for visionaries to predict that scientists would lead the way in making the boundaries of distance obsolete and would be the first to take advantage of new technologies to assemble larger-scale efforts across distance. Yet previous research failed to document some crucial barriers that make scientific collaboration more difficult than expected. There is a key distinction between informal, one-to-one collaborations, which have long been common between scientists, and more tightly coordinated, large-scale organizational structures, which are a less natural fit. In particular, our research has highlighted three types of barriers.

First, scientific knowledge is difficult to aggregate. While *information* has become easy to transmit and store over great distances, *knowledge* is still difficult to transfer (Szulanski 1992). Scientists generally work with ideas that are on the cutting edge of what is understood. This knowledge often requires specialized expertise, is difficult to represent, may be tacit, and changes rapidly. This kind of knowledge is the most difficult to manage over distances or disseminate over large groups. Scientists can often negotiate common understandings with similar experts in extended one-to-one interactions, but may have great difficulty communicating what they know to larger distributed groups. Standard tools for knowledge management may presume an ability to codify and disseminate knowledge that is not realistic in cutting-edge scientific enterprises.

Second, scientists work independently. They generally enjoy a high degree of independence, both in their day-to-day work practices and the larger directions of their work. Scientific researchers have greater freedom to pursue high-risk/high-reward ideas than do individuals in many other professions. Most practicing scientists would strongly resist controls that many corporate employees accept as normal, such as having their work hours, technology choices, and travel schedules dictated by others. The culture of independence benefits science in many ways, but it also makes it more difficult to aggregate scientists' labors. Scientific collaborations must work harder than other organizations to maintain open communication channels, adopt common tool sets, and keep groups focused on common goals.

The third barrier is the difficulty of cross-institutional work. Crossing boundaries between institutions is frequently a greater barrier than mere distance (Cummings and Kiesler 2005; chapter 5, this volume). Even when all of the scientists are ready to proceed, collaborations can run into institutional-related problems—especially legal issues—that cannot be resolved (Stokols et al. 2003, 2005). Universities often guard their intellectual property and funding in ways that hinder multisite collaboration. Since the biggest science funding sources are federal government based, international, or even interstate, collaboration is frequently hindered. In corporate settings, the largest international collaborations are often made possible by mergers, but there has been no such trend in university research, again due to the funding sources. Few universities operate across state lines, much less national boundaries.

These barriers that are specific to scientists are compounded by the normal challenges of working across distance. Distance collaboration challenges coordination and trust building (Jarvenpaa and Leidner 1999), fosters misunderstandings (Cramton 2001), and inhibits the communication of tacit knowledge (Lawson and Lorenz 1999) and transactive knowledge, or the knowledge of what colleagues know (Hollingshead 1998).

The Science of Collaboratories (SOC) was a five-year project funded by the National Science Foundation (NSF) to study large-scale academic research collaborations across many disciplines. The overall goals of the SOC project were to perform a comparative analysis of collaboratory projects, develop theory about this new organizational form, and offer practical advice to collaboratory participants and funding agencies about how to design as well as construct successful collaboratories. Through our research, we identified many of the barriers, both organizational and technological, that made these projects difficult. On a more positive note, we also assembled a database with many success stories. The SOC database contains summaries of collaboratories that achieved some measure of success, and analyses of the technology and other practices that enabled them.[1]

This chapter reports one of the main outputs of the SOC project: a seven-category taxonomy of collaboratories. This taxonomy has proven useful and robust for documenting the diversity of collaboratories that now exists, identifying the associated strengths and key challenges, and framing a research agenda around these types.

Collaboratory Typologies

This is not the first typology of its kind, although it is unique in its scale and purpose. A great deal of previous work in computer-supported cooperative work (e.g., Grudin 1994; DeSanctis and Gallupe 1987) has classified technology as to how well it supported different task types as well as different configurations of local and distant workers. Georgia Bafoutsou and Gregoris Mentzas (2002) reviewed this literature, and mapped it on to the specific technology functionalities of modern groupware systems. This type of classification yields insights about what kinds of task/technology matches are most apt (e.g., text chat is a good choice for maintaining awareness, but a poor one for negotiation). The SOC project conducted a similar technology inventory as part of its research, but this level of classification is not as useful for large-scale projects because these projects perform many different task types using numerous tools over the course of their lives. Any single project will at different times engage in negotiation, decision making, and brainstorming, and will make use of e-mail, face-to-face meetings, and real-time communication tools. Low-level task/technology matching may be one factor in a project's success, but it is not a sufficient predictor of overall success.

Ivan Chompalov and Wesley Shrum (1999) developed a larger-scale classification scheme based on data from phase one of the American Institute of Physics (AIP) Study of Multi-Institutional Collaborations (1992, 1995, 1999). This large-scale, three-phase study looked at a large number of collaborations in high-energy physics, space science, and geophysics. Chompalov and Shrum analyzed data from a subset of twenty-three of these projects, and performed a cluster analysis that made use of seven measured dimensions: project formation and composition, magnitude, interdependence, communication, bureaucracy, participation, and technological practice. Their analysis sought to find relationships between these dimensions and the outcome measures of trust, stress, perceived conflict, documentary process, and perceived success. Most of these categories had little relationship to success measures, and nor did they correspond strongly to particular subdisciplines. One of the researchers' findings was particularly intriguing: the technological dimension (whether the project designed and/or built its own equipment, and whether this technology advanced the state of the art) corresponded to all five of the success measures. It is unclear from these data whether the technology measures actually caused better success or corresponded in some other way—that is, led to a different sort of project. It is difficult to believe that every project should design its technology to work on the "bleeding edge" in order to ensure success (nor do Chompalov and Shrum make any such claim). It seems more likely that other features of these cutting-edge design projects, such as intrinsic interest, tangible products, or funding levels, contributed to their success.

By observing the value that could be obtained from "bottom-up" studies using large data sets of heterogeneous projects, our project learned a great deal from the groundbreaking AIP studies. The classification system we developed, however, differs fundamentally in purpose from that of Chompalov and Shrum. While they sought to explain success after the fact, our project attempted to identify organizational patterns, somewhat similar to design patterns (after Alexander, Ishikawa, and Silverstein 1977), which then could be used by funders and project managers in designing new collaborations. Rather than focusing on the technology or the emergent organizational features, the scheme is tightly focused on the goals of the projects. The result of this classification is the identification of key challenges along with the recommendation of practices, technology, and organizational structures that are appropriate for a stated set of goals.

Data Set and Sampling Methods

In spring 2002, the SOC project started putting together a database of collaboratories that would be the most comprehensive analysis of such projects to date. The database currently contains 212 records of collaboratories. Of these, 150 have received a classification, and summaries have been published for more than 70 of them. Nine broad disciplinary categories are represented using the NSF's field of study classifications.

As noted in the introduction to this volume, attendees of an SOC workshop together constructed and agreed to this definition of a collaboratory:

A collaboratory is an organizational entity that spans distance, supports rich and recurring human interaction oriented to a common research area, and fosters contact between researchers who are both known and unknown to each other, and provides access to data sources, artifacts, and tools required to accomplish research tasks.

This definition is restricted to scientific endeavors, thus excluding many (albeit not all) corporate and government projects. Within the sciences, however, it is quite broad, covering many disciplines and many more organizational forms than did previous studies, such as those of the AIP. For the purposes of data collection, the notion of distance was operationalized to include only collaborations that crossed some kind of organizational boundary (in this case following the AIP lead). For academic research, this usually meant that nominees would have to be multiuniversity or university/ other partnerships; most that were merely cross-departmental or cross-campus were excluded. Few other restrictions were placed on entry, though, in order to be as inclusive as possible.

The breadth of this definition of a collaboratory complicated the choice of a sampling technique. There did not seem to be any way to create a truly representative sample, because the true boundaries of the population to be sampled were unknown. Some options were to choose to sample certain subsets of the population, such as all multisite projects sponsored by the NSF, all projects appearing in Google searches of the word collaboratory, or all projects nominated by members of a certain professional organization. Each of these possibilities would inevitably exclude interesting areas of inquiry.

Our choice required a type of nonrandom sampling—namely, purposive sampling. Michael Patton (1990) provides a taxonomy of purposive sampling techniques. The technique used in this project is similar to what Patton calls *stratified purposeful sampling*, which organizes observations to cover different "strata" or categories of the sample. The complication of this project was that the groups were themselves unknown at the beginning of the study. The technique chosen needed to be flexible enough to both classify and describe, so elements of *extreme and deviant case sampling*, which pays special attention to unusual or atypical cases, were incorporated.

A purposive sampling method called "landscape sampling" was devised to produce a sample as comprehensive as possible in type, but not in frequency. It is similar to what an ecologist would do in a new area: focus on finding and documenting every unique species, but put off the job of assessing how prevalent each species is in a population. An ecologist in this kind of study concentrates on novelty rather than representativeness; once a particular species is identified from a few instances, most other members of that species are disregarded unless they have unusual or exemplary features.

In searching out new cases, we cast the net broadly, using convenience and snowballing techniques, along with other more deliberate strategies. Any type of project could be nominated by having an initial entry created in the database. Nominations were also solicited from the following sources: SOC project staff, SOC workshop attendees, three major funding sources (the NSF, the National Institutes of Health, and the Department of Energy), program officers of each of those sources, and review articles in publications such as the annual database list published in *Nucleic Acids*

Research (see, e.g., Baxevanis 2002). Throughout the project the SOC Web site included a form for nominating projects that any visitor could fill out, and some nominations were received this way. Finally, a snowball technique was used, whereby project interviewees were asked to nominate other projects. These methods led to the nomination of more than two hundred projects, a richer and broader sample than could have been obtained otherwise.

Landscape samples must have criteria for the inclusion/exclusion of cases that fit the definition. Resources were not available to investigate every project that fit the definition of a collaboratory. Instead, energy was focused where the most learning could happen and the most interesting sample could be obtained. The criteria for collaboratories that would be included were:

• *Novelty*: The sampling technique was strongly biased toward finding examples of collaboratories that were different than what had been seen before. Projects were pursued that were novel in their use of technology, their organizational or governance structures, or the scientific discipline that they covered. The emergence of identifiable types (discussed below) greatly aided the identification of novel cases.

• *Success*: Projects that were particularly successful were also of special interest, regardless of whether they were novel. The success criterion had also been explored at a project workshop (SOC Research Group 2001). Success usually manifested as either producing a strong body of scientific research, or attracting and retaining a large number of participants, but there were other possible criteria as well, such as generativity.

• *Prototypicality*: In some cases, collaboratories were included not because they were novel but because they seemed prototypical of a certain type. (The identification of types aided this process.) This helped us correct and re-center the data set when it turned out that the first one or two collaboratories of a certain type were atypical in some respects, just as the first member of a species to be identified may happen to be an outlier on some category.

Social vetting was also used to check and validate these decisions. Few collaboratory nominees were either included or excluded on the basis of one person's judgment. The process was for one investigator to do an initial summary of the project, and report back to a subcommittee of three to five researchers who would make the decision whether to pursue the investigation further. This served to improve the decision process in the same way that multirater coding improves other qualitative rating methods.

Landscape sampling is useful for expanding the horizons of a particular area of inquiry and producing a rough map of a new problem space. It is not useful for making some kinds of generalizations about a sample. For example, the collaboratories database could not be used to make claims about the average size of collaboratories or average success rate; for that, a representative sampling method would be needed. A landscape sample is useful for identifying characteristics, such as identifying key organizational and technology issues.

Seven Types of Collaboratories

The process of categorizing collaboratories was a social one, as described above and resulted in seven types of collaboratories. A small group of experienced investigators examined the data and decided which classification best fit each project. Many projects were also given multiple classifications. One category was always chosen to be primary, but projects could have any number of secondary classifications. Often this was because a project had multiple components. For example, the main work of the Alliance for Cellular Signaling is coordinated multisite lab work, making it a clear-cut distributed research center.[2] This project was also managing the "molecule pages" Community Data System on a related topic with different participants. Sometimes projects were given multiple classifications because they legitimately had multiple goals. Many of the projects, for instance, listed the training of new scientists as one of their goals, but in most cases this is not the primary goal. Therefore, many projects are assigned a secondary category of a virtual learning community. A few, on further investigation, actually did prioritize training and dissemination ahead of new research; these were assigned the primary categorization of a virtual learning community.

Our seven-category classification system is presented below. For each classification, the following information is given:

- Collaboratory type definition
- An example collaboratory of this type
- Key technology issues of this collaboratory type
- Key organizational issues of this collaboratory type

Shared Instrument

Definition   This type of collaboratory's main function is to increase access to a scientific instrument. Shared instrument collaboratories often provide remote access to expensive scientific instruments such as telescopes, which are frequently supplemented with videoconferencing, chat, electronic lab notebooks, or other communications tools.[3]

Example   The Keck Observatory, atop the Mauna Kea summit in Hawaii, houses the twin Keck Telescopes, the world's largest optical and infrared telescopes. Keck has been a leader in the development of remote operations (Kibrick, Conrad, and Perala 1998). Observing time on the Keck Telescope is shared between astronomers from Keck's four funders: the University of California system, the California Institute of Technology, the National Aeronautics and Space Administration, and the University of Hawaii. Each institution is allocated time in proportion to its financial contribution. Because of the extreme altitude of the observatory, Keck's instruments have been made remotely accessible from Waimea, Hawaii, thirty-two kilometers away. Remote observation employs a high-speed data link that connects observatories on Mauna Kea with Internet-2 and runs on UNIX. To prevent data loss, remote sites also have automated backup access via an integrated services digital network. Remote scientists have contact with technicians and scientists at the summit and Waimea through H.323 Polycom videoconferencing equipment. Future plans include online data archiving. Remote access facilities have also been constructed at the University of California at Santa Cruz, the University of California at San Diego, and the California Institute of Technology. These remote facilities allow astronomers to do short observation runs (one night or less) without traveling to Hawaii, and allow late cancellations to be filled, increasing productivity.

Technology Issues   Shared instrument collaboratories have often pushed the envelope of synchronous (real-time) communications and remote-access technology. Keck's recent innovation of allowing access to the Hawaii-based observatory from California is extending the current limits of what has been done in this area. Other interesting technology problems that frequently arise are those involved with managing large instrument output data sets and providing security around data. One product of the Environmental Molecular Sciences Laboratory collaboratory (Myers, Chappell, and Elder 2003) was a high-end electronic notebook that improved on paper notebooks by saving instrument output automatically, allowing access from many locations, and providing the level of security needed for lab notebooks.

Organizational Issues   Shared instrument collaboratories must solve the problem of allocating access, which becomes trickier when instruments are oversubscribed (i.e., there is more demand than the time available). Collaboratories typically solve this by appointing committees to award time based on merit. A less well-handled problem is providing technical support. Local technicians are often critical to using the instruments effectively; remote participants may not have the social relationships and contextual knowledge to work with them effectively.

Community Data Systems
Definition   A community data system is an information resource that is created, maintained, or improved by a geographically distributed community. The information resources are semipublic and of wide interest; a small team of people with an online file space of team documents would not be considered a community data system. Model organism projects in biology are prototypical community data systems.

Example   The Protein Data Bank (PDB) is the single worldwide repository for the processing and distribution of 3-D structure data of large molecules of proteins and nucleic acids (Berman, Bourne, and Westbrook 2004). The PDB was founded in 1971 and was a pioneer in community data systems. As of October 2003, the PDB archive contained approximately 23,000 released structures, and the Web site received over 160,000 hits per day. Government funding and many journals have adopted guidelines set up by the International Union of Crystallography for the deposition and release of structures into the PDB prior to publication. The union was additionally instrumental in establishing the macromolecular Crystallographic Information File, now a standard for data representation.

Technology Issues   Community data systems are often on the forefront of data standardization efforts. Large shared data sets can neither be constructed nor used until their user communities commit to formats for both storing and searching data. The PDB's role in creating the macromolecular Crystallographic Information File standard is typical; there are many other examples of standards and protocols that have emerged in conjunction with community data systems.

A second area of advanced technology that frequently seems to coevolve with community data sets is modeling and visualization techniques. Modelers find opportunities among these large public data sets to both develop new techniques and make contact with potential users. The Visible Human Project, for example, has unexpectedly become a touchstone for new developments in 3-D anatomical visualization because of the data set and user base it provides.[4]

Organizational Issues   Community data systems can be viewed as public goods projects that may find themselves in a social dilemma related to motivating contributions (chapter 14, this volume; Connolly, Thorn, and Heminger 1992). In addition to figuring out how to motivate contributors, these projects also must develop large-scale decision-making methods. Decisions about data formats and new developments for such community resources must take into account the views of many different stakeholders from many different locations.

Open Community Contribution System

Definition   An open community contribution system is an open project that aggregates the efforts of many geographically separate individuals toward a common research problem. It differs from a community data system in that contributions come in the form of work rather than data. It differs from a distributed research center in that its participant base is more open, often including any member of the general public who wants to contribute.

Example   The Open Mind project is an online system for collecting "commonsense" judgments from volunteer participants ("netizens") via its Web site (Stork 1999). Participants contribute by making simple commonsense judgments and submitting answers via a Web form. Participation is open, and contributors are encouraged to return to the site often. The aggregated data are made available to artificial intelligence projects requiring such data. Two currently active projects are on handwriting recognition and commonsense knowledge. The site is hosted by Ricoh Innovations, and individual projects are designed and run by academic project teams. Current project teams are from MIT, Stanford University, and Johns Hopkins University.

The inspiration for this system came when David Stork, the project's founder, reviewed many different pattern-recognition systems and came to the conclusion that rapid advances in this field could take place if large data sets were available. These data sets would generally be too large for hired project staff to construct, but they might be assembled with help from many online volunteers.

The Open Mind initiative only collects and aggregates data; it does not develop products (although Ricoh Innovations does). Data from the project are made freely available to both commercial and noncommercial users.

Technology Issues   The main technology challenge for these collaboratories is to create a system that operates across platforms, and is easy to learn and use. Users must be able to do productive work in the system quickly, without much advanced training. The administrators of such collaboratories do well to utilize the tools of user-centered design early and often. These projects also must address the challenge of standardized data formatting, without expecting the contributors to learn complex entry methods.

Organizational Issues   Open systems must address the problem of maintaining quality control among a large and distributed body of contributors. Some projects rely on the sheer mass of data to render mistakes or inconsistencies harmless. The National Aeronautics and Space Administration's Clickworkers project, for example, found that by averaging together the crater-identification work of several community volunteers, it could create a data set as high in quality as would be produced by a smaller number of trained workers. Wikipedia uses community vetting in a different way. Knowledgeable readers usually catch mistakes in the data by repetitive viewing and vetting. Intentional biases, editorializing, or vandalizing of the data are also generally caught and corrected quickly. Some volunteer editors take on the responsibility of being notified automatically when certain controversial entries, such as the "Abortion" one, are edited (Viégas, Wattenber, and Dave 2004). As with community data systems, open community contribution systems must also address the challenge of reaching and motivating contributors.

Virtual Community of Practice

Definition   This collaboratory is a network of individuals who share a research area and communicate about it online. Virtual communities may share news of professional interest, advice, techniques, or pointers to other online resources. Virtual communities of practice are different from distributed research centers in that they are not focused on actually undertaking joint projects. The term *community of practice* is taken from Etienne Wenger and Jean Lave (1998).

Example   Ocean.US is an electronic meeting place for researchers studying oceans, with a focus on U.S. coastal waters (Hesse et al. 1993). The project runs an active set of bulletin boards/e-mail Listservs used to exchange professional information (e.g., job openings), along with some political and scientific issues. Ocean.US also provides online workspace for specific projects, and develops online support for workshops and distance education in this field. The project began in 1979 as ScienceNet, providing subscription-based electronic discussions and other services before e-mail and Web services were widely available. ScienceNet was shut down in the mid-1990s when the technology became ubiquitous and the project could no longer be supported with paid subscriptions. It was reimplemented as a set of Web-based services and renamed Ocean.US. The service is owned and run by a for-profit company, Omnet.

Technology Issues   As with open community contributions systems, the main technology issue is usability. Successful communities of practice tend to make good use of Internet-standard technologies such as Listservs, bulletin boards, and accessible Web technologies. A key technology decision for these projects is whether to emphasize asynchronous technologies such as bulletin boards, or invest time and energy into synchronous events such as online symposia.

Organizational Issues   Communities of practice, like other for-profit e-communities, must work hard to maintain energy and participation rates with a shifting set of participants. Faced with stiff competition for online attention, many community of practice Web sites are moving away from all-volunteer efforts toward professional or for-profit management.

Virtual Learning Community

Definition   This type of project's main goal is to increase the knowledge of the participants, but not necessarily to conduct original research. This usually involves formal education—that is, education by a degree-granting institution—but can also consist of in-service training or professional development.

Example   The Ecological Circuitry Collaboratory is an effort to "close the circuit" between empiricists and theoreticians in the ecological sciences, and create a group of quantitatively strong, young researchers. The collaboratory is comprised of a set of seven investigators and their students. The NSF's Ecosystem Studies and Ecology programs fund this collaboratory. Participant researchers study the relationship between a system structure (i.e., biodiversity) and the function of that system, and they also do work in terrestrial and aquatic habitats, including forests, streams, estuaries, and grasslands.

The goal of the project is to educate young ecologists to combine empirical research methods with quantitative modeling as well as to show that ecological modeling is a valuable resource in an ecologist's tool kit. Toward this end, students and investigators meet regularly for short courses as well as the exchange of ideas and information. The collaboratory also includes a postdoctoral researcher who leads the team in integration and synthesis activities, coordinates distributed activities, and supports faculty mentors.

Technology Issues   In multi-institutional educational projects there is often a large disparity in technology infrastructure, especially when well-equipped U.S. universities collaborate with K-12 institutions or non-Western universities. Educational projects can make use of specialized e-learning software, but there are frequently trade-offs involved. In currently available software, one usually has to choose between software primarily designed for one-to-many broadcasts (e.g., lectures) and those designed to support small groups working in parallel. Many software packages are designed only for Windows-based systems, despite the continued prevalence of Macintoshes and the growing popularity of Linux in educational settings.

Organizational Issues   Compared to other collaboratory types, the organizational issues related to virtual learning communities are relatively easy to address. The key challenges are aligning educational goals and assessments so that learners from multiple sites are having their needs met. Projects such as the VaNTH biomedical engineering collaboratory (Brophy 2003) have spent a great deal of up-front time negotiating goals, and project staff have spent much time and energy developing cross-site assessments with good success, demonstrating viability. Despite this, only a few virtual learning communities were found and added to the database, suggesting that they are not common.

Distributed Research Center
Definition   This collaboratory functions like a university research center but at a distance. It is an attempt to aggregate scientific talent, effort, and resources beyond the level of individual researchers. Distributed research centers are unified by a topic area of interest and joint projects in that area. Most of the communication is human to human.[5]

Example   Inflammation and the Host Response to Injury is a large-scale collaborative program that aims to uncover the biological reasons why patients can have dramatically different outcomes after suffering similar traumatic injuries (chapter 11, this volume). This research aims to explain the molecular underpinnings that lead to organ injury and organ failure, while also helping to clarify how burn and trauma patients recover from injury. The Inflammation and the Host Response to Injury collaborative consists of an interdisciplinary network of investigators from U.S. academic research centers. Participating institutions include hospitals that take part in clinical research studies, academic medical centers that perform analytic studies on blood and tissue samples, and informatics and statistics centers that develop databases and analyze data.

The program is organized into seven core groups. Each of the core groups is composed of a core director, participating investigators, and other experts. The core personnel are accomplished and highly successful basic scientists working in the areas of research relevant to the focus of each individual core. In addition to researchers who are experts in identifying and quantifying molecular events that occur after injury, the program includes experts who have not traditionally been involved in injury research but have been integrated into the program to expand the multidisciplinary character of the team. These experts include biologists who are leaders in genomewide expression analysis, engineers who do genomewide computational analysis, and bioinformatics experts who construct and analyze complex relational databases. The program scientists are mutually supported by core resources, which provide the expertise, technology, and comprehensive, consensus-based databases that define the success of this program.

Technology Issues   Distributed research centers encounter all of the technology issues of other collaboratory types, including the standardization of data and providing long-distance technical support. They also should pay attention to technologies for workplace awareness, which try to approximate the convenience of face-to-face collaboration. Awareness technologies such as instant messaging and more exotic variants (Gutwin and Greenberg 2004) allow distant collaborators to know when others are interruptible, in order to engage in the quick consultations and informal chat that are the glue of colocated interaction.

Organizational Issues   As the most organizationally ambitious project type, these collaboratories experience all previously mentioned issues with a few additional concerns. They must gain and maintain participation among diverse contributors, work to standardize protocols over distance, facilitate distributed decision making, and provide long-distance administrative support. Distributed research centers also must settle questions of cross-institutional intellectual property. Universities have gotten more proactive about protecting in-house intellectual property, and getting them to agree to the multisite sharing agreements necessary for open collaboration often proves challenging. Both the Alliance for Cellular Signaling and the Center for Innovative

Learning Technologies spent much up-front time negotiating intellectual property policies with partner institutions.

Distributed research centers must think about the career issues of younger participants as well. What does it mean for young scholars to be lower authors on one or two large, potentially important papers, rather than first authors on a set of smaller works? Is it a good career decision for them to get involved in projects where they will spend considerable amounts of their time on managerial tasks and in meetings, rather than on individual data analysis and writing? These are very real trade-offs that should be addressed explicitly for junior researchers and graduate students involved in distributed research centers.

Community Infrastructure Project

Definition   Community infrastructure projects seek to develop infrastructure to further work in a particular domain. By infrastructure we mean common resources that facilitate science, such as software tools, standardized protocols, new types of scientific instruments, and educational methods. Community infrastructure projects are often interdisciplinary, bringing together domain scientists from multiple specialties, private-sector contractors, funding officers, and computer scientists.[6]

Example   The Grid Physics Network (GriPhyN) is a team of experimental physicists and information technology researchers planning to implement the first petabyte-scale computational environments for data-intensive science. The GriPhyN will deploy computational environments called Petascale Virtual Data Grids to meet the data-intensive computational needs of the diverse community of international scientists involved in the related research. The term *petascale* in the name emphasizes the massive central processing unit resources (petaflops) and the enormous data sets (petabytes) that must be harnessed, while *virtual* refers to the many required data products that may not be physically stored but exist only as specifications for how they may be derived from other data.

The GriPhyN was funded by the NSF as a large information technology research project. The group is focused on the creation of a number of tools for managing "virtual data." This approach to dealing with data acknowledges that all data except for "raw" data need exist only as a specification for how they can be derived. Strategies for reproducing or regenerating data on the grid are key areas of research for the virtual data community. The main deliverable of the GriPhyN project is the Chimera Virtual Data System, a software package for managing virtual data.

The collaboratory team is composed of seven information technology research groups and members of four NSF-funded frontier physics experiments: Laser Interferometer Gravitational-Wave Observatory, the Sloan Digital Sky Survey, and the CMS and ATLAS experiments at the Large Hadron Collider at CERN. The GriPhyN will oversee the development of a set of production data grids, which will allow scientists to extract small signals from enormous backgrounds via computationally demanding analyses of data sets that will grow from the hundred-terabyte to the hundred-petabyte scale over the next decade. The computing and storage resources required will be distributed for both technical and strategic reasons, and across national centers, regional centers, university computing centers, and individual desktops.

Technology Issues As with other collaboratories, infrastructure projects often necessitate the development of new field standards for data and data collection protocols. Current infrastructure projects like the GriPhyN are also tackling the problem of managing large data sets. Associated issues also arise in data provenance, which is keeping track of the editing and transformations that have occurred on data sets.

Organizational Issues A critical issue for interdisciplinary projects is the negotiation of goals among disciplinary partners. Whose research agenda will be paramount? In partnerships between disciplinary experts and computer scientists, there is often conflict between pursuing the most technologically advanced solutions (which are of research interest to the computer scientists) and more immediately practical solutions (chapter 17, this volume; Weedman 1998).

Infrastructure projects sometimes must decide between having academic managers and private-sector management. Phase III of the AIP Study of Multi-Institutional Collaborations (1999) compared these and found trade-offs; private-sector managers were better at finishing projects on time and on budget, while academic managers were better at accommodating the idiosyncratic needs of researchers.

A third common issue is how work on infrastructure projects should fit into the careers of the younger scientists who participate in them. Should building infrastructure "count" as a contribution to the discipline in the same way as other publishable works? If not, should junior faculty and younger scholars avoid working on such projects?

Conclusions

Sample Limitation

Despite the precautions taken, the SOC database has some limitations that could not be corrected during the time frame of the SOC project. One area of missing projects is military-funded collaborations. Although the military has a strong interest in long-distance collaboration, there was not sufficient information gathered to be able to enter any of them into the database. Informants were difficult to find, and those located could not provide the information requested. This may have been affected by the timing of the project: the years after the 9/11 terrorist attacks were marked by strong concerns about security, and the strict control of information about military projects and procedures.

Another known area of missing data is international projects. The attention was focused primarily on U.S. projects and concentrated on U.S. funders as informants. This was partly due to the limitations of language (the data collection relied on phone interviews) and was partly a practical decision regarding the allocation of resources. Nevertheless, European Union projects, particularly Framework 7 projects that mandate the assembly of broad international teams, would be excellent candidates for future study.

Key Dimensions: Resources and Activities

Other categorization schemes have used a priori dimensions based on technology, scientific disciplines, or consideration of theoretical issues. This system was intended to be a more "bottom-up" exercise, working from a large data set, and letting the relevant categories emerge with time and understanding. Having done this, it is useful now to go back and examine the categories again to ask what dimensions tend to differentiate the projects.

The 2-D classification shown in table 3.1 seems to capture many of the important distinctions. Each collaboratory type is placed in one cell, based on its dominant type of resource and activity. The first dimension, along the x axis, differentiates based on the type of resource to be shared. In the case of shared instrument and community infrastructure collaboratories, the resources are scientific tools or instruments, such as telescopes or laboratory equipment. Other categories are information and knowledge. The sharing of each of these types of resource requires different technologies, practices, and organizational structures. The second dimension, along the y axis, is the type of activity to be performed. This distinction corresponds to the one often made in organizational studies between loosely coupled and tightly coupled work.

In general, the collaborations become more difficult to manage and sustain from the top left of this table to the bottom right. It is generally more difficult to share knowledge than data or tools, and it is generally more difficult to cocreate than to aggregate.

Table 3.1
Collaboratory types by resource and activity

	Tools (Instruments)	Information (Data)	Knowledge (New findings)
Aggregating across distance (loose coupling, often asynchronously)	Shared instrument	Community data system	Virtual learning community, virtual community of practice
Cocreating across distance (requires tighter coupling, often synchronously)	Infrastructure	Open community contribution system	Distributed research center

This dimensional classification offers some insights. Over time, the field of collaboratories has been observed to move from the top left to the bottom right. The AIP studies (1992, 1995, 1999) and early collaboratory writings (National Research Council 1993) focused largely on tool sharing, with some of the greatest recent successes moving into data sharing. Some individual collaboratory efforts have also been observed to move along these dimensions in both directions. Recognizing that further effort is needed more in one direction than in the other may help to manage and plan these projects.

These dimensions also help to differentiate some of the types from each other. The distinction between a community data system and an open community contribution system was murky even to the research team, but understanding the distinction between aggregating and cocreating helped guide classifications and provide insight into the most difficult aspects of these projects.

The Use of Collaboratory Typology

The SOC collaboratory taxonomy has proven useful in guiding both research and assessment within the SOC project. A question that arose early on in the project was, What technology should be recommended for collaboratories? The nature of the projects that were being generalized across, however, was so diverse as to make the question specious. The technology needs of a shared instrument collaboratory are quite different from those of a virtual community of practice, for example. The identification of types enables more focused practitioner advice to be provided. Understanding these types has also framed research questions, such as helping to narrow the scope of our study of contributor motivation, and how collaboratories change in purpose as they evolve over time. Our future plans include continuing to develop this understanding of types. In the near future, we will focus on identifying best practices for different types. The expansion of types also seems inevitable. Finally, the differentiation of subtypes within the classification system is another potentially rich area for exploration.

Acknowledgments

This material is based on work supported by the NSF under grant no. IIS 0085951. Any opinions, findings, and conclusions or recommendations expressed in this material are those of the authors, and do not necessarily reflect the views of the NSF.

A similar version of this chapter appeared in the online *Journal of Computer-Mediated Communication* 12, no. 2 (2007); minor modifications have been made from the original.

Notes

1. For additional information about the SOC project and the collaboratories database, see the Introduction (this volume).

2. The Alliance for Cellular Signaling is discussed in greater detail in chapter 11 (this volume).

3. For case studies of shared instrument collaboratories, see chapters 6, 8, 9, and 10 (this volume).

4. Mark S. Ackerman, personal communication with authors, June 14, 2002.

5. Distributed research centers are the focus of several chapters in this volume; see, for example, chapters 11, 13, and 19.

6. For in-depth analyses of particular community infrastructure projects, see chapters 17 and 18 (this volume). Most community infrastructure projects can also be classified as distributed research centers.

References

Alexander, C., S. Ishikawa, and M. Silverstein. 1977. *A pattern language*. New York: Oxford University Press.

American Institute of Physics (AIP) Study of Multi-Institutional Collaborations. 1992. *Phase I: High-energy physics*. 4 vols. New York: American Institute of Physics. Available at ⟨http://www.aip.org/history/pubs/collabs/hephome.htm⟩ (accessed June 28, 2007).

American Institute of Physics (AIP) Study of Multi-Institutional Collaborations. 1995. *Phase II: Space science and geophysics*. 2 vols. College Park, MD: American Institute of Physics. Available at ⟨http://www.aip.org/history/pubs/collabs/ssghome.htm⟩ (accessed June 28, 2007).

American Institute of Physics (AIP) Study of Multi-Institutional Collaborations. 1999. *Phase III: Ground-based astronomy, materials science, heavy-ion and nuclear physics, medical physics, and computer-mediated collaborations*. 2 vols. College Park, MD: American Institute of Physics. Available at ⟨http://www.aip.org/history/pubs/collabs/phase3rep1.htm⟩ (accessed June 28, 2007).

Bafoutsou, G., and G. Mentzas. 2002. Review and functional classification of collaborative systems. *International Journal of Information Management* 22:281–305.

Baxevanis, A. D. 2002. The molecular biology database collection: 2002 update. *Nucleic Acids Research* 30 (1): 1–12.

Berman, H. M., P. E. Bourne, and J. Westbrook. 2004. The Protein Data Bank: A case study in management of community data. *Current Proteomics* 1:49–57.

Brophy, S. P. 2003. Constructing shareable learning materials in bioengineering education. *IEEE Engineering in Medicine and Biology Magazine* 22 (4): 39–46.

Chompalov, I., and W. Shrum. 1999. Institutional collaboration in science: A typology of technological practice. *Science, Technology, and Human Values* 24 (3): 338–372.

Collins, H. M. 1998. The meaning of data: Open and closed evidential cultures in the search for gravitational waves. *American Journal of Sociology* 104 (2): 293–338.

Connolly, T., B. K. Thorn, and A. Heminger. 1992. *Social dilemmas: Theoretical issues and research findings*. Oxford: Pergamon.

Cramton, C. 2001. The mutual knowledge problem and its consequences for dispersed collaboration. *Organization Science* 12:346–371.

Crane, D. 1972. *Invisible colleges*. Chicago: University of Chicago Press.

Cummings, J. N., and S. Kiesler. 2005. Collaborative research across disciplinary and organizational boundaries. *Social Studies of Science* 35 (5): 703–722.

DeSanctis, G., and R. B. Gallupe. 1987. A foundation for the study of group decision support systems. *Management Science* 23 (5): 589–609.

Grudin, J. 1994. Computer-supported cooperative work: History and focus. *IEEE Computer* 2 (5): 19–26.

Gutwin, C., and S. Greenberg. 2004. The importance of awareness for team cognition in distributed collaboration. In *Team cognition: Understanding the factors that drive process and performance*, ed. E. Salas and S. M. Fiore, 177–201. Washington, DC: APA Press.

Hesse, B. W., L. S. Sproull, S. B. Kiesler, and J. P. Walsh. 1993. Returns to science: Computer networks in oceanography. *Communications of the ACM* 36 (8): 90–101.

Hollingshead, A. B. 1998. Retrieval processes in transactive memory systems. *Journal of Personality and Social Psychology* 74 (3): 659–671.

Jarvenpaa, S., and D. Leidner. 1999. Communication and trust in global virtual teams. *Organization Science* 10:791–815.

Kibrick, R., A. Conrad, and A. Perala. 1998. Through the far looking glass: Collaborative remote observing with the W. M. Keck Observatory. *Interactions* 5 (3): 32–39.

Kuhn, T. S. 1963. *The structure of scientific revolutions*. Chicago: University of Chicago Press.

Latour, B., and S. Woolgar. 1979. *Laboratory life: The social construction of scientific facts*. Beverly Hills, CA: Sage Publications.

Lawson, C., and E. Lorenz. 1999. Collective learning, tacit knowledge, and regional innovative capacity. *Regional Studies* 33 (4): 305–317.

Myers, J. D., A. R. Chappell, and M. Elder. 2003. Re-integrating the research record. *Computing in Science and Engineering* (May–June): 44–50.

National Research Council. 1993. *National collaboratories: Applying information technology for scientific research*. Washington, DC: National Academies Press.

Newman, M. 2001. The structure of scientific collaboration networks. *Proceedings of the National Academies of Sciences* 98 (2): 404–409.

Olson, G. M., and J. S. Olson. 2000. Distance matters. *Human Computer Interaction* 15:139–179.

Patton, M. Q. 1990. *Qualitative evaluation and research methods*. 2nd ed. Newbury Park, CA: Sage Publications.

Science of Collaboratories (SOC) Research Group. 2001. *Social underpinnings workshop report*. Available at ⟨http://www.scienceofcollaboratories.org/Workshops/WorkshopJune42001/index.php⟩ (accessed June 28, 2007).

Stokols, D., J. Fuqua, J. Gress, R. Harvey, K. Phillips, L. Baezconde-Garbanati et al. 2003. Evaluating transdisciplinary science. *Nicotine and Tobacco Research* 5 (suppl. 1): S21–S39.

Stokols, D., R. Harvey, J. Gress, J. Fuqua, and K. Phillips. 2005. In vivo studies of transdisciplinary scientific collaboration: Lessons learned and implications for active living research. *American Journal of Preventive Medicine* 28 (suppl. 2): 202–213.

Stork, D. G. 1999. Character and document research in the open mind initiative. In *Proceedings of the fifth international conference on document analysis and recognition*, 1–12. Washington, DC: IEEE Computer Press.

Szulanski, G. 1992. *Sticky knowledge: Barriers to knowing in the firm*. London: Sage Publications.

Viégas, F. B., M. Wattenberg, and K. Dave. 2004. Studying cooperation and conflict between authors with history flow visualizations. In *Proceedings of the SIGCHI conference on human factors in computing systems*, 575–582. New York: ACM Press.

Watts, D. J., and S. H. Strogatz. 1998. Collective dynamics of "small world" networks. *Nature* 393:440–442.

Weedman, J. 1998. The structure of incentive: Design and client roles in application-oriented research. *Science, Technology, and Human Values* 23 (3): 315–345.

Wenger, E., and J. Lave. 1998. *Communities of practice: Learning, meaning, and identity*. New York: Cambridge University Press.

Wulf, W. A. 1989. The national collaboratory: A white paper. In *Towards a national collaboratory: Report of an invitational workshop at the Rockefeller University, March 17–18, 1989*, ed. J. Lederberg and K. Uncaphar, appendix A. Washington, DC: National Science Foundation, Directorate for Computer and Information Science Engineering.

Wulf, W. A. 1993. The collaboratory opportunity. *Science* 261 (5123): 854–855.

4   A Theory of Remote Scientific Collaboration

Judith S. Olson, Erik C. Hofer, Nathan Bos, Ann Zimmerman, Gary M. Olson,
Daniel Cooney, and Ixchel Faniel

In the past fifteen years, a great deal has been learned about the particular challenges of
distant collaboration. Overall, we have learned that even when advanced technologies
are available, distance still matters (Olson and Olson 2000). In addition, a recent seminal study of sixty-two projects sponsored by the National Science Foundation (NSF)
showed that the major indicator of lower success was the number of institutions
involved (Cummings and Kiesler 2005; chapter 5, this volume). The greater the number of institutions involved, the less well coordinated a project was and the fewer the
positive outcomes.

There are a number of reasons for these challenges. For one, distance threatens context and common ground (Cramton 2001). Second, trust is more difficult to establish
and maintain when the collaborators are separated from each other (Shrum, Chompalov, and Genuth 2001; Kramer and Tyler 1995). Third, poorly designed incentive
systems can inhibit collaborations and prevent the adoption of new collaboration
technology (Orlikowski 1992; Grudin 1988). Finally, organizational structures and governance systems, along with the nature of the work, can either contribute to or inhibit
collaboration (Larson et al. 2002; Mazur and Boyko 1981; Hesse et al. 1993; Sonnenwald 2007). This chapter describes our attempt to synthesize these findings and enumerate those factors that we (and others) believe are important in determining the
success of remote collaboration in science. In working toward a theory of remote scientific collaboration (TORSC), we have drawn from data collected as part of the Science
of Collaboratories (SOC) project, studies in the sociology of science, and investigations
of distance collaboration in general.

The Developing Theory

Success

We begin by discussing what we might mean by success in remote collaboration, since
in the literature it can vary from revolutionary new thinking in the science to simply
having some new software used. Different sets of factors may lead to different kinds of

success. These outputs include effects on the science itself, science careers, learning and science education, funding and public perception, and inspiration to develop new collaboratories and new collaborative tools. The details are listed in short form in table 4.1.

Effects on the Science Itself   Early goals for collaboratories included that they would increase productivity and the number of participants, and democratize science through improved access to elite researchers (Finholt and Olson 1997; Hesse et al. 1993; Walsh and Bayma 1996). Similar assumptions were made with regard to interdisciplinary research (Steele and Stier 2000). These goals have to date not been tested. Today, scholars, policymakers, and scientists no longer take these assumptions for granted. Increasingly, they recognize that to define and evaluate the success of distributed and large-scale scientific collaborations is a complex task.

Traditional measures of success in science are geared toward the individual, and include metrics such as productivity (e.g., counts of publications, presentations, patents, and graduate students mentored), awards and honors, and the impact of the work as determined by the prestige of the publication outlet or the number of times other researchers cite an individual scientist's papers (Merton 1988; Prpic 1996; Shrum, Chompalov, and Genuth 2001). Some of these measures can be used to evaluate the outcomes of large-scale, interdisciplinary, distributed collaborations, but most of them are inadequate to assess the full spectrum of goals of many current projects. Findings from the SOC project show that collaboratory participants and funding agency personnel frequently describe success in terms of the transformations to scientific practice along with the scale, scope, and complexity of the questions that can be answered. Both scientists and policymakers acknowledge that these outcomes take a long time to achieve and are difficult to assess using traditional measures.

Social scientists have made some attempts to identify appropriate success measures and then evaluate collaborative science projects against these criteria. Methods based on the scientific outcomes of collaboration are the most common means to define and assess success. In the case of cross-disciplinary collaborations, the degree of intellectual integration, innovation (e.g., the generation of new ideas, tools, and infrastructure), and training are used as success measures (Cummings and Kiesler 2005; chapter 5, this volume; Jeffrey 2003; Stokols et al. 2003, 2005). Bradford Hesse and his colleagues (1993) used three scientific outcomes—publication, professional recognition, and social integration—to measure success among oceanographers who used computer networks to communicate with other researchers and access shared resources.

We believe that both more scientists working on a common problem and the diversity among scientists working in a collaboratory can lead to bigger discoveries as well as breakthroughs, such as new ways of working, more revolutionary science, conceptual revolutions, and new models of science emerging. These are the highest-level goals.

Table 4.1
Kinds of outcomes that would count as "success"

Effects on the science itself	Improved quality of life and higher satisfaction of researchers
New and bigger discoveries are made and are made more quickly	**Learning and science education**
New ways of working are demonstrated, and then sustained	New (diverse) scientists are attracted to the field (capacity building)
There is a change in the mix of normal vs. revolutionary science	More students are mentored
A conceptual revolution is enabled	Extended reach of seminars
New models of science emerge (e.g., microparticipation)	Material is used in a classroom setting
There is more high-quality research	New distance-learning paradigms emerge
Existing collaborations work more easily	**Inspiration to others**
More and new collaborations are formed	New collaboratories are developed as a result
Collaborations have a wide geographic and disciplinary spread	Other software is built inspired by it
More jointly authored papers are written and are written more quickly	**Funding and public perception**
More papers are published and patents are issued	A particular collaboratory is re-funded
Greater willingness to share early ideas	Public become more interested and literacy increases
Findings are shared more quickly among more people	Public participates more (e.g., microcontributions)
Artifacts that are shared are richer	Congress becomes more interested
Theoretical discussions are accelerated and enriched	New funding initiatives appear for science and collaboratories
Less undesirable duplication	**Tool use**
Fewer disruptive activities	New software is built
Greater success in competitive arenas	Builder demos the tools working
Science careers	Users use the software and complain when it is taken away
Greater diversity of scientists	New users try it and continue to use it
Participation reaches beyond U.S. R1 universities	Tools move from research prototypes to production quality
Stronger tenure cases because young faculty are known through their collaborations	Tools are reused elsewhere

For instance, the goal of the high-energy physics community (chapter 8, this volume) and the Alliance for Cellular Signaling (AfCS) (chapter 11, this volume) are to do research on a scale that has not been attempted previously. In the AfCS, for example, the work is centered around the identification of all the proteins that comprise the various signaling systems, the assessment of time-dependent information flow through the systems in both normal and pathological states, and the reduction of the mass of detailed data into a set of interacting theoretical models that describe cellular signaling. This type of success cannot be achieved without a large coordinated effort.

Another type of success could be an increase in the productivity of existing projects, in that they overcome the barrier of distance more easily. Researchers who use the large instruments like Pacific Northwest National Laboratory's nuclear magnetic resonance instruments (chapter 6, this volume) or Keck Observatory telescopes (Kibrick, Conrad, and Perala 1998; see also chapter 3, this volume) without traveling are clearly experiencing an opportunity for more productivity. They can gain access without the time and effort involved in a trip, and furthermore can take advantage of securing time on the instrument when someone else releases it unexpectedly. And when scientists discover people of like mind and goals, new collaborations can ensue, including those with people from distant geography.

Even earlier indicators of success are that there are more jointly authored papers, more papers published overall, and a greater willingness to share early ideas. Although these factors do not define ultimate success in and of themselves, they are often thought to be precursors to scientific breakthroughs. The technology adopted is intended to help people share richer artifacts than allowed by text alone, sharing computational analyses, programs, and visualizations. This should lead to better, richer theoretical discussions. If the tools are indeed off-loading some of the tedious work to technology, then it can be expected that scientists are doing more high-level cognitive work and less of the routine work (such as cleaning data or preparing samples). With higher communication comes less duplication of effort. By allowing people to participate from their home locations, less time is wasted in travel and the disruptions to one's daily life are fewer.

If indeed the higher productivity is evident early on, then various collaboratories would have greater success in competing for funding than those that do not collaborate as well. This pours more research dollars into successful collaborations, creating a measure of desired productivity.

Effects on Science Careers   Because long-distance work is possible, we can expect a more diverse set of people working in the field, leading to the desired diversity and possibility for conceptual revolutions. For example, before the Upper Atmospheric Research Collaboratory/Space Physics and Aeronomy Research Collaboratory (UARC/SPARC), going to the sites of the upper atmospheric radar, incoherent scatter radar, imaging riometer, all-sky camera, and Fabry-Perot interferometer often required flights on military transport as well as stays of two weeks or more in unfavorable and uncomfortable conditions (chapter 9, this volume). Only those scientists willing to tolerate such extreme sacrifices for their science are attracted to the field. Now that the same data and some control can be accessed anywhere, a much broader set of people (especially women) could be attracted to the field.

Collaboratories can also build capacity in areas outside the highest-level research (R1) universities, extending to smaller colleges, those with underrepresented minorities, and research institutes and universities in developing countries (chapter 20, this volume), thus broadening the pool of talent working on important problems. For instance, one of the major goals in the International AIDS Research Collaboratory was to build capacity in South Africa to do the data collection and analysis for AIDS research (chapter 19, this volume). This not only speeds the science in general but also allows people to develop the skills to work on problems in science.

In addition, participation in collaboratories can define a cohort of similarly minded scientists, who would otherwise not be known to each other. Although not hugely successful in itself, the Learning through Collaborative Visualization, a five-year project ending in 1998, brought together a cohort of interdisciplinary people who still interact (Gomez, Fishman, and Pea 1998).

Effects on Learning and Science Education   Many collaboratories give graduate students opportunities for hands-on experience. Some are even mentored by remote senior scientists. Students, who often cannot afford to travel, can attend seminars. The Ecological Circuitry Collaboratory and the VaNTH Education Research Center were collaboratories that made specialized training more available at the graduate level, contributing to a new distance-learning paradigm (see also chapter 3, this volume).

Some collaboratories have educational outreach as one of their goals. If the collaboratory has outreach to public schools, it may inspire students to follow a science career. The Beckman Center at the University of Illinois, for example, offered two such outreaches: Chickscope and Bugscope. Chickscope allowed children to view a chicken embryo through an MRI machine from their classrooms (Bruce et al. 1997). Similarly, for Bugscope, time on an electron microscope was devoted to classroom use where students could send in sample insects and then view them from afar through the microscope's magnification. The goal was to inspire students to enter careers in science.

There is, additionally, the possibility of a different kind of distance learning. Instead of lectures from remote researchers, technology can afford remote mentoring and observation along with participation in the science itself. UARC/SPARC witnessed remote mentoring; Bugscope and Chickscope allowed remote participation in the science.

Collaboratories can also increase the visibility of scientific disciplines. Visibility can lead younger students to be inspired by such work. The same kind of visibility and outreach can motivate scientists in related fields to become involved. Also, visibility of details of the ongoing work can reduce a duplication of effort.

Effects by Inspiring Others   Occasionally, there is a collaboratory effort, like UARC/ SPARC, that is not transformative of its own science but serves as an example of what others can do. UARC/SPARC, described earlier, was an inspiration to the George E. Brown Jr. Network for Earthquake Engineering Simulation (NEES) (chapter 18, this volume), and the Diesel Combustion Collaboratory influenced the Collaboratory for Multi-Scale Chemical Sciences. Key personnel are involved in these pairs. People in the Geosciences Network (GEON) (chapter 17, this volume) helped others in the Linked Environments for Atmospheric Discovery early in their project conception. The Cochrane Collaboration inspired the Campbell Collaboration, the first in evidence-based medicine and the second in social interventions.

Effects on Funding and Public Perception   Science requires funding to succeed. The re-funding of a collaboratory is one measure of perceived success. InterPARES1 was funded again under InterPARES2, and the funding for the Biomedical Informatics Research Network (BIRN) was renewed (chapter 12, this volume). If through the collaboratory the public becomes more aware of science, this can in turn influence Congress and funding agencies. New funding initiatives appear, such as those managed by NSF's Office of Cyberinfrastructure. The more funding and the greater the efficiency, the greater is the likelihood of scientific breakthroughs.

Public policy outcomes are another way that success has been defined and measured, although it sometimes takes decades to assess (Stokols et al. 2003, 2005).

Effects by Measuring the Levels of New Tool Use   For those collaboratories that create new tools or infrastructure, success may be measured by the degree of technology adoption within the collaboratory and elsewhere. Some projects are able only to demonstrate a new capability, which though not affecting the science itself, may inspire others to try things in their fields. Some of the new powerful visualization techniques, for instance, are demonstrated and then picked up in other fields.

If the tools are designed well, not only to fit the work at hand and for the ease of use, then it is likely that the tools will be utilized. The greater the ease of learning and use, the less is required of local support. If the tool is a recognized aid to productivity, it is likely that others will begin to use it. If research technologies are useful but unreliable, as many are, the clamor for reliability may cause funds to be devoted to making tools "production quality." And better yet, tools may be reused elsewhere. For example, NEES used the Electronic Notebook from the Environmental Molecular Science Laboratory; GEON and the Scientific Environment for Ecological Knowledge both use Kepler, a visual modeling language; and the AfCS and Lipids Metabolites and Pathways

Strategy are both using the Laboratory Information Management System, made available from the National Institutes of Health (NIH), with the modifications that AfCS made.

Factors That Lead to Success

Five major clusters of components are important to success, as shown in detail in table 4.2: the nature of the work, the amount of common ground among participants, participants' readiness to collaborate, participants' management style and leadership, and technology readiness.

The major categories, with the exception of the management issues, were first described in Olson and Olson (2000). We have since identified the key management and decision-making practices that are crucial as well as detailed the significant components within these clusters.

The Nature of the Work

One of the keys to success is dividing the work of the team so that it can get done without a lot of communication across distance. The more modularized the work at the different locations, the more likely is success. Sometimes work requires participants to continually define and refine their understanding of what to do as well as how to do it because it is new, somewhat ambiguous, or highly interdependent, requiring what has been called "tight coupling" (Olson et al. 2002) or what James Thompson (1967) referred to as reciprocal interdependence. We have seen a number of projects fail because the tightly coupled work spanned people in different locations. For example, a software development team located in two places, the United States and Mexico, attempted to build a system to assess the manufacturability of an engineering design. Even though there were regular videoconferencing meetings and a lot of e-mail exchange, the project suffered. After a period of struggle, the team redistributed the tightly coupled work to people who were collocated—giving the algorithm design to one site and the task of populating the database to the other (Olson and Olson 2000). In other cases, ambiguous, highly interdependent work was done at one location with others traveling to meet face-to-face, or the work was more modularized, so that tight interdependencies did not cross distance or institutional boundaries. Distance creates significant barriers to the frequency and richness of communication, which makes it difficult to reconcile ambiguities and keep in synch on many interdependencies (Birnholtz 2005; Chompalov, Genuth, and Shrum 2002).

Common Ground

In order to make collective progress, people engaged in a collaboration need to have mutual knowledge, beliefs, and/or assumptions, and know that they have this (Clark

Table 4.2
Factors that lead to success in collaboratories

The nature of the work	Exhibits strong leadership qualities
Participants can work somewhat independently from one another	A communication plan is in place
The work is unambiguous	The plan has room for reflection and redirection
Common ground	No legal issues remain (e.g., IP)
Previous collaboration with these people was successful	No financial issues remain (e.g., money is distributed to fit the work, not politics)
Participants share a common vocabulary	A knowledge management system is in place
If not, there is a dictionary	Decision making is free of favoritism
Participants share a common management or working style	Decisions are based on fair and open criteria
	Everyone has an opportunity to influence or challenge decisions
Collaboration readiness	Leadership sets culture, management plan, and makes the collaboratory visible
The culture is naturally collaborative	
The goals are aligned in each subcommunity	**Technology readiness**
Participants have a motivation to work together that includes mix of skills required, greater productivity, they like working together, there is something in it for everyone, not a mandate from the funder, the only way to get the money, asymmetries in value, etc.	Collaboration technologies provide the right functionality and are easy to use
	If technologies need to be built, user-centered practices are in place
	Participants are comfortable with the collaboration technologies
	Technologies give benefit to the participants
Participants trust each other to be reliable, produce with high quality, and have their best interests at heart	Technologies are reliable
	Agreement exists among participants as to what platform to use
Participants have a sense of collective efficacy (able to complete tasks in spite of barriers)	Networking supports the work that needs to be done
Management, planning, and decision making	Technical support resides at each location
The principals have time to do this work	An overall technical coordinator is in place
The distributed players can communicate with each other in real time more than four hours a day	*Special issues:* If data sharing is one of the goals, de facto standards are in place and shared by all participants, and a plan for archiving is in place
There is critical mass at each location	
There is a point person at each location	
A management plan is in place	
The project manager is: Respected	If instrument sharing is part of the collaboration, a plan to certify remote users is in place
Has real project management experience	

1996; Clark and Brennan 1991). Collaborations can be hindered if one or more of these aspects of common ground are absent. The ability to work toward common ground is more difficult when the collaborators are geographically distributed.

Mutual Knowledge   If people have worked successfully together in the past, they are likely to have achieved common ground, which will improve their chance of success in subsequent collaborations. If they are from different disciplinary backgrounds, however, they are unlikely to share a common vocabulary; misunderstandings are likely to ensue. Time and attention must be paid to the activity of developing a common vocabulary. For example, Mouse BIRN is a collaboratory that joins different kinds of scientists all focusing on multiple levels of the mouse brain, from its molecular structure to its morphometry (chapter 12, this volume). The collaborators recognized early on that they did not all speak the same language, particularly when it came to referencing the anatomy of the mouse brain. In response, they jointly built an "atlas" that like the Rosetta stone, shows the relationship between the terms. The interface to the database is a simple spatial layout, with scientists able to point to the areas of interest, without having to specify the terms. In this way, the search engine can find all the data and views relevant to this area, even though the different scientists label that area differently. GEON, likewise, developed an ontology as a way to deal with some of the semantic differences in classification systems used by state geologic survey offices.

Beliefs and Assumptions in Management   Interestingly, it also helps if the participants have a common management style, so that their interactions and expectations are aligned. For example, those used to a hierarchical management style with specified deliverables and reports at various intervals will likely not function well with those used to a more open and informal style of management. In the UARC/SPARC collaboratory, for instance, the designers of the interface were used to a software development method that included explicit user requirements followed by a coordinated design of the multitude of features. In contrast, the developers themselves were following a more open and informal style, using a rapid-prototyping development method that sought explicit input from the users, not the user-interface designers, and rapidly changed the interface to suit requests.

Collaboration Readiness

Understanding what motivates people to collaborate, whether they trust each other, how well their goals are aligned, and how empowered they feel are all important to success—a concept we collectively call collaboration readiness. These factors can be related to work or personal and social dimensions, as detailed below.

Work-Related Dimensions Some domains in science are naturally collaborative. High-energy physics, for example, and space physics have long histories of large collaborations. Theoretical computer science does not. The AIDS collaboratories experienced some competition among postdocs (to stand out in order to be chosen for regular faculty positions) and among the lead researchers themselves, competing for recognition and maybe even the Nobel Prize. It is easier to have a successful collaboratory if the scientists themselves are already collaborative.

The goals of the subgroups need to be aligned (Birnholtz 2005; Chompalov, Genuth, and Shrum 2002). For instance, collaborations in which domain scientists (e.g., physics, biochemistry, etc.) and computer scientists work together to develop scientific software (e.g., UARC) are often plagued by competing goals. The computer scientists see the computer system as an object of research, and want the freedom to experiment and make changes with the software. Their goal is to publish novel ideas. The domain scientists, on the other hand, see the system as a research tool, and need it to be hardened and reliable (Weedman 1998). The computer scientists do not want to take time away from their research to continuously improve and support previous projects. Some more recent projects (e.g., BIRN) do not include computer science researchers as much as high-quality developers, whose goal is to make the software work for the users and work reliably overall.

In some cases, people recognize that others have reciprocally needed skills. That is, some collaboratories exist to share the equipment or unique skill sets of various laboratories. At the Great Lakes Center for AIDS Research, for example, the collaborators had complementary skills, making them natural collaborators (see also chapter 13, this volume).

Social Dimensions We have noted that when people *like* working together there is sufficient motivation to succeed. We also have seen that the collaboration is more likely to succeed when there is some benefit for all participants (Grudin 1988). On the other hand, we have seen difficulties when there are asymmetries in value to the participants. For example, a funder mandate to include non-R1 universities in a collaboratory often embodies unequal benefits, with the R1 universities feeling that they have more to give than receive. Additionally, a collaboration frequently fails when the prime motivation for it is driven by funding agency requirements (i.e., in order to get funded, you must collaborate). The Great Lakes Center for AIDS Research mentioned above, where the institutions were mandated to work together to secure funding, continued only until the funding source that mandated the collaboration ran out.

In a similar vein, it is important that people trust each other. If they do not, they must take time and attention to create contracts and sanctions for noncompliance (Shrum, Chompalov, and Genuth 2001). The three major aspects of trust are that (Rousseau et al. 1998):

- Others will keep their promises, called "confident expectations"
- They will produce with high quality
- One will not take advantage of the other's vulnerability

A group that feels empowered has a higher chance of succeeding than a group that does not—a concept called "collective efficacy" (Carroll, Rosson, and Zhou 2005). Building on the personal self-efficacy work of Bandura (1977), John Carroll and his colleagues developed a set of questions assessing how well the members of a team think that the *team* can overcome things like a shortage of funding or unforeseen events. Carroll and his colleagues have shown that groups that have high collective efficacy in the beginning are more likely to succeed in the end.

Management, Planning, and Decision Making

The way in which the work of a distributed collaboration is organized and carried out is critical to its success. The skills that leaders possess and the time they have to devote to running the collaboration, the effectiveness and timeliness of communication, the mechanisms for decision making, and the clarity of institutional and individual roles as well as responsibilities are all critical aspects of management. The larger the collaboration, the more significant these elements become (Cummings and Kiesler 2005; chapter 5, this volume).

Time and Attention   It is important that scientists have time and resources to commit to a collaborative project. In science, it is common to have multiple projects going at the same time. A researcher proposes different research plans to a number of funding agencies, and with some probability each gets funded. It is possible, therefore, to have too many commitments to spend sufficient time on one or more of them to succeed. We have found that participants' overcommitments can be a serious problem for collaboratories. Recent research has shown that when working on multiple projects, some with people collocated and others with people who are remote, the collocated people get the time and attention, even though the projects are of equal importance (Bos et al. 2004; Fussell et al. 2004).

In collaboratories that span many time zones, it is difficult to find times in the normal working day when real-time conversations can take place. For example, one international AIDS collaboratory includes researchers from the United States, the United Kingdom, and South Africa (chapter 19, this volume), and a high-energy physics collaboratory we studied spans researchers from one hundred countries. Both have to schedule their meetings during the small workday overlap. With less overlap in the working day, participants have fewer opportunities to clarify information, develop common ground, align goals, and so on. All of these activities are necessary for difficult work to succeed, especially at the beginning of a project, before things have a chance of becoming less ambiguous and more routine. A key feature of science, to be sure, is that it is rarely routine. In addition, when participants are working in different time zones, their "body clocks" are set locally. When conversations exclude any cues as to the real time of day in the remote location, misunderstandings can occur. In a study of transatlantic collaboration among automotive engineers, we saw engineers in Detroit on a Friday late morning carry on a conversation too long, insensitive to the fact that their French counterparts were increasingly irritated because they were being kept from going home.

When people are remote and isolated, they are often ignored. Having a critical mass of people at each location ameliorates some of this. When people feel isolated, they feel less motivated to contribute, not owning the problem and not being asked to contribute in any way as frequently as those who are visible to each other and "at hand." Projects should designate a point person at each location who will be responsible for making sure that all participants there are informed and contributing. One business strategy that may work in collaboratories is including a "rotator" at each location, someone from the other location(s) to serve as the eyes and ears for the remote people (Olson and Olson 2000).

Management   A number of key factors leading to success in large collaboratories have to do with management. First, if there is not a critical mass at each location, the larger sites dominate. The smaller sites are likely to be "out of sight, out of mind." When multiple institutions and/or different departments (disciplines) within the same university are involved, it is crucial to know who is serving in what role. It is particularly important to have a point person—one person to whom outsiders can go to in order to find out who can help in a specific situation (Sonnenwald 2003). Those projects left loose suffer when the participants' directions begin to diverge; if they have not assigned someone to take leadership to get the group back on track, or have not bought in to that person having that authority, failure is likely. Most funding agencies now require a management plan as part of the proposal. For example, the National Institute for General Medical Sciences, one of twenty specialized institutes within the NIH, requires applicants to its "glue grant" program to provide detailed descriptions of project management and organizational structure (chapter 11, this volume). The more seriously the scientists take that plan, working out exactly who will do what as well as what the dependencies are among the players and tasks (and assuring that few tightly coupled tasks cross organizational boundaries), the more likely the success.

We have found on numerous occasions that having someone with good project management experience is essential. Few scientists have been trained in project management, a set of known skills to ensure that roles are clear, planning is grounded in reality, and someone monitors the progress and helps resolve problems arising from unexpected events. Some collaboratories find that having a scientist serve as project manager helps to create respect and trust that decisions are made to further the science. Attendees at the NIH's Catalyzing Team Science (2003) workshop reported that having a postdoctoral fellow in a managerial role was an important benefit to distributed projects, and a major recommendation of that workshop was to create career paths for those who provide infrastructure to teams. Certainly understanding the scientific domain is critical, but in some cases it is wise to have a nonscientist project manager so that the scientists are relieved from administrative duties (Mazur and Boyko 1981). Some later collaboratories (e.g., BIRN) have made a case for hiring a project manager who is not a key scientist but has the skills to keep things on track. Ultimate decision authority resides in the principal investigators, but the day-to-day planning and monitoring is in the hands of the project manager. Funders and some scientists themselves balk at spending money on project managers instead of additional scientists, yet when the key to success involves the coordination of a large number of people, such skill has been found to be essential.

Strong leaders not only manage the collaboration well internally but are also effective externally, making the project visible. Visibility has several important effects: it can inspire other scientists to attempt such collaborations, and through public awareness can both increase science literacy and influence Congress to fund more research, as it did post–World War II.

Communication and Possibilities for Redirection   We have also found that collaboratories do well to have a communication plan in place—one that clarifies expectations about when meetings will take place, who is expected to attend, how often e-mail will be answered, how to reach everyone, and who is responsible for what. The BIRN yearly meetings are "all-hands" events, with everyone expected to attend. This is a common practice in many of the collaboratories we have studied. Additionally, the more complex and interdependent the project, the more complex and frequent the communication has to be (Maznevski and Chudoba 2000).

Occasionally, a collaboratory discovers something that is unexpected, making the original plan of work no longer appropriate. For example, a large cellular biology collaboratory found that after two years of work, it needed to change its target molecules. Changing the directions of large projects in midcourse can be difficult, but this collaboratory had a strong decision-making process and management structure in place, thereby allowing the change to occur. Similarly, because of issues of trust or motivation, not all parties may turn out to participate as expected, yet funds are locked in for multiple years. Good management facilitates reflection, redirection, and a reallocation of resources. Successful collaboratories should do this as well. Many collaboratories have oversight committees or advisory boards that can provide this function; the NIH glue grants require them.

Institutional Issues   Even when all of the scientists are ready to proceed, collaboratories can run into institutional-related problems, especially legal issues that cannot be resolved (Sonnenwald 2007; Stokols et al. 2003, 2005). A number of potential collaboratories have been stymied by their institutions' rigid policies about intellectual property. Some universities want to own or control what their professors discover or invent, especially in the highly commercial areas of biomedicine. Collaboratories that succeed have found ways to share the intellectual property and cooperate on other legal matters as well.

Similarly, financial issues can be barriers. In the international AIDS research collaboratory mentioned previously, a South African university required that the money be in hand before anything could be purchased, whereas the U.S. funder would issue a check only after the purchase had been made. This impasse was finally resolved after the U.S. and South African financial officers met in person (a trust-building move) and together worked out a compromise that fit both systems. They managed to arrange a local South African loan to allow the scientists there to purchase what they needed and the U.S. funder to reimburse them once the appropriate paperwork was in place, essentially paying off the loan.

Knowledge Management   We have also noted that those collaboratories without good knowledge management plans often discover too late that data or records are lost. It is common for people to set up informal schemes for keeping records (e.g., minutes of meetings) only to find them inadequate when someone later tries to query the past. This is particularly important when the collaboratory includes people from a number of institutions and is active over a number of years, with key people rotating in and out of the project.

A critical part of today's knowledge management systems is a plan to migrate data when information technology becomes obsolete. For example, today's MRIs are born digital. The whole purpose of BIRN is to collect large enough samples of people with various kinds of schizophrenia and other mental disorders like Alzheimer's to make progress in diagnosis and cure (chapter 12, this volume). One of the challenges they will have to face is how to migrate the data to new technologies as they emerge so that the data are still accessible, say, twenty years from now. Digital preservation is an underappreciated problem that can have costly repercussions. The Protein Data Bank, established in 1971, is a good example of successful migration. It began with punched cards, but now has migrated to servers to hold its results of crystal structural analysis (Berman, Bourne, and Westbrook 2004).

Decision Making and Leadership   Carl Larson and his colleagues (LaFasto and Larson 2001; Larson et al. 2002), in their study of six thousand team members and six hundred managers, found that certain aspects of collaborative decision making were important to the success of various projects. Decision making needs to be free of favoritism, and have fair and open criteria. Everyone has to have an opportunity to influence or challenge decisions. These are the seeds of trust, referred to in the organizational behavior literature as "procedural justice" (Kurland and Egan 1999).

All of the above management factors imply that an effective leader is heading up the collaboratory. An effective leader establishes the collaborative culture, ensures that the plans are in place, and sets the tone of inclusiveness. Collaboratory leaders also must be external spokespersons, keeping the projects visible and managing public impressions. The early visibility of UARC led to the re-funding of a modified project in SPARC. The NEES project was also aware of UARC/SPARC in its early deliberations in forming.

Technology Readiness

Virtually all collaboratories connect people via technology for both communication and core work. Many collaboratories use generic or commercially available tools like e-mail, instant messaging, data or videoconferencing (like WebEx or Centra Symposium), and basic file servers. Others use specially designed and built software, like the Environmental Molecular Science Laboratory's online laboratory notebook (chapter 6, this volume). The adoption of any technology, whether off the shelf or custom designed, is driven by its fit to the work (providing the right functionality) and ease of use (Olson et al. 2000).

The key is to understand the real needs of the end users, not to push "cool" technologies on people. The more user centered the development process, the more likely the technology will be used. The significance of the design process being user centered instead of technology centered cannot be overestimated (Beyer and Holtzblatt 1998). One of the issues with the slow uptake of the grid is the technology push rather than the users' pull (Daniel Atkins, personal communication to authors, 2005).

Similarly, scientists must feel comfortable using the technology. For instance, scientists who are just learning to make efficient use of e-mail will find it challenging to use desktop videoconferencing. It is too big a leap. Interestingly, the early versions of SPARC interfaces mimicked the physical instrument displays (looking the same as the original meters and dials) while the scientists got used to working online. When the scientists later became more comfortable with other online tools, they asked for—and the developers designed—more powerful integrated displays that collected information from a variety of sources. People's beliefs in their abilities to use computers correlate highly with their adoption of technology (Compeau, Higgins, and Huff 1999).

It is also important that all essential technologies give benefit to those expected to use them. As Jonathan Grudin (1988) has pointed out, if some users have to put in effort that only benefits others, the technology will not succeed. An early knowledge management system deployed at the National Aeronautics and Space Administration's

Astrobiology Institute was not adopted widely because it was cumbersome and people were uncertain what advantages the tool provided them. Additionally, in many of the community data systems, there is some concern that one will submit one's data only to have others get credit for the analyses, which could not have taken place without the accumulation of data (chapter 14, this volume). Solutions to this have been few but varied. For instance, the high-energy physicists put *everyone* involved in a project as authors, sometimes running in the thousands (Birnholtz 2006). BIRN has developed an authorship policy that acknowledges the BIRN database at a particular moment in time, and one can look up who the contributors were up to that point.

Technology readiness also involves reliability. If the technology is unstable (as some research proof-of-concept prototypes can be), people will be unlikely to use it. One aspect of reliability, interoperability, is an ever-present challenge for collaborative projects. Few applications are truly compatible across different platforms. Browsers, for example, render the same Web site differently, and some Word documents created on a Macintosh cannot be read successfully on a Windows machine. The success in collaboration is greater if the participants agree on a single platform. Notably, the early SPARC software ran on a NeXT machine; part of the grant budget was spent on giving NeXT machines to all participants (chapter 9, this volume). Similarly, BIRN developed and configured the hardware and software centrally, and shipped it off to each participating institution. The Astrobiology Institute attempted to standardize the tools that its members use for synchronous and asynchronous communication. For instance, it adopted and successfully deployed WebEx for its online meetings and seminars (Blumberg 2003).

It is crucial, too, to ensure that networking infrastructure supports the intended technology. For example, high-energy physicists from Morocco participating in ATLAS have serious bandwidth limitations, which in turn prevent them from participating in videoconferences. They are also even more concerned about getting the large amount of data that will be produced once the detector is operational.

Additionally, technical support at each location is important, especially when technologies are complex or there are new users. Remote systems support is inadequate; computers are physical devices that need onsite technical support. A technical coordinator is helpful in overseeing technical issues. BIRN, for example, is a cluster of four collaboratories, and has a "coordinating center" in support of all of them that handles all technical issues for the cluster (chapter 12, this volume).

There are some special technical issues with particular types of collaboratories as well. If data sharing is the goal, standards must be agreed on and adhered to by all participants (Hesse et al. 1993). Also, data archiving must be planned so that as technology becomes obsolete, the data integrity is maintained. If instrument sharing is part of the collaboratory, then there should be a plan to certify the users. In a high-energy physics collaboratory, say, the operators from different countries have different back-

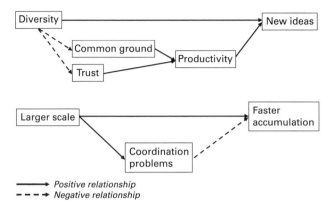

Figure 4.1
The key variables in TORSC showing the inherent benefits and costs of larger-scale efforts and multidisciplinary projects in science and engineering

grounds; in Japan they are technical staff, whereas in the United States they have PhDs in physics. The U.S. operators are having difficulty accepting the fact that the Japanese operators have enough skill for the job.

Discussion

The goals of all collaboratories are to enhance scientific discovery by having more people coordinate their work, use expensive instruments remotely, and engage in more creative activity by allowing people from diverse disciplines and backgrounds to come together. Five factors—the nature of the work, common ground, collaboration readiness, management, and technical readiness—all contribute to the success of a collaboratory.

Two key tensions (see figure 4.1) affecting the achievement of these goals have been identified: the greater the diversity, the less common ground and trust, which together impede the understanding of each other and the production of new ideas; and the larger the scale, the greater the coordination overhead, increasing exponentially rather than linearly (Brooks 1995).

Standards, management, and expectations all play a role in making these tensions as small as possible by finding ways to increase common ground and trust, and addressing the coordination problems by good management and decision making along with trust.

At its core, the theory states that revolutionary science will come about when scientists can work collectively and diverse points of view are brought to bear on a common problem (see figure 4.1). Technology, then, has its effect by allowing more diverse and

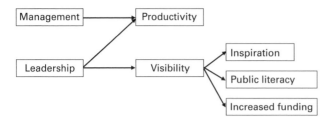

Figure 4.2
Additional key variables showing the importance of good management and leadership

distant groups of scientists to communicate with each other so that their collective work is coordinated (e.g., standards are developed or data are aggregated), and that some aspects of the work can be automated or enhanced (e.g., through visualization and computational aids). But coordinating across diversity and distance offers some particular challenges. As the community of scientists grows, management issues loom large (Kraut et al. 1990). How do we coordinate the various legal and intellectual property issues across the institutions involved? How do we develop standards that satisfy all parties? By the same token, as the diversity of the community grows (e.g., having molecular neuroscientists talking to anatomists to uncover the early signs and perhaps cures of schizophrenia), issues of trust and common ground loom large. How do we assure that we are using the same words in the same way? How do we trust the methods of data collection of others who were not trained in the way we were? TORSC highlights these key trade-offs, and points to areas where particular emphases or new remedial actions are called for. For example, larger and more diverse projects require a more detailed management plan led by experienced project managers, and may call for explicit workshops to engender trust and a common vocabulary.

Good management and leadership not only affect internal productivity but also make the project visible (see figure 4.2). Visibility leads to the possibility of inspiring other scientists to work in new ways, and to borrow tools and lessons learned from earlier efforts. It also can lead to public science literacy, and with pressure on Congress, the possibility of additional funding.

Using TORSC

There is nothing so practical as a good theory.
—Kurt Lewin, "Problems of Research in Social Psychology"

We foresee TORSC as having a number of uses: it can guide the design of high-value technologies; it can provide a framework for conducting evaluations of existing collaborative projects; and it informs strategic planning.

Implications for the Design of High-Value Technologies

TORSC provides guidance to technology designers by highlighting the key social and organizational processes that contribute to the success of collaborations. By identifying those processes that are important for collaboration, TORSC can help developers understand how to design technologies to specifically improve these processes in order to overcome the challenges of relying solely on general-purpose collaborative tools. In particular, TORSC suggests that there are opportunities to improve collaboration support by exploring technologies that create tools targeted to specific social processes as a way to supplement the shortcomings of using general-purpose tools alone, and by searching for abstract representations of information related to critical processes, rather than simply supporting conversations.

In geographically distributed projects, different information and communication technologies are often used in an effort to reproduce (or exceed) the benefits of collocated work (Hollan and Stornetta 1992). While collaboration technologies have yet to completely eliminate the effects of distance, many tools have made strides in helping groups to work well over distance. A common goal of many technologies, including videoconferencing, e-mail, and instant messaging is to enable frequent and ongoing conversation between individuals. This approach to supporting collaboration—emulating the constant conversation that goes on in collocated environments—is extremely widespread and successful.

During the course of the study of collaboratories that led to the development of TORSC, we observed a number of project teams taking a different approach to collaborative tool design. In contrast to technologies that leverage conversation to build trust and awareness, many of these projects were increasing the effectiveness of their collaborations by using technologies that specifically targeted one or more social processes related to collaboration success, using a highly specialized tool to alleviate a particular problem. In all cases, these specialized tools were used alongside general-purpose collaborative tools, but point to an alternate approach to designing collaborative tools based on the specific requirements of antecedents to collaboration success.

One example of these alternate design approaches can be found in the different ways projects have employed technology to support the establishment of common ground. The Mouse BIRN project (discussed above) developed a formal atlas to mediate the different languages of the subdomains involved in the project to support database federation, but scientists have also used it to facilitate cross-domain discussions.

A physical sciences project we studied employed data modeling to build common understandings of subdomains. The formalization of the data model was not nearly as important as the general relationships between concepts, as many data model presentations included the disclaimer "I realize this isn't proper UML, but I think it gets the point across." The value of the modeling language was as a collaboration tool rather than a modeling one. In contrast, a distributed engineering project held weekly technical meetings by videoconference to allow the sites involved in the project to present aspects of their work to other members of the collaboration. These meetings allowed the different sites to build a shared understanding of what was going on at other sites, but were also crucial in reconciling vocabulary misunderstandings and subtle domain differences between sites that represented different scientific fields. Frequent e-mail-list conversation supplemented these meetings.

One commonality in each of these cases is that the projects knew that the creation of a shared understanding was a critical problem facing the collaboration. Once the problem of common ground was well understood and identified, a number of different approaches to design were possible. The distributed engineering group took a mimetic approach, using communication technologies to build and maintain common ground through constant communication, as they would do if collocated. The Mouse BIRN repurposed a technology (the atlas) developed to mediate human-computer communications to support human-human communication. The physical sciences project adapted a methodology intended for another purpose, benefiting from the flexibility of using it incorrectly, rather than limiting its value but following all of the rules.

A Framework for Conducting Evaluations

In scientific research, evaluation is most frequently associated with summative evaluation that measures the outcomes of a scientific project. These outcomes often focus on the quantity and impact of the publications produced, the effectiveness of clinical trials, or the development of technologies that can be adapted for public use. Unfortunately, the true value of a project's output is usually not known until long after the project is finished. To supplement summative evaluations, we need to know more about what processes tend to produce high-value science. TORSC provides an opportunity for distributed projects to identify process and outcome metrics that can be observed early and often in projects, allowing evaluation to become a valuable tool for monitoring project progress and correcting problems along the way.

Formative evaluation is a method used widely in the field of human-computer interaction to understand the requirements of systems, and evaluate existing systems or initial prototypes in order to guide further system design. Formative evaluation frequently employs a variety of analytic methods (e.g., checklists, modeling, or heuristic evaluations) used by experts to predict potential problems or system performance. TORSC can be used as a framework for these kinds of analytic evaluations early in projects to provide administrators or technical coordinators with an understanding of where collaboration problems are likely to arise, and how investments in process changes or technologies might preempt those problems. The identification of key factors can be adapted for checklists or heuristic evaluations. By paying special attention to these processes, we believe distributed projects are much more likely to identify, understand,

Table 4.3

A portion of a script that could be used as a diagnostic tool in an ongoing collaboration

Interviewer: First, let's talk a little bit about your work in general.

1. To begin, tell me a little bit about the type of work you do, who you work with, where they are located, and your relationship with them.

2. For each of the remote workers, how dependent are you on their day-to-day activities? Do you have to coordinate often?

3. How routine is the work that you do? Does everyone know what they're doing? Are you following a standard practice, or are you making it up as you go?

and resolve process breakdowns as they occur, rather than leaving them unaddressed and out of control.

For example, one could imagine building a diagnostic script that asks various questions such as that in table 4.3, which is a portion of an interview script focusing on our first concept: the nature of the work.

The answers to a set of questions such as this would highlight the areas where management might want to put some attention and effort to ensure that the collaboration has the greatest chance of success. And where questions indicate some trouble—for example, a lack of trust—management consultants might recommend various remedies—say, trust-building activities or the use of contractual arrangements.

In providing an understanding of what factors contribute to collaboration success, TORSC helps make the collaboration process measurable and understandable, enabling new kinds of evaluation for distributed scientific projects. By embracing formative and ongoing evaluations, evaluation becomes a tool for maximizing project success rather than simply measuring it after a project is complete.

A Tool for Strategic Planning

In much the same way that TORSC can be used as a framework for ongoing evaluation within a project, the theory can be used as a strategic planning tool. It can help collaboratories decide what kind of geographically distributed projects to participate in and inform how they build capacity in key areas in order to improve their ability to succeed. By providing a set of criteria for comparing different organizations, TORSC offers some insight into the size and nature of the challenges that two organizations are likely to face in trying to work with each other. By understanding the magnitude and likelihood of these challenges before committing to a joint project, organizations can work to develop projects that are likely to match their capabilities. Similarly, organizations that wish to take on more ambitious joint projects can work to build up capacity in key areas. They can build common ground with a particular field, for instance, by hiring candidates with some background in that area or improving documentation practices to make the work more transparent to outsiders. As a strategic planning tool, TORSC offers a way to help organizations systematically improve their ability to collaborate across all projects in addition to within the context of a single project.

Summary

In TORSC, we have gathered the major factors that appear to be important in producing success in science and engineering collaboratories. Research is needed to illuminate the logical connections between the factors, and identify which factors are the most significant and under what circumstances they are operative.

We acknowledge that success can come in a number of forms, from encouraging the use of new tools, to changing the pool of people who become scientists, to enhancing the careers of those in the field, and ultimately, to providing revolutionary breakthroughs in both the conduct and outcome of science. These come about mainly through the judicious design and use of technology, and are enabled by social factors such as the development of common ground, trust, explicit management structures across sites, and the partitioning of work appropriately across sites. The major tensions come from the goal of having larger and more diverse sets of scientists working together, and the tendency in such large and diverse groups to have less common ground, lower degrees of trust, and the need for stricter coordination and management. By facing these tensions and finding remedies in a new focus on key factors, we expect to see an increase of successful collaboratories in the future.

Acknowledgments

This material is based on work supported by the NSF under grant no. IIS 0085951. Any opinions, findings, and conclusions or recommendations expressed in this material are those of the authors, and do not necessarily reflect the views of the NSF.

References

Bandura, A. 1977. Self-efficacy: Toward a unifying theory of behavioral change. *Psychological Review* 84 (2): 191–215.

Berman, H. M., P. E. Bourne, and J. Westbrook. 2004. The Protein Data Bank: A case study in management of community data. *Current Proteomics* 1 (1): 49–57.

Beyer, H., and K. Holtzblatt. 1998. *Contextual design: Defining customer centered systems.* New York: Academic Press.

Birnholtz, J. P. 2005. *When do researchers collaborate? Toward a model of collaboration propensity in science and engineering research.* PhD diss., University of Michigan.

Birnholtz, J. P. 2006. What does it mean to be an author? The intersection of credit, contribution, and collaboration in science. *Journal of the American Society for Information Science and Technology* 57 (13): 1758–1770.

Blumberg, B. S. 2003. The NASA Astrobiology Institute: Early history and organization. *Astrobiology* 3 (3): 463–470.

Bos, N., N. S. Shami, J. S. Olson, A. Cheshin, and N. Nan. 2004. In-group/out-group effects in distributed teams: An experimental simulation. In *Proceedings of the 2004 ACM conference on computer-supported cooperative work*, 429–436. New York: ACM Press.

Brooks, F. P. 1975. *The mythical man-month: Essays on software engineering*. Reading, MA: Addison-Wesley.

Bruce, B. C., B. O. Carragher, B. M. Damon, M. J. Dawson, J. A. Eurell, C. D. Gregory et al. 1997. Chickscope: An interactive MRI classroom curriculum innovation for K-12. *Computers and Education* 29:73–87.

Carroll, J. M., M. B. Rosson, and J. Zhou. 2005. Collective efficacy as a measure of community. In *Proceedings of the SIGCHI conference on human factors in computing systems*, 1–10. New York: ACM Press.

Catalyzing team science: Report from the 2003 BECON symposium. 2003. National Institutes of Health. Available at ⟨http://www.becon.nih.gov/symposia_2003/becon2003_symposium_final.pdf⟩ (accessed April 24, 2007).

Chompalov, I., J. Genuth, and W. Shrum. 2002. The organization of scientific collaborations. *Research Policy* 31:749–767.

Clark, H. H. 1996. *Using language*. New York: Cambridge University Press.

Clark, H. H., and S. E. Brennan. 1991. Grounding in communication. In *Perspectives on socially shared cognition*, ed. L. B. Resnick, J. Levine, and S. D. Teasley, 127–149. Washington, DC: American Psychological Association.

Compeau, D., C. A. Higgins, and S. Huff. 1999. Social cognitive theory and individual reactions to computing technology: A longitudinal study. *Management Information Systems Quarterly* 23 (2): 145–158.

Cramton, C. D. 2001. The mutual knowledge problem and its consequences for dispersed collaboration. *Organization Science* 12 (3): 346–371.

Cummings, J. N., and S. Kiesler. 2005. Collaborative research across disciplinary and institutional boundaries. *Social Studies of Science* 35 (5): 703–722.

Finholt, T. A., and G. M. Olson. 1997. From laboratories to collaboratories: A new organizational form for scientific collaboration. *Psychological Science* 8:28–36.

Fussell, S. R., S. Kiesler, L. D. Setlock, P. Scupelli, and S. Weisband. 2004. Effects of instant messaging on the management of multiple project trajectories. In *Proceedings of the SIGCHI conference on human factors in computing systems*, 191–198. New York: ACM Press.

Gomez, L. M., B. J. Fishman, and R. D. Pea. 1998. The CoVis project: Building a large-scale science education testbed. *Interactive Learning Environments* 6 (1–2): 59–92.

Grudin, J. 1988. Why CSCW applications fail: Problems in the design and evaluation of organizational interfaces. In *Proceedings of the 1988 ACM conference on computer-supported cooperative work*, 85–93. New York: ACM Press.

Hesse, B. W., L. S. Sproull, S. B. Kiesler, and J. P. Walsh. 1993. Returns to science: Computer networks in oceanography. *Communications of the ACM* 36 (8): 90–101.

Hollan, J. D., and S. Stornetta. 1992. Beyond being there. In *Proceedings of the SIGCHI conference on human factors in computing systems*, 119–125. New York: ACM Press.

Jeffrey, P. 2003. Smoothing the waters: Observations on the process of cross-disciplinary research collaboration. *Social Studies of Science* 33 (4): 539–562.

Kibrick, R., A. Conrad, and A. Perala. 1998. Through the far looking glass: Collaborative remote observing with the W. M. Keck Observatory. *Interactions* 5 (3): 32–39.

Kramer, R. M., and T. R. Tyler. 1995. *Trust in organizations: Frontiers of theory and research*. Thousand Oaks, CA: Sage Publications.

Kraut, R. E., R. Fish, R. Root, and B. Chalfonte. 1990. Informal communication in organizations: Form, function, and technology. In *Human reactions to technology: Claremont symposium on applied social psychology*, ed. S. Oskamp and S. Spacapan, 145–199. Beverly Hills, CA: Sage Publications.

Kurland, B., and T. D. Egan. 1999. Telecommuting: Justice and control in the virtual organization. *Organization Science* 10 (4): 500–513.

Larson, C., A. Christian, L. Olson, D. Hicks, and C. Sweeney. 2002. *Colorado Healthy Communities Initiative: Ten years later*. Denver: Colorado Trust.

LeFasto, M. F. J., and C. Larson. 2001. *When teams work best: 6,000 team members and leaders tell what it takes to succeed*. Thousand Oaks, CA: Sage Publications.

Lewin, K. 1951. Problems of research in social psychology. In *Field theory in social science: Selected theoretical papers*, ed. D. Cartwright, 155–169. New York: Harper and Row.

Maznevski, M. L., and K. M. Chudoba. 2000. Bridging space over time: Global virtual team dynamics and effectiveness. *Organization Science* 11 (5): 473–492.

Mazur, A., and E. Boyko. 1981. Large-scale ocean research projects: What makes them succeed or fail? *Social Studies of Science* 11:425–449.

Merton, R. K. 1988. The Matthew effect in science, II: Cumulative advantage and the symbolism of intellectual property. *Isis* 79 (4): 606–623.

Olson, G. M., and J. S. Olson. 2000. Distance matters. *Human Computer Interaction* 15:139–179.

Olson, J. S., S. Teasley, L. Covi, and G. M. Olson. 2002. The (currently) unique advantages of being collocated. In *Distributed Work*, ed. P. Hinds and S. Kiesler, 113–135. Cambridge, MA: MIT Press.

Orlikowski, W. J. 1992. Learning from Notes: Organizational issues in groupware implementation. In *Proceedings of the 1992 ACM conference on computer-supported cooperative work*, ed. J. Turner and R. Kraut, 362–369. New York: ACM Press.

Prpic, K. 1996. Scientific fields and eminent scientists' productivity patterns and factors. *Scientometrics* 37 (3): 445–471.

Rousseau, D. M., S. B. Sitkin, R. S. Burt, and C. Camerer. 1998. Not so different after all: A cross discipline view of trust. *Academy of Management Review* 23 (3): 393–404.

Shrum, W., I. Chompalov, and J. Genuth. 2001. Trust, conflict, and performance in scientific collaborations. *Social Studies of Science* 31 (5): 681–730.

Sonnenwald, D. H. 2003. Managing cognitive and affective trust in the conceptual R&D organization. In *Trust in knowledge management and systems in organizations*, ed. M. Huotari and M. Iivonen, 82–106. Hershey, PA: Idea Publishing.

Sonnenwald, D. H. 2007. Scientific collaboration: A synthesis of challenges and strategies. In *Annual review of information science and technology*, ed. B. Cronin, 41:643–681. Medford, NJ: Information Today.

Steele, T. W., and J. C. Stier. 2000. The impact of interdisciplinary research in the environmental sciences: A forestry case study. *Journal of the American Society for Information Science* 51 (5): 476–484.

Stokols, D., J. Fuqua, J. Gress, R. Harvey, K. Phillips, L. Baezconde-Garbanati et al. 2003. Evaluating transdisciplinary science. *Nicotine and Tobacco Research* 5 (Suppl. 1): S21–S39.

Stokols, D., R. Harvey, J. Gress, J. Fuqua, and K. Phillips. 2005. In vivo studies of transdisciplinary scientific collaboration: Lessons learned and implications for active living research. *American Journal of Preventive Medicine* 28 (Suppl. 2): 202–213.

Thompson, J. D. 1967. *Organizations in action: Social science bases of administrative theory.* New York: McGraw-Hill.

Walsh, J. P., and T. Bayma. 1996. The virtual college: Computer-mediated communication and scientific work. *Information Society* 2 (4): 343–363.

Weedman, J. 1998. The structure of incentive: Design and client roles in application-oriented research. *Science, Technology, and Human Values* 23 (3): 315–345.

5 Collaborative Research across Disciplinary and Organizational Boundaries

Jonathon N. Cummings and Sara Kiesler

Scientists have collaborated with one another for centuries (Finholt and Olson 1997). Recently, policymakers have begun to encourage and support two or more disciplines working together in applied and basic science—that is, multidisciplinary collaboration (Grinter, Herbsleb, and Perry 1999; Teasley and Wolinsky 2001; Chin, Myers, and Hoyt 2002). Important fields such as oceanography and cognitive science have developed out of multidisciplinary collaborations (Hesse et al. 1993; Schunn, Crowley, and Okada 2002). Because the formal organization of science and engineering in universities and industrial laboratories usually follows disciplinary boundaries, multidisciplinary collaboration often requires crossing organizational boundaries, too. The geologist who collaborates with a computer scientist frequently works in another department or university as well as a different field.

In the past, dispersed forms of collaboration would have been made difficult by physical distance between scientists, which not only reduced the likelihood of collaboration, but also had a negative impact on success (Allen 1977; Kraut, Egido, and Galegher 1990; Kiesler and Cummings 2002). Today, dispersed collaborations are more feasible because communication technologies allow scientists to exchange news, data, reports, equipment, instruments, and other resources (Hesse et al. 1993; Kouzes, Myers, and Wulf 1996; Finholt 2002). Fields such as particle physics and mathematics have relied on computer-mediated communication for several decades (Walsh and Bayma 1996). Funding agencies such as the National Science Foundation (NSF) in the United States and the European Union's Framework Programmes, which aim for diverse organizational representation, have spawned an explosion of late in dispersed collaboration.

Recent research suggests that even with some signs of progress (Sonnenwald 2003), technology has not yet conquered distance (Mark, Grudin, and Poltrock 1999; Herbsleb et al. 2000; Cramton 2001; Hinds and Bailey 2003). A major challenge for dispersed scientific collaborations is coordinating work so that scientists can effectively use one another's ideas and expertise without frequent face-to-face interaction. Coordination is the integration or linking together of different pieces of a project to accomplish a collective task (Van de Ven, Delbecq, and Koenig 1976). Although some coordination can be accomplished through project structure—for example, by creating clear lines of authority and a division of labor—science is dynamic, and members of the collaboration still must talk out common problems, discuss shared resources, and monitor and review the work to make joint progress (Malone and Crowston 1994; Kraut and Streeter 1995).

Multidisciplinary collaborations also must manage interpersonal relationships within the project. Scientists from different disciplines have usually trained in different departments, have had different advisers, publish in different journals, and attend different conferences. Their social bonds are likely to be comparatively weak (Granovetter 1973), increasing the difficulty of developing trust and effective interdependence.

Innovation in Multidisciplinary Collaborations

An important claim favoring multidisciplinary collaborations is that they promote innovation. We define innovation as the successful implementation of creative ideas, tasks, or procedures (Amabile 1988). In science and engineering, innovations are technical discoveries or insights, new ways to use existing technologies, or radical approaches to problems (Henderson and Clark 1990; Utterback 1994; Hargadon 1998; O'Connor and Rice 2001). Multidisciplinary projects should increase the likelihood of innovation due to their juxtaposition of ideas, tools, and people from different domains. As the Internet and other forms of computing have enhanced the potential for this "distributed intelligence," policymakers in science and engineering expect greater innovation from such projects (Zare 1997).

There is a tension between the benefits to innovation of working across disciplinary and organizational boundaries versus the risks that arise from the costs of coordination and relationship development in these collaborations. Dispersed science and engineering projects are forms of innovation systems that are meant to create, diffuse, and use diverse sources of knowledge (Carlsson et al. 2002). How researchers manage such projects and organize work to be productive has been the subject of much discussion over the years (Hagstrom 1964). Some authors distinguish between the amount of bureaucracy versus the amount of participation in the scientific collaboration (Chompalov, Genuth, and Shrum 2002), whereas others focus on the extent to which work is project based (Hobday 2000). The existing literature provides no clear guidelines to managing coordination and relationship development in multidisciplinary collaborations.

Multidisciplinary projects may require new approaches to coordination to get the work done and foster trust. Working with other disciplines requires working across organizational boundaries. For example, when a biologist at one university collaborates with a computer scientist at another university, the need for coordination increases due to field differences and geographic dispersion. The research question we pose in this chapter is how collaborations involving multidisciplinary and multiorganizational relationships achieve successful coordination.

Methods

We studied a research program created by the NSF's Computer and Information Science and Engineering Directorate called Knowledge and Distributed Intelligence (KDI). Its purpose was "to span the scientific and engineering communities ... to generate, model, and represent more complex and cross-disciplinary scientific data from new sources and at enormously varying scales." The program was highly competitive. It supported only 40 awards out of 697 proposals in 1998, and 31 awards out of 554 preproposals and 163 full proposals in 1999. These projects were supported at US$1.5 million each over three years. We report the analyses of 62 of the 71 projects awarded this funding.

In fall 2001, the NSF asked us to organize a workshop of research grantees to assess what had happened in the KDI research projects. The NSF invited the principal investigator (PI) and one co-PI from each of the 71 KDI projects to the workshop. Researchers from 52 research projects attended the workshop, held in late April 2002. At this workshop we asked researchers, organized into small randomly assigned groups, to discuss with one another how their research projects were organized and managed, the kinds of outcomes they generated, and the ways in which their research experience could inform future program evaluation. During three mornings of group discussion, note takers as well as participants compiled lists of experiences, outcomes, and suggestions. We asked the participants to send us copies of reports they had written and links to their Web sites.

During the workshop and when reviewing our notes later, we observed that almost all of the projects faced serious obstacles to collaboration. These obstacles ranged from different teaching schedules to different visions of project objectives. For example, one PI, whose university followed the semester system, ran into difficulty finding times to meet with his co-PIs, whose university ran on the quarter system. Another PI spoke of how he had to negotiate budgets, contract language, intellectual property, indirect costs, and human subjects procedures across universities. Still another discussed how students at different universities had been trained with different statistical software—an obstacle to sharing analyses until everyone could agree on a common approach. Many PIs mentioned distance as a barrier to meeting, and recounted how their early enthusiasm for travel to one another's sites was dampened over the course of the project. To overcome these obstacles, project PIs or co-PIs employed traditional approaches to coordination, such as weekly laboratory meetings, as well as mechanisms they invented to maintain communication and keep the project on track. For instance, a few PIs arranged for graduate student exchanges to promote the cross-training of students in the project.

We observed considerable variation in the number and types of outcomes of these projects. Some of the projects produced mainly computer-based tools or resources, such as shared data repositories that could be used in other scientific projects. In other projects, PIs' publications, presentations, and workshops opened up an entirely new field of endeavor. Others were effective in training graduate students who later went on to fill top research jobs, or they gave undergraduates the experience they needed to earn places in graduate programs. Still others worked with community groups by, for example, creating museum exhibits, elementary school classroom materials, or Web sites designed for public use.

Postworkshop Survey

From the workshop notes along with the documentation from PIs' Web sites and reports, we created an online survey to systematically assess the coordination mechanisms and project outcomes that workshop participants had described in connection with their own projects. We created items that represented the most frequent coordination mechanisms and project outcomes mentioned in the workshop. In fall 2002, we surveyed all the KDI PIs and co-PIs, and a random sample of students and staff in each project. We asked this entire sample whether or not their project had used each mechanism, or had produced that outcome. Our questionnaire included the following items designed to measure coordination: direct supervision of work; use of special events, such as workshops, to get people together in the same place; travel in order to work together or meet; and regular use of face-to-face meetings, e-mail, and telephone. If the respondents checked an item, they were asked to describe how they used the respective mechanism in their project. They also could add items that were not otherwise listed, though no single item was mentioned often enough to warrant inclusion in our analysis. The items measuring project outcomes were grouped into categories corresponding to the NSF's goals: generation of new ideas and knowledge (for example, publications, patents, and grants), generation of tools and infrastructure for research (such as software applications and databases), training of scientists and engineers (say, PhD students and undergraduates), and outreach and public understanding and use of science and engineering (school and community projects, for instance, or links with industry). The respondents checked whether their project had achieved outcomes within each of these categories; if so, they were asked to describe these outcomes.

Results

We report results for sixty-two (87 percent) of the seventy-one research projects in which at least one PI or co-PI answered the survey and provided documentation of project outcomes. PIs or co-PIs usually said they spoke for the entire project, inflating scores for those projects where more than one PI responded to the survey. Therefore, we report data for the most senior respondent on each project, either the PI ($n = 37$) or, when the PI did not respond, the co-PI ($n = 25$). Preliminary analyses show that the reports by PIs and co-PIs were equivalent. For example, PIs and co-PIs were equally

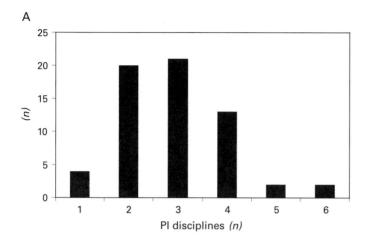

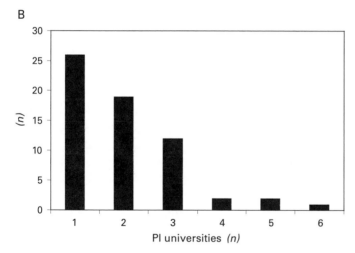

Figure 5.1
Distribution of principal investigator (PI) disciplines (*A*) and PI universities (*B*) (*N* = 64)

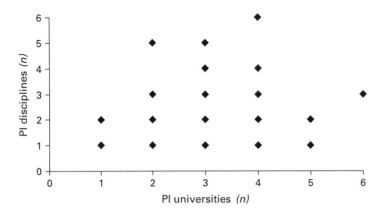

Figure 5.2
Scatter plot showing the relationship between the number of principal investigator (PI) disciplines in a project and the number of PI universities in a project ($r = .29$)

likely to report positive outcomes, regardless of their projects' size, or the number of disciplines or universities involved in their projects. We used data available from the Web, NSF reports, and other NSF data to verify factual information such as project size, disciplines, and universities.

Each project in the sample of sixty-two projects had one PI and up to five co-PIs; the average number of co-PIs was three. The PIs and co-PIs represented forty disciplines, including computer science (16 percent), electrical engineering (13 percent), other engineering disciplines (12 percent), psychology (12 percent), physics (9 percent), mathematics (9 percent), and biology (8 percent). These PIs and co-PIs were employed by nearly a hundred organizations. All but five of these organizations were universities. Henceforth in this chapter we refer to the PI organizations as "universities," in that these were 95 percent of the sample. Of the research projects, twenty-six were at a single university and thirty-six, a majority, were collaborations of multiple universities, up to six (see figure 5.1). A greater number of universities was particularly characteristic of those projects involving more disciplines (correlation $r = 0.29$; see figure 5.2). This finding supports our argument that multidisciplinary projects are likely to require coordination across organizations and over distance.

The mechanisms used for coordination across projects varied in popularity. At least 20 percent of the projects used the coordination mechanisms reported in table 5.1. A few projects used communication technologies other than regular telephone and e-mail at least once a month, such as conference calls (13 percent), videoconferencing (8 percent), instant messaging (3 percent), and online forum discussions (8 percent). Nevertheless, these were too few to include in the subsequent analyses.

Table 5.1

Coordination mechanisms used by projects ($N = 62$ projects)

Coordination mechanism items (0 no: 1 yes)	Projects (%)
Faculty supervised tasks	84
Postdoctoral supervised tasks	44
Graduate student supervised tasks	34
Held seminar or invited speakers	60
At least monthly face-to-face project meetings	55
At least monthly phone or e-mail on project	84
Held conference or workshop	55
Worked on project during conference or workshop	52
Sabbatical to work with collaborators	21
Traveled by airplane to work with collaborators	52

The respondents reported many different project outcomes and products, ranging from an algorithm for large-scale predictive species distribution to a blood-flow simulation for prosthetic heart valves, a system to support the manual manipulation of virtual objects, an undergraduate thesis published in a top journal, and a partnership with a major corporation. We ran a confirmatory factor analysis, which showed that the items were clustered into four independent categories of outcomes that mapped onto the four NSF goals we had previously specified: ideas and knowledge (Ideas), tools and infrastructure (Tools), student training (Training), and outreach (Outreach) (table 5.2). For subsequent analyses, we used items from the four factors that loaded together at least at the 0.4 level on each factor. Every project received a score for each of four categories, Ideas (Cronbach's alpha = 0.55), Tools (Cronbach's alpha = 0.51), Training (Cronbach's alpha = 0.54), and Outreach (Cronbach's alpha = 0.28), depending on the number of items to which the PI or co-PI responded "yes." For instance, in the Ideas category, a project could receive up to four points if the PI or co-PI reported that their project started a new field or area of research, came up with new grants or spin-off projects, developed new methodologies, and was recognized with an award for contributions to the field. Projects' average score in this category was two points. The respondents who answered "yes" to any item had to document their answer by describing the specific outcome, giving a citation, naming the student, and so forth. We intended this requirement to discourage gratuitous entries.

Effects of Multiple Disciplines and Universities on Project Coordination

We argued that more disciplines and/or universities involved in a research project might impair project coordination. We performed statistical tests, using ordinary least squares regression, to examine the simultaneous effects of the main predictor variables, the number of PI disciplines and the number of PI universities, on their projects' use of

Table 5.2
Project outcomes ($N = 62$ projects)

Project outcome items (yes/no)	Projects saying "yes" (%)
Ideas	
Started new field or area of research	58
Created new grants or spin-off projects	58
Developed new methodologies	66
Recognized with award for contribution to field	19
Tools	
Created new software	71
Created new hardware	13
Generated new datasets	47
Submitted patent application	15
Training	
Undergraduate/graduate student finished thesis or dissertation	76
Undergraduate/graduate/postdoc got academic job	48
Undergraduate/graduate/postdoc got industry job	42
Outreach	
Formed partnership with industry	27
Formed community relationships through research	27
Formed collaborations with different researchers	65

Note: The items above loaded above .4 on four separate factors, as categorized above. Each project could have 0 to 4 points in the Ideas and Tools categories, and 0 to 3 points in the Training and Outreach categories.

each of the coordination mechanisms. The regression analyses statistically control for the year the project started, the size of the project in budget and people, and the level of research and development in the main PI's university. Table 5.3 shows these analyses. The findings were that to a statistically significant degree, more PI universities involved in a project predicted fewer coordination mechanisms used in that project. More PI universities on a project predicted a lower level of faculty, postdoctoral, and graduate student direct supervision, a reduced likelihood of having created a project-related course, seminar, or invited speakers, and a much lower likelihood of having at least monthly project meetings. The results also show that with more universities involved, the pattern of coordination mechanisms changed. PIs were more likely to hold a conference or workshop, and to work on the project at a conference or workshop. (Holding a conference or workshop, however, was less likely when the PIs were from different disciplines.) The analyses taken as a whole suggest that distance and organizational boundaries interfered with those coordination mechanisms that involve frequent, spontaneous conversation and problem solving (direct supervision, face-to-face meetings, seminars, or courses). Distance and organizational boundaries impelled

Table 5.3

Regression analyses predicting the amount of project coordination from the number of principal investigator (PI) disciplines and number of PI universities in the project ($N = 62$ projects)

	Coordination mechanisms used in projects									
	Faculty supervised tasks	Postdoc supervised tasks	Graduate student supervised tasks	Held seminar or invited speakers	At least monthly face-to-face project meetings	At least monthly phone or e-mail on project	Held conference or workshop	Worked on project during conference or workshop	Sabbatical to work with collaborators	Traveled by airplane to work with collaborators
Predictor variables										
Number of PI disciplines	−.18	.17	−.01	−.07	−.07	−.03	−.43†	−.29	.67†	.08
Number of PI universities	−.22†	−.39†	−.56*	−.62**	−.64**	.07	.37*	.38†	−.06	.23
Controls										
Year started	1.25**	1.31**	.44	1.09**	1.41**	.66**	.91*	.77†	.86†	.43
Budget	−.16	−.26	.04	−.04	−.13	.09	.08	−.14	−.11	−.23
University research and development	−.05	−.14	.05	−.08	−.04	.12	.00	.05	.00	.10
Number of PIs	.19	−.18	.49	.36	.17	.05	−.18	−.04	−.85*	.02
Number of postdocs	.09	.39**	.20	.25*	.11	.00	.27*	.14	−.09	.03
Number of graduate students	−.02	−.18	.00	−.1	−.17	−.01	−.18	−.07	−.04	.21
R^2	.86	.56	.44	.71	.66	.85	.65	.56	.31	.57

Note: Values in table are beta coefficients. Statistical significance is indicated by : † $p < .10$; * $p < .05$; ** $p < .01$. Positive beta values indicate that a higher value of the predictor (or control) variable predicts a higher likelihood that the coordination mechanism was used in a project. Negative beta values indicate that a higher value of the predictor (or control) variable predicts a lower likelihood that the coordination mechanism was used in a project. For instance, the significant negative beta (−.64**) for number of universities predicting monthly face-to-face project meetings means that when more PI universities were involved in a project, the project team was less likely to have held at least monthly face-to-face project meetings.

researchers to use other means of getting together, such as putting together a workshop to which all the collaborators could travel. Our data do not show that PIs from multiple universities used technology or traveled more than PIs who were collocated.

Effects of Multiple Disciplines and Universities on Project Outcomes

Table 5.4 (Model 1) shows the results from regression analyses of the impact of the number of PI disciplines and the number of PI universities on project outcomes. The number of disciplines and control variables had little impact, except that more disciplines in the project tended to be less beneficial for student training. The strongest statistical effects derived from the number of universities. Having more PI universities on a project was significantly negatively associated with the generation of new ideas and knowledge, and was also negatively associated with student training and project outreach, though this association did not reach statistical significance.

Mediation Analysis

We conducted an analysis to examine how coordination mechanisms were related to outcomes. We found that controlling for the number of universities, coordination mechanisms predicted the outcomes of projects. The most effective coordination mechanism overall was direct supervision, especially by faculty and graduate students; this mechanism was used more by single university projects. Face-to-face mechanisms, such as holding a seminar, inviting outside speakers, and having face-to-face laboratory meetings, were especially important in student training. The mechanisms used in multiple university projects, such as travel as well as holding a workshop or conference, were somewhat effective in helping the project generate new ideas.

To test whether coordination mechanisms partly caused the negative relationship between the number of universities and project outcomes, we conducted a mediation analysis (Baron and Kenny 1986). We compared a model using only the number of PI universities and disciplines (plus controls) to predict project outcomes (Model 1 in table 5.4), with a model adding in all the coordination variables (Model 2). If negative beta coefficients for the number of PI universities are smaller or reversed in Model 2 compared with Model 1, that difference suggests that coordination mechanisms could account for the lower degree of success of projects with more PI universities. The beta coefficients for the number of PI universities in Model 2 versus Model 1 is indeed smaller in predicting Ideas outcomes (−0.33 versus −0.40), Training outcomes (0.27 versus −0.22), and Outreach outcomes (−0.17 versus −0.26), showing some support for the idea that a lack of coordination was associated with poorer outcomes of these types.

Note that the opposite occurred in predicting outcomes in the Tools category. That is, the beta coefficients for the number of PI universities become significant and positive when coordination is added to the model. This finding suggests that controlling

Table 5.4

Regression analyses testing the effects of number of principal investigator (PI) disciplines, number of PI universities, and number of coordination mechanisms onproject outcomes (N= 62 projects)

	Ideas		Tools		Training		Outreach	
	Model 1	Model 2	Model 1	Model 2	Model 1	Model 2	Model 1	Model 2
Controls (not shown)								
Predictor variables								
Number of PI disciplines	−.08	.09	.25	.16	.00	.01	.25	.25
Number of PI universities	−.40**	−.33 †	.00	.39 †	−.22	.27	−.26	−.17
Coordination mechanisms								
Faculty supervised tasks		.35*		.42 †		.38*		.26
Postdoc supervised tasks		.01		.02		−.13		.00
Graduate student supervised tasks		.13		.24*		.17*		.05
Held seminar or invited speaker		−.07		.08		.31*		−.10
At least monthly face-to-face project meetings		.17		.12		.24*		.17
At least monthly phone or email on project		.03		−.19		−.23		.12
Held conference or workshop		.13		−.05		−.11		−.03
Worked on project during conference or workshop		.11		−.07		.01		.06
Sabbatical to work with collaborators		−.04		.19*		.08		.08
Traveled by airplane to work with collaborators		.24*		.16		.17 †		.13
R^2	.87	.77	.78	.68	.87	.77	.73	.68

Note: Values in table are beta coefficients. Statistical significance is indicated by : † $p < .10$; * $p < .05$; ** $p < .01$. Model 1 shows the effects of number of PI disciplines and number of PI universities on project outcomes. A positive beta indicates that the predictor is associated with more outcomes in each category shown. A negative beta indicates that the predictor is associated with fewer outcomes in each category shown. Model 2 shows the combined effects of number of PI disciplines, number of PI universities, and number of coordination mechanisms on outcomes. The comparison is a mediation analysis (Baron and Kenny, 1986). If the beta for number of disciplines or universities is lower in Model 2 than in Model 1, one can infer that coordination mechanisms are partly mediating (causing) the effect of the predictor on outcomes.

for coordination effects (which are all positively associated with good outcomes, as in the other models), more PI universities contributed to better Tools outcomes. The finding indicates that research to produce computer-based tools might be qualitatively different from other kinds of research.

In sum, the results show that more PI universities rather than more PI disciplines were problematic for collaborations, and that using more coordination mechanisms could reduce the negative impact somewhat. Unfortunately, having PI universities involved in a project significantly reduced the likelihood that PIs would actually employ sufficient coordination mechanisms.

Discussion

Despite the widespread excitement about dispersed collaboration reflected in terms like *virtual team*, *e-Science*, and *cyberinfrastructure*, there appear to remain a number of challenges that scientists encounter when they work across organizational boundaries. The multiuniversity projects we studied were less successful, on average, than projects located at a single university. We show these trends in figure 5.3. The overall trend in figure 5.3 is a downward slope from single university to multiple universities. Also, the figure indicates a marginally significant overall interaction effect, suggesting that multidisciplinary projects can be highly successful in producing new ideas and knowledge, and outreach, when they are carried out within one university. Projects with many disciplines involved excelled when they were carried out within one university. We also found that when projects used more coordination mechanisms, they were more successful, but projects involving more universities used fewer coordination mechanisms than did projects involving fewer universities. Using more coordination mechanisms partly made up for distance and organizational boundaries, but even controlling for the number of coordination mechanisms used, projects involving more universities were less successful.

Our findings are open to alternative explanations that need to be examined before drawing strong inferences. One problem is that the projects investigated here represent only 6 percent of all the proposals sent to the program. We do not know what forms of selection bias operated. For example, did peer reviewers give higher scores to multiuniversity projects because they liked the number of organizations and regions represented? If reviewers gave multiuniversity proposals extra points for including many organizations, and if doing so is independent of scientific merit, then the poorer outcomes of multiuniversity projects could be explained by a difference in intrinsic merit. To check on this possibility, it will be necessary to examine the peer review process.

Another problem is that our analysis represents a case study of one funding agency's program, and especially, the beginning of this agency's attempts to support interdisciplinary research on a grander scale. The research program had a number of distinctive

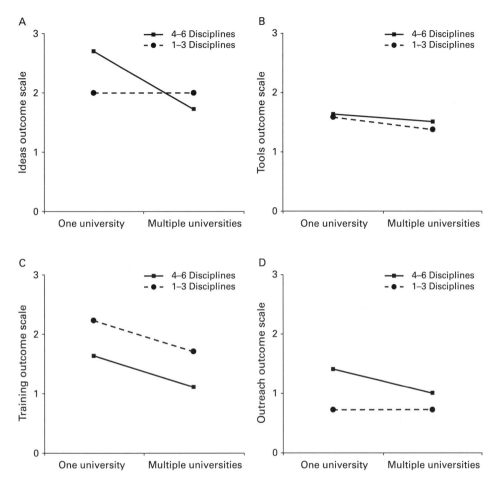

Figure 5.3
Project outcomes in a single university and multiuniversity project (*N* = 62 projects). *A*, Ideas; *B*, Tools; *C*, Training; *D*, Outreach. The unit of measurement on the y-axis is the number of items checked on the postworkshop survey for each outcome. Based on a median split, there were thirty projects with one to three principal investigator (PI) disciplines and thirty-two projects with four to six disciplines.

attributes that might have influenced the results: for example, that funding was provided for only three years, probably insufficient time to create effective coordination for the multiuniversity projects.

Implications for Theory

Research on innovation and social networks suggests that multidisciplinary collaborations should generate innovations in science and engineering. Multidisciplinary collaborations can bring new ideas and approaches to a problem. The work arrangements that make these collaborations possible, though, require a deliberate strategy for coordination because the natural forces of propinquity and similarity are absent or reduced. In our data, the pattern of coordination in multiuniversity projects was indeed different than in single university projects.

In managing their projects, the PIs of multiuniversity projects were less able to supervise all the work directly (and supervision was related strongly to outcomes), hold regular weekly face-to-face meetings involving the whole group, or create mechanisms such as cotaught seminars and reading groups that would help the research staff and students share information, learn from one another, and develop professional relationships. They had to travel more and arrange other ways to communicate with participants in the project. Some project leaders jump-started their projects by holding a workshop or conference in which they brought everyone together. Others scheduled monthly telephone meetings. And other groups shared an application, a piece of equipment, or a database. These mechanisms were sometimes successful, particularly if they were sustained. Monthly phone calls as well as regular e-mail and workshops improved outcomes. But investigators complained that funding agencies did not recognize the costs incurred, budgets did not support the extra coordination efforts needed, and communication tended to fall off as the dispersed investigators discovered it was easier to work on their own tasks, rather than try to work together. These behaviors suggest that technology did not overcome distance. In multiuniversity collaborations, leaders and members had to figure out how to keep communication going to create successful projects.

Theories of innovation and social networks have not yet addressed this problem. Social network research mainly focuses on the importance of strong ties for achieving deep exchanges of knowledge and effective learning, and such research is only beginning to address how groups with comparatively weak ties can achieve innovative outcomes (Hansen 1999). Research on innovation has examined mainly single organization projects in which the ties are comparatively strong (Clark and Wheelwright 1992). Our study suggests that theories of innovation and social networks could benefit from further investigations of how weak ties change into strong ones during the collaboration process. Longitudinal data with measures taken at multiple time periods would be required for such analysis, and cannot be addressed with our cross-sectional data.

Currently, we have no theory of the "ideal" level of collaboration in science, especially in interdisciplinary science. Our results suggest that student training benefits from less collaboration across disciplines or universities (see figure 5.3). The most successful training outcomes were in one university with fewer disciplines involved in the project. In future research, we should examine how different kinds of science use different forms of coordination, and how the use of those mechanisms changes the nature of the collaboration. It may be the case that some mechanisms are more effective than others for tightly coupled—compared with loosely coupled—projects (Weick 1979). For example, the data in figure 5.3 indicate that work on tools and infrastructure (especially software projects) is not impeded at all by multiple disciplines or universities. This is work that can be decomposed, managed, and evaluated across distance and organizational boundaries, as is indicated by the success of many open-source projects (for example, Linux or Mozilla).

Implications for Practice

Our findings should stimulate discussion about the organization and management of funding agencies' multidisciplinary programs and large-scale initiatives, and also about approaches that researchers themselves can use to manage multidisciplinary projects. Given the importance of face-to-face supervision and coordination, which is apparent in our data, perhaps more project-related conferences, workshops, sabbaticals, and travel to other sites would improve the opportunity for supervision in multiuniversity collaborations. Additional research is needed to identify the incentives that would encourage multiorganizational collaborations to explicitly use coordination mechanisms in their projects.

The use of communication technology (e-mail, instant messages, phone conferences, and videoconferences) did not give PIs at multiple universities an added advantage, at least as far as we could determine. Web sites were common, though they were rarely used for ongoing work. Our impression from the workshop was that e-mail was used a great deal, but that it failed to help people coordinate project work across many investigators located at different places. Using e-mail sometimes encouraged too much task decomposition and too little intraproject sharing and learning. What kinds of technology might help? Our data and comments at the workshop suggest the requirements of such technology would include tools to:

- Manage and track the trajectory of tasks over time
- Reduce information overload
- Facilitate ongoing conversation (perhaps some version of instant messages for scientists)

- Encourage awareness with reasonable interruption for spontaneous talk
- Support simultaneous group decision making
- Schedule presentations and meetings across distance

It is likely that these suggestions apply not only to the comparatively small multiuniversity collaborations we studied but also to bigger projects focused on large-scale data analysis and visualization, such as the Biomedical Informatics Research Network, the Network for Earthquake Engineering Simulation, and the Grid Physics Network.

Implications for Policy

Policymakers in the research establishment must understand the difficulties of projects that cross distance and organizational boundaries, and decide if they are willing to invest in their extra coordination costs to make them successful. What really accounts for the difficulties associated with such projects? Are they inherently more difficult? Does it simply take more time and effort to get them started? Or do investigators have too little skill or time to manage distributed work arrangements? At the KDI workshop, a litany of issues was raised ranging from the difficulty of arranging meetings and joint courses when different universities have different teaching calendars, to the difficulty of meeting expectations of different researchers in different departments. Some university departments, believing that they were on the periphery of the problem, did not reward investigators for their work. Some projects fell apart when their budgets were cut and the resources had to be redistributed. (For example, in one project whose budget was cut, one of the co-PIs at a distant university was cut out of the grant entirely.) In some cases, the subcontracting mechanism delayed progress while co-PIs waited for funding. It is not difficult to imagine that the problems become even more severe when national and language boundaries are introduced, as in the case of the European Union Framework Programmes.

The experiences expressed at the workshop and analyzed by our survey suggest that funding agencies should consider a number of changes to meet the challenges of multiorganizational collaborations. Changes were made in some programs—for instance, longer-term funding to build infrastructure and relationships, and collaborative grant mechanisms instituted in the NSF's Information Technology Research program. Further changes that funding agencies should make include, for example, budgets to support an infrastructure for multiuniversity collaborations and PI salary support. In addition, the practice of encouraging a funding target and then cutting budgets has caused needless stress as well as resentment for researchers who developed proposals while assuming a particular distribution of resources. The entire community should reconsider the costs of "proposal pressure." Researchers, like everyone else, respond to the promise of large-scale funding despite the poor chances of funding. More than one thousand researchers wrote full applications for KDI research funding and did not receive awards. These proposals were required to be innovative and interdisciplinary, but it seems likely that many involved work that the investigators would have done anyway. If under a conservative estimate it took each group only three weeks to write its proposal, then the aggregate effort represents three thousand weeks of wasted scientific labor. Because funding agencies do not currently study unfunded proposals and unsuccessful applicants, we cannot answer this question.

Conclusion

The question of how to promote collaboration across disciplines and organizations applies to innovation systems beyond science. Hence the trade-off we have characterized here—innovation opportunities versus coordination costs—is a general question. We show that the dilemma is serious. There may be organizational and technological ways to alleviate it.

Acknowledgments

This chapter was adapted from Cummings, J. N., and Kiesler, S. (2005). Collaborative research across disciplinary and organizational boundaries. *Social Studies of Science*, 35(5), 703–722. For a replication and extension of these results with the NSF ITR program, also see Cummings, J. N., and Kiesler, S. (2007). Coordination costs and project outcomes in multi-university collaborations. *Research Policy*, 36(10), 1620–1634. This work on scientific collaboration was supported by NSF awards IIS-9872996/IIS-0603836 Duke/IIS-0432638 CMU. We thank Allyson Pottmeyer and Maria Ines Garcia for their excellent research assistance throughout the project. We also thank Suzanne Iacono for her helpful research suggestions and critiques of the findings.

Note

This chapter was first published in *Social Studies of Science* 35, no. 5 (October 2005): 703–722. © SSS and SAGE Publications. ISSN 0306-3127 DOI: 10.1177/0306312705055535.

References

Allen, T. 1977. *Managing the flow of technology*. Cambridge, MA: MIT Press.

Amabile, T. M. 1988. A model of creativity and innovation in organizations. *Research in Organizational Behavior* 10:123–167.

Baron, R. M., and D. A. Kenny. 1986. The moderator-mediator variable distinction in social psychological research: Conceptual, strategic, and statistical considerations. *Journal of Personality and Social Psychology* 51:1173–1182.

Carlsson, B., S. Jacobsson, M. Holm'en, and A. Rickne. 2002. Innovation systems: Analytical and methodological issues. *Research Policy* 31:233–245.

Chin, G., J. Myers, and D. Hoyt. 2002. Social networks in the virtual science laboratory. *Communications of the ACM* 45 (8): 87–92.

Chompalov, I., J. Genuth, and W. Shrum. 2002. The organization of scientific collaborations. *Research Policy* 31:749–767.

Clark, K. B., and S. C. Wheelwright. 1992. Organizing and leading "heavyweight" development teams. *California Management Review* 34 (3): 9–28.

Cramton, C. D. 2001. The mutual knowledge problem and its consequences in dispersed collaboration. *Organization Science* 12 (3): 346–371.

Finholt, T. A. 2002. Collaboratories. *Annual Review of Information Science and Technology* 36:73–107.

Finholt, T. A., and G. M. Olson. 1997. From laboratories to collaboratories: A new organizational form for scientific collaboration. *Psychological Science* 8 (1): 28–36.

Granovetter, M. S. 1973. The strength of weak ties. *American Journal of Sociology* 78:1360–1380.

Grinter, R. E., J. D. Herbsleb, and D. E. Perry. 1999. The geography of coordination: Dealing with distance in R&D work. In *GROUP*. Phoenix, AZ: ACM.

Hagstrom, W. O. 1964. Traditional and modern forms of scientific teamwork. *Administrative Science Quarterly* 9 (3): 241–264.

Hansen, M. T. 1999. The search-transfer problem: The role of weak ties in sharing knowledge across organization subunits. *Administrative Science Quarterly* 44:82–111.

Hargadon, A. B. 1998. Firms as knowledge brokers: Lessons in pursuing continuous innovation. *California Management Review* 40 (3): 209–227.

Henderson, R. M., and K. B. Clark. 1990. Architectural innovation: The reconfiguration of existing product technologies and the failure of established firms. *Administrative Science Quarterly* 35 (1): 9–30.

Herbsleb, J. D., A. Mockus, T. A. Finholt, and R. E. Grinter. 2000. Distance, dependencies, and delay in a global collaboration. In *Proceedings of the 2000 ACM conference on computer-supported cooperative work*, 319–328. New York: ACM Press.

Hesse, B. W., L. S. Sproull, S. B. Kiesler, and J. P. Walsh. 1993. Returns to science: Computer networks and scientific research in oceanography. *Communications of the ACM* 36 (8): 90–101.

Hinds, P., and D. Bailey. 2003. Out of sight, out of sync: Understanding conflict in distributed teams. *Organization Science* 14 (6): 615–632.

Hobday, M. 2000. The project-based organisation: An ideal form for managing complex products and systems? *Research Policy* 29:871–893.

Kiesler, S., and J. Cummings. 2002. What do we know about proximity and distance in work groups? In *Distributed work*, ed. P. Hinds and S. Kiesler, 57–80. Cambridge, MA: MIT Press.

Kouzes, R. T., J. D. Myers, and W. A. Wulf. 1996. Collaboratories: Doing science on the Internet. *IEEE Computer* 29 (8): 40–46.

Kraut, R. E., C. Egido, and J. Galegher. 1990. Patterns of contact and communication in scientific research collaboration. In *Intellectual teamwork: Social and technological bases of cooperative work*, ed. J. Galegher, R. Kraut, and C. Egido, 149–171. Hillsdale, NJ: Lawrence Erlbaum.

Kraut, R. E., and L. A. Streeter. 1995. Coordination in software development. *Communications of the ACM* 38 (3): 69–81.

Malone, T. W., and K. Crowston. 1994. The interdisciplinary study of coordination. *ACM Computing Surveys* 26 (1): 87–119.

Mark, G., J. Grudin, and S. E. Poltrock. 1999. Meeting at the desktop: An empirical study of virtually collocated teams. Paper presented at the European Conference on Computer Supported Cooperative Work, Copenhagen, September 12–16.

O'Connor, G., and M. P. Rice. 2001. Opportunity recognition and breakthrough innovation in large established firms. *California Management Review* 43 (2): 95–116.

Schunn, C., K. Crowley, and T. Okada. 2002. What makes collaborations across a distance succeed? The case of the cognitive science community. In *Distributed work*, ed. P. Hinds and S. Kiesler, 407–430. Cambridge, MA: MIT Press.

Sonnenwald, D. S. 2003. The conceptual organization: An emergent organizational form for collaborative R&D. *Science and Public Policy* 30 (4): 261–272.

Teasley, S., and S. Wolinsky. 2001. Scientific collaborations at a distance. *Science* 292:2254–2255.

Utterback, J. M. 1994. *Mastering the dynamics of innovation*. Boston: Harvard Business School Press.

Van de Ven, A. H., A. L. Delbecq, and R. Koenig Jr. 1976. Determinants of coordination modes within organizations. *American Sociological Review* 41:322–338.

Walsh, J., and T. Bayma. 1996. Computer networks and scientific work. *Social Studies of Science* 26:661–703.

Weick, K. E. 1979. *The social psychology of organizing*. Reading, MA: Addison-Wesley.

Zare, R. N. 1997. Knowledge and distributed intelligence. *Science* 275:1047.

III Physical Sciences

6 A National User Facility That Fits on Your Desk: The Evolution of Collaboratories at the Pacific Northwest National Laboratory

James D. Myers

In late 1993, as the Pacific Northwest National Laboratory's (PNNL) 200,000-square-foot Environmental Molecular Sciences Laboratory (EMSL) was being approved by the Department of Energy (DOE) for construction, the National Research Council's (1993) National Collaboratories report helped catalyze a vision of EMSL as a new type of user facility—one that was "just down the hall" from any researcher in the nation. Further, a collaboratory was seen as a way for EMSL and PNNL to bring cutting-edge science to the classroom, and have a much more significant role as a regional educational resource than would have been possible by traditional means. With a plan to house two hundred researchers and more than seventy instruments spanning multiple scientific disciplines, and a mission to be a resource for hundreds of researchers across the nation each year, EMSL was seen as a natural focus for a collaboratory.

With EMSL's broad disciplinary and cultural scope, and technologies such as the World Wide Web and Java in their infancies in the early 1990s, realizing the EMSL Collaboratory was also clearly a long-term grand challenge research and development endeavor. Today, a decade beyond the initial planning workshops, the EMSL Collaboratory includes successful research and operations components; it has produced software tools downloaded by thousands, and enabled numerous projects between PNNL researchers and scientists, educators, and students across the nation.

While the EMSL Collaboratory has had broad success in practice and as an example for other developing collaboratories, it remains a work in progress in terms of fulfilling the grand EMSL-wide vision espoused in its early days (see figure 6.1). The collaboratory's most notable success in terms of operational impact and visibility is its adoption by the EMSL High-Field Magnetic Resonance Facility, in which collaborative technologies have become a standard part of operations, supporting a significant fraction (20 to 25 percent) of the facility's users. Collaboratory technologies such as screen sharing, lab cameras, or electronic notebooks have also found recurring use in many parts of EMSL, supporting individual projects rather than facilities as a whole.

EMSL's Mission

The EMSL will serve as a national scientific user facility, focusing basic research on solving critical environmental problems. EMSL scientists will

- seek molecular-level understanding of the physical, chemical, and biological processes needed to solve environmental problems

- advance molecular science in support of long-term missions of the U.S. Department of Energy

- create a collaboratory, where unique research capabilities are made available to the broader scientific community using both traditional collaborations and the latest communications technology

- provide opportunities to educate and recruit the next generation of molecular scientists for tomorrow's challenges.

Figure 6.1
Original EMSL mission statement, from brochure dated October 16, 1996

Initial Developments

The collaboratory project at EMSL began even before the EMSL building itself existed and coincided roughly with the first release of the Mosaic browser. The earliest technology development efforts focused on the creation of cross-platform chat and screen-sharing tools (such as the EMSL TeleViewer) integrated with the early VIC and VAT multicast-based videoconferencing tools (Eriksson 1994). A shared whiteboard, the Virtual Notebook System electronic notebook (Burger et al. 1991), and a shared Web-browsing capability were soon added.

In parallel with these initial technology efforts, we organized a workshop to guide a program linking research and development of collaborative software with deployment to support EMSL research and education projects as well as with investigation of the processes and dynamics of scientific collaboration.[2] The workshop participants heartily endorsed the idea of an EMSL Collaboratory, and helped to identify a wide range of technical and social challenges that would have to be overcome for the collaboratory to succeed. The proposed scope of the effort, at the level of a facility spanning many scientific disciplines, brought to light issues ranging from the need to integrate heterogeneous data, to the proper attribution of online research contributions, to funding mechanisms for shared facilities and long-term infrastructure.

By 1996, the EMSL Collaboratory tools had coalesced into the Collaborative Research Environment (CORE), and a number of proof-of-concept remote lectures, remote instrument control sessions, and collaborative data analysis sessions had demonstrated the collaboratory's capabilities. These experiences led us to categorize collaboration technologies in terms of axes such as "information dissemination versus interaction" and "synchronous versus asynchronous," and to map these to the overlapping needs of various types of group-level collaborations (peer to peer, mentor-student, interdisciplinary, and producer-consumer) (Kouzes, Myers, and Wulf 1996). With a set of working technologies and along with researchers from the Lawrence Berkeley National Laboratory (LBNL), EMSL embarked on the creation of the Virtual Nuclear Magnetic Resonance (NMR) Facility, envisioned as a persistent mechanism for accessing the instruments, software, and expertise of EMSL's High-Field NMR Research Facility.

In 1996, the collaboratory's education activities also expanded in the form of the Collaboratory for Undergraduate Research and Education (CURE). Through a series of workshops, demonstrations, and pilot projects, CURE developed a number of innovative frameworks for distance collaboration, including, for example, the concept of "research triangles." Research triangles involved expanding traditional summer undergraduate fellowships at the national laboratories to include ongoing interaction between the student, a faculty adviser, and a lab researcher, coupling research and class work at the student's home institution with experiments or modeling performed on state-of-the-art equipment during a summer stay at the lab (Myers et al. 1997). Unfortunately, as CURE aimed to expand beyond isolated pilot projects under joint NSF and DOE funding, the DOE eliminated its program providing direct funding for education-related activities, leaving many of the ideas generated in CURE unexplored.

The Toolkit for Collaboratory Development

In 1997, funding obtained through the DOE's DOE2000 National Collaboratories program put EMSL's efforts on a solid footing and enabled the initial collaborative tools to evolve into the downloadable Toolkit for Collaboratory Development. The toolkit was developed through a coordinated set of projects, involving a number of external collaborators, that focused on real-time collaboration tools, electronic laboratory notebooks, and secure collaborative instrument control. While the real-time collaboration suite is no longer under development, it and contemporary versions of the electronic notebook and instrument control software are available on the EMSL Collaboratory Web site.[1]

The toolkit marked a shift toward a more Java- and Web-centric technology base, and an increased emphasis on providing technologies to external projects, although use within EMSL and in support of the Virtual NMR Facility remained a key driver. Adopting new collaborative tools to extend the toolkit's range and adding extension interfaces to enable future integration were additional motivations. The toolkit moniker was intended to emphasize the idea of a comprehensive general suite of capabilities for remote scientific collaboration that could then be easily integrated with specific instruments and analysis tools to create a customized collaboratory environment tailored to the needs of individual communities, although in practice the toolkit was often used without further customization.

CORE2000

The suite of real-time collaboration tools in the toolkit extends the National Center for Supercomputing Applications' (2002) Java-based Habanero environment. CORE2000 adds shared computer screens, remote cameras, and third-party audio and videoconferencing to Habanero's whiteboard, chat box, and other tools. The CORE2000 client allows users to start or join sessions by supplying the session name, the server hostname (or Internet protocol number), and an optional port number. When a user starts or joins a session, they see a palette of icons representing the available tools (figure 6.2), which can be launched at any time by any session participant. CORE2000 starts each tool simultaneously on whatever mixture of personal computer, Mac, and UNIX systems the remote collaborators are using. Over time, a mechanism to start, monitor, and join CORE2000 sessions via a Web page was added, but it was neither well advertised nor heavily used.

CORE2000 offers a variety of collaboration capabilities. The third-party audio and video tools allow participants to converse and see each other. CORE2000 can launch the publicly available Mbone tools—the option used in our Virtual NMR Facility project (Lawrence Berkeley National Laboratory Network Research Group 2002)—or CU-SeeMe—limited to non-UNIX participants (Dorcey 1995). The chat box tool is used to exchange short text messages. The whiteboard tool allows users to create sketches and diagrams together using a variety of pen colors. Users can drag and drop geometric shapes (lines, rectangles, ellipses, etc.), type text, or draw freehand on the whiteboard. They can also import GIF or JPEG images, such as NMR spectra, pulse sequence diagrams, electrophoresis gels, or molecular models on to the whiteboard, and mark them up as the discussion proceeds. The TeleViewer, CORE2000's initial dynamic screen-sharing tool, allows users to transmit a live view of any rectangle or window on their screen to all session participants. It also allows any user to share information with the group—there was no static notion of one computer being the source during a session, and any person in a given session could click and drag a rectangle on their screen and become the source as desired. CORE2000 eventually switched to using Virtual Network Computing (VNC) (Richardson et al. 1998), which despite having a static sender-receivers model and initially lacking support for sharing a rectangle instead of the full screen, proved more central processing unit efficient and provided support for more display types. Finally, two tools are included in CORE2000 specifically for viewing 3-D molecular models: the Molecular Modeler displays Protein Data Bank formatted molecular structures, and the 3-D XYZ tool displays molecules stored in the .xyz format.

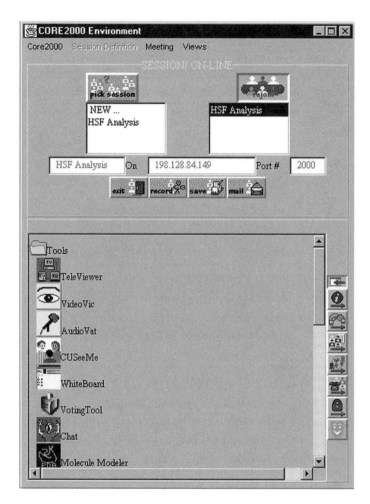

Figure 6.2
CORE2000 screen capture

CORE2000 also has a simple programming interface in common with Habanero that allows new tools to be added as needed. Various groups have used this interface to develop sophisticated, domain-specific tools including collaboratively controlled geographic information system viewers as well as image analysis software for the Visible Human project (Keating et al. 2000). At PNNL, a data acquisition system for a mass spectrometer was developed using CORE2000's programming interface. During the Virtual NMR Facility project, the project team used this interface to develop a collaborative remote pan-tilt-zoom controller for cameras (i.e., the Canon VC-C1 Communication

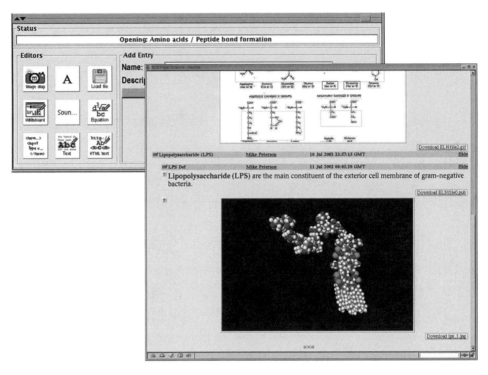

Figure 6.3
Electronic Notebook screen captures showing editor features and a sample graphic

Camera) positioned in EMSL NMR labs, allowing researchers to get a sense of lab activity and view some important noncomputerized instrument status displays.

Electronic Laboratory Notebook

An electronic notebook is an analog of a paper laboratory notebook, designed to allow distributed teams to record and share a wide range of notes, sketches, graphs, pictures, and other information. The Web-based EMSL/PNNL Electronic Laboratory Notebook (ELN) (figure 6.3) was developed as part of a collaboration with researchers at the LBNL and the Oak Ridge National Laboratory.

The ELN was designed to manage a wide range of information, including literature references, experimental procedures, equipment design drawings, observations, summary tables, annotated graphs, and visualizations. After the user logs in, the ELN displays a main window containing a table of contents with a user-defined hierarchy of chapters, pages, and notes. The contents of the currently selected page appear in a separate browser window. All entries are keyword searchable. Notes on a page are created using a variety of "entry editors," which are launched from the main window. The base set of editors includes ones to create text (plain, HTML, or rich text), equations (LaTeX), and whiteboard sketches (using the CORE2000 whiteboard); capture screen images; and upload arbitrary files. Once a note is created, the user hits "submit" and publishes it to the notebook page, making it available to other authorized users of the notebook. Entries are shown as part of a page, tagged with the author's name along with the date and time of the entry.

The text and images in each "note" can be rendered by the browser with external applications such as Microsoft Word, or in the case of equations, molecular structures, and the like, with Java applets. The creation and display of entries is fully customizable via simple editor and viewer programming interfaces. Over the course of the Virtual NMR Facility project, these interfaces were used to create an NMR Spectroscopists' version of the ELN. One of the first customizations of the notebook involved linking in a Java applet viewer for protein structures entered into the ELN as Protein Data Bank–formatted files. After a brief search and some initial tests, we integrated the WebMol Java applet (Walther 1997). WebMol displays Protein Data Bank–formatted molecular structures in a 3-D, rotatable format, and allows users to display interatom distances and angles—enough information to allow quick analysis and comparisons without having to launch a stand-alone analysis package. We have also developed some Java applets for the ELN, including one to display NMR parameter files. This applet shows the parameters not in a long text list but in a more usable interactive window format that displays only the lines of text associated with the selected parameter. In addition, we have extended the ELN by creating an "ELNWizard" that can be called from within other programs—for instance, from the spectrometer control software—to automate the transfer of parameter sets and screen snapshots immediately to a user-specified chapter and page. The ELNWizard can also be used to create scripts that automatically record instrument status at predefined intervals or in response to events.

Although the ELN was configured within PNNL to use usernames and passwords transmitted over the secure https protocol, the ELN includes a full public key certificate-based authentication and digital signature capability to provide stronger protection as well as address the issues related to using an electronic notebook as a legally defensible document (Myers 2003). Recent work on the ELN within the DOE-funded Scientific Annotation Middleware (SAM) project has repositioned it as just one tool contributing to a semantically rich end-to-end data context created by problem-solving environments, workflow engines, data curation portals, and applications (Myers et al. 2003).

Secure Instrument Control and Data Access

At the beginning of the Virtual NMR Facility project, EMSL already had mechanisms in place to allow remote users to access EMSL's computer resources and data. Since the NMR spectrometer console software is based on UNIX and X Windows, these mechanisms were also sufficient to allow remote users to control the spectrometer (the spectrometer manufacturer would take advantage of this to install and trouble-shoot spectrometers over the Internet). This simple mechanism, however, was insecure against "session hijacking," and provided no mechanism to allow a local instrument operator and remote researcher to both see the spectrometer display and work together on setting up and interpreting experimental results. We felt that both increased security and the ability for multiple researchers to view the spectrometer software in collaboration would be needed to support the advertised continuous availability of EMSL's high-field, high-profile spectrometers as part of the facility's user program. The EMSL NMR operations staff collaborated with EMSL's Computing and Network Services group to set up and use secure shell (ssh) for authenticated, encrypted connections along with tools for shared X Windows displays, EMSL TeleViewer, and eventually VNC. After settling on secure shell and VNC, significant work was done to hide the details of setting up connections and enable long-running sessions (on the order of weeks) that shared the spectrometer control software for an entire course of experiments.

Hardware and Network Setup

By modern standards, the hardware requirements for using the toolkit are modest. In the late 1990s we were recommending fairly standard desktop computers and workstations, such as 400 MHz Windows 95 PCs and Sun Ultra series machines with 128 Mbytes of memory, as sufficient to run all necessary client and server software. We recommended cameras and echo cancellers. We also experimented with small scanners to allow researchers to conveniently scan gels of the purified protein samples and other paper "documents" into the ELN.

A research team with members at PNNL and the LBNL did the first Virtual NMR Facility experiments over a T3 network link (45 Mbits per second) between the laboratories as part of the DOE's Energy Sciences Network. Other projects used a shared campus T1 (1.2 to 1.4 Mbits per second) network connection and found it sufficient for small group (two to three participants) collaboration, although video could be temporarily frozen by spikes in other network traffic. Basic notebook access and screen sharing were also demonstrated over 56K modem lines, supporting use from homes and to international institutions. (By 2000, I was able to run the toolkit well enough over a $200 per month digital subscriber line from my home near Philadelphia to enable a full-time telecommuting arrangement with PNNL and continue leading PNNL Collaboratory development efforts remotely through 2005.)

Collaboratories in Practice

During the late 1990s, we used the evolving toolkit to enable a wide range of research and education projects involving areas such as mass spectroscopy, theoretical chem-

U.W. Chem 155 - Live from the EMSL

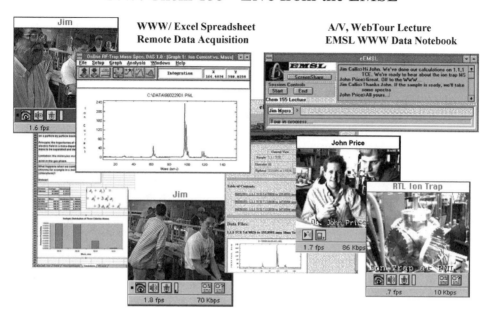

Figure 6.4
Screen captures from remote lecture given conducted with EMSL collaboratory tools

istry, surface science, subsurface fluid transport, and even collaboratory software development itself. The projects ranged from remote guest lectures by PNNL staff to semester- and year-long high school, undergraduate, and graduate student research projects involving remote instrument use and/or collaborative data analysis. As an example of this style of project, figure 6.4 shows John Price of EMSL remotely giving a guest mass spectroscopy lecture to a first-year chemistry laboratory class at the University of Washington (UW). At the conclusion of the lecture, the students performed an experiment using an ion trap mass spectrometer at EMSL, and later analyzed their data using an electronic notebook and analysis spreadsheets posted on the UW Web site by the course's regular instructor, James Callis of the UW Department of Chemistry.

The ELN found continuing use in clean labs where paper dust was a contaminant and returning to the lab to retrieve a paper notebook entailed donning a clean suit, where capturing an image from the data acquisition software was simpler than hand-transcribing individual parameters, and where iterative datacentric collaboration was required. Screen-sharing capabilities found use in remote (single-user) and collaborative data acquisition, analysis, and presentation of results. Internet audio and video remained part of lecture-style interactions, but were largely replaced by telephone audio in experiment operations, with the exception of video-only laboratory cameras.

The continuing stream of demonstrations and pilot projects with various communities was critical to prioritizing enhancements to the toolkit. Nevertheless, of all these activities, only the Virtual NMR Facility provided an ongoing laboratory with multiple similar experiments performed by multiple teams (usually one of several NMR operators employed at EMSL with a remote researcher along with one or more graduate students and postdocs) on a continuing basis. The operations focus of this effort helped the combined team of collaboratory and NMR researchers at EMSL explore, over the course of years, how to maximize the scientific impact of the available technologies. A number of the lessons learned during these efforts are discussed in the following section. Ultimately, as the funding priorities and organizational structure changed at PNNL, the Virtual NMR Facility made a transition from an operational pilot leveraging research grants to a capability solely supported by EMSL's operations funds and its computing support staff as a service to users. Secure shell and VNC were already used to support collaborative instrument control, but this transition led to the Virtual NMR Facility decision to drop support for the CORE2000 environment in favor of leveraging secure shell/VNC in combination with desktop text and drawing tools to support collaboration. Laboratory camera support was provided by new self-contained pan-tilt-zoom cameras that incorporated a Web server and Ethernet connectivity directly into the camera hardware. Electronic notebooks were retained as an option, although most postpilot projects have not set them up.

With the incorporation of VNC into the toolkit (stand-alone or integrated with CORE2000), we had theoretically developed the capability to remote enable any instrument or analysis software suite at EMSL. In practice, a combination of technical, social, and institutional issues stalled progress toward an overall EMSL Collaboratory. Some instruments had numerous manually controlled adjustments, such as the alignment of laser mirrors, which made remote control difficult. Many instruments as well as the associated experimental and analysis protocols were complex and evolving, and required long-term, immersive partnerships to master. At the level of management, staff changes, reorganizations, changes in funding priorities, and perhaps the length of time between the initial vision and when collaborative technologies became robust and the idea of collaboratories became more generally accepted all made progress difficult.

Lessons Learned

From its inception, the EMSL Collaboratory was always about enabling scientific research and education. Thus, despite the lack of explicit funding for the social science analysis of collaborating groups, the team was deeply engaged in trying to understand how science was "performed" and how collaborative tools shifted practices. From the mix of short- and long-term projects at EMSL, our conclusion, based on anecdotal evidence and a few surveys, was that "working together apart" worked, and that it worked best for those who adapted to use its strengths. The nearly decade-long use of the Virtual NMR Facility and the author's own six-year-long telecommuting experience further demonstrated that the cost-benefit ratio could be large enough to transition from pilot use to normal practice.

Some of the most interesting observations came from the Virtual NMR Facility project. Jeff Pelton, the first remote user from the LBNL, likened the remote operation of a high-end spectrometer to "driving a Cadillac": while it may be a luxury vehicle, it has no "road feel" (Keating et al. 2000). In general, users noted that remote collaboration required extra start-up time (both in terms of training and the daily launching of tools), but that the ability to access more advanced instruments and get rapid feedback from remote colleagues provided overall payback in terms of time savings and improved quality. Although Pelton did not visit EMSL prior to beginning experiments, subsequent groups have reported that their initial visit to the facility was useful (particularly if it was a new spectrometer type to them). Being able to make introductions, observe spectrometers, and see collaborative tools in action before having to start getting accounts and installing software both helped create initial momentum. Video appears to play a similar role within collaborative sessions; in the early years, after the initial start-up of the video tool and an exchange of greetings, the video window was often minimized and not reopened during the remainder of the session, and conference (versus laboratory) video was eventually dropped from the offered capabilities.

As new best practices were developed, many groups slowly shifted the way in which they used tools. For example, over time, researchers began using the chat box for two purposes in particular: to notify remote colleagues when they stepped away from their desk, and to transmit unfamiliar terms and numbers that could be misunderstood when spoken. Verbal dialogue also changed slightly. The relative lack of feedback from remote participants and their lack of "presence" were compensated by instrument operators learning to ask confirmation questions ("Do you see that in the Tele-Viewer?"), and to type messages in the chat box to confirm that they were seeing updated information ("got it"), explain long pauses, or inform their colleagues of local (off-camera) events.

With sufficient use, however, the technologies truly became second nature to the extent that users came to depend on them. For example, collaboratory participants would feel frustrated when listening to uninitiated colleagues attempting to describe complex phenomena by phone alone instead of sharing their computer displays. More striking were the changes in the overall distribution and scheduling of tasks within distributed groups. Researchers working with local colleagues expect to see them in the hallway, discover problems, brainstorm solutions, and change plans as needed on a daily or weekly basis. With remote colleagues, collaboratory users initially divided their work into larger, more independent chunks, and expected to perform most of the sample preparation and data analysis alone. Over time, geographically remote collaborators gradually became more like their local counterparts, checking with their colleagues to discuss analysis options, comparing notes at intermediate stages, and so forth. At the facility level, this type of change was evident in the ability of remote collaboratory users to make opportunistic use of spectrometers when time suddenly became available because another user had canceled. The collaboratory thus put off-site users on an equal footing with on-site researchers.

Toward a Ubiquitous Collaboration Infrastructure

The EMSL Collaboratory project, our interactions with the collaboratory community, and our interactions with interested researchers and educators from a wide range of disciplines also allowed us to speculate beyond the confines of current technology, culture, and practice. Would chemists eventually be able to "follow a molecule" and investigate it via numerous techniques at remote facilities versus studying one aspect of many molecules via the one technique for which they had equipment? Would the role of teachers shift more toward mentoring as lectures, curricular materials, data, and lab resources became accessible via the Internet? Would summer fellowships at national laboratories become part of a researcher-student-faculty triangle that would be more enriching for all concerned? What would the role of a paper scientific publication be if it were possible to directly publish data and keep live electronic documents that always reflected the latest understanding?

Envisioning these types of shifts also led us to question whether then-current collaboratory designs were capable of supporting such advanced uses. For example, while integrated environments with plug-in interfaces and standardized data formats are sufficient for isolated pilot projects, they cause problems as a ubiquitous mechanism. Tool developers must commit to a single environment, thus becoming dependent on its longer-term viability. Users must perform all of their work through the lens of the environment. These issues emerged during the development of CORE2000. Developers were concerned about whether it would be feasible to build advanced capabilities such as collaborative instrument control into the system because of funding uncertainties beyond the end of our projects. Conversely, users were hesitant to commit to the environment when it did not have all the tools they desired and because it made them launch the collaboration system in order to access data acquisition capabilities. We heard analogous issues from other cyberinfrastructure developers—integrated suite architectures impose an unnatural single hierarchy on developers and users.

In subsequent work by the EMSL Collaboratory team at PNNL and more recently at the National Center for Supercomputing Applications, NCSA, we have focused on looking for design patterns that address these "social" issues. Our work within the Collaboratory for Multiscale Chemical Science (CMCS) (Myers et al. 2005) identified a metadata-rich content management pattern, which allowed CMCS to accept data in all formats and offer translation capabilities versus imposing its own "standard" formats, as a key element in decoupling cyberinfrastructure from individual and community decisions about data standards. Similarly, we now see workflow and provenance (data history) capabilities as necessities for simplifying the transfer of best-practice processes between both communities and software systems. At NCSA, we've coined the term *cyberenvironment* to represent systems built on these types of design patterns and focused on enabling individuals to maximize their contribution to overall scientific progress.

Conclusions

The EMSL Collaboratory has shown that it is possible for a National User Facility to "fit" on your desk. As the subject of literally hundreds of demonstrations in its early years, it helped showcase the potential of collaboratories and real-time collaboration over the Internet to a wide range of scientists and educators. The EMSL Collaboratory was able to transition aspects of the effort such as the Virtual NMR Facility to operations. At the same time, it contributed to the state of the art in understanding the potential of collaboratories for research and education. Arguably, this was because of the focus on the development of capabilities aimed at realistic use cases rather than technology development per se. A dozen years beyond the kickoff workshop, both the technology landscape and the scope of the collaboratory/grid/cyberinfrastructure vision has evolved and broadened. The EMSL Collaboratory has contributed to the growth of this field as an operational proof of concept, and along with its intellectual progeny, a source of design ideas and lessons learned in how to enable more science, and more complex science, through collaborative technologies.

Acknowledgments

The author wishes to acknowledge the contribution of many individuals to the development of the collaborative technologies described and the operational success of the Virtual NMR Facility. This work was supported by the DOE through the DOE2000 program sponsored by the Mathematical, Information, and Computational Sciences Division of the Office of Science. The PNNL is operated by Battelle for the DOE. The W. R. Wiley EMSL is a national scientific user facility sponsored by the DOE's Office of Biological and Environmental Research, and located at PNNL.

Notes

1. See ⟨http://collaboratory.pnl.gov⟩.

2. "Environmental and Molecular Sciences Collaboratory Workshop," U.S. Department of Energy's (DOE) Pacific Northwest Laboratory (PNL) March 17–19, 1994, organized by Richard

Kouzes, James Myers, and John Price. A white paper written to discuss the concept and the workshop is "Building a Collaboratory in Environmental and Molecular Science, Richard Kouzes, James Myers, Mike Devaney, Thom Dunning, Jim Wise (*PNL-SA-23921*) ⟨http://collaboratory.emsl.pnl.gov/resources/publications/collaboratory.WP.html⟩.

References

Burger, M., B. D. Meyer, C. P. Jung, and K. B. Long. 1991. The virtual notebook system. In *Proceedings of ACM hypertext '91*, 395–401. New York: ACM Press.

Dorcey, T. 1995. CU-SeeMe [computer software]. Ithaca, NY: Cornell University.

Eriksson, H. 1994. MBONE: The multicast backbone. *Communications of the ACM* 37 (8): 54–60.

Keating, K., J. Myers, J. Pelton, R. Bair, D. Wemmer, and P. Ellis. 2000. Development and use of a virtual NMR facility. *Journal of Magnetic Resonance* 143:172–183.

Kouzes, R. T., J. Myers, and W. Wulf. 1996. Collaboratories: Doing science on the Internet. *IEEE Computer* 29 (8): 40–46.

Lawrence Berkeley National Laboratory Network Research Group. 2002. MBone tools [computer software]. Available at ⟨http://www-nrg.ee.lbl.gov/⟩ (accessed April 17, 2007).

Myers, J. 2003. Collaborative electronic notebooks as electronic records: Design issues for the secure Electronic Laboratory Notebook (ELN). In *Proceedings of the fourth international symposium on collaborative technologies and systems*, ed. W. W. Smari and W. McQuay, 13–22. San Diego, CA: Simulation Council.

Myers, J., T. Allison, S. Bittner, B. Didier, M. Frenklach, W. Green et al. 2005. A collaborative informatics infrastructure for multi-scale science. *Cluster Computing* 8 (4): 243–253.

Myers, J., A. R. Chappell, M. Elder, A. Geist, and J. Schwidder. 2003. Re-integrating the research record. *Computing in Science and Engineering* 5 (3): 44–50.

Myers, J., N. Chonacky, T. Dunning, and E. Leber. 1997. Collaboratories: Bringing national laboratories into the undergraduate classroom and laboratory via the Internet. *Council on Undergraduate Research Quarterly* 17 (3): 116–120.

National Center for Supercomputing Applications. 2001. Habanero (version 3.0 alpha) [computer software]. Available at ⟨http://www.isrl.uiuc.edu/isaac/Habanero/⟩ (accessed April 17, 2007).

National Research Council. 1993. *National collaboratories: Applying information technology for scientific research*. Washington, DC: National Academies Press.

Richardson, T., Q. Stafford-Fraser, K. Wood, and A. Hopper. 1998. Virtual network computing. *IEEE Internet Computing* 2 (1): 33–38.

Walther, D. 1997. WebMol: A Java based PDB viewer. *Trends in Biochemical Sciences* 22 (7): 274–275.

7 The National Virtual Observatory

Mark S. Ackerman, Erik C. Hofer, and Robert J. Hanisch

Like many scientific communities, the astronomy community faces a coming avalanche of data as instrumentation improves in quality as well as in its ability to integrate with computational and data resources. Unlike scientific fields that are oriented around a small number of major instruments, such as high-energy physics, astronomers use a large number of telescopes located around the world that are designed and calibrated to look at celestial objects in fundamentally different ways. Both space and terrestrial telescopes are designed to observe objects across a narrow part of the energy spectrum, typically focusing on a small part of the spectrum from the infrared to X-ray wavelengths. While each telescope has the potential to reveal and characterize new astronomical objects, even more powerful would be the ability to combine the data produced by each of these instruments to create a unified picture of the observable universe. This data fusion requires federating a large number of data sets, and developing the search and analysis routines that allow investigation across multiple wavelengths.

The National Virtual Observatory (NVO) project is funded by the National Science Foundation (NSF) to provide the cyberinfrastructure necessary to support the federation of a large number of astronomical data sets, allowing search across multiple data sets and the development of simulations that incorporate many types of astronomical data.[1] Through the development of tools and standardized data models, the NVO hopes to enable the combination of multiple pointed-observation telescopes and sky surveys into a large, unified data set that effectively functions as a broadband, worldwide telescope. The NVO is part of a larger effort, known as the International Virtual Observatory Alliance (IVOA), to support data federation and exchange across a number of national and regional virtual observatories.[2]

The Coming Data Avalanche

Astronomy is undergoing several revolutions. Like many sciences, new instruments and digital capture provide orders of magnitude more data. One example project, the Sloan Digital Sky Survey, will map more than one hundred million distinct objects.[3]

At present (Sloan Digital Sky Survey data release 1) it has mapped only 1.6 percent of the sky, but has already obtained data on fifty-three million objects (see also chapter 1, this volume). Many of these objects, stars, quasars, and galaxies will be mapped multiple times with photometry and spectroscopic measurements. Gaia, a European space-based observatory, will survey one billion objects.[4] Target stars will be monitored in detail about one hundred times over its five-year mission. These surveys will not only map the sky in more detail than ever before; astronomers will also use them to find new objects (such as new brown dwarfs)—and hope to find new classes of objects. They will also find sources for subsequent investigations, such as sources for later X-ray or gamma ray bursts and microlensed (small-scale gravitational lensing) events.

These two surveys are only some of the new observatories coming online. Of the National Aeronautics and Space Administration's four "Great Observatories," Hubble is the most famous.[5] The other two existing Great Observatories are the Spitzer Space Telescope (formerly SIRTF) to observe in the infrared and Chandra to observe in the X-ray. (The Compton gamma ray observatory mission has already ended.) In addition to these four, there are other space- and earth-based observatories, all producing data. Some are current, such as the FUSE (far ultraviolet spectroscopic explorer) mission. Others are planned, such as the James Webb observatory, the successor to Hubble, in process for a launch in 2011. There are also numerous European and Japanese efforts.

These observatories are all exceptional instruments. As an example, the Chandra X-Ray Observatory cost $1.65 billion for development, $350 million for launch costs, and $750 million for operations and data analysis in the first five years. It is able to obtain images at twenty-five to fifty times better resolution than previous X-ray telescopes. The resolution is the equivalent, according to the Chandra science Web site, "to the ability to read a newspaper at a distance of half a mile."[6] In addition to being able to observe black holes and supernovas, this capability provides the ability to do detailed studies of dark matter.

As might be expected from occasional development costs of a billion dollars, these are also extremely complex projects. Four factors contribute to this complexity.

First, these projects can differ in their goals. While all produce huge data streams, the surveys obviously produce the most. Space-based missions tend to target specific objects, based on astronomers' observing-time proposals, but this is shifting toward survey work as well.

Second, different observatories operate in different "wavelength regimes." Spitzer, for example, observes the infrared (between visible and microwave wavelengths at between approximately 0.75 μm and 0.1 mm), but it does not even cover that entire spectrum. As mentioned, Chandra operates in the X-ray, and Compton operated in the gamma ray. Hubble operates in the visible as well as near infrared and ultraviolet (both close to visible light). This mirrors the traditional division of the astronomy community. Each wavelength regime and subcommunity has its own data formats, which are unlikely to change, since the detectors and data can be quite different.

Third, the complexity and costs of the observatories and projects themselves are reflected in the complexity of the institutional arrangements. The Sloan Digital Sky Survey telescopes are at Apache Point Observatory, operated by a consortium of astrophysical institutions. The Sloan Digital Sky Survey itself is a joint effort of thirteen universities and research institutions. While a single institution often controls satellite missions (for example, the Center for Astrophysics at Harvard runs Chandra), the planning is multi-institutional and frequently international.

Finally, as will be discussed below, the data capture and storage are similarly complex, and often idiosyncratic to the institutions and mission involved.

The Coming Revolution in Astronomical Data Analysis

The revolution of increasing capabilities of the observational instruments and the resulting huge volumes of data are likely to be mirrored in a second revolution. It is thought that a substantial transformation in astronomical and astrophysical work is about to occur. Traditionally, astronomers working across wavelength regimes were rare. It is clear, however, that some research question can be studied best by combining data in different wavelengths. This is particularly true with phenomena that are changing—for example, bursts or supernovas. Additionally, the large quantities of data and their automatic capture make it possible to watch for dynamic situations— that is, to provide triggers for the automatic detection of changing phenomena. Astronomers to date have lost the precious minutes after the detection of a supernova to bring many instruments to bear on the new supernova.

While the availability (or rather, the potential availability) of data makes new analysis possible, it cannot be overstated that this is a fundamental shift in the nature of the analysis work. Currently astronomers work within a wavelength regime. Like any scientist, their sources of expertise and help are all within their own subcommunities; they understand the instruments and data sets within their own subcommunities, and publish and garner credentials within those subcommunities.

We have also been constantly struck with the concern by astronomers that the next generation will be "armchair astronomers." As stated in study interviews and at conferences, they believe that it will be possible in the near future for astronomers to no longer spend observational time taking data and controlling an instrument, but to merely be able to summon data from these vast data repositories for analysis. This concern, regardless of its merit, clearly reflects an understanding that astronomical analysis—always considered to be at the heart of the profession—is changing and will continue to change in nature.

Building a New Kind of Observatory

To enable the kind of inquiry that will allow astronomers to rely on a shared data resource rather than a shared instrument resource, a new type of observatory has to be built. This new observatory will not focus on a single instrument as the focal data provider but rather will engage a network of existing and future instruments, enabling the publication and federation of data from that instrument network. As noted in the chapter opening, the NVO is an NSF project to design and build the cyberinfrastructure needed to support this new kind of observatory. The goal of the NVO project is to prototype this new type of observatory. Using information technology to federate the newly available quantities of data, the hope is that astronomers can work in multiple wavelengths, consider temporal phenomena, and perform new forms of statistically based analyses. It is, in fact, an answer to the increasing amount of data, and the astronomers' inability to find, access, or utilize most of it.

A large number of institutions are participating in the NVO project. Members of the collaboration include astronomers, astronomy programmers, and computer scientists from universities and observatories across the United States. The project is co-led by an astronomer and a computer scientist, and is funded by the Information Technology Research program at the NSF (chapter 17, this volume), with oversight from both the Computer and Information Science and Engineering Directorate and the Astronomy and Astrophysics Division. The NVO's external advisory board also reflects this disciplinary split between computer science and astronomy, with membership of prominent researchers from each field. As with many cyberinfrastructure projects, managing the research interests of both computer and domain scientists can be challenging (see also chapters 17 and 18, this volume). While this problem of competing interests has been problematic for some other collaborations, the technical sophistication of the astronomers working on the project spans many of the gaps that would be expected, causing this partnership between computer science and an application science to work extremely well.

In addition to this internal diversity, the NVO is also the U.S. participant in the IVOA, a larger federation project (see also chapter 1, this volume). The IVOA consists of fifteen similar virtual observatory projects around the world. This coordinating organization serves as a venue for interoperability testing and standardization to ensure that the kind of federation possible on a national scale can also occur on an international scale. The NVO has been critical to the creation of several standards for data formatting and interchange, but must also work to coevolve with other virtual observatories to identify and meet the common needs of IVOA members.

Technical Overview

Technically, the NVO consists of six layers and many components. In this, it is like many other cyberinfrastructure projects. The following is a brief description of the

NVO from a technical point of view. (The details are simplified here for clarity; this description will only overview what is required technically.) The NVO includes several efforts that show the requirements for coalition infrastructures. These are being developed by groups of highly geographically distributed people. These efforts include:

• Virtual observatory registries: Registries allow users and applications to search for data. They indicate what observational or derived data are in the archives.
• Query services: These allow astronomer-users to query registries and search for data. As mentioned, this is not simple, as the search occurs within a 3-D space, and on potentially noisy, differently formatted, and incomplete data.
• Portals, analysis procedures, and client tools: These present the NVO capabilities to the astronomer-user. They include, for example, the OpenSkyQuery tool, which can provide data from ten different astronomical surveys.
• A data-access layer: This layer maps the retrieval to actual physical data. An interesting problem is how to provide a common format for data, and there is considerable work being done on standardizing these formats. An international effort has been made to create a standards process for virtual observatory projects.
• Data models: These are detailed data models of various entities important to the NVO. Currently, work is going on to model observational data and a few other simple entities. Additional work is going on to model data tables in archives—how the data are currently stored in archives and what can be simply compared.
• Metadata: Metadata will be automatically attached to queries, and it is hoped that archives will provide more metadata. Currently, there is little standardization within astronomy of this metadata. The initial efforts within the NVO are to standardize coordinate system and provenance metadata.

Figure 7.1, from an NVO report, shows the NVO system architecture.[7] The figure pays more attention to the data services layers. The user layer, which consists of NVO services, applications, and portals, gets short shrift in this figure. Nonetheless, it shows that the NVO architecture is distributed, multilayered, and reasonably complex. New services can be introduced at any layer without affecting the others.

The architecture is perhaps less interesting than what the NVO must do. Figure 7.2 depicts what astronomers want to do.[8] In practice, astronomers would deal with more raw images or data, but figure 7.2 shows that important details are provided in different wavelengths.

One should note that this type of data federation has never occurred within astronomy before. While the automation of this process is desired, the NVO team understands that it is more likely that astronomers will not accept a solution that does not allow them to understand the entire retrieval and conversion process. To scientifically interpret any image (or other astronomical data) requires a complete understanding of the observing conditions, the source instrument, and the transformations applied to

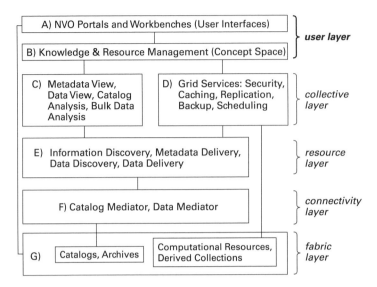

Figure 7.1
The NVO architecture

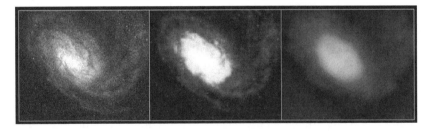

Figure 7.2
A galaxy in visible, radio, and X-ray (original is in color and has additional detail)

the collected data. Astronomers require a detailed understanding of their data; it is an open question how to facilitate that understanding.

Another key area of technical effort has been the standardization of protocols, data formats, and data models. Astronomers have long understood the significance of data standards in data preservation and interoperability. The Flexible Image Transport System (FITS) data format was developed as a standard to solve exactly these problems.[9] The group that created FITS, however, was large and represented many different subcommunities with many different technical goals—the end result being a standard that was extremely general. The huge number of variations due to the different use conventions of FITS has lead to a data standard that is extendable to the point that the standard is virtually unenforceable. Even so, the standard has been crucial to the astronomy community, not just for its intrinsic value as a format, but also as an example of what can happen when standardization efforts do not force difficult decisions to be made.

Largely because of FITS, the NVO group and the larger IVOA community are actively pursuing standards that are meaningful, and balance the need for extendability and adaptability to many uses with the need for some things to remain the same. Presentations, discussions, and arguments about the details of and the need for standards are a major component of the IVOA interoperability meetings that are held twice a year.

Challenges and Outreach

Notably absent from this technical description of project deliverables are the new analysis and comparison tools that will need to be built in order to take advantage of these federated data. A major challenge of the project, which has been funded to provide the basic framework for the NVO cyberinfrastructure, is how to stimulate use of the tools to support the new types of scientific inquiry that the project will enable. Some technology demonstrations, such as producing a merged, multiwavelength image of a single object, are relatively simple given the tools that the NVO has developed for matching and reorienting different data sets so that they are comparable. All that is required is to adapt the existing imaging tools to import data from the NVO. More sophisticated as well as challenging are efforts to build new applications that integrate simulations and analyses with the NVO-federated data, such as a demonstration presented at the 2004 winter American Astronomical Society conference that allowed users to compare theoretical simulations of globular clusters with observed globular clusters in the NVO.

Building these applications faces two challenges, and the NVO is developing solutions for both of them. The first is that astronomers have to be trained how to write programs that leverage the powers of the NVO. This requirement creates a dependence on scientists to do the articulation work (Strauss 1993) (or coordination work) required to connect the NVO capabilities and current scientific practice. The NVO team is only providing the infrastructure and the interfaces required to use that infrastructure; widespread scientific advancement because of the NVO depends on the ability and willingness of others to create the applications that enable discovery. To meet this challenge, the NVO team is targeting junior members of the community by hosting an annual applications "boot camp." This camp allows members of the project team to work with students, postdocs, and junior faculty to help them build applications to introduce them to working with the NVO. This strategy has so far proved successful, with the 2004 summer school resulting in a number of application- and infrastructure-focused student projects.

The second challenge the NVO faces in realizing the scientific vision of the project is the difficulties in training young astronomers to work across wavelength regimes. As noted previously, most astronomers are trained to work within a single wavelength regime. They become experts in the physics of a particular type of observation, and focus their observation at the limits of what is observable. Moving into a different wavelength regime requires mastering an understanding of an entirely new set of observational physics. Furthermore, trying to combine these different observational techniques is even more challenging. In short, the challenge of multiwavelength astronomy is not going to be met just by technical infrastructure. New students must be trained to work across regimes, and think about observation and analysis in fundamentally different ways. The big question now is who will train them—only a handful of astronomers are attempting to work across wavelengths, and many of them are not yet out of graduate school.

Project leaders are hopeful both of these challenges will be overcome. As the possibilities of new discoveries grow, astronomical practice will follow.

In summary, the National Virtual Observatory and the International Virtual Observatoryoffer a cyberinfrastructure for a critical next step in astronomy. As more and more space-based observatories as well as earth-based surveys come online, the NVO offers the possibility of doing new types of science, providing astronomers with more data capabilities than they have ever had before. The NVO is likely to change—and revolutionize—astronomy.

Notes

1. More information about the NVO is available at ⟨http://www.us-vo.org⟩.

2. More information about the IVOA is available at ⟨http://www.ivoa.net⟩.

3. More information about Sloan Digital Sky Survey is available at ⟨http://www.sdss.org⟩.

4. More information about the Gaia mission is available at ⟨http://sci.esa.int/science-e/www/object/index.cfm?fobjectid=28820⟩.

5. More information about all of the Great Observatories is available at ⟨http://www.nasa.gov⟩.

6. Chandra X-ray Observatory, available at ⟨http://chandra.harvard.edu/about/telescope_system3.html⟩.

7. Figure 7.1 is from ⟨http://www.us-vo.org/pubs/files/Y2-annual-report1.pdf⟩.

8. Figure 7.2 is from ⟨http://www.euro-vo.org/avo/gallery/diff_wavelengths_1000.jpg⟩.

9. More information about FITS is available at ⟨http://heasarc.gsfc.nasa.gov/docs/heasarc/fits.html⟩.

Reference

Strauss, A. L. 1993. *Continual permutations of action.* New York: Aldine de Gruyter.

8   High-Energy Physics: The Large Hadron Collider Collaborations

Erik C. Hofer, Shawn McKee, Jeremy P. Birnholtz, and Paul Avery

High-energy physics (HEP) is widely recognized as a highly collaborative field, organizing huge project teams to undertake the construction as well as operation of large and highly specialized research infrastructure and analyzing the resulting data. In this chapter, we focus on the major organizational and technical challenges that have arisen as the HEP community has increased the scale of its scientific projects from institutional or regional collaborations to a coordinated, global scientific investigation centered around the Large Hadron Collider (LHC), housed at the European Center for Nuclear Research (CERN) in Geneva, Switzerland.

A History of Large, Shared Instruments

HEP explores the relationship between the fundamental particles that make up the universe (Galison 1997). Critical to understanding the behavior of these particles is the ability to observe matter under conditions that do not readily occur in the natural world. The particle accelerators needed to produce these collisions are massive in size and complexity, and require highly skilled teams of scientists to construct and operate them. In the 1930s, institutions such as the University of California at Berkeley, and individual leaders including Ernest O. Lawrence, were able to marshal the human and financial capital to build these devices (Heilbron and Seidel 1989). As the boundaries of scientific understanding grew, higher-powered and more complicated devices were increasingly needed, making state-of-the-art accelerators regional and national resources rather than institutional ones. HEP has become "big science" as signified by massive capital investments in expensive and sophisticated instrumentation and infrastructure along with large teams drawn from many institutions (Galison and Hevly 1992). Teams, instruments, and funding today are all multinational and highly distributed, but work together within a coordinated effort to answer specific research questions. Few scientific projects reflect this more than the LHC at CERN. This multibillion dollar apparatus is comprised of circular underground tunnels 27 kilometers in circumference and sits 280 feet underground. The ATLAS detector, one of four that sit inside of the

LHC tunnels, will be 20 meters in diameter when complete and weigh 7,000 tons. For reasons of technical complexity, scale, and facility scarcity, the human scale of HEP research is correspondingly large. The ATLAS experiment, a large experiment at the LHC, involves over 1,800 physicists at 140 institutes in 34 countries around the world.

While high-energy physicists have long worked in large collaborations and with shared instrumentation, the complexity of the LHC, the size of the collaboration, and the volume of the data that will result from the experiments have introduced the need for serious changes in the social and technical infrastructures that support HEP collaborations.

Social and Organizational Challenges

The increasing size and the complexity of the HEP community's scientific goals have introduced challenges to the ways that experiments are organized and managed due to underlying changes in the social and organizational structures of the field. New forms of authority, attribution of credit, and training have emerged in response to these challenges of scale and complexity.

Leading by Persuasion and Managing by Coffee

Consider first the challenge of leadership. CERN is governed and has historically been funded primarily by its twenty-five European member states. But its status as perhaps the leading HEP facility in the world puts it in a global spotlight, and its experiments have attracted participants from institutes around the world, thereby complicating the issue of governance. Participating institutes not in CERN member states must secure funding from their home country and volunteer to make some contribution to the experiment (e.g., constructing some component of the detector or writing software). But as the number of non-CERN-member-state participants increases, so too does the fraction of experimental resources not under the direct control of CERN and the elected leaders of the experiments (for a detailed description of the HEP collaboration structure, see Knorr Cetina 1999, 166–191).

As of 2004, only about 25 percent of the resources in the ATLAS experiment that come from CERN member states are routed through CERN's internal accounting systems. This means that only 25 percent is controlled directly by the formal experiment leadership. Researchers from other participating institutes control the remaining 75 percent of the resources. Some of these researchers may also be leaders of specific subprojects, but these resources are not formally controlled by CERN. Effectively, because any non-member-state institute is free to withdraw its voluntary contribution to ATLAS at any time (to be sure, there would be substantial intangible costs to the institute, but withdrawal is not unprecedented), this means that the elected leaders have little real power beyond persuasion and a technique that one project team leader describes as "managing by coffee." In other words, leadership in this environment becomes an exercise in continuous consensus building through informal meetings (usually held over coffee at CERN), formal presentations, and peer review panels for making certain important decisions. The LHC experiments have evolved (and are continuing to evolve) a fascinating array of techniques for organizing themselves to take action and make decisions in an environment where leadership and power are highly ambiguous.

One example of this is the election of a "technical coordinator" for each of the large experiments. This individual has direct responsibility for the construction and installation of the detector, despite (as noted above) having minimal control over the resources. On the ATLAS experiment, this is accomplished through a constant process of technical review that is tied both to ATLAS's technical requirements and those of the funding agencies that support the work of participating institutes. These reviews, in other words, assess the suitability of work for installation in the detector, but can also be used by individual institutes in justifying their efforts to funding agencies in their home countries. While ATLAS members reported that it was difficult initially to get institutes to agree to submit to this extensive review process, these were later widely felt to be quite useful, and the technical coordinator indicated that institutes were eager to undergo these reviews.

Beyond this, the experiment has an elaborate hierarchy with coordinators of resources and efforts at multiple levels, but it is widely acknowledged that this hierarchy is not absolute. When there are disputes about how a particular component should be designed or constructed, multiple competing proposals may take shape and move forward until a crucial decision point is reached. At this point the leader of the work group in which the dispute has occurred may try to bring the group to a shared solution, or if there is insufficient common ground, may turn to a panel of peer reviewers to resolve the dispute. Some physicists also acknowledge that politics and economics play a role in this process. An institute that is contributing large amounts of money, materials, and/or effort toward the construction of a detector component will have more influence on how that component gets constructed, because in the end it is their responsibility to contribute to a working detector, and nobody wants to build something they think will not function.

There are similar disputes when it comes to the analysis of physics data. The experiment hierarchy assigns data to physics groups for analysis, and assigns shared computing resources for these analysis tasks. It is widely acknowledged, however, that some data sets will be more desirable than others, as they are more likely to result in a high-profile discovery. Thus, the assignment of data to physics groups is a highly contentious process that is watched closely by all collaborating institutes. Yet despite these assignments, the data are available (without accompanying computing resources for analysis) to anyone who wishes to analyze them. Some LHC physicists have therefore described colleagues attempting to amass private clusters of personal computers for conducting their own analyses. Once again, there is the potential for conflict here in that multiple groups might be analyzing the same data and attempting the same discovery. To address this potential, the experiment has a strict policy that no results can be released without prior authorization and approval from the publication committee. In the event of multiple papers on the same topic, the publication committee will decide which result gets published or if the results must be combined. Additionally, all papers released by the collaboration must bear the name of all collaborators as authors.

Standing Out in a Crowd: Getting Credit When You Have 1,699 Coauthors

Another issue that becomes problematic as the size of HEP collaborations continues to increase is the attribution of credit for research discoveries. Historically, the scientific research enterprise has used reputation as its primary currency (Whitley 2000), and one's reputation is earned through first- and single-author publications, awards, and similar clear measures of individual contribution. Promotion and tenure, in turn, are awarded based on tangible evidence of scientific productivity provided by first-author publications as well as the peer assessment of a researcher's ability to carry out high-quality independent research. Where collaboration occurs in other fields, researchers usually demonstrate that they played an important role in the collaborative work by publishing some results as a first author. This mode of operation becomes quite difficult in HEP, where there is a long-standing tradition of listing all collaborators as authors on every paper, always in alphabetical order.

The idea behind this practice is to render individual reputation subservient to the collaboration, and recognize that everybody plays a crucial part in carrying out the work, even if they do not all participate in the final analysis that yields the highest-profile results. At the same time, individuals must nonetheless find ways to differentiate themselves from the crowd if they are to remain competitive in applying for jobs, promotions, and even desirable assignments within the experiment itself. As the author list on the current CERN experiments approaches two thousand names, one can easily imagine the difficulties in attempting to evaluate individuals via a list of publications alone. In fact, many in HEP argue that authorships have become meaningless; what really matters for individuals are letters of recommendation, informal reputation within the experiment, and the number of conference presentations given on behalf of the entire collaboration. This argument has given rise to a contentious debate within the HEP community—a debate that is described in greater detail in Birnholtz (2006).

On the one hand, some contend that the current system of authorship (long, alphabetical author lists) is the only way to ensure that credit is attributed to everybody involved in the project, such as those whose primary contribution was in the design of the apparatus and who will not be actively involved in the data analysis. On the other hand, others assert that this system, by virtue of rendering all individual contributions highly ambiguous, does not really effectively recognize people like detector designers, and also deprives the truly clever contributors to specific papers and discoveries of the individual recognition they deserve. Many alternatives have been proposed, such as listing the major contributors to a paper before an alphabetical list of the rest of the authors or removing authors who do not feel they could effectively defend or explain the results presented in a particular paper. The system that ultimately takes shape will not likely be put to the test until the LHC becomes operational and collaborations of unprecedented size begin publishing results. It will likely have important implications, however, for credit attribution in many big science disciplines.

Designing for Our Progeny: The Impact of Long Time Horizons

Another critical issue that emerges in a discussion of the social effects of the large physical scale of HEP research is the concomitant increase in the time scale of experiments. One example of a long-lived project is the ATLAS experiment, which began its life around 1989 as a "proto-collaboration," a type of working group that is critical to the development of an experiment, called Eagle. The current experiment is not likely to have publishable results until at least 2008. This means that those most actively involved in this experiment will have a twenty-year gap in their publications based on data from "real" experiments (as contrasted with, say, Monte Carlo simulation data, which is often used as a supplement to instrument data). For junior faculty and graduate students in the United States, this is widely acknowledged to be tantamount to career suicide. (This is less of a factor in Europe, where publications and dissertations based on simulation data are more accepted.) The unsurprising effect of the long time horizon, therefore, is that there are few junior faculty or graduate students from U.S. institutes involved in the LHC experiments.

Before discussing the implications of this, it bears mentioning that time scale was a problem historically as well. In the past, though, it was common for graduate students to participate in the detector design for one experiment, while simultaneously taking and analyzing data from another. As such, students got exposure to both analysis and design tasks, had publications based on real experimental data, and had a logical career path to follow that frequently led them to work on the experiment for which they assisted with detector design. Today, experiments take so long and there are so few of them in progress that such arrangements are no longer possible.

It is thus primarily senior faculty from the United States that are involved in the LHC experiments—and many of them will be ready to retire (or will have already retired) when the experiment begins taking data and their junior colleagues become involved. This seems likely to put the U.S. institutes, which are located physically far from CERN, and whose junior faculty will have less experience and familiarity with the detectors than their European and Asian colleagues, at a significant disadvantage. The actual outcomes remain to be seen, however.

Building a Cyberinfrastructure to Support the LHC Experiments

Because of the significant amount of data anticipated from the LHC (over fifteen peta-bytes per year from the four experiments) as well as the large, globally distributed col-laborations (typically fifteen hundred to two thousand PhD physicists per experiment), the LHC physicists are striving to create a cyberinfrastructure that can harness more physical and intellectual resources to enable scientific discovery at the LHC. The com-putational needs for an LHC experiment are so large (typically about one hundred thousand of today's most powerful workstations) that LHC physicists need a system that allows their collaborations to utilize all the computational resources available, wherever they are physically located in the world. Given the extraordinary amount of data (about ten petabytes per year per experiment when simulated data are included in the total), the collaborations also must be able to access storage resources wher-ever they exist. The common component that ties storage, computers, and people to-gether is the network. The network is thus a critical component of the LHC global infrastructure.

Computational and Data Grids

LHC physicists have extensively studied how to build an infrastructure that will pro-vide the needed computational and storage resources, and that will ensure their ef-fective and efficient use. They have concluded that a grid-based cyberinfrastructure composed of hundreds of computing sites linked by high-speed networks offers the most cost-effective means of sharing resources and expertise, since large geographic clusters of users are likely to be close to the data sets and resources that they employ (chapter 1, this volume). Such a distributed configuration is also preferred from a socio-logical perspective as it enables distributed control, and therefore facilitates autonomy in pursuing research objectives. In the Compact Muon Solenoid detector (the other large detector in the LHC), for example, the computing resources will be arranged in a tiered "hierarchy" of regional computing centers, interconnected by regional, na-tional, and international networks. The levels include Tier-0, the central facility at CERN where the experimental data is taken, and where all the raw data are stored and initially reconstructed; Tier-1, a major national center (located typically at a major lab-oratory) supporting the full range of computing, data handling, and support services required by a large scientific community; Tier-2, a university-based system supporting analysis and reconstruction on demand by a community of typically thirty to fifty physicists; Tier-3, a work-group cluster specific to a university department or a single physics group; and Tier-4, an access device such as an individual user's desktop, laptop, or even mobile device. Each Tier-1 will have about 40 percent of the computing and storage capability of the Tier-0 CERN facility, and each Tier-2 site will have about 10 to 20 percent of the capability of a Tier-1.

The grid framework described above is expected to play a key role in realizing the LHC collaboration's scientific potential by integrating all resources, from desktops and clusters at universities to the high-performance computing centers and national labs, into a coherent environment that can be utilized by any collaboration member. Such a collaboration-wide computing fabric will permit enhanced participation in the LHC research programs by physicists at their home institutes—a point that is particularly relevant for participants in remote or distant regions. Since grids enable distributed resources to be fairly shared while taking into account experiment policies as well as local ownership and control, a highly distributed, hierarchical computing infrastructure exploiting grid technologies is a central element of the LHC worldwide computing model.

In the United States, several key initiatives were undertaken in support of this vision of building worldwide grid-based cyberinfrastructures (Avery 2003). The Grid Physics Network (GriPhyN) project, funded by the National Science Foundation in 2000 for $11.9 million, involved a collaboration of physicists, astronomers, and computer scientists from fifteen institutions, including universities and national laboratories. Its computer science research was aimed at developing grid "middleware" capable of supporting large grid-based cyberinfrastructures. The GriPhyN Virtual Data Toolkit—a comprehensive packaging of grid software from GriPhyN and other projects—has been adopted by the international grid community.

The International Virtual Data Grid Laboratory (iVDGL) was funded by the National Science Foundation in 2001 for $13.7 million and is composed of approximately twenty institutions, including universities and national laboratories. The iVDGL is deploying a grid laboratory where advanced grid and networking technologies can be tested on a large scale by multiple disciplines. In 2003, the iVDGL, in partnership with GriPhyN and the Particle Physics Data Grid (PPDG), deployed Grid3, a general-purpose grid of approximately thirty sites and thirty-five hundred processors that operated for two years, and supported applications in HEP, gravitational wave searches, digital astronomy, molecular genomics, and computer science. Grid3 sites are now part of the Open Science Grid, a distributed computing infrastructure for large-scale scientific research that integrates computing and storage resources for more than fifty sites in North America, Asia, and South America.

The PPDG is another example of a U.S.-based project to deploy, use, and extend grid technologies to serve the data management and computing needs of HEP (Bunn and Newman 2003). It began in 1999 as a joint project between several laboratories and universities funded by the U.S. Department of Energy under the Next Generation Internet program, and has continued through ongoing support from the Department of Energy's Mathematical, Information, and Computational Sciences Division base program along with funding from the Scientific Discovery through Advanced Computing program. The PPDG has played a critical role in hardening grid technologies, promoting service specifications, deploying different service implementations, and developing the security policy and architecture that allows these different elements to be integrated into a common grid fabric.

The three grid projects described above each played a unique role in deployment, operation, and integration that contributed to the community's ability to build a production-ready cyberinfrastructure with the Open Science Grid. While there have been similar grid technologies efforts internationally as well, these projects illustrate the complexity of building a cyberinfrastructure to support a global-scale collaboration, and the effort required to direct proper attention and resources to the development, packaging, integration, and operation that are required to produce a production-ready cyberinfrastructure.

Networking

HEP has a long history of involvement in networking, and has been one of the primary proponents and developers of wide-area networks in support of science. This involvement started with analog 9.6 Kbit per second leased lines that composed HEPNet in 1985 and continues to multiple 10-gigabit transatlantic links supported by LHCNet today. Networks are critical to a discipline like HEP since they have such large distributed collaborations. Robust, ubiquitous networks are key enablers of large international collaborations.

Today's best-effort networks with their rapidly increasing bandwidth will be vital to the success of HEP in the future. Shared network infrastructures like Internet2 and ESnet have gone a long way in enabling HEP, but physicists are finding that even more capabilities are required to deliver an efficient, effective infrastructure to support LHC-scale collaborations. Current networks, though highly performing and reliable, are still only best-effort networks that are unable to adapt their behavior or modify their delivered service in response to demanding applications or high-priority tasks.

In preparation for the LHC turn-on in 2008, physicists, in collaboration with computer scientists and network engineers, are working on numerous projects to advance the network from a "black box" into a dynamic managed component of their infrastructure through projects in the United States (like UltraLight, LambdaStation, Terapaths, and UltraScienceNet) and internationally (like the Global Lambda Integrated Facility, national-scale user- and application-managed network projects such as the User-Controlled Lightpath Project (UCLP) with CA4Net in Canada, and many others). The goal is to create a network infrastructure that is dynamic, manageable, and integrated within the HEP infrastructure. Physicists need to have the network support numerous types of data flows: real-time, interactive uses like videoconferencing, remote-control rooms, shared interactive applications, and remote presence; high-bandwidth data transfers from storage elements to compute elements; and low-priority bulk transfers between storage elements and varying priority user analysis applications accessing widely distributed copies of data sets.

Conclusion

The HEP community represents project-based collaborations of remarkable scale. Achieving the capacity to organize collaborations consisting of thousands of individual investigators took many decades to achieve, and introduces new social and technical challenges with each new experiment. Currently, the HEP community depends not only on a unique set of social and organizational processes but also an advanced cyberinfrastructure that the community continues to build and invest in that encompasses data, computing, and networking. Continued development of and reliance on this type of cyberinfrastructure is a critical enabling factor that allows HEP to conduct global-scale "big science".

References

Avery, P. 2004. Grid computing in high-energy physics. In *Proceedings of the 9th international conference on B physics at Hadron Machines—BEAUTY 2003: AIP conference proceedings, vol. 722*, ed. M. Paulini and S. Erhan, 131–140. Melville, NY: American Institute of Physics.

Birnholtz, J. 2006. What does it mean to be an author? The intersection of credit, contribution, and collaboration in science. *Journal of the American Society for Information Science and Technology* 57 (13): 1758–1770.

Bunn, J., and H. Newman. 2002. Data-intensive grids for high-energy physics. In *Grid computing: Making the global infrastructure a reality*, ed. F. Berman, G. E. Fox, and A. J. C. Hey, 859–906. New York: Wiley.

Galison, P. 1997. *Image and logic: A material culture of microphysics*. Chicago: University of Chicago Press.

Galison, P., and B. Hevly. 1992. *Big science: The growth of large-scale research*. Stanford, CA: Stanford University Press.

Heilbron, J. L., and R. W. Seidel. 1989. *Lawrence and his laboratory: A history of the Lawrence Berkeley Laboratory, volume 1*. Berkeley: University of California Press.

Knorr Cetina, K. 1999. *Epistemic cultures: How the sciences make knowledge*. Cambridge, MA: Harvard University Press.

Whitley, R. 2000. *The intellectual and social organization of the sciences*. Oxford: Oxford University Press.

9   The Upper Atmospheric Research Collaboratory and the Space Physics and Aeronomy Research Collaboratory

Gary M. Olson, Timothy L. Killeen, and Thomas A. Finholt

This chapter reviews the decade-long history of a collaboratory project in upper atmospheric physics. The project was both one of the earliest collaboratories funded by the National Science Foundation (NSF) and certainly the longest. Many important collaboratory functions were explored in the project, and detailed studies of collaboratory usage were carried out. The project had a number of significant outcomes and influenced the development of subsequent collaboratories. It also influenced the development of technologies that later had widespread usage.

Upper atmospheric physics was an ideal scientific community for an early collaboratory effort. Indeed, this area of research was highlighted in the National Research Council's (1993) early report on collaboratories. It is a relatively small field, and had a long-standing tradition of collaboration prior to the emergence of collaboratories. Thus, in our nomenclature, the field was for the most part collaboration ready (chapter 4, this volume). Upper atmospheric physicists study the interactions among the earth's upper atmosphere, the earth's magnetic field, and the stream of charged particles that constitute the solar wind. A common manifestation of this is the aurora borealis, or "northern lights," and the corresponding phenomenon in the southern hemisphere, the aurora australis. As in much of physics, there is a divide between experimentalists and theoreticians, and by the early 1990s, when the Upper Atmospheric Research Collaboratory (UARC) began, there were already established supercomputing modelers who were using data to test models of the upper atmosphere. Among the experimentalists, data were collected in three ways: ground-based instruments, satellites, and rockets. The first two were the most dominant forms of data collection.

The UARC project started in 1992 and initially focused on a community of upper atmospheric physicists who used ground-based instruments in Greenland. Our initial goal was to provide this geographically distributed community of physicists with real-time access to those remote instruments, and supply collaborative tools that would allow them to interact with each other over the real-time data. We hoped that as they became familiar with these basic capabilities new ideas about how their science might be practiced would lead to the development of new collaboratory capabilities. This

Figure 9.1
The observatory in Greenland; this picture highlights the radar and the buildings in which additional observational equipment is housed

indeed happened. Thus, in this chapter we trace the progress of the UARC project and its successor, the Space Physics and Aeronomy Research Collaboratory (SPARC), reflecting on the practice of science through the use of these emerging tools.

At the time of the UARC effort, the Sondrestrom Upper Atmospheric Research Facility at Kangerlussuaq, Greenland, had as its core instrument an incoherent scatter radar (ISR) that was supported jointly by the NSF and the Danish Meteorological Institute. SRI International in Menlo Park, California, provided overall management for the facility. In addition, there were a number of other instruments at the site that were managed by a variety of principal investigators (PIs). Figure 9.1 shows a view of the Sondrestrom facility as it appeared in the early 1990s. At that time, the ISR was the most complex and expensive instrument at the site. It operated about 150 hours per month and was attended by a small local staff. Its operation was usually scheduled in advance by making requests to SRI. An ISR can operate in many data gathering modes, and some of them require extensive real-time decision making depending on ionospheric conditions. Other instruments vary in their complexity and need for interaction. Some, such as the Imaging Riometer for Ionospheric Studies, run 24 hours a day, 365 days a year, and have no settings that can be varied. Others, such as optical instruments like an all-sky camera, are used during darkness, which at Kangerlussuaq is abundant during the winter months but scarce in the summer. Some have different modes of operation or adjustable parameters—for example, various optical filters that can be set on an all-sky camera.

In the past, most data collection required the physicists to be in Greenland to operate the instruments and monitor the ionospheric conditions. If multiple instruments were involved, several scientists might arrange to be in Greenland at the same time. The physicists call such coordinated activity a "data campaign." A campaign usually has a particular scientific focus and may involve simultaneous observations using several instruments. Campaigns are generally scheduled to take advantage of particular viewing conditions (e.g., moonless nights) or coincide with other data collection events (e.g., a satellite passing overhead). Within a campaign period, observations often take place only when relevant conditions are present. Campaigns involving the coordination of the radar with optical instruments are particularly frequent during the winter months.

In 1990, the National Aeronautics and Space Administration installed a fifty-six-kilobyte data link to the Sondrestrom facility. This enabled access to data on local discs over the network, and opened the door to the possibility of remote interactions with the instruments. The UARC project took advantage of this link to provide access to the instruments at the facility. The initial set of UARC users came from five sites: the Danish Meteorological Institute in Copenhagen, the University of Maryland, the University of Michigan, SRI International, and Lockheed Palo Alto, in California. During the early years several new sites were added: Cornell University, the University of Alaska, the University of New Hampshire, Phillips Laboratory, Florida Institute of Technology, and the High Altitude Observatory in Boulder, Colorado. Thus, even by the end of the early phase of UARC (see below) the user community had grown considerably.

The NSF funded the UARC project in 1992 for a five-year period. A no-cost extension took the project through a sixth year. In 1998, the project was renamed SPARC and funded for an initial three-year period. A fourth year extended the entire length of the project to ten years, a duration that is remarkable among the variety of collaboratories in the Science of Collaboratories database (see the Introduction to this volume). Over the decade of this project we went through a series of phases. These are briefly summarized here, as well as in table 9.1.

Phase I: NeXTStep

This phase focused on getting the Sondrestrom instruments online to support observational campaigns. An early project decision was to develop software using the NeXT-Step programming environment, with distributed objects written in Objective C. The rapid prototyping capability of this software development environment was an extremely important feature since it facilitated the evolution of the software in response to how the scientists actually used it. The initial version of the UARC application allowed users to access radar data in real time and provided a simple public chat window for communication. All messages exchanged through the chat window and all

Table 9.1
The phases of the UARC/SPARC project

Phase	Dates	Science focus	Technical focus	Usage
I (UARC)	92–95	Sondrestrom instruments	NeXTStep	Widest usage
II (UARC)	95–98	Expanded data sources	Java implementation; CBE	Slow, unreliable, limited Web browsers; showed entire chain of ISRs
III (SPARC)	98–02	Added simulation models, workshop support	Thin client	Reliable; modest usage

user actions were time stamped and saved in log files. We used user-centered design methods to facilitate the development of software that was both useful and usable (McDaniel, Olson, and Olson 1996; Olson, Finholt, and Teasley 2000).

The decision to use a homogeneous computing environment for the entire project was possible because of the small number of sites. This, of course, simplified interoperability. The project equipped each site with a NeXT workstation. The subsequent expansion of the project to additional sites used NeXTStep running on Intel 486 platforms. This phase of the project ended in 1996 when UARC software development shifted to a new architecture and a Web-based user environment. The NeXTStep version of the software was available after 1996, although few users continued to use it.

The initial version of the software was first used in a scientific campaign in April 1993. A senior space physicist was in Greenland, and his graduate student participated from Ann Arbor, Michigan. A member of the development group observed this campaign from Greenland. The campaign provided valuable user-performance data, and extensive revisions were made in the UARC software as a result of the experience. In June 1993, this revised version of the software was used in another campaign with the same scientific focus, but with the same senior physicist in Ann Arbor and the same student in Greenland.

Based on the June campaign, further extensive revisions to the software were made. In addition, two new instruments, the imaging riometer and the magnetometer, were added. By fall 1993, campaigns using these three instruments were supported. In December 1993, the second annual project workshop was held. Prototype versions of new collaboration capabilities, an annotation feature, and the ability to share windows were demonstrated. Shortly after this workshop, the NSF held an external review of the project and approved plans for the remaining years of the project.

During 1994, the UARC software developed amid extensive experience with users. By the annual workshop in Ann Arbor in December 1994, the basic design of UARC ver-

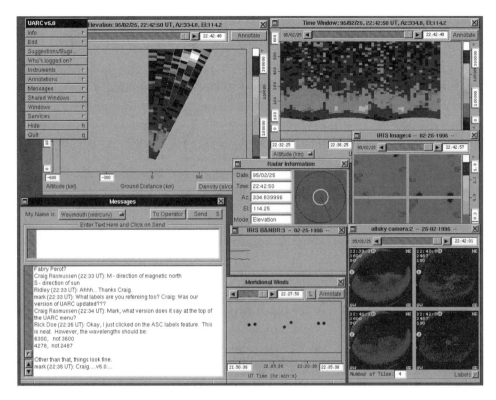

Figure 9.2
A screen capture from UARC5.2 during an observational campaign in February 1995; several instrument data displays and status displays are shown

sion 5.0 was set. UARC 5.3 was the final version of the software built using the NeXT-Step environment. At this stage the software was reasonably reliable and was being used regularly by a core set of users. A number of scientific campaigns were held, and some experiments with asynchronous replay campaigns were attempted. A replay consisted of playing back a recorded version of an earlier campaign for further reflection and analysis. Figure 9.2 shows a representative screen from this phase of the project.

Phase II: Web Based

During these early years of the project, the World Wide Web emerged and had a dramatic effect. It was clear that a Web-based tool suite would allow much better growth of the user base. Also, looking ahead a bit, it was clear that many in the upper atmospheric physics community would be putting their instruments, models, and data sets online, making expansion of the capabilities of the project easier. On the basis of experience gained during the first three years of the project, the technical goal shifted to develop a more generic tool kit to support a broader range of collaboratories across multiple platforms. This tool kit was called the Collaboratory Builders Environment. The UARC software itself was rebuilt during 1995–1996 into a series of modules that captured the key functionality and interface clients that allowed the UARC displays to be shown on any platform from a Web browser. This allowed for considerable expansion of users and data sources, allowing UARC functionality to extend to other ground-based facilities, satellite data, and model outputs. Several reports on the software architecture for this phase are available (Prakash and Shim 1994; Hall et al. 1996; Lee et al. 1996).

The first version of the Web-based interface, called Mural, was available in October 1996. A major campaign that featured a coronal mass ejection from the sun was conducted in April 1997. While the Web-based strategy made functional sense, there were many technical obstacles during this period, and the software was so unreliable that it seriously affected usage. For instance, while the vision of the Web-based model was that any hardware/operating system platform and any Web browser could be used to access the suite of tools, in the end only a small combination of these actually worked. Further, during this phase the Java-based client software was downloaded and ran on the user's workstation. This made for slow, often unreliable performance.

Nonetheless, some important landmarks were achieved. Prodded by the NSF, we sought to cover the entire chain of ISRs that included: two European Incoherent Scatter Scientific Association radars in Norway at Longyearbyen and Tromso; Sondrestrom, Greenland; Millstone Hill, Massachusetts; Arecibo, Puerto Rico; and Jicamarca, Peru. In April 1998 we achieved this, and at a major demonstration of the software at the NSF, showed all six ISRs running in real time.

Phase III: Thin Client

The project, renamed SPARC, received continued funding through an NSF Knowledge and Distributed Intelligence grant in 1998. The new name reflected in part the broader science goals during this phase of the project as well as a shift in the lead upper atmospheric physicist on the project. By now numerous useful data sources had come online, through the individual efforts of upper atmospheric physicists all over the world. So our focus shifted to providing a data viewer that would allow access to any arbitrary data source, either in real time or retrospectively. We also added an option to look at time-based supercomputer model output, so data and theory could be compared in more or less real time. In the words of one of our users, this dramatically "closed the data-theory loop."

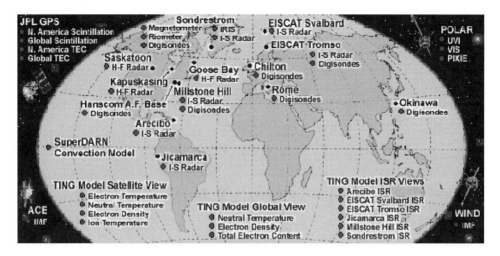

Figure 9.3
Extent of the SPARC data feeds in 1998

The changes in Phase III had a dramatic effect on the usefulness of SPARC. By 2002, when the NSF support of the project ended, we had several hundred data sources available online for viewing. There were ground-based data from all over the world, satellite data, and archival data from a variety of sources. Output from several supercomputer models was also available. Figure 9.3 shows the extent of data available in 1998 during the Phase III expansion.

On the technical side, given the performance problems experienced in Phase II, we shifted to a thin client strategy. What this meant was that on the user side, the viewer would display images that had been assembled by a server elsewhere. This dramatically reduced the load on the client side, though it also somewhat limited the flexibility we had sought to view the data in any arbitrary way the user wanted during Phases I and II. Now a data format had to be specified at the server, so the appropriate images could be generated. We gave high priority to reliability, and indeed in the last several years of the project the system was running 24–7 on a regular basis, with no unscheduled downtime.

While much of the focus of the UARC/SPARC project was on providing support for remote real-time data acquisition, in the later stages of SPARC we began offering online support for workshops. The scientists had a tradition of convening periodically for intense, face-to-face sessions called Coordinated Data Analysis Workshops. They would use these events to study data from past campaigns and plan future ones. We took initial steps in SPARC to support virtual Coordinated Data Analysis Workshops. In particular, we adapted a course management system developed at the University of Michigan called CourseTools to create a support site for a distributed project, called WorkTools. CourseTools was built on a Lotus Notes infrastructure, and provided support for managing content, organizing a calendar, creating an e-mail archive, and other useful features. The WorkTools adaptation was used for several space physics meetings late in the project. The WorkTools environment continued to evolve after the end of SPARC, and indeed became quite successful and was adopted for several thousand projects. This is one kind of success for the SPARC project.

Observation of the Use of the System

Early UARC Usage

The NeXTStep version of the UARC software was used extensively from April 1993 until spring 1996. We captured the behavior of our users in several ways. First, all user actions with the software were recorded and time stamped in an action log. Second, the message server saved the contents of the message window for later analysis. Third, we hired behavioral observers in each of the major sites, and they directly observed the physicists using the software. The observers often asked questions about the software or made notes about how the scientists used it. Sometimes they videotaped these sessions for later analysis. Fourth, users themselves volunteered their reactions to the software, often via e-mail. Starting in fall 1994, the software itself had a feature where users could report bugs and suggestions directly within the application to make this even easier, and it was used extensively.

We concentrated our behavioral observations on campaigns. As noted earlier, the campaigns in 1993 were collecting data on the phenomenon of convection boundary reversals (i.e., movements among different bodies of plasma at the boundary of Earth's magnetosphere as revealed through high-latitude ISR studies). Only ISR data were available over the network. By fall 1993, the Imaging Riometer for Ionospheric Studies and magnetometer data were available, and in early winter 1994 engineering data from a Fabry-Perot Interferometer were available. During the winter campaign season in 1993–1994 the UARC software was used extensively. Some particularly noteworthy events were: a January 1994 campaign that led to the conduct of a replay campaign in March 1994 (see the specific description of this below), and a February 1994 campaign where two space scientists from outside the UARC sites came to Michigan rather than go to Greenland. One of these scientists was a theoretician who had never before seen data collection in real time. Throughout this time, scientists throughout the UARC network observed monthly "World Days," when the Greenland ISR operated in a standard, predefined mode. In May 1994, there were further convection boundary reversal observations.

Further extensive revisions of the software were made in summer and fall 1994. A full complement of Fabry-Perot Interferometer data displays were added, an all-sky camera was brought online, a separate operator's window to support the Greenland site crew was added, the annotation and shared window capabilities were added, and numerous small fixes and additions were made to make the client application more useful and usable, and to make the server more reliable.

To give an impression of what these campaigns were like, we include some data obtained between April 1993 and November 1995, during the use of the NeXTStep system for access to the Greenland facility. The first set of data is based on analyses of the message window files. We coded the content of the messages using a five-category scheme:

- Science: Space science phenomena, data, and methods
- Session: Scheduling, timing, and planning
- Technology: UARC system, NeXT, and network
- Display: Orienting to data displays
- Socializing: Greeting, jokes, and personal matters

This scheme was developed from earlier experiences with coding conversations while people used collaborative technology (e.g., Olson et al. 1993). Coders were trained so they had acceptable reliability in the coding of the messages.

Figure 9.4 shows the distribution of messages by these categories for four different classes of users, summed over all campaigns between April 1993 and November 1994.

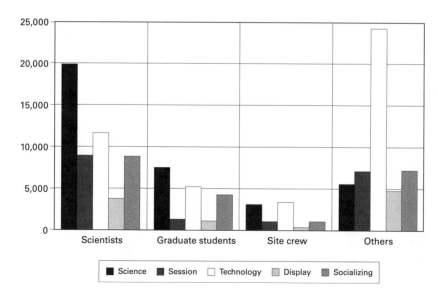

Figure 9.4
Messages classified by category of usage over four different classes of user, summarized over all the major campaigns, 1993–1994

It is encouraging that for the scientists themselves, the most frequent communications were about the science itself. This suggests that the UARC software, even at this early stage, was serving a useful purpose in the conduct of the scientists' science—a suggestion confirmed by detailed observations of their work, and discussions with them during and after the campaigns. The discussion of the "Technology" by the "Others" is primarily the programmers and the behavioral scientists, who often used the message window to query users online about the functionality and usability of the software.

How do these electronic conversations compare with face-to-face behavior? As one example, we compared transcripts of face-to-face conversations at the Sondrestrom site in March 1993 with a selection of episodes from electronic conversations using the UARC chat facility. The episodes selected for both the face-to-face and electronic conversations were from campaigns that involved similar science goals. The conversations focused primarily on the real-time data from the ISR. In the case of the face-to-face conversations the data were displayed on a bank of monitors along a wall, while in the UARC case they were in windows on the individual participants' workstations.

Figure 9.5 shows the relative amounts of conversation in the five coding categories. Both kinds of conversation were dominated by science talk, particularly when interesting things were happening in the displays. During the times when upper atmospheric activity was limited, the face-to-face groups tended to socialize, whereas the UARC users tended to talk about the technology. Such talk was about improvements, bugs, problems, and wish lists of added functionality. Interestingly, there was also socializing in the UARC chat window. Most of it was greetings and good-byes as participants came and went. But there were periods of jokes, teasing, weather discussions, and even talk about an ongoing National College Athletic Association tournament basketball game.

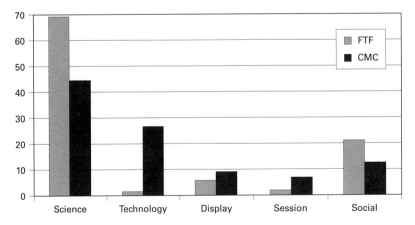

Figure 9.5
Comparison of content for face-to-face and computer-mediated conversations

The elevated levels of display and session coordination in UARC were due to the greater difficulty of coordination using the technology. Yet there was an interesting amount of display coordination in the face-to-face setting, reflecting the need to coordinate what people were looking at as they talked about data in front of a large bank of monitors.

Overall, the conversations in the two situations were quite similar. This indicated to us that the technology did not significantly interfere with the object of the scientists' work. The technology clearly got in the way from time to time, reflecting in part its prototype status. But the overall pattern of conversation in the electronic medium was surprisingly similar to the in-person interactions. For more details about these two conversational situations, see McDaniel, Olson, and Magee (1996).

There has been considerable interest in the literature as to whether computer-mediated communication, with its reduced social cues, equalizes the participation among the participants (e.g., Sproull and Kiesler 1991). We found no evidence of this when we compared patterns of participation between face-to-face and UARC-based conversations. Figure 9.6 shows data for the same set of transcripts that we analyzed in figure 9.5. The participation patterns are similar for the two kinds of conversations, though significantly, there is a much longer tail in the case of UARC, indicating that the technology allowed a large number of "lurkers," people who observed but did not participate much. This long tail is important, since it shows how it is possible for the technology to bring the real-time practice of science to a much broader community.

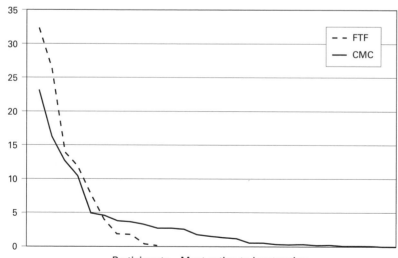

Participants – Most active to least active

Figure 9.6
Percentage of time taken up by different participants, ranked by frequency

The Replay Campaign of March 1994

As mentioned earlier, there was a campaign in January 1994 with a number of events of great interest to the scientists. Since the data for this session were archived at the University of Michigan for other purposes, several of the scientists asked if it would be possible to replay the two days in question so the phenomena that passed by in real time could be examined more carefully. The Michigan programmers set up a "replay campaign" for this purpose. The archived data were replayed, under the hand control of a programmer in Ann Arbor. The principal participants were in Copenhagen, Boston, and Menlo Park. The participants reported that it was extremely valuable to reexamine the session, being able to fast forward over quiet periods, pause or replay interesting periods, and converse through the message window about the phenomena.

This mode of operation had not been anticipated. Nevertheless, the scientists reported that this kind of replay campaign was useful for both the science itself and the training of students and junior scientists. We decided not to explicitly support this capability in the NeXTStep-based versions of the UARC software. Yet replay capabilities were important parts of the later evolution of SPARC, particularly in Phase III.

Use of UARC for Graduate Student Mentoring

One feature of the UARC software that was crucial was its role in the training of graduate students. Previously, when data were collected by means of trips to Greenland, graduate students would rarely be able to participate. But with UARC making this phase of the science available online, students could join in any campaign, even if only as an observer. This allowed students to observe the interactions among a wider range of scientists than would typically be available in their home laboratory, and indeed we frequently saw episodes of intense interaction between students at one site and senior scientists at different sites.

Summary of Use of UARC Software

The early UARC software was used extensively by a growing community of scientists for real-time data acquisition from Greenland. This provided a foundation for expanding the community of UARC users, making similar capabilities available for other sites where space scientists collect data, and making UARC available for the examination and analysis of archived data. Thus, the early phase of UARC represented a strong beginning for transforming the practice of upper atmospheric physics.

SPARC Usage

As mentioned earlier, the change to Web-based technology that coincided with the second round of funding led to dramatic changes in usage. The Mural version of the system had severe performance problems, and the spotty availability by browser/

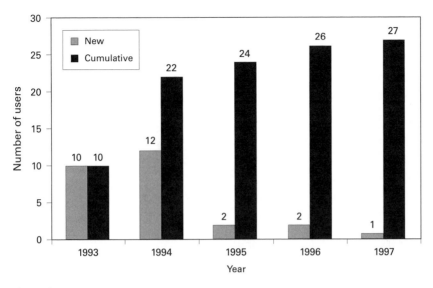

Figure 9.7
Pattern of usage across 1993–1997

operating system combinations seriously eroded usage. While the thin client version of the software in the latter stages of the project had a dramatic effect on the availability and reliability, the number of new users dropped significantly, and many old users became former users.

Figure 9.7 depicts the pattern of usage over the UARC phase of the project, and the dramatic shifts that occurred during the 1996–1997 shift to the Web-based technology. Figure 9.8 portrays some representative usage data over the 1999–2000 period of SPARC. This was due to a high rate of usage by a small number of scientists, primarily from the University of Michigan, where the project was centered.

As mentioned earlier, beyond the expansion of data sources and the marked improvement in reliability, the newest feature of this phase of the project was the incorporation of simulation output in the system. While the addition of simulation capability introduced a critical new type of user to the UARC/SPARC community, running the simulations often depended on contingencies outside the control of the UARC/SPARC project, such as the availability of high-performance computing resources to run relevant models (e.g., the Thermosphere-Ionosphere Nested Grid model developed at the University of Michigan). As a result, while the potential of side-by-side comparison of modeled output and real-time data was demonstrated, particularly in Phases II and III, in reality it wasn't feasible to provide this functionality "on demand."

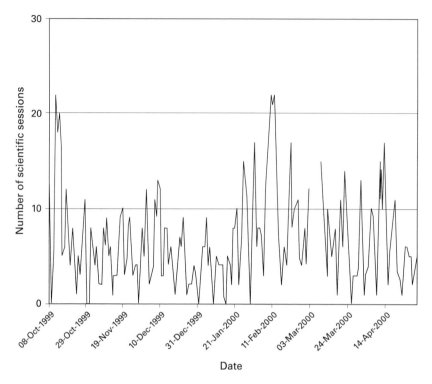

Figure 9.8
Use of SPARC, 1999–2000

Analysis of User Attitudes

We conducted several surveys during the UARC/SPARC project. There were six waves of surveys administered, with the earliest conducted in 1993, and the final one in 2001. There were two samples of respondents: those who had used the UARC/SPARC technology, and a matched control sample drawn from the membership roles of relevant sections of the American Geophysical Union (e.g., the Space Physics and Aeronomy section). Typically, these samples consisted of several hundred respondents, and we obtained response rates of between 40 to 60 percent.

The results of these surveys gave us a picture of the changing nature of technology use across the decade of the project. One clear finding was that by 2001, e-mail was a dominant form of communication, displacing such modes as the telephone and fax. This was more pronounced for the control subjects. Also, consistent with our direct observations, UARC users reported substantially less use of the system after 1994. One conjecture we had was that some other Web-based resource had substituted for UARC/

SPARC use. But while the survey indicated there was an increased use of the Web, only a small proportion of the respondents used data-intensive Web sites, and there was no predominant Web site that members of the community were using. There was also no evidence that in 2001 they were reading their core science journals online. Finally, there was little reported use of collaboration technologies such as data conferencing or videoconferencing.

Post-SPARC

With the end of the NSF funding, SPARC operations continued briefly as a joint effort of the University of Michigan and the National Center for Atmospheric Research in Boulder, Colorado. Eventually, SPARC capabilities were available elsewhere, particularly from various space weather sites (e.g., the National Aeronautics and Space Administration's Space Weather Bureau and National Oceanic and Atmospheric Administration's Space Environment Center). The core technology of SPARC went on to become the basis for Sakai, a successful open-source collaboration and learning environment developed by the University of Michigan along with partners at Stanford University, MIT, the University of California at Berkeley, and Indiana University. Many of the UARC/SPARC collaborators became the PIs on second-generation collaboratory projects funded by the NSF, such as the George E. Brown Jr. Network for Earthquake Engineering Simulation (chapter 18, this volume). Similarly, one of the UARC/SPARC PIs (Dan Atkins) went on to author the influential NSF Blue Ribbon Advisory Panel Report on Cyberinfrastructure and became the first head of the NSF's Office of Cyberinfrastucture (Atkins et al. 2003), while another PI (Tim Killeen) became the director of the National Center for Atmospheric Research. Finally, the UARC/SPARC effort spun off at least one successful business, Arbor Networks, founded by one of the SPARC participants (Farnam Jahanian).

Summary

The UARC/SPARC project played an important role in the history of collaboratories. On the positive side, it was the first collaboratory project supported by the NSF, and it lasted for an astonishing decade. In 1998, UARC was a finalist for the Smithsonian/ Computerworld computer honors in the science category. As noted above, PIs on UARC/SPARC went on to fill key roles in shaping the emergence of the NSF's cyberinfrastructure initiative. While in the end there was no sustained use of the system, it provided a rich proof of concept of what could be done with collaboratory infrastructure. Finally, the project was also an inspiration for other subsequent collaboratory projects, notably the Network for Earthquake Engineering Simulation at the NSF.

On the negative side, while use of the Web increased throughout the decade of the UARC/SPARC project, there was little evidence that this use revolutionized the practice of upper atmospheric physics. Some additional flexibility in carrying out data collection activities was achieved, and some initial explorations of other aspects of the science such as modeling and workshops were carried out. For the most part, however, the introduction of Web technologies did not achieve the hypothesized broadening of participation in upper atmospheric physics. One reason for this failure might have been the emphasis in UARC and the early SPARC on the acquisition and interpretation of real-time data. Second- and third-generation cyberinfrastructure projects have placed a much greater emphasis on data federation and reuse, with preliminary evidence (particularly in the case of biomedical and astronomical research) that this strategy can produce profound shifts in research practice. For example, projects like the Sloan Digital Sky Survey and the National Virtual Observatory (chapter 7, this volume) are transforming astronomy from an observationally intensive to a data-intensive science (see also chapter 1, this volume).

Acknowledgments

The UARC project was supported by an NSF Cooperative Agreement (IIS 9216848), while SPARC was supported by a Knowledge and Distributed Intelligence grant, also from the NSF (ATM 9873025). An earlier conference grant (NSF IIS 9123840) laid the groundwork for the UARC project. Over the years, numerous people were involved in the project—too many to list here. Dan Atkins served as the PI during both UARC and SPARC. Bob Clauer was the lead space physicist during UARC, while Tim Killeen served in that role during SPARC. Others with extensive involvement in the project included Terry Weymouth, Atul Prakash, Farnam Jahanian, Craig Rasmussen, Sushila Subramanian, and Peter Knoop.

References

Atkins, D. E., K. Droegemeier, S. Feldman, H. Garcia-Molina, M. L. Klein, D. G. Messerschmitt et al. 2003. *Revolutionizing science and engineering through cyberinfrastructure: Report of the National Science Foundation Blue-Ribbon Advisory Panel on Cyberinfrastructure*. Arlington, VA: National Science Foundation.

Hall, R. W., A. Mathur, F. Jahanian, A. Prakash, and C. Rasmussen. 1996. Corona: A communication service for scalable, reliable group collaboration systems. In *Proceedings of the 1996 ACM conference on computer-supported cooperative work*, 140–149. New York: ACM Press.

Lee, J. H., A. Prakash, T. Jaeger, and G. Wu. 1996. Supporting multi-user, multi-applet workspaces in CBE. In *Proceedings of the 1996 ACM conference on computer-supported cooperative work*, 344–353. New York: ACM Press

McDaniel, S. E., G. M. Olson, and J. McGee. 1996. Identifying and analyzing multiple threads in computer-mediated and face-to-face conversations. In *Proceedings of the 1996 ACM conference on computer-supported cooperative work*, 39–47. New York: ACM Press.

McDaniel, S. E., G. M. Olson, and J. S. Olson. 1994. Methods in search of methodology: Combining HCI and object orientation. In *Proceedings of the SIGCHI conference on human factors in computing systems: Celebrating interdependence*, ed. B. Adelson, S. Dumais, and J. Olson, 145–151. New York: ACM Press.

National Research Council. 1993. *National collaboratories: Applying information technology for scientific research*. Washington, DC: National Academies Press.

Olson, G. M., T. A. Finholt, and S. D. Teasley. 2000. Behavioral aspects of collaboratories. In *Electronic collaboration in science*, ed. S. H. Koslow and M. F. Huerta, 1–14. Mahwah, NJ: Lawrence Erlbaum.

Olson, G. M., J. S. Olson, M. Carter, and M. Storrøsten. 1992. Small group design meetings: An analysis of collaboration. *Human Computer Interaction* 7:347–374.

Prakash, A., and H. S. Shim. 1994. DistView: Support for building efficient collaborative applications using replicated active objects. In *Proceedings of the 1994 ACM conference on computer-supported cooperative work*, 153–164. New York: ACM Press.

Sproull, L., and S. Kiesler. 1991. *Connections: New ways of working in the networked organization*. Cambridge, MA: MIT Press.

10 Evaluation of a Scientific Collaboratory System: Investigating Utility before Deployment

Diane H. Sonnenwald, Mary C. Whitton, and Kelly L. Maglaughlin

The evaluation of scientific collaboratories has lagged behind their development, and fundamental questions have yet to be answered: Can distributed scientific research produce high-quality results? Do the capabilities afforded by collaboratories outweigh their disadvantages from scientists' perspectives? Are there system features and performance characteristics that are common to successful collaboratory systems? Our goal is to help answer such fundamental questions by evaluating a specific scientific collaboratory system called the nanoManipulator Collaboratory System. The system is a set of tools that provide collaborative interactive access to a specialized scientific instrument and office applications.

To evaluate the system, we conducted a repeated measures controlled experiment that compared the process and outcomes of scientific work completed by twenty pairs of participants (upper-level undergraduate science students) working face-to-face and remotely. We collected scientific outcomes (graded lab reports) to investigate the quality of scientific work, postquestionnaire data to measure the intentions to adopt the system, and postinterviews to understand the participants' views of doing science under both conditions. We hypothesized that the study participants would be less effective, report more difficulty, and be less favorably inclined to adopt the system when collaborating remotely. Yet the quantitative data showed no statistically significant differences with respect to effectiveness and adoption. Furthermore, in the postinterviews, the participants reported advantages and disadvantages working under both conditions, but developed work-arounds to cope with the perceived disadvantages of collaborating remotely. A theoretical explanation for the results can be found in the theory of the "life-world" (Schutz and Luckmann 1973, 1989). Considered as a whole, the analysis leads us to conclude that there is a positive potential for the development and adoption of scientific collaboratory systems.

Evaluation Design and Hypotheses

The goals of our evaluation included providing insights regarding the efficacy of scientific collaboratories, increasing our understanding of collaborative scientific work processes mediated by technology, and informing the design of collaboratory technology. To address these goals we choose a controlled experiment approach to evaluation. The experimental approach gave us three advantages. The first advantage is that the evaluation can take place before all the necessary infrastructure components are developed and deployed. The collaboratory system we evaluated requires the high-speed, robust, and secure Internet connections that are only now emerging. Our approach permitted evaluation without waiting for new networking technology to be developed and deployed.

The second advantage is that the time before results are available is shorter compared to other evaluation methods, such as field studies. In field studies, because of the rhythm of science, long periods of time can pass when scientists do not actively collaborate due to differences in their schedules and available resources. An experiment is not dependent on these cycles of inactivity and activity, enabling us to offer feedback to system developers and funders in a timely fashion.

The third advantage is that the risk of obtaining no evaluation data is reduced. Science is dynamic and highly specialized. Scientists may be enthusiastic about using a collaboratory system during the initial research funding and system design process, but by the time the system is developed and ready for use, any number of factors such as modifying the direction of their research and moving to another university may have reduced their need for or ability to utilize the system. Finding other scientists to participate in the evaluation increases the costs of and time to results, especially if new technical infrastructure is needed to support the system.

A primary disadvantage with respect to the controlled experiment approach is its inherent artificiality. To reduce the artificial nature of the experiment the tasks used in the control experiment were replications of actual experiments performed by scientists. Task completion took up to four hours, more closely replicating real-world scientific practice than is typically done in controlled experiments. This reduction in the gap between the real-world, intended use of the collaboratory system and the evaluated use increases the validity of the evaluation results.

Previous research in computer-supported cooperative work (e.g., Dourish et al. 1996; Olson and Olson 2000) and the theory of language (Clark 1996) would predict that working remotely would lack the richness of collocation and face-to-face interaction. The multiple and redundant communication channels, implicit cues, and spatial co-references are difficult to support via computer-mediated communications. This lack of richness is thought to impair performance because it is more difficult to establish the common ground that enables individuals to understand the meaning of each other's utterances. Other research (e.g., Star and Ruhleder 1996; Orlikowski 1993; Olson and Teasley 1996) predicts that working remotely may not be compatible with many structural elements of work, such as existing reward systems and common work practices. As a result, a collaboratory system is not likely to be adopted by individuals, especially when individuals can themselves decide whether they work face-to-face or remotely. Thus, our evaluation hypotheses were:

• H1: The study participants will be less effective collaborating remotely than collaborating face-to-face
• H2: The study participants will report more difficulty collaborating remotely than collaborating face-to-face
• H3: The study participants will report they are more likely to adopt the system after using it face-to-face than remotely

In the following sections we report on the controlled experiment study conducted to test these hypotheses, including discussions of the context of the evaluation, the study design, data collection and analysis, and the results of the controlled lab study and their implications.

Evaluation Context: The nanoManipulator Collaboratory

The collaboratory system we evaluated provides distributed, collaborative access to a specialized scientific instrument called a nanoManipulator (nM). The single-user nM supplies haptic and 3-D visualization interfaces to a local (colocated) atomic force microscope, providing a natural scientist with the ability to interact directly with physical samples ranging in size from DNA to single cells. A nM can be used in live and replay modes. In live mode, a nM is used to both display and record data from an atomic force microscope and to control the microscope. The recorded data, including all data produced by the microscope, is saved in a "stream file" so that it can be replayed later for analysis. In replay mode, the nM is a display device where the stream file, instead of the live microscope, provides the data for the visual and haptic displays. Approximately 80 percent of nM use is in replay mode where scientists move forward and backward through the data, stopping at critical points to perform visualization and analysis. (Details regarding the nM and its uses are described in Finch et al. 1995; Taylor and Superfine 1999; Guthold et al. 1999, 2000.)

The collaboratory version of the nM was designed based on the results of an ethnographic study from which we developed an understanding of scientific collaborative work practices, the role of an nM as a scientific instrument, and scientists' expectations regarding technology to support scientific collaborations across distances (Sonnenwald et al. 2001; Sonnenwald 2003; Sonnenwald, Maglaughlin, and Whitton 2004).

The collaboratory system (figure 10.1) is based on two personal computers. One personal computer provides an interface to the scientific instrument and the other supports shared productivity applications and videoconferencing tool.

The first personal computer, equipped with a Sensable Devices Phantom forcefeedback device, provides haptic and 3-D visualization interfaces to a local or remote

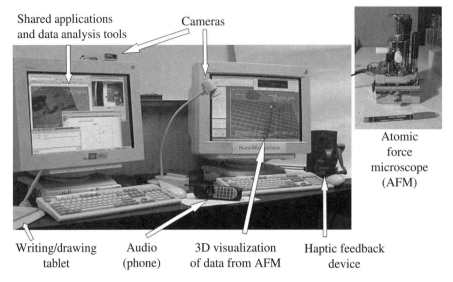

Shared applications
and data analysis tools

Cameras

Atomic
force
microscope
(AFM)

Writing/drawing   Audio   3D visualization   Haptic feedback
tablet   (phone)   of data from AFM   device

Figure 10.1
NanoManipulator Collaboratory System

atomic force microscope. It also supports the collaborative manipulation and exploration of scientific data in live and replay modes.

Via a menu option, scientists can dynamically switch between working together in a *shared* mode and working independently in a *private* mode (see figure 10.2). In the shared mode, remote (that is, noncollocated) collaborators view and analyze the same (scientific) data. Mutual awareness is supported via multiple pointers, each showing the focus of attention and interaction state for one collaborator. As illustrated in figure 10.2, the cone is the remote scientist's pointer and the text label on the cone indicates the function that the remote scientist is performing. In this example, the remote scientist is positioning measure points that are displayed as red, green, and blue lines. The double green arrows indicate that the local scientist is zooming out or enlarging the magnification of the sample.

We use optimistic concurrency techniques in the shared mode (Hudson et al. 2004), eliminating explicit floor control and allowing collaborators to perform almost all operations synchronously. Because of the risk of damage to an atomic force microscope, control of the microscope tip is explicitly passed between collaborators. In private mode, each collaborator can independently analyze the same or different data from previously generated stream files. When switching back to the private from the shared mode, collaborators return to the exact data and setting they were using previously.

The second personal computer supports shared application functionality and video-conferencing (via Microsoft NetMeeting) along with an electronic writing/drawing

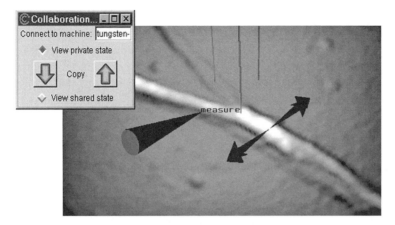

Figure 10.2
Shared menu and screen view

tablet. This personal computer allows users to collaborate using a variety of domain-specific and off-the-shelf applications, including specialized data analysis, word processing, and whiteboard applications. Two cameras support the videoconferencing. One camera is mounted on a gooseneck stand so it can be pointed at the scientist's hands, sketches, or other physical artifacts that scientists may use during experiments; the other is generally positioned to capture a head-and-shoulders view of the user. Collaborators have software control of which camera view is broadcast from their site. Previous research (e.g., Bellotti and Dourish 1997; Harrison, Bly, and Anderson 1997) has illustrated the importance of providing the ability to switch between multiple camera views as well as repositioning and refocusing the cameras.

A wireless telephone connected to a commercial telephone network offers high-quality audio communications for collaborators. Telephone headset and speakerphone options are also included to allow users mobility, and provide the option of having others in the room participate in a conversation with a remote collaborator.

The Controlled Experiment Study

The controlled experiment study was a repeated measures design comparing working face-to-face and working remotely with the order of conditions counterbalanced. This type of experiment is also referred to as a "mixed design" because it allows comparisons both within and between groups.

Twenty pairs of study participants conducted two realistic scientific research activities—each requiring two to three hours to complete. The participants worked face-to-face on one occasion, and on a different day, collaborated remotely (in different locations). When face-to-face, the participants shared a single collaboratory system; when collaborating remotely, each location was equipped with a complete collaboratory system. We collected a variety of quantitative and qualitative evaluation data, including task-performance measures to compare the quality of scientific work produced in the two collaboration conditions, postinterviews to gain, from the participants' perspectives, a more in-depth understanding of the scientific process in both conditions, and postquestionnaire data.

The Study Participants

The study participants were upper-level undergraduate natural science students from local Research I universities. We chose this population because it is relatively large as well as representative of individuals who perform scientific research, most often under the direction of faculty or postdoctoral fellows. The science and math skills of this pool are somewhat consistent, as they have taken a similar set of core science and math courses as first- and second-year students. The study participants were recruited through announcements in classes and student newspaper advertisements, on posters, and via e-mail.

The majority of the forty participants reported they were majoring in biology and reported A or B grade point averages; none of the participants reported a grade point average lower than a C. Thirty-six of the participants were Caucasian, two were African American, and two were Asian or Indian. All were fluent in English, and all but one appeared to be a native English speaker. The participants were assigned to pairs without respect to their undergraduate major, self-reported grade point average, and ethnicity. Pair assignments did not change over the course of the experiment. To reduce the possibility of gender bias in our results, we strove for a mix of gender composition in the pairs; nine pairs were of mixed gender, six pairs were female only, and five pairs were male only. To avoid bias or confounding results, we selected participants who had no experience collaborating across distances or using the nanoManipulator. In addition, none of the participants had any substantive knowledge of fibrin, the biological material under investigation in the collaborative activities.

All of the study participants had previous experience collaborating face-to-face with others while conducting scientific experiments and working on class projects. Twenty-five percent of the study participants (five pairs out of twenty) knew their partner before participating in the experiment—a situation that mirrors scientific and teaching practice. Scientists who collaborate may know each other, but they frequently have their students or postdoctoral fellows, who do not know each other, work together to design and conduct the actual experiments and data analysis for their collaborative project. Collaboratories, in particular, bring together scientists who are from different disciplines and locations, and who do not know each other. One scientist may have knowledge of the scientific tool and methodology, while the other may have knowledge of the sample to be investigated. Due to the small number of previously acquainted pairs in our study, it was not possible to determine if the previous acquaintance statistically affected the experimental outcome measures. Nevertheless, the outcome measures of the participants who knew each other already follow the same trends as the measures from the participants who had not known each other beforehand.

Experiment Design

The controlled experiment consisted of three sessions: an introduction and two task sessions. The introduction entailed a presentation providing background information on the controlled experiment, a thorough introduction to the natural science used in the controlled experiment, and a brief hands-on demonstration of the collaboratory system. During the presentation and demonstration, the participants were encouraged to ask questions. The study participants signed an informed consent document and completed a demographic questionnaire. This session typically lasted forty-five minutes.

Task sessions 1 and 2 were performed on different days and under different conditions: face-to-face and remote. The order of the conditions was counterbalanced (see table 10.1), and the pairs were randomly assigned to the two order conditions. Each task session had three parts: a tutorial, a scientific research lab, and a postquestionnaire and postinterview.

The hands-on tutorial led the participants through instructions on how to use the features of the collaboratory system required for that day's lab. The tutorial before the remote collaboration session also included instructions on the videoconferencing system, shared applications, and the collaboration-specific features of the system. Each participant completed the tutorial in a separate location, and was accompanied by a researcher/observer who was available to assist and answer questions. The participants were allowed to spend as much time as they wanted on the tutorial; typically they spent forty-five minutes.

The scientific research labs in both task sessions were designed in collaboration with natural scientists who regularly use the nanoManipulator to conduct their scientific

Table 10.1

Conceptual experiment design: Repeated measures with the order of conditions counterbalanced

Condition	Order of conditions	
Type of interaction	Task session 1	Task session 2
Face-to-face	Pairs 1–10	Pairs 11–20
Remote	Pairs 11–20	Pairs 1–10

research. The tasks were actual activities that the scientists completed and documented during the course of their investigations. The labs were designed to be similar in difficulty as judged by the natural scientists and the pilot study participants. To complete the labs, the participants had to engage in the following activities typical of scientific research: operate the scientific equipment properly; capture and record data in their (electronic) notebooks; perform analysis using scientific data analysis software applications, and include the results of that analysis in their notebooks; draw conclusions, create hypotheses, and support those hypotheses based on their data and analysis; and prepare a formal report of their work. We did not require the study participants to design a natural science experiment or write a paper describing the experiment because the collaboratory system under evaluation was not designed to explicitly support these components of the scientific research cycle.

During each scientific research lab, the study participants were asked to work together, using the collaboratory system in replay mode to manipulate and analyze data recorded previously during an experiment conducted by a physicist (Guthold et al. 2000). As discussed above, the prerecorded stream file contained an exact and complete record of all data collected from an atomic force microscope when the experiment was originally performed. All visualization options and controls on the system, except "live" microscope control, were available to the study participants in replay mode.

The subject of the scientific research labs was the structure of fibrin, a substance critical for blood clotting. In the first lab, the participants were asked to measure the distances between the branch points of fibrin fibers and discuss the possible relationship between these distances and the blood-clotting process. In the second lab, the participants were asked to measure additional structural properties of fibrin and, based on these measurements, discuss its possible interior structure.

The study participants were asked to document their results—recording the data they collected and their analysis of that data—in a lab report. The lab report mirrored the lab notes created by the scientists when they originally conducted their fibrin investigation. The lab reports created by the participants contain data images, tables of data values, explanatory text, and annotated graphs illustrating their analysis of their data (figure 10.3). A single report was requested from each pair of study participants for each task session.

After each lab, each study participant was asked to complete a postquestionnaire and participate in a one-on-one interview with a researcher. The postquestionnaire took approximately twenty minutes to complete, and postinterviews lasted between thirty and sixty minutes. The questionnaires and interviews provided data regarding the participants' perceptions of the lab activities, the technology in the collaboration system, and the collaborative process as discussed below. The sessions and data collection instruments were tested and refined in a pilot study.

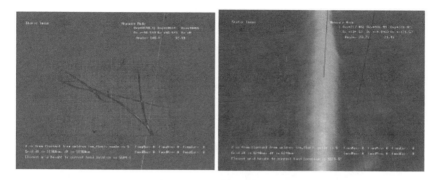

Path	Length
From 1 to 2	3.1173um
From 1 to 3	5.7696um
From 2 to 3	3.8581um
From 1 to 4	4.0473um
From 3 to 4	1.7766um
From 3 to 5	1.3337um
From 4 to 5	3.0141um

By the nature of clotting, we would expect that the distance between juncture points would be smaller than the diameter of a red blood cell. The average length between juncture points is 3.2738um; this is less than 7.5um, implying that a red blood cell would get caught in the fibrin mesh. The effectiveness of the clot at stopping red blood cells increases as the distance between the juncture decreases. There could be an upper limit on the number of junctures related to the energy to produce fibrin.

The measured width was 350nm, approximately twice the measured height. Either the width of the fiber was overestimated or the cylindrical model for the fibrin fiber is not accurate. The width of the fiber at half height was 210nm. We conclude that the tip is conical and rounded at the tip because the slope of the cross section is not steep and there is a change of inflection at the measured edges of the fiber.

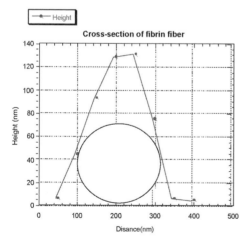

Figure 10.3

Sample lab report page including microscope data capture, measurement data recording, and data analysis

(a)

(b)

Figures 10.4a and 10.4b
Overhead view of participants working remotely

Figures 10.4a and 10.4b show two study participants collaborating remotely during a task session, and figure 10.c shows the same study participants collaborating face-to-face during a subsequent task session.

Evaluation Measures
Three evaluation measures assess three different perspectives of the collaboratory system. A task-performance measure assesses the quality of science produced when using the system. Postinterviews assess participants' perceptions regarding working collaboratively, and postquestionnaires assess participants' opinions regarding the adoptablity of the system. Together these measures gave us a rich, and ultimately consistent, evaluation of the system.

Figure 10.5
Overhead view of participants working face-to-face

Task-Performance (Outcome) Measure: Lab Reports A primary goal of our overall evaluation study is to compare the quality of science produced in face-to-face collaborations with that produced in remote collaborations. Typically statistics such as the number of publications, citation counts, the number of grants and patents awarded, and peer reviews are used to measure science quality. These measures, however, require years of performance and data collection that are not possible in evaluation studies with a limited time frame. Therefore, we chose to have the study participants create laboratory reports that are modeled on scientists' lab notes documenting their data collection and analysis progress. We graded the reports and used the grades as a task-performance measure—that is, as a measure of the quality of science conducted face-to-face and remotely.

The instructions for the lab activities and what should be included in the laboratory reports were designed in collaboration with natural scientists. As is typical in controlled experiments, the instructions were specific and guided the participants' actions. The information that the participants were asked to provide in the reports mirrored the information found in the scientists' lab notes created when they conducted their original research on fibrin. Each pair of study participants collaboratively created a lab report under each condition, generating a total of forty lab reports—twenty created working remotely, and twenty created working face-to-face.

The lab reports were graded blindly; the graders had no knowledge of the lab report authors or under which condition the report was created. Intercoder reliability was calculated for these assigned grades using Cohen's Kappa (Robson 2002). Values of 0.75 and 0.79 were calculated for graded lab reports from the first and second task sessions, respectively. Values above 0.70 are considered excellent (Robson 2002).

The Participants' Perceptions: Postinterviews   To further our understanding of the participants' perceptions of the system, we conducted semistructured interviews with each participant after each task session. The study participants were asked what they thought about their experience, including the most satisfying and dissatisfying aspects of their experience (Flanagan 1954). In addition, we inquired about specific incidents that were noted by the observer, work patterns that emerged during the experience, and the impact that technology may have had on their interactions with their collaborator. After task session 2, the participants were also asked to compare working face-to-face and remotely. To better learn each participant's perspective, the participants were interviewed individually, for a total of eighty interviews, each lasting from thirty to sixty minutes. Each interview was audiotaped and transcribed.

The interviews were analyzed using both open and axial coding (Berg 1989). During open coding, a subset of the interviews was read thoroughly and carefully by two researchers, who identified coding categories or coding frames. For example, a category that emerged was negative references to aspects of the technology. During axial coding, we looked for relationships among the categories. After the initial set of categories and their relationships were discussed among the research team, three team members analyzed another subset of interviews. Definitions of coding categories and relationships among the categories were further refined during this analysis. All three researchers analyzed an additional subset of interviews. No new coding categories or relationships emerged, and researchers were in agreement regarding the application of the codes. Intercoder reliability, calculated using Cohen's Kappa, yielded values of 0.86 and 0.81. Values above 0.70 are considered excellent (Robson 2002). In the final step, all the interviews were reread and analyzed using the coding categories. For the purposes of this chapter, we analyzed the following codes: references to working face-to-face, references to working remotely, a comparison between working face-to-face and remotely, positive aspects of the technology, and negative aspects of the technology.

Innovation Adoption Measure: Postquestionnaires   Innovation adoption and diffusion theory provided us with a foundation for investigating the potential of the collaboratory system for adoption by scientists. Synthesizing over five decades of innovation adoption and diffusion research, Rogers (2003) identifies five attributes of innovations that are correlated with the adoption of innovations. The five innovation attributes are: relative advantage, compatibility, complexity, trialability, and observability.

Relative advantage is the degree to which the potential adopters perceive that an innovation surpasses current practices. *Compatibility* is the degree to which an innovation is perceived to be consistent with the adopters' existing values, past experiences, and needs. It includes individual, group, and organizational goals, needs, and culture, and is concerned with the level of congruence between a group's traditional work patterns and the work patterns required by the innovation. *Complexity* refers to the perceived difficulty of learning to use and understand a new system or technology. When a system is perceived as complex, it is less likely to be adopted. *Trialability* refers to the ease of experimenting with an innovation. It includes the level of effort needed and the risk involved in observing as well as participating in small-scale demonstrations of the system, including the ease with which you can recover from (or "undo") an action taken using the system and the cost of reversing the decision to adopt. *Observability* is the degree to which the results of the innovation are easily seen and understood.

Numerous researchers have validated these attributes in a variety of domains including medicine, engineering, and airline reservation information systems (Rogers 2003; Tornatzky and Fleischer 1990). Researchers—for instance, Grudin (1994), Shniederman (1997), Olson and Teasley (1996), and Orlikowski (1993)—have also identified the importance of the attributes in computer-supported cooperative work contexts. Rogers's theory and the five attributes guided the construction of our postquestionnaire.

We used the same questionnaire under both collaboration conditions to enable a comparison of results. As upper-level undergraduate natural science students, the participants had many previous experiences conducting scientific experiments using a variety of scientific instruments and could assess the innovation attributes, including relative advantage and compatibility, based on these earlier experiences. Details regarding the construction and validation of the questionnaire instrument can be found in Sonnenwald, Maglaughlin, and Whitton (2001).

Results and Discussion

The quantitative data analysis did not support the hypotheses. No statistically significant negative differences in the measures of scientific outcomes and intentions to adopt the system that are attributable to condition emerged. The analysis of the qualitative interview data helped explain this null result. The participants reported advantages and disadvantages working under both conditions, and developed work-arounds to cope with the perceived disadvantages of collaborating remotely.

We present the detailed results in several parts. We look at data from each measure, examining similarities and differences that arise when working face-to-face and remotely, with respect to our hypotheses regarding scientific outcomes, the participants' perceptions of the scientific work process and technology, and collaboratory adoption.

Task-Performance (Scientific Outcomes): Analysis of the Graded Lab Reports
Hypothesis H1 suggests that collaborating remotely would have a negative impact on scientific task-performance outcome measures. Only minimal support was found for this hypothesis. The average lab report scores for the first task session were identical

Table 10.2

Graded lab report scores (max. score = 100)

	Lab A					Lab B				
	Mean	SD	Max	Min	Range	Mean	SD	Max	Min	Range
Face-to-face	70.0	16.75	88	42	46	86.4	10.52	98	70	28
Remote	70.0	8.89	80	55	25	75.1	10.49	89	56	33

Table 10.3

Multivariate analysis of variance of differences between lab report scores

	Multivariate analysis of variance results		
Type of comparison	Df	F	p
Between group			
Condition: Face-to-face vs. remote	1	2.67	0.1198
Condition and order: Face-to-face first and remote second vs. remote first and face-to-face second	1	9.66	**0.0061**
Within group			
Face-to-face first vs. remote second	1	1.09	0.3110
Remote first vs. face-to-face second	1	11.24	**0.0035**

(70/100) for both the face-to-face and remote condition (table 10.2). Furthermore, using a multivariate analysis of variance test (row 1 in table 10.3), the differences in scores for the face-to-face and remote conditions are not statistically significant.[1]

Yet the data suggest that collaborating remotely first may have a positive effect on scientific outcomes in this context. When order is taken into account using a multivariate analysis of variance test (row 2 in table 10.3), the participants who collaborated remotely first scored significantly higher on the second task than did those who collaborated face-to-face first ($p < 0.01$). Furthermore, there is no statistically significant difference between face-to-face and remote lab scores for those participants who collaborated face-to-face first (row 3 in table 10.2). There is a statistically significant difference ($p < 0.01$), however, between the face-to-face and remote lab scores for those participants who collaborated remotely first (row 4 in table 10.3).

The only statistically significant correlation (at the 0.05 level) between scores across conditions and order occurs among scores within the group who collaborated remotely first. Using a Pearson correlation test, the value of the correlation between scores is 0.698, $p = 0.025$. That is, if the participants received a high grade on their first lab report created when collaborating remotely, then they were likely to receive a high grade when collaborating face-to-face. The converse is not supported; that is, the score that the participants received when collaborating face-to-face did not predict their score when collaborating remotely.

Previous research (e.g., Olson and Olson 2000) would predict that scores from a remote first session would be lower because the remote session would lack the richness of collocation and face-to-face interaction, including multiple and redundant communication channels, implicit cues, and spatial coreferences that are difficult to support via computer-mediated communications. This lack of richness is often thought to impair performance. Perhaps technical features such as seeing a partner's pointer and functions, optimistic shared control of scientific instrumentation and applications, improved videoconferencing providing multiple views, and high-quality audio communications are "good enough" for scientific tasks focusing on collecting, analyzing, and interpreting data.

Moreover, the literature would predict that the participants would learn more working together face-to-face and thus have higher scores afterward, whereas our data indicate that the participants performed better in a second, face-to-face collaboration after first collaborating remotely. One explanation for the difference in scores is that the activities in the second task were inherently more difficult to perform remotely than face-to-face. Replication of the study using a Solomon four-group design to obtain data from two consecutive face-to-face and remote sessions is needed to provide additional insights regarding any possible task effect. We looked to the postinterview data for further insights regarding these results.

The Participants' Perceptions of the Scientific Process: Postinterview Analysis

Hypothesis H2 proposes that the participants would find working remotely more difficult than working face-to-face. Analysis of the interviews provided only partial support for this hypothesis. As expected, the participants reported disadvantages to collaborating remotely. Nevertheless, the participants also reported that some of these disadvantages are not significant in scientific work contexts, and that coping strategies or work-arounds can reduce the impact of other disadvantages. Furthermore, the participants reported that remote collaboration offered several relative advantages compared with face-to-face collaboration (table 10.4).

Similar to previous studies (e.g., Olson and Olson 2000; Olson and Teasley 1996), the study participants reported face-to-face collaboration was more personal than remote collaboration. They said that working face-to-face was "more personal," "made it easier to express oneself," and "allowed for more chatting."

Of course, problems can also arise when working face-to-face. As one participant reported: "It was a little difficult at times to determine if ... [my partner] had

Table 10.4

Interview analysis: Participants' comments on remote collaboration compared to face-to-face collaboration

Disadvantage	Significance, coping strategy, or relative advantage
Interaction less personal	Doesn't matter for this work
Fewer cues from partner	Need to talk more frequently and descriptively
Some tasks are more difficult	Easier to explore system and ideas independently Having identical views of data visualization is better Working simultaneously on the data visualization increases productivity

something to say and she just wasn't saying it or she just wasn't sure.... I found it a little hard to communicate." Many of the participants reported that a lack of personal interaction when working remotely did not have a negative impact on their work. The impersonal nature of remote collaboration increased their productivity and facilitated collaborative intellectual contributions. As some of the participants explained:

If we were ... working side by side, we might tell more stories or something like that.... [Yet] if you're trying to get something done, sometimes the stories and stuff can get in your way.

It does make for a less interpersonal experience if you're not working right beside someone ... but [when working remotely] I had time to figure things out for myself instead of [my partner] just doing it and me just accepting what he was doing, or me doing it and him accepting what I did. This time [working remotely], we both got to figure it out and say "hey, look at this" in collaboration.

I think that being in separate rooms helps a little bit because it's more impersonal.... [You] just throw stuff back and forth more easily.

The participants also reported that when working remotely, they received fewer implicit cues about what their partner was doing and thinking. Similar to previous research (e.g., Clark 1996), the study participants explained that without these cues, it could be difficult to follow social interaction norms and assist one's collaborator:

[When collaborating face-to-face] it was a lot easier to ask questions of each other ... since you have a feeling [about] when to interrupt them.... If you're in the same room ... you'll wait [to ask a question] until the other person is not doing as much or not doing something very specific.

It is hard to get the context of any question that's asked because you're not paying attention to what the other person is doing because they're in a little [videoconferencing] screen.

To compensate for this lack of cues, several of the participants reported they needed to talk more frequently and descriptively when collaborating remotely. Some of the participants reported that:

even though we were in separate rooms, it kind of seemed like there was more interaction compared to being face-to-face, which seems kind of strange. . . . It just seemed more interaction was expected . . . maybe needed.

We had a really good interaction [when collaborating remotely]. . . . You're conscious that you're not together and you can't see [some things, and] so you think more about [interacting. For example, you think,] "I need to let this person know that I'm about to do this" or "this is what I'm seeing and I'm trying to let you know so, and you're like doing the same to me." Yeah, so [our interaction] was probably more. Interaction was really easier. It made [working together] better.

You have to be more descriptive with your words.

Thus, to compensate for the absence of implicit cues in the remote condition, many of the participants provided explicit cues for their partner. When working remotely, it appears that some individuals recognize they do not have a common shared physical reality and subsequently may not have a shared cognitive reality. Humans, though, are intrinsically motivated to develop a shared reality (Schutz and Luckmann 1973, 1989). Subsequently, the study participants developed and adopted a strategy of providing explicit cues to their partner to develop a shared reality. These explicit cues appear to be joint actions (Clark 1996) that help coordinate activities between the participants. The cues may contribute to a faster and more accurate formation of common ground and mutual understanding.

It is interesting to note that even with the disadvantages of remote collaboration and the need for coping strategies, many of the participants reported they could work and assume the roles similar to those they typically do when collaborating face-to-face. Two participants commented that:

[collaborating remotely] was just like if we had to sit down and do a group project and we were sitting right next to each other.

I tend to naturally take on the role of coordinator. So if anything seems like it's not getting done fast enough, I'll go and say, 'Well, you need to do this' or 'I need to do that.' So I think I . . . did this [collaborating remotely] because I do that with everything I do.

Schutz and Luckmann (1973, 1989) suggest that when developing a shared reality or acting within the context of different realities, individuals believe that differences will not keep them from achieving their goals. In Schutz and Luckmann's terms, individuals assume there is a congruence of relevance systems. This may explain why the participants assumed similar roles as if working face-to-face and succeeded working remotely.

In addition to receiving fewer cues from a partner when collaborating remotely, the participants also reported that some physical tasks are more difficult. These tasks include creating and sharing sketches of scientific structures, manipulating mathematical equations, and jointly using shared applications in NetMeeting. Some of these problems may be remedied by including more tools in the systems, such as MATLAB. Others may be remedied by advances in technology, such as shared applications that support multiple pointers and use optimistic concurrency for floor control. As two of the participants explained,

[when collaborating face-to-face] you could draw more easily, communicate diagrams more easily, and you could look at the other person and see their level of understanding more easily. The thing that frustrated me the most [collaborating remotely] was the shared applications [NetMeeting;] ... you could see the other person doing things but you couldn't do anything [simultaneously].

I caught myself pointing at my screen sometimes but [my partner] couldn't see my finger pointing at the screen.

Although technology made some tasks more difficult, the study participants also reported that the collaboratory system provides advantages over collaborating face-to-face. These advantages include the ability to work independently as well as collaboratively, having identical and unconstrained views of the data visualization, and working simultaneously with the data visualization.

I liked that we were separate. I think it gave a whole new twist on the interactions, and if one of us got snagged up with something the other could independently work and get it done rather than both of us being bogged down by having to work on it simultaneously.

I think the technology helped the interaction ... because ... one person could do a task and then the other ... has the chance to say, "OK, well maybe we can do it this way."

Sometimes when you're working side by side with somebody, you have to deal with "Well, you're looking at [the data] from a different angle than I am, and so you're seeing a different perspective there." Now [working remotely] we could both of us be straight on, having the exact same perspective from where we're sitting. It made it easier.

[My partner] could be changing the light focusing somewhere, while I could be zooming or moving [the plane] around. And that was really helpful because you're thinking, "OK, as soon as I'm done moving the light I want to go ahead and shift [the plane]" ... [to be able to] say to [my partner], "Why don't you [shift the plane] while I'm shining the light," was really cool. It was really helpful.

The participants in this study reported experiencing disadvantages of remote collaboration and the system that is similar to others that have been previously reported in the literature. Still, the study participants also reported that some disadvantages had minimal impact on their scientific work, and that they developed and used coping strategies to compensate for the disadvantages. They also perceived remote collaboration to provide some advantages relative to face-to-face collaboration. In addition, they reported that collaborating remotely was compatible with their previous ways of collaborating face-to-face. These findings elucidate our null result regarding scientific outcomes. Next we look at our data on innovation adoption.

Table 10.5

Mean questionnaire responses for collaboratory system attributes

	Mean (and SD) questionnaire responses scale: 1 (low) to 5 (high)					
Adoption Attribute	Face-to-face (n = 40)	Remote (n = 40)	Face-to-face session 1 (n = 20)	Remote session 1 (n = 20)	Face-to-face session 2 (n = 20)	Remote session 2 (n = 20)
Relative advantage	4.13 (0.60)	4.05 (0.72)	3.94 (0.54)	3.83 (0.87)	4.31 (0.61)	4.27 (0.45)
Compatibility	4.15 (0.64)	4.20 (0.60)	3.97 (0.60)	4.20 (0.66)	4.33 (0.64)	4.19 (0.55)
Complexity	1.26 (0.62)	1.30 (0.75)	1.41 (0.61)	1.25 (0.78)	1.10 (0.62)	1.35 (0.73)
Trialability	4.10 (0.80)	3.89 (0.82)	4.30 (0.49)	3.78 (0.96)	3.90 (1.00)	4.00 (0.65)
Observability	3.42 (0.85)	3.50 (0.72)	3.38 (0.83)	3.45 (0.77)	3.47 (0.89)	3.55 (0.68)

Collaboratory Adoption: Postquestionnaire Data Analysis

An analysis of the collaboratory adoption postquestionnaire data (table 10.5) yielded no support for hypothesis H3, that is, there was no support that study participants were more likely to adopt the system after using it face-to-face than remotely. We performed a multivariate analysis of variance test using a general linear model to investigate whether differences in the adoption questionnaire responses can be attributed to either condition—that is, working face-to-face or remotely—or any interaction effect between condition and order—that is, working face-to-face or remotely first.

The results indicate another null result. The differences in questionnaire responses due to condition are not statistically significant (at the $p < 0.05$ level). That is, the participants' perceptions of the system's relative advantage, compatibility, complexity, trialability, and observability were not significantly different from their perceptions after using the system face-to-face.

The data analysis indicates that there is only one statistically significant difference in questionnaire responses due to the interaction between condition and order. This difference is for relative advantage ($p < 0.01$). The participants' mean score for relative advantage was always greater after their second lab session, irrespective of the order of conditions.

The null results are surprising because intuition suggests the participants would perceive that the system provides fewer relative advantages when working remotely, and that using the system face-to-face would be more compatible with the participants' existing work patterns, norms, and values, developed primarily from face-to-face experiences. Furthermore, we expected the system would be perceived as less complex when working face-to-face because a partner who could offer assistance was collocated, and that the participants would not be able to observe their partner as well remotely as face-to-face. Even when working remotely, however, there was always a remote partner who could provide help and be observed to some extent, which may account for no statistically significant differences in the perceptions of complexity and observability between conditions. These results are consistent with the interview data.

The null results also help to eliminate some possible explanations for the other results. For example, one possible explanation for the task-performance results described earlier is that collaborating remotely first provided more time for the participants to independently learn to operate the system. Therefore, when subsequently working face-to-face, they understood the system better and could perform tasks more effectively. Yet there were no significant differences reported regarding trialability, observability, or complexity between the conditions, which one would expect if working remotely first let participants learn more about the system. Indeed, there is a slight trend for trialability to be perceived as higher when working face-to-face in general (4.10 versus 3.89) and after working face-to-face second (3.78 versus 3.90). These results, in sum, help eliminate this possible explanation for the task-performance results.

Limitations

This study has several limitations resulting in suggestions for further research. One limitation is the repeated measure design. A Solomon four-group design would allow additional comparisons among data from two consecutive face-to-face sessions and two consecutive remote sessions. These comparisons could increase our understanding of the differences between working face-to-face and remotely, including the differences caused by varying the order of working face-to-face and remotely, and the impact of any differences between the first and second task.

A second limitation can be found in our population sample. We used upper-level undergraduate science students, one segment of the overall population who conduct scientific research and are potential collaboratory users. This overall population also includes graduate and undergraduate research assistants, postdoctoral fellows, and faculty. The small number of individuals in these groups locally, the variance in their scientific knowledge, and the demands on their time kept us from including them in our population sample. The entire participant sample for the ongoing ethnographic study of the collaboratory system is taken from this working scientist population. The presence or lack of correlation between data from the two studies will help confirm or refute the validity and reliability of the current study.

A third limitation focuses on the tasks. Although the tasks are representative of natural science data collection, analysis, and interpretation, they do not encompass the entire life cycle of the scientific process. Problem formulation, research design, and research dissemination were not included in the tasks. Furthermore, the tasks in session 1 and 2 differed. Although designed to be similar in complexity, additional investigation may uncover aspects of the tasks that are inherently impacted by an interaction condition.

Discussion

The data from the scientific task outcome measures, postinterviews, and collaboratory adoption postquestionnaires do not support the hypotheses that working remotely would be less effective and more difficult than working face-to-face, or that working remotely would have a negative impact on the participants' perceptions regarding innovation adoption. This leads us to conclude that there is a positive potential for the development and adoption of scientific collaboratory systems. The participants were able to adequately complete scientific work when collaborating remotely, readily developed and used strategies to compensate for system deficiencies, and developed positive attitudes toward adoption.

Schutz and Luckmann's theory of the life-world (1973, 1989) may be used to explain some of the behaviors and responses we saw. Working remotely can be considered an example of a problematic situation in which individuals cannot assume their physical world is the same as that of their collaborators'. At the same time, humans have a desire to develop a shared reality. Although individuals may have different types and degrees of motivation in establishing a shared reality, we strive to assume a shared reality, an intersubjectivity, at least to the degree necessary for our current purposes (Clark 1996).

When developing a shared reality or acting within the context of different realities, Schutz and Luckmann propose that individuals assume that differences will not keep them from achieving their goals. That is, individuals assume there is a congruence of relevance systems. Schutz and Luckmann further propose that individuals assume that were they together, they would experience things the same way—that is, individuals assume there is an interchangeability of standpoints.

When working remotely, the participants' different physical locations and the system's limitations in fully as well as accurately representing the remote location may provide strong evidence that causes the participants to believe they do not have a shared reality. Their motivation to develop a shared reality, however, makes them seem willing to work proactively at developing that shared reality, and to assume that the physical location differences will not keep them from completing their tasks (a congruence of relevance systems). For example, none of the study participants reported an inability to do science when working with their partner remotely. This is especially interesting considering that 75 percent of the study participants had not worked with their partner previously. The participants appear further to assume an interchangeability of standpoints. They take explicit joint actions to develop a shared reality, using language to share their experiences and standpoint. For example, the participants said that when collaborating remotely, they discussed what they were currently doing with their partner more frequently and in greater detail than when working face-to-face. These explicit joint actions may help to create a shared reality and assist in task performance. The joint actions compensate for a lack of physical collocation as well as limitations in the system's ability to represent the remote physical location fully and accurately.

In comparison, when working face-to-face, the shared physical location helps individuals believe there is also a shared reality. Individuals may, perhaps erroneously, assume a shared reality already exists or that it is more comprehensive than it really is. Knowledge about each other gained through the interpersonal interactions that commonly occur in face-to-face situations may also reinforce the perception of an existing shared reality. For instance, the study participants reported they have more interpersonal interactions when collaborating face-to-face. Personal knowledge about a collaborator and a shared physical location may influence or strengthen an individual's assumptions about a shared reality, and subsequently reduce the type and number of joint actions whose purpose is to develop a shared reality.

More research is needed to explore whether Schutz and Luckmann's life-world theory definitively explains our results, and if so, what the implications are for collaboratory system design. The theory of the life-world seems to imply, for example, that situation awareness is critical to collaboratory systems. Yet are all system features, including multiple communication channels, synchronous task execution, and haptics, equally important for situation awareness? In other work (Sonnenwald, Maglaughlin, and Whitton 2004) we begin to explore these issues, proposing that contextual, task and process, and socioemotional information is needed to create and maintain situation awareness when performing tasks collaboratively across distances. We further suggest that when designing collaboratory systems, control, sensory, distraction, and realism attributes of technology should be considered with respect to their ability to facilitate access to these types of information. Continued evaluation of emerging collaboratory systems is required to explore these issues, and enable us to realize the full potential of e-Science and e-Social Science.

Acknowledgments

Our thanks to the study participants; to Martin Guthold, Richard Superfine, and Dorothy Erie, who generously shared their natural science expertise and data in developing the scientific tasks and lab reports; to Leila Plummer, Ron Bergquist, and Atsuko Negishi, who helped run the experiment sessions; to Bin Li, who helped with interview data analysis; and to the team who developed the nanoManipulator, including Frederick P. Brooks Jr., Aron Helser, Tom Hudson, Kevin Jeffay, Don Smith, and Russell M. Taylor II. This research was supported by the National Institutes of Health's National Center for Research Resources, NCRR 5-P41-RR02170. This chapter is based on a paper originally published in *ACM Transactions on Human-Computer Interaction* 10, no. 2 (2003): 150–176. © 2003 ACM, Inc. Included here by permission.

Note

1. The average lab report scores were greater in the second task session for both conditions, indicating a possible learning effect. This difference is accounted for in the analysis of variance computation.

References

Bellotti, V., and P. Dourish. 1997. Rant and RAVE: Experimental and experiential accounts of a media space. In *Video-mediated communication*, ed. K. Finn, A. Sellen, and S. Wilbur, 245–272. Mahwah, NJ: Lawrence Erlbaum.

Berg, B. L. 1989. *Qualitative research methods for the social sciences*. Boston: Allyn and Bacon.

Clark, H. 1996. *Using language*. Cambridge: Cambridge University Press.

Dourish, P., A. Adler, V. Bellotti, and A. Henderson. 1996. Your place or mine? Learning from long-term use of audio-video communication. *Computer Supported Cooperative Work* 5 (1): 33–62.

Finch, M., V. Chi, R. M. Taylor II, M. Falvo, S. Washburn, and R. Superfine. 1995. Surface modification tools in a virtual environment interface to a scanning probe microscope. In *Proceedings of the ACM symposium on interactive 3D graphics: Special issue of computer graphics*, 13–18. New York: ACM Press.

Flanagan, J. C. 1954. The critical incidence technique. *Psychological Bulletin* 51:1–22.

Grudin, J. 1994. Eight challenges for developers. *Communications of the ACM* 37 (1): 92–105.

Guthold, M., M. R. Falvo, W. G. Matthews, S. Paulson, S. Washburn, D. A. Erie et al. 2000. Controlled manipulation of molecular samples with the nanoManipulator. *IEEE/ASME Transactions on Mechatronics* 5 (2): 189–198.

Guthold, M., G. Matthews, A. Negishi, R. M. Taylor, D. Erie, F. P. Brooks et al. 1999. Quantitative manipulation of DNA and viruses with the nanoManipulator scanning force microscope. *Surface Interfacial Analysis* 27 (5–6): 437–443.

Harrison, S., S. Bly, and A. Anderson. 1997. The media space. In *Video-mediated communication*, ed. K. Finn, A. Sellen, and S. Wilbur, 273–300. Mahwah, NJ: Lawrence Erlbaum.

Hudson, T., A. Helser, M. Whitton, and D. H. Sonnenwald. 2004. Managing collaboration in the nanoManipulator. *Presence: Teleoperators and Virtual Environments* 13 (2): 193–210.

Olson, G. M., and J. S. Olson. 2000. Distance matters. *Human-Computer Interaction* 15 (2–3): 139–178.

Olson, J. S., and S. Teasley. 1996. Groupware in the wild: Lessons learned from a year of virtual collocation. In *Proceedings of the 1996 ACM conference on computer-supported cooperative work*, 419–427. New York: ACM Press.

Orlikowski, W. 1993. Learning from Notes: Organizational issues in groupware implementation. *Information Society* 9 (3): 237–252.

Robson, C. 2002. *Real world research, 2nd ed.* Cambridge, MA: Blackwell.

Rogers, E. 2003. *Diffusion of innovations, 5th ed.* New York: Free Press.

Schutz, A., and T. Luckmann. 1973. *The structures of the life-world, vol. I.* Evanston, IL: Northwestern University Press.

Schutz, A., and T. Luckmann. 1989. *The structures of the life-world, vol. II.* Evanston, IL: Northwestern University Press.

Shneiderman, B. 1997. *Designing the user interface.* Boston: Addison-Wesley.

Sonnenwald, D. H. 2003. Expectations for a scientific collaboratory: A case study. In *Proceedings of the ACM GROUP 2003 conference*, 68–74. New York: ACM Press.

Sonnenwald, D. H., R. Berquist, K. L. Maglaughlin, E. Kupstas-Soo, and M. C. Whitton. 2001. Designing to support collaborative scientific research across distances: The nanoManipulator example. In *Collaborative virtual environments*, ed. E. Churchill, D. Snowdon, and A. Munro, 202–224. London: Springer Verlag.

Sonnenwald, D. H., K. L. Maglaughlin, and M. C. Whitton. 2001. Using innovation diffusion theory to guide collaboration technology evaluation: Work in progress. In *IEEE 10th international workshop on enabling technologies: Infrastructure for collaborative enterprises (WETICE)*, 114–119. New York: IEEE Press.

Sonnenwald, D. H., K. L. Maglaughlin, and M. C. Whitton. 2004. Designing to support situational awareness across distances: An example from a scientific collaboratory. *Information Processing and Management* 40 (6): 989–1011.

Star, S. L., and K. Ruhleder. 1996. Steps toward an ecology of infrastructure. *Information Systems Research* 7:111–134.

Taylor, R. M., II, and R. Superfine. 1999. Advanced interfaces to scanning probe microscopes. In *Handbook of nanostructured materials and nanotechnology, vol. II*, ed. H. S. Malwa, 271–308. New York: Academic Press.

Tornatzky, L. G., and M. Fleischer. 1990. *The process of technological innovation.* Lexington, MA: Lexington Books.

IV Biological and Health Sciences

11 The National Institute of General Medical Sciences Glue Grant Program

Michael E. Rogers and James Onken

This chapter describes the history and development of the National Institute of General Medical Sciences (NIGMS) glue grant program. It includes an overview of the initial five consortia funded through this program. Our goal is to convey the rationale for this program and provide sufficient descriptions of these initial programs to show that each consortium represents a different experiment in the conduct of collaborative research on a large scale. The descriptions contained herein reflect the early development of the glue grant program and the nature of the glue grants during the first period of their awards, generally in their first couple of years. Each of these early glue grants is discussed in the present tense but will be further along and may be significantly modified by the time the reader encounters this chapter. The chapter is intended to offer a useful history and background against which changes and future outcomes can be evaluated and understood. In that regard, this chapter also includes a discussion of evaluations planned by the NIGMS of its large grant programs in general, including the glue grant program.

History and Concepts

Science itself not only evolves but so too does the way it is practiced. That an evolutionary leap in the sociology of science had occurred and that science was moving into a more integrative phase seemed evident to the NIGMS staff as a result of meetings held in May 1998. The director of the institute, Dr. Marvin Cassman, asked the division heads to organize these meetings with the scientific community to assess opportunities and barriers in the fields covered by the NIGMS in advance of an anticipated growth in the institute's budget. A common theme that emerged from the meetings was a desire of already-funded investigators to work together on the solution of complex biomedical problems. This represented a major shift: established scientists who held NIGMS-supported individual investigator-initiated basic research ("R01 research") grants were asking for a mechanism to provide support for them to work together in a teamlike fashion. Independent investigators from many disciplines needed processes and an infrastructure to align, coordinate, and integrate their research efforts. This lack constituted a significant barrier to solving major complex biological problems. Existing grant mechanisms were not viewed as adequate for this purpose.

Over the last fifty years, reductionist science has and continues to supply spectacular advances in the understanding of organisms and cells at increasingly lower levels of organization as well as higher levels of resolution, down to the single molecule level. This work is carried out primarily in the laboratories of individual investigators. Now, individual investigators have a growing desire to understand how their parts of the puzzle fit to make the functional whole, to understand how a complex system operates in a mechanistic, predictable fashion. Such a goal requires the combined efforts of scientists from different fields and the use of sophisticated, expensive tools that are difficult to justify for an individual project alone. It also requires the involvement of physical scientists used to thinking about tool development and engineers used to thinking about how systems function. The trend is toward cooperation, collaboration, and integration. The human genome project has provided validation for both team approaches and doing less hypothesis-driven discovery research where the goal is the collection of data that provide a basis for generating hypotheses later. Both of these approaches are typically necessary to make integrative efforts successful. Biological systems add new layers of complexity. And the integration of all these efforts requires a substantial investment in the newly developing fields of bioinformatics and computational biology. In 1998, it seemed clear that a mechanism was needed to support large-scale, collaborative approaches beyond the capabilities of any one laboratory, and that these would require a substantial investment.

The institute was challenged to respond to this new development, and a significant response was enabled by the fact that the National Institutes of Health (NIH) was just beginning the period of the doubling of its budget (1999–2003). Thus, funds were likely to be available to support new initiatives and programs. The NIGMS staff began to develop a new initiative and coined the term glue grants in summer 1998 because the support mechanism being formulated was meant to "glue" the investigators together into a collaborative and integrative team. Each participating investigator in a glue grant is required to already have independent research support for their individual efforts in order to be part of the consortium. A follow-up meeting of outside consultants in November 1998 led to the recommendation that the NIGMS initiate two glue grant programs—a large one and a smaller one—to accommodate two different needs. The upper limit for the large-scale projects was recommended at $5 million in direct costs per year, and the upper limit for the smaller glues was $300,000 per year in direct costs. Eventually, the name glue grants became associated with the large-scale projects, and the NIGMS later began to refer to the smaller awards as Collaborative Project Grants instead of small glue grants.

The NIGMS request for applications for Large-Scale Collaborative Projects went out in May 1999 and the three subsequent years. The first awards, phase I, provided a $25,000 planning grant to enable successful initial applicants to submit phase II applications for the full-scale award. Because of growing uncertainties over future increases in the institute's budget, applications were not accepted for phase II funding that would begin in either fiscal year 2004 or 2005. This institute did reissue an announcement in fiscal year 2004 for glue grants for phase II funding that would begin in either fiscal year 2006, 2007, or 2008. This most recent issuance was made as a program announcement rather than a request for applications, which meant that there was no set-aside of funds and that applications would have to compete more directly with other institute priorities. But by offering the funding opportunity for a three-year period, the NIGMS relieved applicants of time pressure to meet a particular deadline. In essence, the institute chose to continue to offer the glue grants to the scientific community as one of many mechanisms that investigators can employ to conduct science.

As preparation for drafting the first announcement for large glue grants, institute staff consulted with staff in other NIH institutes and funding agencies who managed large-scale programs. The National Science Foundation's (NSF) experiences with its Science and Technology Centers (STC) program was particularly valuable. One staff member from the NSF stated that an important lesson learned was that "you don't give an investigator several million dollars and say tell me in five years what you have done," no matter how much you believe in investigator-initiated research. The NIGMS staff took this message—the need for both strong agency oversight and investigators to propose a sound project management plan up front—to heart. First, the institute set the bar high in requiring investigators to propose a solution to the complex biomedical problem within ten years, not just to make progress on the biomedical problem being investigated. Glue grants are limited to an initial period of support of up to five years, and if successful on renewal application, one additional period of up to five years, for a ten-year maximum. The NIGMS also built in several measures of accountability: proposed annual milestones that had to be addressed in the application and updated in annual progress reports; a requirement for a steering committee to assist in governance; a required committee of outside experts to advise the principal investigator; annual progress reports on each glue grant made to the National Advisory General Medical Sciences Council; and a required internal plan for evaluation. Because these awards would be spending up to $100,000 in research funds per week, it was crucial to maintain consistent forward progress. Thus, a project management plan was a required element of the application and the awards were issued as cooperative agreements, instead of grants, so that an NIGMS staff member could work closely with the grantees (including serving on the steering committee).

Designing a large grant program where the funds were to go for collaborative activities—the glue—and not individual efforts was a challenge. Up to that point, the

NIGMS had not offered an award specifically for collaborations. Even in its larger multi-investigator funding mechanisms—program project grants or center grants—the research efforts were primarily focused on individual projects within those overall awards. In addressing this need for a new mechanism, the institute wished to provide investigators with maximum flexibility to design a project that fit the needs of the biomedical problem being solved, but did not want to support research that was more appropriately supported by the R01 mechanism and individual efforts. It was anticipated that a lot of the funds would go to supporting cores, which are organizational subunits devoted to the production of data or resources of a specific type, such as an instrument facility, a facility for cell culture, or a data analysis laboratory. Cores serve all or most of the investigators within the consortium. It was also recognized, however, that research in individual laboratories would be necessary to fill in gaps and bridge R01 efforts to the work of the consortium, to add to the cohesiveness of the overall project. In addition to core laboratories, support was allowed for such bridging projects. To add investigators with relevant expertise yet no relevant support in the area, a limited number of pilot projects were also allowed. The NIGMS later further increased the flexibility in how these different elements could be assembled and combined based on feedback from the applicant community. Nevertheless, applicants and reviewers were instructed that if research in any of the elements proposed was more appropriate as R01-styled projects, then that element was not appropriate as part of the glue grant. The mechanism to support individual projects already existed, and it was important that the glue grant funds go to support consortium activities—that is, the glue.

It was also clear that projects of this magnitude could encompass a substantial portion of the leading researchers in an area, or perhaps the field in its entirety. The logical conclusion was that these efforts would serve not just the participating investigators but also the field in general. Furthermore, there was a concern about how large-scale projects would affect other researchers in the area, especially new investigators. The applicants were therefore required to propose measures by which each large-scale project would consider and respond to concerns of the scientific community directly affected, and a consideration of community views was to be included on the agenda for meetings of the glue grant steering committee with its advisory committee. To serve this role, ease this concern, and be consistent with NIH goals, the open sharing of research resources was mandated. These resources included data, reagents, genetically modified animals, and software. A data dissemination core was required of all applications. Specific research resource-sharing requirements were negotiated for each glue grant, depending on the types of data and resources being generated (for example, data versus transgenic animals) as well as the overall approach of the glue grant (say, linear or parallel data flow), and were made part of the grant award notice. Variations in approach were allowed as long as the policies used were consistent with NIH research resource-sharing policy. In general, awardees, being cognizant of how they served larger communities, proposed and agreed to more stringent data- and resource-sharing policies than required by the NIH. Each glue grant has a Web site, and lists available resources and how to access consortium databases.

The NIGMS itself was presented with a number of administrative challenges. Having staff serve on the steering committees for each of the glue grants represented a deeper level of involvement in awards than was typical. It consumed a great deal of staff time and raised questions of how to protect staff from appearances of conflict of interest; for instance, it was decided that the NIGMS project officers for the glue grants would not be allowed to attend the review of the renewal applications. This deeper involvement led quickly in the early years of the initial glue grants to the conclusion that bioinformatics efforts needed to be enhanced in each of the existing glue grants, and supplements were made to fund these efforts. The wide involvement of so many researchers raised concerns with management of the peer review of glue grant applications. When one considers that a sizable fraction of the researchers in an area and up to twenty universities are included, who will be left to participate in the study section and advisory council reviews? Fortunately, while this aspect has made review difficult, experience has shown it not to be an insurmountable problem. One has to keep in mind that the fundamental independent work has already been reviewed as R01s, and that what is being reviewed in the phase I and II applications are the glue efforts. Thus, the primary considerations in phase I and II glue reviews revolve around whether this self-selected group of investigators should be supported to work together on the problem chosen, in the way proposed, and at what cost.

The Existing Glue Grants

The normal mode of operation for R01-styled research is for a PhD or MD investigator to head a project that would also include students, postdoctoral scientists still in training, and technicians. These principal-investigator-led teams usually comprise three to five people. For a glue grant, a principal investigator heads a team of equals, involving a much larger number of PhD and/or MD participating investigators, and comprising many, if not most, of the leading investigators in the relevant areas. Once a problem had been selected, the grantees faced a number of challenges: Who would lead? Who would be included? What would be the basic strategy of the collaboration? How would the participants communicate and coordinate over distance within the collaboration and with the larger community? What would be the incentives to participate and be productive? How would credit be apportioned? What would the career impact be for junior investigators and technical personnel? What would the priorities be for access to the resulting research resources? How would intellectual property be assigned or shared? The NIGMS did not prescribe answers to these questions but only insisted that they be addressed. It was anticipated that different administrative and managerial

Table 11.1
The existing glue grants and principal investigators are listed below in order of date first supported

Glue grant name	Start date	Lead principal investigator	No. of institutions/ participants*	Web site
Alliance for Cellular Signaling	2000	Alfred Gilman, University of Texas Health Sciences Center at Dallas	20/50	⟨http://www.signaling-gateway.org⟩
Cell Migration Consortium	2001	Alan R. Horwitz, University of Virginia	12/31	⟨http://www.cellmigration.org⟩
Consortium for Functional Glycomics	2001	James Paulson, Scripps Research Institute	12/44	⟨http://www.functionalglycomics.org⟩
Inflammation and the Host Response to Injury	2001	Ronald Tompkins, Massachusetts General Hospital	19/46	⟨http://www.gluegrant.org⟩
LIPID MAPS Consortium	2003	Edward Dennis, University of California at San Diego	8/40	⟨http://www.lipidmaps.org⟩

*These numbers are approximate as of the date of application; actual numbers usually increased during the course of the award.

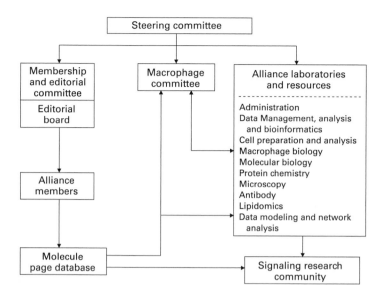

Figure 11.1
Alliance for Cellular Signaling

structures might be required for different scientific problems depending on the scale, scope, and present level of development of the problem. Therefore, each glue grant was expected to be an experiment in itself in supporting a new approach to solving a major biological problem.

The Alliance for Cellular Signaling

The goal of the Alliance for Cellular Signaling (AfCS) is a descriptive and quantitative understanding of intracellular signaling in a mammalian cell—that is, a molecular- and mathematical-level understanding of how external inputs lead to functional outputs, enabling the creation of a "virtual cell." The alliance's approach is to collect input/output data on a large scale using highly standardized cells and reagents, and accomplish this in AfCS laboratories that are distinct from the participating investigator laboratories to further ensure the reproducibility of results. Concurrently, the AfCS would organize and analyze this data computationally to eventually develop testable models and hypotheses. The goals are to generate high-throughput data, relationships between inputs and outputs, and predictive models that can be investigated in hypothesis-driven, R01-style research in individual investigator laboratories, both those associated with the AfCS and those that are unassociated.

The AfCS is often viewed as the archetypal glue grant, probably because it was the first to be funded and is headed by a well-known leader in the field, Nobel laureate, Dr. Alfred Gilman. In fact, the alliance and the other glue grants differ from each other, not only scientifically but also organizationally. All work is done in AfCS laboratories, and is initiated and developed as separate and freestanding entities to support the specifications of the alliance management for the production of the data and reagents desired. Hence, it functions organizationally somewhat like a small biotech company might. It is unusual in two other respects as well. First, the consortium received significant additional support from two other NIH institutes (the National Institute of Allergy and Infectious Diseases and the National Cancer Institute), and second, by agreement of the participating investigators and the host institutions, all intellectual property rights have been relinquished, except for a few pilot projects. All data are therefore made publicly available as soon as they are validated, and AfCS members do not enjoy preferential access.

The AfCS has an annual meeting for participating investigators and invited guests, including members of the external advisory committee, where the progress from the alliance laboratories is presented. Challenges for the year ahead are also presented and discussed. Time is set aside at this meeting for a get-together of the steering committee and the advisory committee, where a frank assessment and advice are provided to Gilman and the steering committee. The steering committee also meets monthly by a videoconference that includes the NIGMS program director responsible for the glue grant. Videoconferencing is the preferred format for steering committee meetings for most, but not all, of the glue grants.

An early AfCS decision related to how information generated by the consortium would be disseminated to the larger scientific community. The alliance initiated a collaboration with the Nature Publishing Group to set up a user interface that would combine AfCS data with Nature reviews and reports on a Web site called the Signaling Gateway. This Web site was meant to become a major reference for the signaling community. Offered at no charge, the Web site served as the gateway to the AfCS data center and a repository of Molecule Pages, a database of information on signaling molecules. The Molecule Pages were authored by volunteer scientists and were peer-reviewed by the editorial board. As such, they are equivalent to reference articles (with hyperlinks to consortium data) on each signaling molecule. By counting as a publication, they provide additional incentive to participate.

The Cell Migration Consortium

The Cell Migration Consortium (CMC) is codirected by Dr. Alan R. Horwitz and Dr. Thomas Parsons; these two scientists lead as a team, generally sharing the time when presentations about the CMC are made. The CMC employs a distinctly different consortium strategy from the AfCS. The program's goal is to overcome critical technical and conceptual barriers restraining progress on research on cell migration. The aims are to generate reagents, technologies, and information for the cell migration field; catalyze interdisciplinary research in cell migration by recruiting chemists, engineers, physicists, mathematicians, and structural biologists; develop new cross-disciplinary research strategies to study cell movement, signaling, and structure; and generate certain unique scientific outcomes unlikely to arise from individual research efforts. The scientific focus is on catalyzing and enabling progress by the field as a whole, rather than on the mass production of information by the CMC itself. A final aim is to integrate all that is known about cell migration proteins into a cell migration knowledge base.

The primary effort here is to address and overcome barriers to research in the area of cell migration by forming interdisciplinary teams of investigators to address the barriers in several areas. Instead of having the work done in the consortium laboratories and service cores, as with the AfCS, the work is primarily done in individual participating investigator laboratories that receive direct funding from the glue grant. The participating laboratories are aggregated into collaborative clusters directed toward "initiatives" and "facilities" intended to catalyze and facilitate research in cell migration. The initiatives represent clusters of projects, and investigators clustered around a subarea and the facilities represent cores for consortium activities; most also have development activities as well. Thus, there are initiatives to discover new proteins, determine the structures of multimolecular complexes, develop new probes for signaling processes, develop transgenic and knockout mice (laboratory mice in which a gene has been interrupted or displaced by a piece of DNA, thus "knocking out" the gene), and develop mathematical models. There are facilities for biomaterials, patterned substrates and quantitative assays, and the development of imaging/photomanipulation technology. There is also a bioinformatics core to amass data and information, and develop tools for sharing them.

The consortium initiatives and facilities generally meet once monthly by videoconference, although subgroups meet as frequently as daily. The steering committee meets at least two times a year as needed. The CMC also holds an annual meeting once a year for progress review, planning, and development of the next year's milestones.

Information about the activities of the consortium is disseminated via its Web site and through workshops at one or two meetings in the field each year. The consortium has sponsored focused workshops at major annual meetings. Data and other research resources available for sharing are posted on the consortium's Web site. Investigators outside the consortium can request reagent and animal resources by contacting the coprincipal investigators or the principal investigators responsible for the activity listed on the Web site. An interesting facet of the CMC organization is the commitment to sharing research resources with the community as soon as it is released to the consortium members. There is no internal Web site for consortium members, so the results from a particular initiative are unknown to members of other initiatives until they are placed on the public Web site.

The CMC subsequent to funding entered into a collaboration with the Nature Publishing Group to establish the Cell Migration Gateway as the official Web site of the

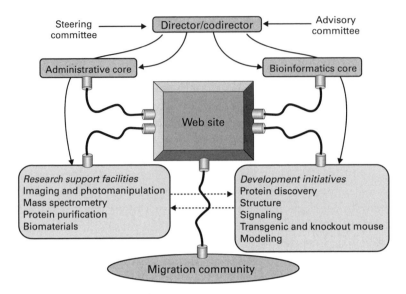

Figure 11.2
Cell Migration Consortium

consortium and a resource center for the field. The Web site includes three components: a Cell Migration Update to provide articles, summaries, and updates on key findings in cell migration research as well as disseminate the results of the consortium's activities; a Cell Migration Knowledgebase to house and integrate data and fact files in the field; and a CMC Activity Center to access information on consortium activities, developments, and data.

The Consortium for Functional Glycomics

The Consortium for Functional Glycomics (CFG) is led by Dr. James Paulson at the Scripps Research Institute. The overarching goal of the CFG is to define the paradigms by which carbohydrate-protein interactions at the cell surface mediate cell-cell communication. An immediate contrast can be drawn between the CFG and the CMC. Whereas the vast majority of the CMC's funding goes to support consortium work done in the labs of the participating investigators, about 90 percent of the CFG's funding goes to support the consortium's cores. The cores include information and bioinformatics, analytic glycotechnology, carbohydrate synthesis/protein expression, gene microarray, mouse transgenics, mouse phenotyping, and protein-carbohydrate interactions.

Membership is open to any investigator worldwide working within the scope of the consortium. The participating investigators now number over two hundred and have two responsibilities: exploring biology using the tools provided by the consortium,

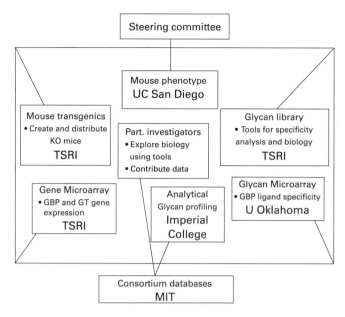

Figure 11.3
Consortium for Functional Glycomics

and contributing the data derived by using consortium tools to the consortium's databases and Web site.

The steering committee led by the principal investigator is the governing body of the consortium. This committee establishes the operating principles, priorities, and milestones for the cores. The steering committee meets for two hours by videoconference every other week to review progress, set and review quarterly goals for each core, and review requests for core resources and services. The cores report progress on these clearly defined goals on a quarterly basis. It was Paulson's experience in industry that led him to institute this quarterly reporting system.

The steering committee utilizes subcommittees and the participating investigator subgroups to aid in priority setting. The participating investigators join subgroups based on the relevance of their research to the carbohydrate-binding protein families studied by the consortium. These subcommittees and subgroups provide the steering committee with recommendations for setting priorities on the production of reagents, models, and technologies to study glycan-binding proteins and the enzymes involved in the expression of carbohydrate ligands.

The CFG holds an annual meeting of the participating investigators to report on progress from both the cores and the participating investigators, and solicit feedback from the participating investigators. The steering committee also holds an annual meeting with the external advisory committee. The codirectors and core directors report progress and solicit the advisory committee's advice. Overall, information and data dissemination are accomplished through the consortium Web site representing a portal to a set of integrated databases, a quarterly letter to members, subgroup e-mail lists, and presentations by the participating investigators and the steering committee members at scientific meetings, including but not limited to Gordon conferences, the annual meeting of the Society for Glycobiology, and the annual meeting of the participating investigators.

Inflammation and the Host Response to Injury

Dr. Ronald Tompkins at the Massachusetts General Hospital heads the Inflammation and the Host Response to Injury glue grant. The overarching goal of this consortium is to discover the biological reasons why different patients with a similar traumatic injury or severe burns have dramatically different outcomes. The immediate, specific goal is to determine whether changes in gene expression in circulating lymphocytes can serve as a predictor for which patients will progress from injury to multiple organ failure. The underlying hypothesis of this effort is that individual differences in the host's inflammatory and immune systems (both the innate and acquired responses) drive the systemic response to traumatic injury, and that many of the mechanistic details may be ascertained from the peripheral blood leukocytes. While pathophysiological mechanisms occur in tissues separate from the circulating blood, these researchers contend that peripheral leukocytes are readily obtainable and can offer a useful window to other compartments. This is the only NIGMS glue grant with a substantial clinical component.

The collaborative effort is performing a time series, whole genome expression analysis on a broad population of critically ill, injured patients. To accomplish these aims, the injury consortium needs to enroll sufficient patients using stringent entry criteria, and use the same or similar standards of care. The investigators first needed to assure that reproducible biological samples actually could be obtained at multiple clinical sites, and that the expression data obtained was usable and of high quality. The group also needed to create a clinical database that included information likely to be necessary for understanding the genomic data. Institutional Review Board approval was required at all clinical, analytic, and storage sites to cover the enrollment of patients and the collection of samples, processing, and the transfer of blood samples and data to the appropriate sites. Moreover, the collaborative effort is developing new methods to analyze the data, and then derive biological meaning from a massive genomic and clinical data set. This glue grant also includes an animal component to compare animal and human responses to determine which animal models are useful predictors of the human situation.

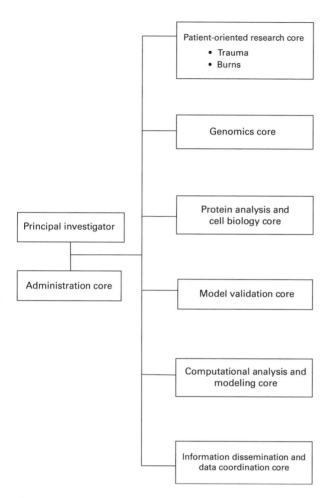

Figure 11.4
Inflammation and the Host Response to Injury

The injury glue grant is organized into seven cores: administrative, information dissemination and data coordination, computational analysis and modeling, model validation, protein analysis and cell biology, genomics, and patient-oriented research. Priority setting and progress for these cores is overseen by the steering committee, which meets four times a year in face-to-face meetings. Numerous other meetings occur during the year within and between core personnel, with individuals traveling to others' laboratories for training or discussions. There is also a weekly teleconference that includes representatives for all the cores where current problems are identified, possible solutions discussed, and plans/timelines agreed on. Most individual cores have weekly or biweekly teleconferences as well. Because of the need to obtain agreement on standards of care for patient research and standards for biological research, this group has preferred face-to-face meetings rather than videoconferencing. An important aspect of this glue grant is the need for coordination among the cores, which must act in a carefully orchestrated sequence.

Data and research resources are disseminated through publications, a database, and a Web site. Researchers in the scientific area of the consortium are invited to join the consortium on agreeing to the standards of conduct statement. Because of the need to protect sensitive patient information, the information in the database is coded; in order to gain entry to the patient core database, researchers must receive approval first by their own Institutional Review Board.

The Lipid Metabolites and Pathways Strategy

The Lipid Metabolites and Pathways Strategy (LIPID MAPS) consortium, headed by Dr. Edward Dennis of the University of California at San Diego, is the most recently awarded NIGMS glue grant. The specific goals are to discover and characterize all the lipids in the macrophage cell (at rest and activated), quantify the six major classes of lipids, determine the subcellular locations of lipids over time, and define the biochemical pathways and interactions for each lipid. One of the consortium's intents is to develop an international infrastructure for lipidomics research.

The LIPID MAPS consortium is organized into six focus areas: administrative, lipidomics, cell biology, lipid detection and quantitation, lipid synthesis and characterization, and informatics. These focus areas include a mixture of cores and/or bridging projects. The lipidomics focus area is further divided into six cores covering different classes of lipids, and two bridging projects covering oxidized lipids and lipid subcellular localization. In addition to the steering committee and the external advisory committee, the administrative structure includes an operating committee and a University of California at San Diego advisory committee.

A challenge for the LIPID MAPS consortium was to improve standardization to enable the comparison of results across laboratories. The consortium developed a bioinformatics infrastructure for the deposition of data on cellular lipids and the enzymes involved in lipid metabolism. This database was made more useful by the establishment of a lipid classification scheme that involved obtaining the consensus of and adoption by lipid researchers from around the world. The consortium has also developed a single, specific form of a commonly used cell activator called lipopolysaccharide as well as a variety of previously unavailable lipid standards for quantitation by mass spectrometry. These reagents along with the protocols for cell preparation and lipid analyses are made available for the broader scientific community interested in lipid and macrophage cell biology and function.

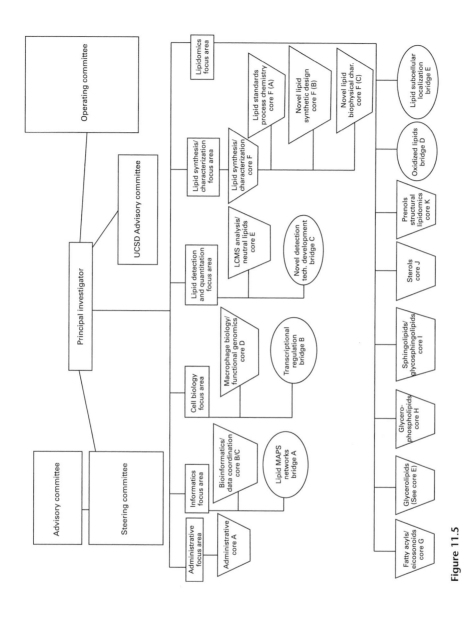

Figure 11.5

Lipid Metabolites and Pathways Strategy

Communication across the consortium is accomplished by an annual meeting, semiannual workshops, and bimonthly videoconferences. Data dissemination is accomplished through these meetings, the LIPID MAPS database and Web site, and peer-reviewed publications. Reagents produced by the consortium will be available to the scientific community at a reasonable cost through industry partners after standardization by the consortium in cases where the demand exceeds what a laboratory can easily produce within its operating budget.

Conclusion: Some Crosscutting Issues

While each glue grant's scientific focus and organizational structure is different, one similarity for all of them stands out: these large-scale efforts are played out in open view. The Web sites present comprehensive and in-depth descriptions of the consortia and their activities. The databases are open to the broader scientific community. An emphasis is placed on making data, information, and research resources available to nonconsortium members as quickly as possible through the use of databases and Web sites. The consortia are also making use of peer-reviewed publications for data and information dissemination. Intellectual property agreements are in place to ensure that the academic use of these resources will not be impeded. They are consistent with both university and NIH guidelines.

A common problem encountered by leaders of glue grants is the difficulty in responding to opportunities as they arise during the course of the award and in dealing with units within the consortium that are not performing well. The principal investigator depends on the willing cooperation of the participating investigators. Moving funds from one investigator to another during the course of the award carries the risk of creating resentment and disharmony within the group. The steering committees have proved valuable in this regard by backing the principal investigators when needed changes had to be implemented. The principal investigators have also expressed a desire for undesignated funds that could be used as needed or as opportunities arise.

The integration and sharing of data through the development of a sound bioinformatics and computational infrastructure has proven to be a much larger problem for each glue grant than anticipated. Applicants should take this into account in the early stages of their planning. Staging is also an issue that needs additional thought. There is a considerable induction period to getting a glue grant started and completely functional. Typically, most of the first two years is spent getting people and equipment in place, and building a working culture of team science. This has implications for budgeting and reviews of progress.

An important issue for consortia and the NIGMS to consider is the continuing need in the scientific community at large for access to data and other research resources generated by these large-scale awards beyond their finite lifetimes. How will the investigators deal with closing out the awards, and how will the NIGMS deal with continuing valuable research resources?

That being said, one gratifying aspect has been evident in all the glue grants. Great emphasis is placed on cooperation, collaboration, and integration within the glue grants themselves as well as the broader scientific community. The engagement of nonconsortium members in these comprehensive efforts is achieved in many ways, such as through the authorship of Molecule Pages for the AfCS or direct participation in the CFG. External advisory committees are in place to aid in linking the glue grants to the communities they serve. Each glue grant team realizes that they are serving a larger team effort—that of the relevant field at large. In fact, it is clear that the excitement for investigators in a glue grant comes from working together with esteemed colleagues from different disciplines for a common purpose, and the incentive for most of the glue participants derives less from what is in it for their laboratories than from a sense of having for the first time the opportunity to solve a biomedical problem of such scale that it can only be addressed by working together with other experts from many disciplines.

Glue Grants and the Evaluation Needs of the NIGMS

There are many examples of past and current evaluations of the process of scientific collaboration, including studies of the organizational structures that facilitate collaboration (Chompalov, Genuth, and Shrum 2002), the social process of collaboration (Bozeman and Corley 2004), and tools and technologies for enhancing collaborative research (Olson et al. 2002). This body of work may serve as a useful resource for academic or industrial organizations that seek to form successful collaborative research teams.

The evaluation needs of the NIGMS are somewhat different, being driven by the unique questions the institute faces as the funding agency for the glue grant program. The questions faced by the NIGMS originate from "stakeholders" in the NIGMS and its programs: the NIGMS and other NIH staff, the U.S. Office of Management and Budget, appropriations committees in the U.S. Congress, and members of the scientific community. These questions most often concern the proper stewardship of the NIGMS's appropriated budget and the allocation of limited resources among competing priorities.

Evaluation for Stewardship

Accountability is one of the primary purposes of the federal government's evaluation efforts, and the need for such studies by federal agencies increased with the passage of the Government Performance and Results Act (GPRA) of 1993. The GPRA (1993) was passed by Congress to "provide for the establishment of strategic planning and performance measurement in the Federal Government." One goal of this broader mandate is "to improve congressional decision making by providing more objective information ... on the relative effectiveness and efficiency of Federal programs and spending." Since its passage, federal agencies have been working to implement the GPRA, and incorporate evaluation into agency planning and budget processes. The broad, government-wide mandate of the GPRA and the absence of specific guidance for implementing major provisions of the law have contributed to uncertainty among agencies as to the best way to comply with the act (GAO 1996, 2000). As a result, the GPRA's implementation continues to be an evolutionary process, although it appears that progress is indeed being made (GAO 2002). The heavy emphasis that most interpretations of the GPRA have placed on establishing and assessing progress toward specific, measurable, and quantitative goals is particularly problematic for those agencies, like the NIGMS and other components of the NIH, that support basic scientific research. The outcomes of basic research are inherently unpredictable. Even negative outcomes (unsuccessful experiments or those with null findings) contribute to our scientific knowledge base, and the outcomes of research that may not appear particularly noteworthy or useful today may ultimately become so at some undetermined point in the future. The federal government has begun to address these problems through a new NSF initiative to develop better measures of research programs (Mervis 2006).

Evaluation for Resource Allocation

In addition to the need faced by all funding agencies to demonstrate proper stewardship of their appropriated resources, agencies that support large-scale collaborative research efforts face a particular need to evaluate these initiatives in the context of competing demands for funding. Individual investigator-initiated basic research, which competes for funding with more targeted large-scale research efforts, is considered by many to have been a major factor contributing to U.S. leadership in biomedical research. More targeted large-scale efforts, on the other hand, still generate some skepticism (see, for example, Russo [2005]). It was possible to both maintain relatively high levels of funding for individual investigators as well as support experimental collaborative projects when the first NIGMS glue grant was funded in fiscal year 2000—the second year of a five-year effort by congressional appropriations committees to double the NIH budget. The NIH budget doubling was completed in 2003, and the NIH has now entered a period in which there is greater competition for a more limited pool of resources.

As noted at the beginning of this chapter, there are significant biological problems that can only be addressed by multidisciplinary teams of scientists, and opportunities for such research appear to be increasing. There are clearly merits to supporting both large- and small-scale research programs, and the need to make trade-offs in the level of support for different-size projects has increased the demand for information on which to base the allocation of limited resources. While data may be used to inform these decisions, there currently exist no formal, widely accepted quantitative evaluation methods for allocating resources among competing scientific priorities. The bases for allocation decisions in the basic biomedical sciences are, and are likely to continue to be, perceived public health needs and the consensus judgment of scientific experts. It was this process (the meetings of representatives of the scientific community held in 1998 by the NIGMS) that led to the creation of the glue grant program, and most likely, it will be this process that is used to evaluate the outcomes of the program and its continuing need.

Previous Evaluations of Collaborative Research Funding Mechanisms

Several successful evaluations of the NIH collaborative research programs have been completed in recent years. In 2003, the National Institute of Arthritis and Musculoskeletal and Skin Diseases (NIAMS 1997) conducted an evaluation of its Specialized Centers of Research (SCOR) program. The purpose of this program is to expedite the development and application of new knowledge related to a specific disease. At each SCOR center, several projects were funded to develop innovative approaches to understanding the mechanism and treatment of disease, elaborate new and significant hypotheses, and elucidate disease mechanisms and new treatment strategies. A key component of the SCOR program is a linkage between basic and clinical research projects, and between basic and clinical researchers, designed to create a synergy and collaboration.

The NIAMS charged a committee of eight members of the scientific and lay communities to evaluate the SCOR program in the context of then-current scientific opportunities for translational research, the NIAMS's priorities, and other opportunities for translational research presented by the newly emerging NIH Roadmap for Medical Research. The committee held several meetings and discussions over a four-month period in which it reviewed the funding history of the SCOR program, descriptions of the funded grants, scientific findings generated by the grantees, and the results of a survey of current and former SCOR program directors. On the basis of this review, the committee concluded that the major scientific contribution of the SCOR program was not consistent with the institute's priority to support translational research. For these reasons, the committee decided not to amend the SCOR program but rather to move toward completely new Centers of Research Translation.

This evaluation might be considered successful by several criteria. The deliberations of the committee were informed by factual data, there was transparency in the decision-making process, the conclusions follow from the facts presented, and the committee was able to reach consensus on several recommendations. One key to the success of this evaluation effort was a close correspondence between the needs of the decision-making body and the data collection. It was through the committee's deliberations that the data needed to inform its decision were identified and the data collection was tailored to specific questions posed by the committee.

The NIAMS evaluation process was modeled, in part, on prior evaluations conducted by the National Heart, Lung, and Blood Institute (NHLBI). In 1971, NHLBI initiated its own SCOR program to encourage translational research in high-priority areas. In 1993, the NHLBI Advisory Committee recommended that each SCOR program be limited to two five-year funding periods unless an evaluation conducted midway through the second funding period demonstrated a continuing need. Like the NIAMS study, the NHLBI evaluations were conducted by knowledgeable panels of experts who met to consider research needs and opportunities, assess the role of the SCOR program in achieving unmet research goals, and provide recommendations to continue, modify, or terminate the program at the end of its ten years of funding. Fact-finding for these evaluations was tailored to the information needs of the panels, and included a standard set of questions posed to SCOR program directors, a review of collaborations fostered by the program, and a review of research findings translated into clinical applications. By 2001, these evaluations were successful in identifying an overemphasis on basic research in several SCOR programs along with an apparent lack of collaboration between basic and clinical investigators that hindered progress toward the translational research goals of the SCOR programs (NHLBI 2001). These evaluations eventually led to a redefinition of the SCOR programs to create NHLBI's current Specialized Centers of Clinically Oriented Research programs, which place a substantially greater stress on clinical research than the old SCOR programs. The NHLBI has retained a mandatory evaluation during the second five-year funding period of these new programs.

The NIAMS and the NHLBI evaluations were founded on consensus opinion among knowledgeable experts. The collection of data used to inform this process was driven by the specific needs of the decision-making body, the data were tailored to its deliberations, and the data were often of a descriptive or qualitative nature. These types of evaluations stand in contrast to more formal evaluation methods—drawn in large part from the social sciences—that have been used to evaluate other types of programs (such as educational or human services programs). These formal methods can involve large-scale data collection efforts, frequently with an emphasis on quantifiable outcome measures and the use of statistical decision criteria. Currently, the applicability of such methods in the evaluation of biomedical research programs is limited by a lack of measures of scientific impact that are at once well-defined, commonly accepted by stakeholders as valid, and comparable across research programs. These methodological shortcomings, along with the high costs usually associated with these types of studies, severely limits the utility of such evaluation approaches in the design of and allocation of resources for federal grant programs to support collaborative science.

The risk faced by funding agencies that invest in large data collection efforts to evaluate research-funding programs was perhaps best exemplified in an evaluation of the NSF's STC program completed in 1996. In a two-year evaluation effort, the NSF conducted a large and systematic collection of quantitative data from the STCs, the results of which were compiled into a four-volume report. The decision-making body assembled by the NSF to review the STC program, however, ultimately did not find these data to be useful (Mervis 1996). While the expert committee strongly endorsed the STC program and recommended that it be continued, it appears that the formal evaluation did little to inform this recommendation, leading the NSF to conclude that future evaluations would be performed through existing scientific committees with less emphasis on quantitative methods.

Evaluation of the NIGMS Large Grant Programs

In addition to funding for glue grants, the NIGMS support for research centers and other large collaborative projects has grown substantially in recent years. Several new programs utilizing large grant mechanisms were established to facilitate new directions in biomedical research that are difficult to support through the NIGMS's more traditional funding mechanisms—research involving collaborative, multidisciplinary teams working on complex problems that are of central importance, but that are beyond the means of any one research group. In this changing scientific environment, and because of the large investments required by these programs, it is crucial for the NIGMS to periodically assess the success of its large grant mechanisms.

To prepare for these evaluations, a Large Grants Working Group of the National Advisory General Medical Sciences Council has been formed to guide the assessment of the institute's large grant programs and develop recommendations to the full advisory council. The primary charge to the working group is to develop guidelines for assessments that will address whether the NIGMS's large grant programs are meeting the goals for which they were established and whether any changes that would improve the programs are needed. In developing these guidelines, the working group will review the original rationales and goals of large grant programs that distinguish them from programs funded through other research grant mechanisms. The working group will suggest the types of information required to assess the continued validity of these rationales and the extent to which the goals are being met, and recommend a process by which the overall assessment of each program is to be performed. It should be noted that these evaluations will be designed to assess the funding mechanisms used to support research and not the component grants themselves. The merit of individual grant proposals, regardless of the funding mechanism, will continue to be evaluated through the well-established NIH peer review process.

The first program to be assessed under this NIGMS large grants evaluation framework is the Protein Structure Initiative (PSI). The PSI, implemented through an integrated group of research centers and smaller projects, is experimentally determining the three-dimensional structure of proteins in pursuit of its overall goal of making the three-dimensional atomic-level structures of most proteins easily obtainable from knowledge of their corresponding DNA sequences. A panel of investigators met in the fall of 2007 to consider the status of the project and its impact on the biomedical research enterprise. The panel received input from members of the scientific community who responded to questions concerning the PSI that were posted on the NIGMS Web site. In addition, the panel heard presentations by PSI project teams and by individuals with reservations about the PSI. The panel submitted its report to the NIGMS Director in December 2007, and the report was presented publicly to the National Advisory General Medical Sciences Council at its January 2008 meeting.

References

Bozeman, B., and E. Corley. 2004. Scientists' collaboration strategies: Implications for scientific and technical human capital. *Research Policy* 33:599–616.

Chompalov, I., J. Genuth, and W. Shrum. 2002. The organization of scientific collaborations. *Research Policy* 31:657–848.

Government Performance and Results Act of 1993 (PL 106-32) (GPRA). 1993. *United States Statutes at Large* 110:285–296.

Mervis, J. 1996. Assessing research: Pilot study teaches NSF costly lesson. *Science* 273 (5280): 1331–1332.

Mervis, J. 2006. NSF begins a push to measure societal impacts of research. *Science* 312:347.

National Heart, Lung, and Blood Institute (NHLBI). 2001. *Report from the committee to redefine the specialized centers of research programs.* Available at ⟨http://www.nhlbi.nih.gov/funding/scor_report .pdf⟩ (accessed April 16, 2007).

National Institute of Arthritis and Musculoskeletal and Skin Diseases (NIAMS). 1997. *Report to the institute director, NIAMS centers working group II.* Available at ⟨http://www.niams.nih.gov/ne/ reports/sci_wrk/1997/cenrptfn.htm⟩ (accessed April 16, 2007).

Olson, G. M., S. Teasley, M. J. Bietz, and D. L. Cogburn. 2002. Collaboratories to support distributed science: The example of international HIV/AIDS research. In *Proceedings of the 2002 annual research conference of the South African Institute of Computer Scientists and Information Technologists on enablement through technology: ACM international conference proceeding series 30,* 44–51. South African Institute for Computer Scientists and Information Technologists, Republic of South Africa.

Russo, E. 2005. NSF National Science Board member questions "center" funding model. *Research Policy Alert,* August 11. Available at ⟨http://www.researchpolicyalert.com/fdcreports/rpa/ showHome.do⟩ (accessed June 30, 2007).

U.S. Government Accountability Office (GAO). 1996. *Managing for results: Key steps and challenges in implementing GPRA in science agencies.* Testimony before the Committee on Science, House of Representatives. GAO/T-GGD/RCED-96-214.

U.S. Government Accountability Office (GAO). 2000. *Managing for results: Continuing challenges to effective GPRA implementation.* Testimony before the Subcommittee on Government Management, Information, and Technology, Committee on Government Reform, House of Representatives. GAO/T-GGD-00-178.

U.S. Government Accountability Office (GAO). 2002. *Managing for results: Agency progress in linking performance plans with budgets and financial statements.* Report to the ranking minority member, Committee on Government Affairs, U.S. Senate. GAO-02-236.

12   The Biomedical Informatics Research Network

Judith S. Olson, Mark Ellisman, Mark James, Jeffrey S. Grethe, and Mary Puetz

The Biomedical Informatics Research Network (BIRN), an infrastructure initiative sponsored by the U.S. National Institutes of Health (NIH), fosters large data- and compute-intensive distributed collaborations in biomedical science with information technology innovations (Grethe et al. 2005; Ellisman and Peltier 2004).[1] Currently, BIRN is composed of a collection of three scientific collaboratories centered around the brain imaging and genetics of human neurological disorders and the associated animal models. To enable these collaborative groups, the BIRN Coordinating Center (BIRN-CC) was established to develop, implement, and support the infrastructure necessary to achieve the large-scale data sharing, computation, and collaboration among the scientific collaboratories. BIRN's overriding goal is to collect data from a number of researchers at different institutions so that for each scientific investigation, the scientists can consider sample sizes in the hundreds or thousands instead of in the tens. This is especially important in research into the causes and cures for relatively rare diseases.

The BIRN collaboratories are:

- *Function BIRN*: Developing multisite functional magnetic resonance (MR) tools focusing on understanding the underlying causes of schizophrenia and treatments for the disease.
- *Brain Morphometry BIRN*: Developing calibration and anatomical analysis tools to investigate the structural variance among brains with an eye to correlating specific structural differences to symptoms such as memory dysfunction or depression.
- *Mouse BIRN*: Focusing on mouse models of human disease, such as multiple sclerosis, schizophrenia, Parkinson's disease, attention deficit hyperactive disorder, Tourette's syndrome, and brain cancer. These researchers are aggregating data from different scales, from molecular information to anatomical imaging, to better understand these neurological disorders.
- *BIRN-CC*: Focusing on common technological issues across the various BIRN collaboratories, supporting the common technology infrastructure, enabling the sharing of

both data and analysis tools, and providing an intuitive Web-based portal for access to these resources.

In addition to the three scientific collaboratories and the coordinating center, BIRN also supports other NIH-funded collaboratories that are using the BIRN infrastructure to advance their research:

- *National Alliance for Medical Image Computing*: A multi-institutional, interdisciplinary team of computer scientists, software engineers, and medical investigators developing computational tools for the analysis and visualization of medical image data.[2]
- *Yerkes National Primate Research Center* of Emory University in Atlanta, Georgia: Studying the linking of brain imaging, behavior, and molecular informatics in primates with neurodegenerative disease.[3] This center is using BIRN resources for developing data-sharing strategies with seven other National Primate Research Centers as well as the existing BIRN collaboratories.

BIRN's originating NIH awards totaled approximately $30 million, with an additional $32.8 million awarded for the continuation of activities for five additional years in early 2005. Funding began in 2001, and current awards anticipate the participants engaging in the development and testing of this shared cyberinfrastructure throughout this decade. An overview of participation in the three collaboratories and the BIRN-CC is shown in table 12.1. It is important to note that members may participate in more than one BIRN collaboratory.

In the section that follows, we describe the three collaboratories and the BIRN-CC in more detail. Then we analyze specific aspects of the BIRN in light of the emerging

Table 12.1

Participation by institution and individuals in the BIRN collaboratories and the BIRN-CC

	Participants	Institutions
Function BIRN	186	University of California at San Diego (UCSD), Duke University, University of California at Los Angeles (UCLA), Brigham Women's Hospital (BWH), Massachusetts General Hospital (MGH), University of California at Irvine (UCI), Stanford University, University of Minnesota, University of Iowa, University of New Mexico, University of North Carolina (UNC)
Morphometry BIRN	153	UCSD, Duke, UCLA, BWH, MGH, Johns Hopkins University, UCI, Washington University at Saint Louis
Mouse BIRN	73	UCSD, Duke, UCLA, California Institute of Technology, University of Tennessee at Memphis
BIRN-CC	33	UCSD

theory of remote scientific collaboration (chapter 4, this volume). The findings in this chapter are based on the University of Michigan authors' interviews with the creators and principals in BIRN, examination of documents on the public Web site, and observation of an all-hands meeting, and on the University of California at San Diego authors' personal ongoing experience as principals in BIRN.

The BIRN Collaboratories

Function BIRN

Function BIRN's goal, as stated above, is to study brain dysfunctions related to the progression and treatment of schizophrenia. In order to get a large enough sample size of the various populations of schizophrenics (e.g., early as well as late onset), data must be integrated across many sites. Major challenges that Function BIRN had to address were the calibration of the functional MR data, the calibration of the MR scanners being done by Morphometry BIRN, and deciding on the cognitive tasks that the participants were to engage in to standardize the results. As a consequence of this work, a truly unique data set has been collected by Function BIRN and has been made available to the scientific community. This data set, a Traveling Subjects study designed to allow for the investigation of calibration methods, used healthy volunteers who traveled to all the sites and were scanned on two days, with the sequence of scans agreed on by the entire collaboratory.

Brain Morphometry BIRN

Brain Morphometry BIRN investigates the structure of the human brain and examines the neuroanatomical correlates of neuropsychiatric illnesses. It utilizes the BIRN infrastructure to facilitate the comparison of findings across the collaboratory in order to identify the unique and common structural features of disorders such as unipolar depression, Alzheimer's disease, and mild cognitive impairment. One of the major issues facing Morphometry BIRN is the calibration of the structural MR data being collected at multiple sites on varying equipment and the subsequent statistical analysis of 3-D shapes, both for analysis and visualization purposes. Different institutions have made inroads in developing these analytic tools; the participants are now allowing others to access not only the data but also the tools themselves, with an eye to building even more powerful, more broadly applicable tools.

Mouse BIRN

The mouse brain has certain correspondences with the human brain, and mice can be genetically modified to manifest more or less the same disease pathologies as seen in human disorders such as Parkinson's and Alzheimer's. Since much more detailed

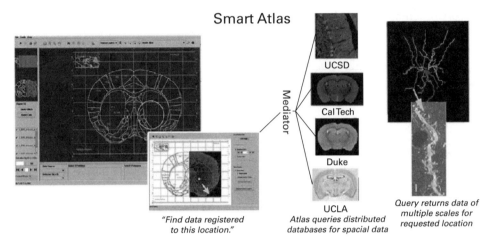

Figure 12.1
The BIRN Smart Atlas (from *BIRNing Issues* 2, no. 3)

investigations can be undertaken in mouse brains, and "preclinical trials" of new treatments can be more rapidly and less expensively carried out on mice, this is a good "model organism." One key issue in this large-scale integration of data is that researchers from different subdisciplines do not always refer to the same location in the brain with the same terminology. Consequently they have had to develop the SmartAtlas, which allows all data to be placed within a common coordinate system, and uses a system of unique terminological identifiers to connect anatomical data to molecular and structural schema (see figure 12.1).

The SmartAtlas allows for spatially registered data to be displayed, queried, and annotated. The spatial registration of data sets involves warping and scaling the data to a standard template, and then referencing the resulting data to the coordinate system.

BIRN-CC

A unique feature of the BIRN collaboratories is that they share not only a common technical core but also a set of social and administrative issues that they resolve together. These are done through the BIRN-CC and a well-designed management structure. The BIRN-CC is housed at the University of California at San Diego, and is commissioned to develop, implement, and support the information infrastructure necessary to achieve large-scale data sharing among the collaboratories. In addition to the development and deployment of the technical infrastructure, the BIRN-CC provides high-level project management, training, and expert-level technical support. It also collects best practices and serves as the management's point of contact. Finally, the BIRN-CC supports many central services, such as a Web site and Web portal services that provide access to data, software, computing clusters, data storage clusters, database servers, and application servers.

The BIRN collaboratories deal not only with large, distributed databases but also with highly heterogeneous sets of data. A query may need to span several relational databases, ontology references, spatial atlases, and collections of information extracted from image files. A major success within the BIRN was the deployment of a data integration environment that enables researchers to submit these multisource queries and navigate freely between distributed databases. This data integration architecture for BIRN builds on work in knowledge-guided mediation for integration across heterogeneous data sources (Gupta, Ludäscher, and Martone 2001; Ludäscher, Gupta, and Martone 2000; Martone, Gupta, and Ellisman 2004). In this approach, the integration environment uses additional knowledge captured in the form of ontologies, spatial atlases, and thesauri to provide the necessary bridges between heterogeneous data. This is unlike a *data warehouse*, which copies (and periodically updates) all local data to a central repository and integrates local schemata through the repository's central schema. The BIRN federated data environment creates the illusion of a single integrated database while maintaining the original set of distributed databases. By federating their data as opposed to storing it in a central location, the original owners can grow their databases and use them with their own tools independent of the BIRN integration environment.

The BIRN-CC does not rely on all the sites to configure their own hardware and software to meet BIRN standards. Instead, people at the BIRN-CC integrate the necessary hardware, which is already loaded and preconfigured with the requisite BIRN software. It is then shipped to the site. We call this BIRN-in-a-box, illustrated in figures 12.2a and 12.2b. In the rack are the grid point-of-presence network tools, network-attached storage, and general-purpose computing nodes, where security and encryption can be uniformly applied. To effectively address and manage the expanding complexity of these hardware/software systems, the BIRN-CC is formalizing and expanding the process of integrating, testing, deploying, and updating the software stack.

Key Aspects to BIRN's Success

The theory of remote scientific collaboration (chapter 4, this volume) identifies five major categories of factors that are critical to the success of collaboratories: technical readiness, aspects of management and decision making, collaboration readiness, the nature of the work, and common ground. In this section, we comment on how these factors play out in BIRN.

(a)   (b)

Figure 12.2
(*a*) BIRN racks are carefully packaged by BIRN-CC staff and shipped to the various test-bed sites. (*b*) Key components are assembled within each rack.

Technical Readiness

The researchers in BIRN are generally technically sophisticated, which they have to be to do research using MR imaging (MRI) and the associated data. They are accustomed to carrying out sophisticated data analysis and developing visualization tools. The advent of BIRN has provided them with a larger database and access to tools developed at other sites. The delivery of the hardware and software as BIRN-in-a-box lightens the load on the local system administrator for the administration and maintenance of the system at that site.

BIRN also supports the development of the technology needed to comply with various federal regulations having to do with privacy and the protection of human research subjects, such as the Federal Policy for the Protection of Human Subjects, often referred to as the "Common Rule," and the Health Insurance Portability and Accountability Act (HIPAA). For example, when sharing data publicly, HIPAA (1996) requires that it be impossible to identify the person whose medical data are being shared. Unfortunately, the MRI data has information that can allow a reconstruction of the person's face, which in turn could identify the person to those who know them. There has thus been considerable effort to build "de-identification" tools for MRI data that will strip away the face without disturbing the actual brain data and will also remove any potential identifiers in the data files themselves.

In addition to merely being "ready" technically, BIRN is leading in the area of cyber-infrastructure (Buetow 2005; Ellisman 2005). BIRN offers a useful example of why scientists need high-end networking and grid technologies (for security, scalability, and performance), and it exposes the social issues that are sometimes invisible to people concentrating on making the technology available. The BIRN participants have had a strong voice in cyberinfrastructure planning, enumerating the real needs for such data aggregation and use to take place.

Management and Decision Making

BIRN has a management plan that follows what the theory of remote science collaboration recommends for complex projects. An oversight committee (the BIRN Executive Committee) is made up of the principal investigators of the BIRN collaboratories and representatives from the National Center for Research Resources at the NIH. This committee commissions a variety of standing and ad hoc committees that tackle important common issues. For instance, one committee is devising standard "template" wording to satisfy the subject consent and data-sharing agreements that must be approved at each institution's Institutional Review Board (IRB). (IRBs are committees that every research institution is required to have to protect the patients/participants in research studies.) IRBs differ in how they interpret the federal guidelines, and states have additional guidelines and laws. Therefore, standard language, expectations, and procedures are critical to getting approval to conduct studies using the BIRN infrastructure. These standing and ad hoc committees are populated with people from each of the BIRN collaboratories. In this way, every participant has a voice and is heard. BIRN has developed a *Cooperative Guidelines Technical Manual* that assists in delineating the technical responsibilities of the BIRN-CC and each site participating in BIRN.

A principal investigator, a scientific coordinator, and a project manager head each of the BIRN collaboratories (test beds) and the BIRN-CC. The project manager is experienced with project management and is, in addition, schooled in the domain. Many of the committees hold biweekly or monthly meetings supported by a mixture of audio and videoconferencing. Each year, in the fall, BIRN organizes an all-hands meeting in which nearly everyone participates (see figure 12.3).

The annual meeting has helped to generate a spirit of open communication and has created opportunities for the participants to express their opinions regarding decisions that affect the project. Annually, in the spring, each scientific test bed holds its own all-hands meeting to focus on domain-related research, the identification of new tools, a review of policies and procedures, and plans for future research and studies. Even with this communication technology and the structure of regular meetings across sites,

Figure 12.3
The fourth annual BIRN all-hands meeting was held in Boston with over 150 participants

however, the participants still identify cross-site communication as one of the major challenges.

Collaboration Readiness

Collaboration readiness is an issue in BIRN. BIRN scientists have raised concerns about releasing data before they have had time to use them. They fear that other researchers will analyze and publish the data before they have the chance to do so. Indeed, while they espouse the value to the community at large for sharing data (bigger sample sizes, the ability to see things at various scales, and better science in general), the field has not evolved new credit mechanisms. Researchers are typically rewarded for peer-reviewed publications, with the first and last position in a multiauthored work counting the most heavily. Those "in the middle" who provide critical analyses, or even those who donate their data to make a discovery possible, receive less recognition. BIRN continues to work on these issues. BIRN scientists have developed a draft "roll-out" scheme and timeline in which the data would first be available only to the originator, then to specified others, then to the BIRN consortium as a whole, and finally to the general public. How well the "big science" aspect is supported in this rollout while individual scientists mine the data for their own discoveries remains an open issue. In support of this data-sharing philosophy, the first large-scale publicly available data sets being offered by BIRN were made available in fall 2005.

The Nature of the Work

The prescription about the nature of work says that if the work is tightly coupled (that is, where the individuals are dependent on each others' input) or is ambiguous (where things have to be clarified), it is difficult to conduct this work long distance. BIRN in its final state may not require tight coupling; the data ought to be clearly identified through the metadata, and their analysis and interpretation ought to be straightforward. With the clarity, people will be able to work on their own hypotheses without having to coordinate with others remotely. Yet at the beginning, when issues of standardization are being worked out, tight communication is important. This makes the times when the participants can get together to work out these issues all that much more significant.

Common Ground

Although many of the BIRN researchers in the currently active test beds are in the same field (neuroscience), they have serious differences in the cultures of their subfields. Those working on Mouse BIRN, for example, are researching brain functions at a wide range of scales. As mentioned above, the scientists in the subfields may refer to the location of a sample (e.g., the microscopy image of a single cell) using different terminologies. The SmartAtlas resolves this problem by placing the integrated data into a common spatial framework so that all the appropriate data can be aggregated. In addition to the common spatial framework, the use of ontologies is required to bridge these differing nomenclatures. The use of ontologies and other "knowledge sources" is critical to the data integration architecture being deployed by BIRN, which allows researchers to submit multisource queries and navigate freely between distributed databases.

There is an additional synergy in the fact that BIRN is a consortium of collaboratories, allowing lessons learned at one site to spread to others. For instance, Function BIRN is taking the lessons gained and methods developed for anatomical imaging in Morphometry BIRN, and is utilizing, extending, and developing novel methods to develop calibration methods for functional imaging.

Successes

As explained in the theory of remote scientific collaboration (chapter 4, this volume), success can be manifested in a variety of ways. There are effects on the science itself, changes in the scientists' careers (e.g., attracting a more diverse population to the field), effects on science education and public awareness, and the reuse of technologies developed in one collaboratory by another.

The Effects on the Science Itself

It is too early to tell whether the discovery of disease markers and the effects of the associated cures is moving more quickly because of BIRN, but the preliminary accomplishments are encouraging. Early measures of BIRN's success are reflected in use. As of June 2006, BIRN had over fifteen million files on the data grid, encompassing over sixteen terabytes. There are nearly four hundred accounts for access to BIRN plus fifty-one guest accounts that are limited to read-only capability. Evidence of collaboration appears in the nearly eighteen million files that were accessed by people who did not create them.

At the time this chapter was written, the BIRN participants had produced ninety-six publications. Most of these publications discuss the building of the infrastructure and the associated software tools, but some that are now coming out report new scientific findings based on the aggregated data that BIRN makes available. The number of co-authors ranges from one to twenty, with the average increasing over the years. Forty-seven publications have BIRN listed as a coauthor.

Advances in the science to date include improved understandings of the hippocampus and amygdala in Alzheimer's patients (Beg et al. 2004; Horne et al. 2004), morphological changes in a mouse model with dopaminergic hyperfunction (Cyr et al. 2005), neurocognitive correlates in patients with schizophrenia (Kemp et al. 2005), genomics and dyslexia (Williams forthcoming), and genomics and hippocampal neurogenesis (Kempermann et al. 2006).

Just as in high-energy physics, there is an entire subfield dedicated to the study of the instrumentation and data analysis. For example, collaborative imaging studies require the standardization and calibration of instruments (e.g., Jovicich et al. 2004), and some tools are necessary for compliance with federal regulations such as HIPAA in the sharing of data (e.g., Fennema-Notestine et al. 2006).

The Effects on Other Collaboratories

In addition to the Yerkes's and the National Alliance for Medical Image Computing's use of the BIRN infrastructure, people from BIRN have been active in sharing their experiences with others. They have participated in global conferences to explain how they have solved problems in instrument calibration and data federation. In the UK Research Council's e-Science program, for example, an architecture similar to that used by BIRN and myGrid was utilized to combine data and databases through a semantic data integration system that bridges different kinds of data, like MRI images and microscopic data.

BIRN was also cited in testimony to the U.S. Congress to illustrate how data aggregation could promote faster scientific discovery. Finally, BIRN leaders have been heavily involved in shaping cyberinfrastructure projects to note which kinds of services (e.g., security) scientific collaboratories will need.

The Reuse of Tools

Others have adopted the tools developed by BIRN. Some of the infrastructure for integrating data has been adopted by the National Ecological Observatory Network, which seeks to foster understanding of the relationship between effects on lakes, rivers, and oceans and land formations (see also chapter 16, this volume). In addition, BIRN is offering its collaboration tools to general clinical research centers.

The University of California at San Diego is fortunate to host a number of grid collaboratories in many different scientific domains. The software engineers hold joint meetings between collaboratories for the express purpose of sharing technologies and techniques that can be applied across grid projects. This open sharing process allows subsequent grid projects to benefit from the lessons learned and the tools developed by projects like BIRN.

Summary

BIRN incorporates a lot of what we believe makes a collaboratory successful. It has made technology adoption easy through the availability of BIRN-in-a-box. The BIRN-CC has developed tools to help in a number of different collaboratories, both within and outside BIRN. Indeed, BIRN has a voice in shaping cyberinfrastructure, so that other sciences that might benefit from large-scale, long-distance collaboration will have access to the shared infrastructure they need.

BIRN also places a strong emphasis on participatory and open management. Standing and ad hoc committees tackle issues common to a number of the BIRN collaboratories (e.g., IRB issues, data sharing, and ontologies). A principal investigator, a lead scientist, and a professional project manager leads each committee, thereby ensuring that best practices from project management are adopted, and that the leadership garners the respect of the participants.

Notes

1. See ⟨http://www.nbirn.net⟩.

2. See ⟨http://www.na-mic.org⟩.

3. See ⟨http://www.yerkes.emory.edu/index/⟩.

References

Beg, M. F., C. Certitoglu, A. E. Kolasny, C. E. Priebe, J. T. Ratnanather, R. Yashinski et al. 2004. Biomedical Informatics Research Network: Multi-site processing pipeline for shape analysis of brain structures. Paper presented at the tenth annual meeting of the Organization for Human Brain Mapping, Budapest, June. Available at ⟨http://www.nbirn.net/publications/abstracts/pdf/Beg_HBM_2004.pdf⟩ (accessed June 22, 2007).

Buetow, K. H. 2005. Cyberinfrastructure: Empowering a "third way" in biomedical research. *Science* 308 (5723): 821–824.

Cyr, M., M. G. Caron, G. A. Johnson, and A. Laakso. 2005. Magnetic resonance imaging at microscopic resolution reveals subtle morphological changes in a mouse model of dopaminergic hyperfucntion. *NeuroImage* 26:83–90.

Ellisman, M. H. 2005. Cyberinfrastucture and the future of collaborative work. *Issues in Science and Technology* 22 (1): 43–50.

Ellisman, M. H., and S. T. Peltier. 2004. Medical data federation: The Biomedical Informatics Research Network. In *The grid: Blueprint for a new computing infrastructure*, ed. I. Foster and C. Kesselman. 2nd ed. San Francisco: Morgan-Kaufman, 109–120.

Fennema-Notestine, C., I. B. Ozyurt, C. P. Clark, S. Morris, A. Bischoff-Grethe, M. W. Bondi et al. 2006. Quantitative evaluation of automated skull-stripping methods applied to contemporary and legacy images: Effects of diagnosis, bias correction, and slice location. *Human Brain Mapping* 27 (2): 99–113.

Grethe, J. S., C. Baru, A. Gupta, M. James, B. Ludäscher, P. M. Papadopoulos et al. 2005. Biomedical Informatics Research Network: Building a national collaboratory to hasten the derivation of new understanding and treatment of disease. *Studies in Health Technology Information* 112:100–109.

Gupta, A., B. Ludäscher, and M. E. Martone. 2001. Model-based mediation with domain maps. *Proceedings of the international conference on data engineering* 17:81–90.

Health Insurance Portability and Accountability Act of 1996 (PL 104-191) (HIPAA). 1996. *United States Statutes at Large* 110:1936.

Horne, N. R., M. W. Bondi, C. Fennema-Notesting, W. S. Houston, G. G. Brown, T. L. Jernigan et al. 2004. Hippocampal and amygdalal brain changes in young-old and very-old with Alzheimer's disease: Association with neuropsychological functioning. Paper presented at the Ninth International Conference on Alzheimer's Disease and Related Disorders, Philadelphia, July.

Jovicich, J., E. Haley, D. Greve, R. Gollub, D. Kennedy, B. Fischl, and A. Dale. 2004. Reliability in multi-site structural MRI studies: Effects of gradient non-linearity correction on volume and displacement of brain subcortical structure. Paper presented at the tenth annual meeting of the Organization for Human Brain Mapping, Budapest, June. Available at ⟨http://www.nbirn.net/publications/presentations/pdf/Jovicich_HBM_2004.pdf⟩ (accessed June 22, 2007).

Kemp, A. S., J. A. Turner, H. J. Lee, L. C. Trondsen, K. N. Gooch, D. Mirski, and S. G. Potkin. 2005. The neurocognitive correlates of BOLD activation in the dorsolateral prefrontal cortex of patients with schizophrenia: An fMRI investigation. Paper presented at the International Congress of Schizophrenia Research, Savannah, Georgia. Available at ⟨http://www.nbirn.net/publications/presentations/pdf/Kemp_ICSR_2005.pdf⟩ (accessed June 22, 2007).

Kempermann, G., E. J. Chesler, L. Lu, E. Lein, J. Nathanson, R. W. Williams, and F. H. Gage. 2006. Natural variation and genetic covariance in adult hippocampal neurogenesis. *Proceedings of the National Academy of Science* 103:780–785.

Ludäscher, B., A. Gupta, and M. E. Martone. 2000. Model-based information integration in a neuroscience mediator system. *Proceedings of International Conference on Very Large Data Bases* 26:639–642.

Martone, M. E., A. Gupta, and M. H. Ellisman. 2004. E-neuroscience: Challenges and triumphs in integrating distributed data from molecules to brains. *Natural Neuroscience* 7:467–472.

Williams, R. W. 2006. Genomics and dyslexia: Bridging the gap. In *Developing new pathways in the study of the dyslexic brain*, ed. G. D. Rosen. Philadelphia, PA: Lawrence Erlbaum Associates.

13 Three Distributed Biomedical Research Centers

Stephanie D. Teasley, Titus Schleyer, Libby Hemphill, and Eric Cook

Research conducted by the Science of Collaboratories group has identified distributed research centers as one generalized instance of collaboratories (chapter 3, this volume). In his original paper on collaboratories, William Wulf (1993) suggests that the ease of interaction through information technology would support informal and ad hoc collaborations between scientists to create "center[s] without walls." As centers have come to play an important role in the conduct of research at large universities and funding agencies, it is not surprising that the promise of Wulf's "collaboratory opportunity" has been applied to support formally established distributed centers of research, and collaboratories have become more widely known and adopted in biomedical research (e.g., chapters 11 and 12, this volume). In this chapter we examine three examples of distributed research centers, all conducting biomedical research, where each center had funding designated specifically to provide and support a collaboratory. A distributed research center is by definition truly a *center* without walls, and the extent to which the collaboratory promise can be realized by these centers will be discussed.

Distributed Centers: Supporting Big Science

The growing pressure for "bigger science" combined with the technological capacity to communicate over distance has lead to the funding of more and more distributed centers for research. These centers are typically structured like traditional single-site centers in terms of supplying funding for specific research projects, making developmental awards to junior colleagues for generating pilot data, bringing in speakers to offer an educational program, and establishing cores and services that provide specific services such as bioinformatics or gene sequencing to center members at special prices and priorities compared to nonmembers. In order to achieve the goals implicit in center funding, however, geographically distributed centers of research face unprecedented challenges in communication and collaboration. The three centers discussed here represent large centers that have specifically incorporated funding and provided infrastructure to facilitate collaboration among geographically distributed center members. Most biomedical research centers do not include funding earmarked to facilitate communication and coordination. Many center directors simply expect traditional methods, such as phone, fax, e-mail, and occasional face-to-face meetings, to support effective and efficient work toward the center's objectives. While centers using more traditional communication methods reduce the technical complexity of their operations, opportunities for more efficient, effective, and novel collaborations through new electronic tools are lost (Cummings and Kiesler 2005; chapter 5, this volume). In each of the centers presented here, we were provided with dedicated funding and personnel to support our dual roles on these projects: *center members* offering services for supporting communication and coordination, and *researchers* studying the use of technology to support the scientific activity of the centers. The requests for these funds were included in the original grant proposals to address the difficulty of communicating and coordinating activities when center members cannot easily or regularly meet face-to-face.

In this chapter, we use the term *center* to refer to the center grant projects and members as a whole. Earlier work limited the definition of the term *collaboratory* to refer to the electronic infrastructure that supports communication and collaboration (Finholt 2002, 2003; Finholt and Olson 1997), but this volume uses *collaboratory* to refer to an organization. Here, we use the term *collaboratory technology* to refer to the infrastructure within each center. The main purpose of this chapter is to comparatively evaluate three centers that used off-the-shelf tools and relatively modest resources to support the scientific activity of distributed biomedical researchers. We first describe the three centers—their institutional participants and personnel. Next, we discuss the requirements for collaboration and communication within each center, the funding provided to support these activities, and our role in supporting these requirements using commercially available electronic tools. Finally, we analyze the barriers and enablers that affected the technology adoption within each center.

Overviews of Three Distributed Biomedical Research Centers

The three geographically distributed research centers we describe in this chapter are the Great Lakes Regional Center for AIDS Research (HIV/AIDS Center), the New York University Oral Cancer Research for Adolescent and Adult Health Promotion Center (Oral Cancer Center), and the Great Lakes Regional Center of Excellence in Biodefense and Emerging Infectious Diseases (Biodefense Center). All three centers are large-scale, cooperative research projects funded by the National Institutes of Health (NIH) and are focused on a single, complex biomedical research problem. The centers range in size from 4 to 23 institutions and from 31 to 105 individual members. Each center has dedicated less than 10 percent of its total funding to collaboration technology and sup-

Table 13.1
Summary of case study centers

	HIV/AIDS center	Oral cancer center	Biodefense center
Funding agency	NIH	NIH (NIDCR)	NIH (NIAID)
Total centers funded	17	5	8
Number of institutions	4	11	23
Members	105	31	187
Cores	8	3	9
Research projects	7	4	6
Eligibility for membership	Open to individuals at member institutions	Limited to personnel listed in grant proposal	Open to individuals at member institutions
Directors/PIs	1/12	1/7	2/6
Funding period	5 years (9/98–9/03)	7 years (8/01–7/08)	5 years (9/03–8/08)
Total budget	$6.75 million	$8.3 million	$38 million
Budget for collaboration technology and support	$559K (8%)	$604K (7%)	$400K (1%)

port. At the time of each application, these three centers were the only awardees to integrate a formal proposal for funding to explicitly support collaboration. Table 13.1 summarizes basic information on the centers, and the following sections examine the centers in detail.

To understand the specific needs of investigators and projects in each of the centers, we conducted interviews with each principal investigator (PI) and key research personnel. Semistructured interviews addressed questions about the tasks related to projects, prior and current interaction between project teams and center members, the project-related information generated or managed, and other project commitments. In addition, we assessed the local computing infrastructure and the applications used by each investigator, including for desktop computers and mobile devices. As each grant progressed, we continued to interact with center members and to collect observations and log data about the activities associated with the research projects funded by the centers. We acted as participant observers in individual projects' lab meetings, the centers' all-hands meetings, and other activities associated with each center as described below.

The HIV/AIDS Center
The HIV/AIDS Center was active in many areas of HIV/AIDS research, including HIV biology, immunology, vaccines, therapeutic trials, and behavioral science. The center

was originally funded for four years starting in September 1998 and received an additional year of bridging funds in 2002. Competitive renewal applications were unsuccessful, leading to the dissolution of the center in September 2003. The total budget for the center was $6.75 million, of which $559,000 was allocated for the support of collaboration technologies.

The HIV/AIDS Center was comprised of eight cores engaged in seven research programs. Its missions were to promote multidisciplinary AIDS research and increase the number of scientists engaged in the research needed to develop more effective measures to prevent, moderate, and treat HIV infection. The original HIV/AIDS Center application proposed several research areas and created an infrastructure in which research projects were developed and supported. This infrastructure led to the development of seven research studies, including HIV molecular biology, HIV/AIDS pathogenesis, and therapeutic research and development. The center also contained eight cores, including genomics and proteomics, single-cell imaging and analysis, and a non-human primate model. The research mandate of the center emphasized collaboration, especially between basic science and clinical researchers.

A center director and twelve principal investigators guided the cores and research studies of the HIV/AIDS Center. Center membership was open to anyone engaged in AIDS and AIDS-related research at the four participating institutions. In June 2001, there were 105 registered members of the HIV/AIDS Center distributed across four sites ranging from 16 to 42 members per site.

The Oral Cancer Center

The goals of the Oral Cancer Center are to conduct research that leads to an understanding of the factors associated with health disparities in oral cancer and to develop, test, and evaluate interventions designed to reduce oral cancer disparities. The total budget is $8.3 million, and the project's funding started in August 2001 and runs through July 2008. The budget for the informatics core is $604,000.

The research studies in this center focus on risk factors for oral epithelial dysplasia (a precursor condition for oral cancer), current and emerging technologies for oral cancer detection, cancer screening and research subject participation by minorities, and personalized risk feedback in dental clinic smokers. In contrast to the HIV/AIDS Center, which established the infrastructure for developing research projects, the Oral Cancer Center grant application clearly defined the four research studies to be conducted. A fifth study will be developed later in the project period. Each of the research proposals clearly framed research questions and methods and described participating research personnel, infrastructure, and budgets. The projects address the overall theme of reducing health disparities in oral cancer, but they are considered (and were reviewed as) separate research grant applications. The four research studies are supported by three cores: the administrative, biostatistics, and informatics cores. The informatics core is the entity that supports the development, implementation, and evaluation of the center's collaboratory.

The Oral Cancer Center personnel consist of four study PIs, three core PIs (one study and one core are directed by the same person), fifteen research personnel (including the PIs), and nine administrative personnel at eleven participating institutions. While some of those institutions are located relatively close to each other (e.g., the Memorial Sloan-Kettering Cancer Center and New York University), others are quite isolated (e.g., the University of Puerto Rico).

The Biodefense Center

The Regional Centers for Excellence in Biodefense and Emerging Infectious Diseases program was created as a response to the Blue Ribbon Panel on Bioterrorism and Its Implications for Biomedical Research convened by the NIH in February 2002. The total budget for the Biodefense Center studied here was $38 million for five years, starting in September 2003. The communications core of the center was funded from September 2003 to March 2006, and its total budget was $400,000. The communications core was established to explicitly address the communication and coordination needs of the center. The center's communications core was dissolved after three years when the NIH provided centralized funding for a national communications core serving all the Biodefense Centers. The Biodefense Center was funded under an NIH program that called for regional centers that would build and maintain infrastructure to support research surrounding the worst bioterror threats. The research promotes basic biology, immunology, vaccines and drugs, and diagnostic tools for pathogens such as anthrax and plague. These diseases are given priority as potential bioterror threats because of their ease of dissemination, potential for high impacts on public health, and requirements of special attention and action for public health preparedness.

Like the Oral Cancer Center, the Biodefense Center included specific research projects in its application—six projects that were selected by peer review in a competition held in advance of the full grant proposal submission. The six original projects funded by the Biodefense Center included research on the Centers for Disease Control "Category A agents," including plague, anthrax, smallpox, hemorrhagic fever, tularemia, and botulism. These six projects varied in the number of collaborators and the relative distances among the participating scientists. The funding also supported nine cores, including the communications core, that provided and supported the collaboration technology for the center members.

During the period we studied this center, the Biodefense Center personnel consisted of 2 codirectors, 6 PIs, 9 core directors, 4 administrative personnel, and 187 center members located at 23 participating institutions in 6 of the Great Lakes states.

Table 13.2
Collaboration and support in three centers

	HIV/AIDS center	Oral cancer center	Biodefense center
Project structure	Emergent: Specific projects grew out of research areas	Fixed: Self-contained, predetermined projects	Evolving: Initially funded self-contained, predetermined projects; had additional funding to support development of new projects
Primary goal for collaboration support	Encourage new collaborations	Support existing collaborations	Support existing collaborations and encourage new collaborations
Temporal mode of interaction	Synchronous: Developing research protocols, discussing data	Asynchronous: Data sharing	Synchronous: Discussing data
Preferred collaborative activities	Videoconferencing and remote instrument sharing	Digital data and protocol sharing	Face-to-face meetings
Recommended technologies	Private Web site, videoconferencing, remote instrument sharing	Private Web site, videoconferencing	Private Web sites for center and each project, videoconferencing, phone conferencing
Technologies implemented	Public and private Web sites, PlaceWare, NetMeeting	Groove, Genesys, Webconferencing	Sakai work sites, public Web site, Access Grid, Polycom, teleconferencing
Supported activities	Administrative tasks, virtual seminar series	Monthly conference call	Data sharing, weekly all-center conference call, sporadic research project videoconferences, administrative tasks

Comparison of the Three Centers

In this section, we provide additional information about the activities of the centers and their corresponding technology needs. We describe the kinds of collaboration the centers wished to support, common collaborative activities in which they engaged, and the technologies they adopted to support those activities. Table 13.2 summarizes this information. The next section will discuss barriers and enablers of technology adoption to meet those needs.

When first funded, few of the investigators, research staff, or administrators in any of the centers had prior exposure to collaborative tools beyond e-mail and locally shared data stores (e.g., shared file servers). They were most comfortable using e-mail and the phone for collaborative activities that did not require physical copresence (e.g., scheduling meetings or sharing files). Some members in each center had participated in videoconferences, typically using Polycom videoconferencing. In the Biodefense Center, several of the center members had experience using the Access Grid for remote collaboration and meetings. The Access Grid uses distributed computing resources (instead of centralized processing) along with high-end audio and visual technology for large-scale distributed work sessions. It requires different equipment from Polycom videoconferencing but similarly allows for multiple sites to be involved in a single videoconference.

Overall, members of the centers seemed open to new technologies, yet had concerns about the security of unfamiliar technologies as well as the time and effort required to learn how to use new systems. Scientists' and administrators' primary activities involved work at the bench, in the clinic, writing grants and papers, and managing budgets. They were not usually first adopters but rather preferred to use well-documented, popular, and familiar technologies. The centers' activities and the corresponding technology tools differed primarily along three dimensions:

- The existence or emergence of collaborations
- The synchronous or asynchronous nature of collaborative activities
- Support for center-sponsored activities

The Existence or Emergence of Collaborations

Each center was charged with encouraging and supporting collaboration at different stages of development, and this difference impacted the degree to which research within the centers was centrally organized. The HIV/AIDS Center emphasized emergent collaborations; therefore, the specific research projects funded by the center grew out of the identified research thrusts. The center was viewed as a mechanism for starting new collaborations between investigators that would not have been likely to occur without the infrastructure of the center. In contrast, both the Oral Cancer Center and the Biodefense Center had predefined research projects, which while supported by the respective center, could also have been funded as stand-alone projects. The projects in the Oral Cancer Center were self-contained, and there was not a strong emphasis placed on interaction between the PIs of each project. As there was some geographic dispersion within each project, the focus for collaboration support was on members within projects but not necessarily across projects. Like the Oral Cancer Center, the Biodefense Center projects function independently of each other, and because they focus on different biological agents, work on one project is unlikely to directly impact other projects.

An important goal of the HIV/AIDS Center was to attract scientists to the center who otherwise would not have engaged in multidisciplinary AIDS research, while the other two centers focused on facilitating preexisting collaborations. Thus, access to the HIV/AIDS Center was open to any scientist active in HIV/AIDS research at any one of the four participating institutions. There were also some structures in place in the Biodefense Center to encourage the emergence of new research projects. Scientists from member institutions joined the Biodefense Center in anticipation of securing funding for new projects to be supported by the center through a number of research competitions, including funding for new research projects, career development grants, and developmental projects. In contrast, the Oral Cancer Center's numbers and roles of research investigators were defined and fixed before the center started. New personnel joined the center only by virtue of study personnel turnover or a specific interest in an existing research project.

The HIV/AIDS Center described potential research areas supported by cores in its application, rather than proposing to fund specific research projects at the beginning of the grant. Thus, an important part of the early work in the HIV/AIDS Center was the development of specific research projects, which required interaction between center members. The Oral Cancer Center and the Biodefense Center, in contrast, started out with well-defined research projects with specific personnel assigned. For the Oral Cancer Center, the stress was primarily on completing those projects, rather than developing new ones. The Biodefense Center had an emphasis on the growth of the center's research portfolio, and therefore required some support for community building, as did the HIV/AIDS Center. This support, however, was not intended to directly impact the primary research projects funded by the center. These goals and their resulting organizational structures impact the kinds of collaboration support each center required. The HIV/AIDS Center needed to support collaboration across projects and across the center; the Oral Cancer Center needed to support collaboration within research projects. The Biodefense Center was interested in supporting collaboration both across and within projects, but its main focus lay within existing projects.

The Synchronous or Asynchronous Nature of Collaborative Activities
The three centers also differed in the timing of the collaborations they wanted to support. Some activities required synchronous interaction (e.g., distributed lab meetings), while others required asynchronous interaction (e.g., sharing data sets). In the HIV/AIDS Center, real-time interaction was important for developing research protocols as well as discussing and analyzing research data. During the first year of the grant, two primary activities emerged for supporting existing collaborations and starting new ones. First, the scientists expressed a need for a way to run distributed lab meetings that would allow conversation over shared data, including, for example, images from a specialized microscope located at only one of the sites. The expectation for this activity was that it be synchronous so that participants, from few to many, could interact with each other in real time. Second, the scientists wanted a way to broadcast seminars

to share information from experts inside and outside the center. Here, the expectation was to be able to broadcast to as many members as possible with the ability for participants to ask questions in real time.

Several off-the-shelf applications were selected to support synchronous interaction among the HIV/AIDS Center scientists. Microsoft NetMeeting was selected for real-time document, image, and equipment sharing. The cross-platform issues involved in using NetMeeting were resolved by having the Macintosh users use Timbuktu Conference, and later, Virtual PC. PlaceWare Auditorium, a Web-based presentation tool, was selected for virtual presentations. Telephones were used in addition to groupware tools in the absence of an Internet-based solution for multipoint audio that provided the same quality as telephony. NetMeeting and PlaceWare were accompanied on occasion with Web-based video provided through iVisit.

The needs assessment of the Oral Cancer Center suggested that the requirements for this center's collaboratory were quite different from those of the HIV/AIDS Center. In the Oral Cancer Center, asynchronous data sharing of several types of data (such as project files, schedules, and research data) was much more important than real-time interaction. Although early discussions with the Oral Cancer Center investigators indicated the need to facilitate synchronous interaction between the participants of the research studies and the cores at large, providing centerwide support became less critical than supporting the increasingly intensive work on the research projects. In this case, the requirements centered on facilitating small group communication; the sharing of protocols, raw research data, and analyses; and workflow support. Instrument sharing was not a consideration for the Oral Cancer Center collaboratory.

Interviews with Oral Cancer Center investigators illustrated the significant differences in the goals and objectives, operations, and personnel roles among the groups. For instance, in the research project on cancer screening and research subject participation by minorities, the work was highly sequenced, and was either performed by one or two individuals at a time, or by a group (such as telephone interviewers) who required no support with collaborative tools. The research project on personalized risk feedback in dental clinic smokers, on the other hand, was highly interactive and data intensive. In this project, the research personnel at the Memorial Sloan-Kettering Cancer Center (who designed the study and analyzed the data) and the clinical personnel at New York University (who handled all the patient interactions) interacted frequently and intensively through e-mail, telephone, and face-to-face meetings. The other two groups suffered operational delays, partially due to several Health Insurance Portability and Account Act (1996) regulations coming into effect, and were therefore less active at the time.

Because of the frequency and depth of the scientists' interactions in the Oral Cancer Center, we deployed a commercial collaboration tool, Groove, on a pilot basis with the Memorial Sloan-Kettering Cancer Center/New York University research group. Groove is a peer-to-peer collaborative application that contains a wide variety of collaborative tools that can be combined individually into a work space.

The first real-time collaborative opportunity emerged in the Oral Cancer Center when survey data needed to be analyzed on cancer screening and research subject participation by minorities. The study PI and three other collaborators (who were all at different institutions) used a commercial Webconferencing service provided by Genesys to discuss raw data and statistical analyses. An Informatics Core research staff member participated in the sessions to help manage the technical aspects (such as uploading materials as well as managing the workflow and the participant interactions).

Based on our experience with the HIV/AIDS Center and the Oral Cancer Center, we anticipated that the Biodefense Center would need tools specifically to support the research needs of the individual research projects funded by the center. To address these needs, shared online work spaces were created using the open-source Sakai project for the center's initial six research projects, ten developmental projects, and two career development projects.[1] Sakai was selected because it provided an integrated framework for both synchronous and asynchronous collaboration functions, including threaded message forums, shared calendaring, real-time multiparticipant text chat, and document sharing. Sakai brings these tools together in an application accessible through a Web browser, and its tools are often collectively referred to as a "Sakai work site."

The six primary research projects in the Biodefense Center were accepted for inclusion in the original center application because they proposed high-quality scientific work that brought together several investigators who crossed disciplines and, for most projects, also crossed institutions. For projects where the PIs were at different institutions, they were not necessarily at great geographic distance from each other (e.g., Argonne National Laboratory and the University of Chicago; the Medical College of Wisconsin at Milwaukee and the University of Wisconsin at Madison). During the first two years of the center, the scientists did not adopt Sakai's tools to support any of the research projects. For projects where several of the members were within the same institution or reasonable driving distance of each other, the scientists preferred meeting face-to-face on a weekly or monthly basis, even though this practice isolated more remote members of a project. One project resolved the isolation of one of the two remote members by adopting the Access Grid videoconferencing system for weekly lab meetings. The other remote scientist on this project could not access the Access Grid, so he participated via audio conference and traveled on the one occasion when his data was the primary focus of the discussion. Because all the members of the Biodefense Center reside in the Great Lakes region, travel among sites is not as problematic or time-consuming as for Oral Cancer Center members where collaborators are distributed between the United States and Puerto Rico.

Synchronous interaction was the preferred mode for Biodefense Center scientists to conduct research, although as we shall see, the lack of enthusiasm for the Sakai tools does not appear to be primarily due to the asynchronous nature of the application. In our initial introduction of Sakai, most of the scientists expressed reservations about using a site where all project members would have access to all information on the site. What the scientists wanted instead were protected areas within a project work site with the ability to control when to move information out to all project members (functionality not available in Sakai at that time). This desire to protect one's own intellectual property, even from collaborators, is a consequence of the center funding creating collaborations between scientists who might otherwise be competitors. While the HIV/AIDS Center scientists worked together because they had complementary expertise, the Biodefense Center scientists agreed to work together because they represented the expertise on a particular agent (e.g., botulism) available within the region. The ability of the collaboration software to protect one's intellectual property from collaborators was not an issue in the Oral Cancer Center projects.

The difference in the utility of synchronous versus asynchronous tools for each center is due to several factors. In the HIV/AIDS Center, the necessity of involving scientists from different fields, sharing the instruments, and interpreting the data, required real-time interaction. The need for asynchronous tools to share data sets arose late in the center's lifetime after the projects matured, and the center was dissolved before any asynchronous tools were widely adopted (e.g., MS DocuShare). In the case of the Oral Cancer Center, there was little need to coordinate between projects, and tasks within the projects were highly distributed, independent, and predefined, so real-time interaction was far less important than making sure that the information needed to work on a particular project was available and up-to-date. In the Biodefense Center, the scientists usually organized the project work using face-to-face interaction, and only one project adopted a synchronous tool (Access Grid) to more tightly couple the work of the three distributed project members.

Support for Center-Sponsored Activities

Even though the centers each contained independent research projects, each center had a set of activities that utilized collaborative technologies such as keeping track of members and holding yearly all-hands meetings. Many of these activities were administrative or public facing, and this section describes the nonscientific collaborative activities the center also needed to support.

A comprehensive HIV/AIDS Center Web site was created for the public and center members. The members-only part of the site informed scientists about the operations of the HIV/AIDS Center, including reports about the progress of the research collaborations, core services being offered to center members, and a searchable database of all existing members. The Web site was also used to accomplish administrative tasks (e.g., to register members, make announcements of upcoming events, distribute applications for developmental grants, archive center presentations, and provide help documents for collaboratory tools) and to evaluate the activity of the center (e.g., collecting survey data, recording observations, and creating usage logs). This Web site also provided links to launch the collaboratory applications such as NetMeeting that were used for meetings and presentations.

The HIV/AIDS Center used PlaceWare Auditorium to provide a virtual seminar series that was available to the full center membership. The seminars were used as a mechanism for sharing prepublished data among the HIV/AIDS Center members. The first virtual seminar occurred at the beginning of the second year of the grant; there were a total of nine seminars presented by center members and speakers from outside the center. There were an average of thirteen computers (the range was five to nineteen) logged into each presentation, located at three to four sites. This figure greatly underestimates the number of participants for each seminar, however, because people were typically assembled in groups around monitors or projected screens. These virtual seminars were important to the center because they enabled members to identify potential collaborators and potential projects while offering feedback and advice about existing data as well as its collection.

Interviews and surveys with the participating HIV/AIDS Center members revealed the value of the virtual seminar series. While not all the participants felt the virtual experience offered the same experience as physical copresence, the participants strongly disagreed with the statement, "Managing the technology gets in the way of learning about the science during the seminar." As the virtual seminars were occasions for presenting prepublished work, the real-time interactivity of the seminars was seen as valuable for accelerating the scientific work of both the speakers and the audience members. One speaker commented, "The feedback on the data was good. I probably would have had the same discussion with folks when I presented the talk at a meeting, but this was useful as I will not be presenting the data publicly for a month or two."

In terms of supporting centerwide activity, the Oral Cancer Center is comparatively low-tech. Initially, there was a plan to create a private Web site with information of interest to all center members. Yet during the development of this site, it became clear that primarily only the PI and the PI's center administrator were interested in providing information for the site. Since there was trouble getting other center members to supply information, the plans for the Web site were abandoned, and the staff focused instead on supporting individual research group work. The center members at large, however, do interact and exchange information. For example, the center administrator distributes information of general interest quite frequently through an e-mail distribution list. There is also an annual two-day meeting of all research project and core directors as well as the External Advisory Board. A monthly conference call of all research project and core directors was instituted by the funding agency, but it serves mainly to update the National Institute of Dental and Craniofacial Research project officer on the study progress.

Although the Sakai work sites were not used for the research projects of the Biodefense Center, there were several work sites created to facilitate coordination and document sharing among researchers, the administrative core, and the other cores and components of the Biodefense Center. Specifically, there was an administrative core work site used for information and activities required of the full membership, such as competition submissions, quarterly and annual reports, and participation in emergency response drills. The cores and components work site contained information about the services and fee structures (when applicable) of the cores, and was also available to all center members. The center leadership, including the Executive Advisory Board, actively contributed to their own work site, which they used to perform the administrative duties of these advisers, including reviewing for the various internal funding competitions. Finally, online interaction was supplemented by bimonthly phone conferencing between the PIs and members of the administrative core. A public Web site was created for the center, and it primarily served as the center's public face. Like the HIV/AIDS Center's Web site, it also provided secure links to tools and forms available only to center members.

Barriers and Enablers of Technology Adoption and Use

As this evaluation has shown, the three collaboratories described in this chapter exhibited some similarities, but they also differed in fundamental ways in terms of both organizational issues and technical needs. The open membership and developmental nature of the HIV/AIDS Center were the primary reasons for the collaboratory's focus on enabling general, cross-site collaborations with the capability of both one-on-one and group interactions. In contrast, the Oral Cancer Center and the Biodefense Center were initiated with much more specific work plans, and therefore the collaboratories emphasized supporting group work within individual projects and the general administrative activities necessary to running these multi-institutional centers. Real-time collaboration in the HIV/AIDS Center used a rich array of tools, resulting in types of collaboration that would not have occurred (for example, a real-time discussion of tissue samples among pathologists and clinicians) using the phone or e-mail only. For the Oral Cancer Center, making sure that the information needed for working on a particular project was available and up-to-date was initially more important than real-time interaction between project PIs. In this center, the need for real-time collaboration emerged only when the first project transitioned to data analysis and interpretation. At the Biodefense Center, the project teams performed primarily independently, and most center members traveled when there was a need for tightly coupled work that required a high degree of trust to succeed. The comparison of these collaboratories highlights several barriers and enablers that affected the outcomes of the respective implementations.

Barriers

Multiple computing platforms   The cross-platform issues were more problematic in the HIV/AIDS Center (with MS Windows, Macintosh, and UNIX platforms) than in the Oral Cancer Center (MS Windows and Macintosh only), but the collaboratory staff of both centers had to use various work-arounds (e.g., Virtual PC on the Macintosh) to allow certain members to participate. The decision to use the Windows-based Access Grid by some members of the Biodefense Center created a challenge for the Macintosh users—a problem that persisted in the initial piloting of the commercial version of the Access Grid to center members nationally.

Network infrastructure complexity   A major hurdle for the Oral Cancer Center was to find Webconferencing software that worked with the firewall configurations of all participants. For the HIV/AIDS Center and the Biodefense Center, firewalls were less of an issue, as the local technical support staff could negotiate with systems administrators to open access as needed.

Variable availability and expertise of local information technology support   The availability of local information technology support personnel facilitated the installation and use of collaboratory tools in the HIV/AIDS Center. On the other hand, limited remote support and lack of sophisticated local support was a major impediment for the Oral Cancer Center and several of the sites in the Biodefense Center.

Low computer and collaborative software literacy   Limited computer literacy with groupware tools hindered the participants' collaboratory adoption and use in all centers. While many of the scientists had some experience collaborating with distant colleagues, these collaborations typically relied on face-to-face meetings and e-mail. In the Biodefense Center, the only project that employed tools for synchronous interactions involved scientists who were already using the Access Grid or had access to local technical support for using the Access Grid. Scientists in all centers needed strong incentives and low risks for adopting new ways of conducting their work.

Insufficient maturity of collaborative software   Many collaborative software applications are still relatively new products. Functional limitations, poor interface design, and bugs had a negative effect on the scientists' perceptions about the value of these tools.

Lack of integration with existing application environments   Collaborative tools should, as much as possible, integrate seamlessly with a user's existing application environment (Mandviwalla and Olfman 1994). This barrier was especially obvious for users of Groove in the Oral Cancer Center, as Groove provided stand-alone calendaring and messaging functions that did not integrate with other applications. Similarly, in the Biodefense Center, the Sakai environment hosting the projects' Web sites was a stand-alone application that required a unique log-in and password, which researchers found difficult to remember given the infrequency of its use.

Despite the problems described above, the comparison of the three collaboratories also identified several factors that promoted collaboratory adoption.

Enablers

Collaboration incentives through continued funding   In all three centers, the continued funding mechanism promoted collaboration between center members, albeit in two different forms. For the HIV/AIDS Center, funding was predicated on the development of projects representing new collaborations between scientists. For the Oral Cancer Center and the Biodefense Center, continued funding depended on adequate progress on predefined research projects.

Collaborative versus competitive relationship of researchers   At both the HIV/AIDS and Oral Cancer Center, the lack of competitive pressures among the researchers led to a general readiness to collaborate with other center members. The HIV/AIDS Center involved researchers with complementary expertise, and the Oral Cancer Center funded research projects with nonoverlapping scientific questions. This structure ensured that each scientist's own individual work did not threaten to "scoop" the work of a center colleague. In contrast, the Biodefense Center projects often brought together members with similar expertise who might be competitors were it not for the center. For these scientists, the use of collaborative tools was not perceived as controlled enough to ensure that they did not scoop each other on work published outside the center.

Leadership by example   At the HIV/AIDS Center, the director led by example, as he was an early adopter and one of the most frequent users of the collaboratory technology in his own center. In addition, several senior scientists not only quickly adopted the technology for their work within the center but also began to use the tools for other collaborations as well. In the case of the Oral Cancer Center, the director actively sought out opportunities for the use of collaborative tools and strongly encouraged members to participate. Enthusiastic leadership did not ensure use, however. At the Biodefense Center, the director's early promotion of the tools seemed to inhibit their use, as he requested that the project work sites be open to the organizational hierarchy of the center, including the NIH program directors.

Tools matched to tasks   In general, the tools in the collaboratories were relatively well matched with the project tasks. For instance, Groove provided the capability to reduce or expand the feature set of a work space depending on the current needs of a project. On the other hand, in the HIV/AIDS Center the general functionality of the document-sharing application did not match the specific clinical needs, and therefore the tool was not adopted. Similarly, the lack of access control of the project sites in the Biodefense Center did not fit the comparatively competitive culture.

Technical progress   During the lifetime of the HIV/AIDS Center, voice over Internet protocol had not matured sufficiently to be a viable option for multicast audio of acceptable quality. By the start of the Oral Cancer Center, however, voice over Internet protocol applications were feasible. Conversely, the bandwidth of Internet connections was sufficient to satisfy the performance demands of the collaboratory applications in the HIV/AIDS Center, where the research sites were interconnected via Internet2. Members who suffered from "the last mile problem" (Bell and Gemmell 1996) (e.g., the wiring in their buildings was not modern enough to capitalize on the bandwidth enabled by Internet2) often solved the problem by participating in the virtual meeting at a colleague's office or in their lab located in a newer facility on campus. Similarly, the availability of the Access Grid technology as a commercial product (inSORS) moved the availability of this tool from one local project in the Biodefense Center to all similar centers nationally.

Conclusions

Applying the collaboratory model to distributed biomedical research will require further research on the factors related to the successful application of the tools to the scientific activity. It is clear from the failure of the HIV/AIDS Center to be refunded that the presence of a collaboratory does not ensure collaboration between all the participants. The success of this center in leveraging Wulf's "collaboratory opportunity" (1993) was judged differently by the NIH review panel and the center participants. A number of center members felt that their research benefited tremendously from the collaboratory and that they produced work with others with whom they would otherwise not have collaborated. In contrast, despite the relatively low use of the collaboratory tools provided to the Biodefense Center, the NIH decided to apply the concept to all the biodefense centers funded under this initiative. It remains to be seen whether these centers will embrace the tools for their scientific work or use them primarily for the administration of the centers, as was seen in the analysis of the Biodefense Center examined here.

As collaboration technology continues to mature and becomes more commonplace in scientists' everyday lives, the challenge will be to figure out how to integrate these tools into routine scientific practice to both supplement and transform these practices in order to increase scientific efficiency and productivity. Funding agencies have made it clear that they value collaboration by implementing programs that require it as a component of the research. Both the National Science Foundation (NSF) and NIH have released research programs and plans for the future that incorporate even more collaborative funding awards (chapters 11 and 17, this volume). Nevertheless, getting scientists to work together is often difficult. In fact, editorials appeared in both *Nature* and *Science* asking why individual researchers would be interested in the kinds of collaborations that the NSF and the NIH want to fund (Kennedy 2003; Who'd want to work in a team? 2003). It is not always clear how individual researchers will benefit from participating in a team project, and the reward structure of biomedical research is still focused on the reputation of individual researchers. For this reason, disciplinary social norms will undoubtedly drive the pace and breadth of the adoption of collaboratory tools. The rise in popularity of bioinformatics tools along with the emphasis on exploiting cyberinfrastructure for data archiving and management suggest that the capacity for sharing data is an increasingly important functionality for collaboration tools. It seems likely, though, that the integration of new tools into collaboratories will be subject to the same pressures and enablers for use that we have seen in the three centers presented in this chapter.

Notes

Portions of this chapter addressing the HIV/AIDS Center and the Oral Cancer Center appear in Titus Schleyer, Stephanie D. Teasley, and Rishi Bhatnagar, "Comparative Case Study of Two Biomedical Research Collaboratories," *Journal of Medical Internet Research* 7, no. 5 (2005): e53.

1. Sakai is a free and open-source online collaboration and learning environment that is built and maintained by the Sakai community. Many users of Sakai deploy it to support teaching and learning, ad hoc group collaboration, and research collaboration. For further information, see ⟨http://www.sakaiproject.org⟩.

References

Bell, G., and J. Gemmell. 1996. On-ramp prospects for the information superhighway dream. *Communications of the ACM* 39 (7): 55–60.

Cummings, J., and S. Kiesler. 2005. Collaborative research across disciplinary and organizational boundaries. *Social Studies of Science* 35:703–722.

Finholt, T. A. 2002. Collaboratories. In *Annual review of information science and technology*, ed. B. Cronin, 74–107. Washington, DC: American Society for Information Science.

Finholt, T. A. 2003. Collaboratories as a new form of scientific organization. *Economics of Innovation and New Technology* 12:5–25.

Finholt, T. A., and G. M. Olson. 1997. From laboratories to collaboratories: A new organizational form for scientific collaboration. *Psychological Science* 8:28–36.

14 Motivation to Contribute to Collaboratories: A Public Goods Approach

Nathan Bos

The first-generation collaboratories were preoccupied with the question of how to create the technology to enable long-distance communication. As is well documented in this book, the 1980s and 1990s saw rapid development in real-time communication, Web-based collaboration, and online database development. The next generation of collaboratories will deal with less technical but equally critical problems of how to motivate and sustain participation in collaborative activities that the new technologies enable.

Many early projects ran into motivation and incentive issues as unanticipated and poorly understood roadblocks. Most of these failures went undocumented but were well-known to insiders in the field. A few high-profile collaboratories have documented these issues, however, including the Upper Atmospheric Research Collaboratory, the Environmental Molecular Sciences Laboratory, SEQUOIA (Weedman 1998), and WormBase (Schatz 1991). Each of these projects developed cutting-edge technology that, at least for a period of time, was underutilized. These projects had by and large done a good job of studying how scientists do their jobs; the core failures were not simply usability or compatibility but the result of a more general problem of understanding how to motivate scientists to take on new and different kinds of work.

This chapter will examine collaboratory participation as a "public goods" problem. The provision of public goods is a well-studied problem in economics. Economists, political scientists, and psychologists have identified many factors and mechanisms that affect people's willingness to contribute to public goods.

This chapter will focus on contributions to one kind of collaboratory: community data systems (CDSs) (chapter 3, this volume), which share some similarity with classic public goods experimental tasks. Drawing from a survey of forty-eight CDS administrators, interviews with participants of ten other databases, and public reports from other projects, I will examine how these projects solve the "social dilemma" of motivating data contributions, and compare these real-world solutions to those that are the most thoroughly studied in laboratory research on public goods.

Public Goods Problems

Public goods is the study of how groups obtain cooperation for a greater good among self-interested individuals. How do societies provide for public goods such as hospitals, charities, and the like, which are too expensive for any one person to fund, but benefit all? How do societies prevent environmental destruction by their members? These public goods problems are difficult because they present social dilemmas—situations where an action that is rational for every individual in a group brings about a group outcome that is suboptimal and sometimes has dire consequences. One of the most well-known social dilemmas is the "tragedy of the commons," described by Garrett Hardin (1968) thusly:

Picture a pasture open to all. It is to be expected that each herdsman will try to keep as many cattle as possible on the commons. Such an arrangement may work reasonably satisfactorily for centuries because tribal wars, poaching, and disease keep the numbers of both man and beast well below the carrying capacity of the land. Finally, however, comes the day of reckoning, that is, the day when the long-desired goal of social stability becomes a reality. At this point, the inherent logic of the commons remorselessly generates tragedy.

As a rational being, each herdsman seeks to maximize his gain. Explicitly or implicitly, more or less consciously, he asks, "What is the utility to me of adding one more animal to my herd?" This utility has one negative and one positive component.

1. The positive component is a function of the increment of one animal. Since the herdsman receives all the proceeds from the sale of the additional animal, the positive utility is nearly +1.

2. The negative component is a function of the additional overgrazing created by one more animal. Since, however, the effects of overgrazing are shared by all the herdsmen, the negative utility for any particular decisionmaking herdsman is only a fraction of −1.

Adding together the component partial utilities, the rational herdsman concludes that the only sensible course for him to pursue is to add another animal to his herd. And another.... But this is the conclusion reached by each and every rational herdsman sharing a commons. Therein is the tragedy. Each man is locked into a system that compels him to increase his herd without limit—in a world that is limited. Ruin is the destination toward which all men rush, each pursuing his own best interest in a society that believes in the freedom of the commons. Freedom in a commons brings ruin to all.

The tragedy of the commons is a prototypical social dilemma. There is a clear greater good, which is a healthy (not overgrazed) common pasture that benefits all. There is also an individually rational course of action (continually increasing the herd size) that when followed by each individual to its logical conclusion, leads to a suboptimal group outcome (the destruction of the commons).

A corollary to the tragedy of the commons is a public goods experiment where instead of preventing the destruction of an existing resource, a group is presented with the challenge of creating a new public good with pooled resources. In a laboratory setting, it might be played this way:

Four male undergraduates from a sociology course are brought to a room and seated at a table. They are each given an endowment of $5. They are then told that each can choose to invest some or all of their $5 in a group project. In particular, each will simultaneously and without discussion put an amount between $0 and $5 in an envelope. The experimenter will collect the "contributions," total them up, double the amount, and then divide this money among the group. The private benefit from the public good, in this case, is one half the total contributions, which is what each receives from the group project. No one, except the experimenter, knows others' contributions but all know the total. The procedure is implemented and the subjects are paid. The data collected, beyond the description of the experimental parameters, is simply the amount contributed by each individual. (Ledyard 1995)

The optimal group outcome for this situation is clear. The group as a whole will make the most money as a group if everyone contributes all of their $5 endowment. In the absence of other interventions, however, this rarely happens.

The worst group solution occurs when each individual contributes nothing. This is considered by many economists to be the "rational" outcome (or at least the outcome that is the result of independent rational individual actions). For every individual, the marginal payoff for contributing $1 more to the group is only 50¢. (Each dollar is doubled by the experimenter to $2, but is then divided by four.) If the individual contributes nothing, they will become what is called a "free rider" on the group and will still get one-fourth of the group payoff.

This worst-possible group outcome rarely happens in practice, though. Faced with the uncertainty of this social dilemma, most groups take a middle ground, and contribute between 40 and 60 percent of the total (Ledyard 1995). If the game is played repeatedly with no other interventions, the contributions tend to drop. If the group is allowed to communicate between rounds, the contributions tend to rise. Many different versions on the above game have been performed in research settings, varying such conditions as the group size, the payoff amount, communication, the information exchanged between the participants, and the amount of background information provided about the participants. An important distinction should be made between the types of public goods. Some public goods offer relatively easy solutions to the dilemma of contribution, in that those who fail to contribute can be excluded from the benefits. A simple example of this would be a public zoo that charges admission (perhaps in the form of a "suggested donation") or a cooperative nursery where parents are expected to take turns staffing. Public goods can be made excludable if their usage is observable, and if there is some means of limiting access. Still, many public goods do not fall into this category, including Hardin's commons.

Discretionary Databases

What if the goods being pooled are not money or tangible goods but information? Information has the interesting property that it can be duplicated and shared with others without being lost to the owner of the information. Does this make the public goods dilemma a moot point? Unfortunately, this is not the case because other costs are often associated with the act of sharing knowledge. There is a cost of effort and time required to transform information into a form that others can use. There is also the potential loss of exclusive control of that knowledge as intellectual property.

Terry Connolly and Brian Thorn (1990) and Terry Connolly, Brian Thorn, and Alan Heminger (1992) explored the nature of pooled public knowledge resources, or what they referred to as discretionary databases. Their main area of interest was intracorporate databases of strategic business information, which sprung up in large numbers during the early period of the Web. These authors conducted experimental studies with a business game in which undergraduate participants had to decide whether to share marketing information from their "region" with the rest of their eight-person group. Sharing the information helped everyone else in the group and did not hurt the sharer because groups were not in direct competition with each other. Terry Connolly and Brian Thorn (1990) modeled the effort cost of sharing with a small monetary cost. When the costs were set low (4 percent of the participants' stake), the participants shared at a relatively high rate (80 percent of the maximum possible), but sharing rates dropped to 32 percent when the costs were increased to 20 percent of their stake. Not surprisingly, the cost of sharing mattered. It was also interesting that even when the costs were nominal, sharing was high but not close to 100 percent, so the participants may have had some reluctance about sharing that went beyond the cost.

Janet Fulk and her colleagues (2004) conducted a field study of discretionary databases at three corporate sites, and delved deeper into the individual variables that predict higher contribution rates. One of the strongest predictors of who would contribute to a database is the measure of who has downloaded information from it. The perceived value of the resource was also a predictor, as was the low perceived cost of contributing.

Online Communities

Some of the research in online communities is also relevant to collaboratories. E-communities, as they are sometimes called, are typically volunteer-staffed bulletin boards, mailing lists, wikis, blogs, or other Web sites devoted to a specialized topic. Commitments of time, effort, and energy, rather than monetary contributions, are what keep the community viable. Brian Butler and his colleagues (2007) surveyed owners and volunteers on 121 active e-mail lists to learn more about who does the work of maintaining these communities and what motivates them to do this task. They found that motivations clustered into three categories: information benefits, social benefits, and altruistic benefits. All three types of motivation seemed to be important as each one was correlated with a higher level of involvement in the site. Interestingly, the social and altruistic motivations were more highly correlated than the informational. These authors also found a strong link between the level of involvement and the number of social connections an individual had in the group, although the causality of this effect could go either way (and probably does go both ways). This study highlights the social motivations and benefits of online communities.

Collaboratories

The public goods framework is beginning to be applied to the arena of distributed science as well. An interesting example of a public goods problem that falls into the category of a collaboratory was funding for Space Station Freedom. In this case, the funding was provided by a consortium of governments. Mark Olson and David Porter (1994) explored the dynamics of funding for this cooperative effort, and they piloted a funding enforcement mechanism that was being considered for use in this situation.

Community Data Systems

CDSs have characteristics that make them a good first target for study in this area. It is relatively easy to define and measure contributions as they come in the tangible form of depositions of data or annotations to existing data. Thus, contributing to a CDS more closely resembles a classic public goods problem than do the more varied types of participation required by other collaboratories.

CDSs are public aggregations of data and are most prevalent in two areas: biology and health science. A CDS is defined as:

An information resource that is created, maintained, or improved by a geographically distributed community. The information resources are semipublic and of wide interest; a small team of people with an online file space of team documents would not be considered a community data system. Model organism projects in biology are prototypical community data systems. (chapter 3, this volume)

CDSs are assuming an increasingly significant role in biology research. The annual review of biology databases published in *Nucleic Acids Research* lists over four hundred such projects (Baxevanis 2002). CDSs are an example of a new organizational form where the motivation of contributors is unclear, and their role in the traditional academic reward system is still in flux. As such, they make an interesting target for the study of participant motivation.

An early example of a CDS is the Zebrafish Information Network (ZFIN), a centralized database for the research community that studies this popular "model" organism. ZFIN obtains data through contributions from individual laboratories that upload their data on a regular basis (Sprague et al. 2006). Many individual labs generate data on ZFIN, but no individual laboratory (to my knowledge) has the motivation or resources to manage these data, or integrate all of them. Yet there is a clear public good in aggregating this knowledge. The data are more useful in the aggregate because duplication of effort can be avoided, and because various modeling and searching functions can be done more thoroughly on a more complete data set. But there is not a large marginal payoff for any individual lab to do the work of "cleaning up," formatting, uploading, and possibly annotating the data it has already collected—the addition of one more piece of information does not increase the value of the entire resource by such a large amount as to make it worthwhile. Further, there is some heterogeneity of payoff, which makes cooperation even more difficult (Bagnoli and McKee 1991; Ledyard 1995). The individuals who benefit the most are those who can avoid the cost and trouble of doing the sequencing themselves, not the individuals who have already expended that cost for their immediate purposes. As such, the organizers and promoters of CDSs, like ZFIN, face the challenges of a full-fledged social dilemma.

Solving social dilemmas in the fields of biological and health research may be particularly difficult. Compared to other fields such as high-energy physics, biology is traditionally more competitive between laboratories (Chompalov, Genuth, and Schrum 2002) and is not always completely open in its data-sharing policies (Cohen 1995).

In the rest of this chapter, I will examine how existing CDSs solve, or attempt to solve, the challenge of obtaining contributions from individual scientists or individual laboratories. These solutions will be compared with those proposed in the literature. Information on current CDS practices will be taken from two data sources: the Science of Collaboratories (SOC) database and a survey conducted of CDSs.

Data Sources and Methods

The SOC project has assembled a database of more than two hundred projects that meet the definition of a collaboratory. It then further investigated almost seventy of them by analyzing written reports and conducting interviews with key personnel. In the course of these investigations, we conducted phone interviews with administrators from ten CDSs in biology or health sciences, and analyzed published information from a number of others. I will use these data to provide examples of how database managers are solving the social dilemma of motivating contributors. Further description of the collaboratories database can be found in chapter 3 of this volume.

A Survey of CDSs

A second data source is a survey we conducted of CDS managers in spring 2003. To identify a sample for this survey, we started with the review of biological databases published annually in *Nucleic Acids Research* (Baxevanis 2002), supplemented with a few other projects we knew of from the SOC database. This yielded a sample of 347 databases. However, most of these databases generate all data in-house, rather than soliciting contributions from outside researchers, and so were excluded from our sample. Some databases also use an enforcement mechanism whereby they partner with relevant journals in their field rather than relying on voluntary submissions; these were also excluded. (This journal partnership system will be described later.) We reviewed the Web sites of these 347 databases, and identified 105 that openly solicited additions, annotations, corrections, bibliographic references, or other types of contributions. We sent a message to the e-mail contact listed on the Web site of these 105 databases and asked them to participate in an online survey, requesting that the survey be completed by a database administrator (who sometimes, but not always, gave their contact e-mail on the Web site).

In addition, we asked the survey respondents for general statistical data about their database's size and usage, reports of how they solicited contributions, what they perceived to be important contributor motivations, and some miscellaneous management issues relevant to CDSs. Questions from this survey and the response rates are listed in appendix A. We received an acceptable response rate of 46 percent, or forty-eight total responses, as detailed below.

Profile of Survey Respondents   Tables 14.1 and 14.2 give a profile of responding collaboratories according to type of data collected and level of data processing expected. Tables 14.3, 14.4, and 14.5 shows the distribution of databases according to page views and unique users.

Table 14.1
Which of these types of information are collected in your database? (select all that apply)

Genomic databases	39%
Comparative genomics	20%
Gene expression	26%
Gene identification and structure	22%
Genetic and physical maps	17%
Intermolecular interactions	9%
Metabolic pathways and cellular regulation	11%
Mutation databases	24%
Pathology	7%
Protein databases	39%
Protein sequence motifs	24%
Proteome resources	11%
Retrieval systems and database structure	11%
RNA sequences	22%
Structure	22%
Transgenics	7%

Table 14.2
Which of these best characterizes the information in your database? (select all that apply)

Data pulled from other databases	58%
New data from various laboratories	70%
Annotations of existing data	63%
New original analyses of data	40%
Visualizations or other value-added analyses of data	56%
Bibliographic information	60%

Table 14.3
Site traffic

	Mean	Low	High
Page views	58,298 (n = 22 respondents)	50	500,000
Unique users	2,346 (n = 21 respondents)	50	20,000

Table 14.4
Distribution of databases by reported Web traffic

	0–1000	1001–10000	>10000
Page views	1	12	8
Unique users	5	7	4

Table 14.5
How many outside researchers have contributed information to your database so far? (please estimate if the exact number is unknown)

Less than 10	22%
10 to 20	16%
21 to 100	27%
100+	31%

These site traffic results are higher than expected. Web sites with an average of five thousand or more unique visits per month appear to be serving healthy-size academic communities. The highest in terms of page views is the Protein Data Bank (Berman et al. 2000), which is a database almost as well established as GenBank with a similar journal partnership mechanism (see the discussion below), so this is a definite outlier.[1]

Results and Discussion

How do the real-world policies of CDSss compare with interventions of social psychologists that attempt to "solve" the social dilemma of public goods problems? I identified common solutions from our CDS survey, supplemented by SOC interviews and other data sources. The solutions can be divided into two broad categories: economic solutions and social/organizational ones. Within each of these categories, three types of solutions can be distinguished.

Economic Solutions

I define economic solutions as changes to the external reward system that make contribution more attractive, or alternately, that make it less attractive to withhold contributions. I distinguish between three types of economic solutions: sanctions, rewards, and funding contingencies.

Sanctions Not surprisingly, contribution in public goods games increases when the participants can be sanctioned or punished for not contributing. Sanctions can be imposed if contributions (or the lack thereof) are observable and if some enforcement mechanism is available. Sanctions do not necessarily require a central authority to be enforced. Elinor Ostrom, James Walker, and Roy Gardner (1992) experimented with a decentralized sanctioning mechanism whereby individual participants could levy fines on other individuals for uncooperative behavior. Individuals had to pay a fee in order to levy fines against another player, thus making it less likely that they would do so casually or maliciously. These researchers found that the peer-sanctioning method was effective in increasing cooperation and was even more effective when paired with the possibility of communicating with other players.

Sanctions per se are rarely used to enforce contributions to CDSs because it is difficult to determine when an individual is withholding data. Researchers do sometimes complain to a higher authority, such as the agency that funded the research for which the data were collected, or malign a researcher's reputation among their peers to punish those who do not share reagents freely (Cohen 1995). This is regarded as a clumsy and ineffective mechanism, however, and it is likely to backfire on the individual complainant.

As already discussed, it is also not possible to withhold access to scientific data to noncontributors. Most data generated in academic settings is funded either by the federal government or another source that requires the public release of the data (although as noted, this is difficult to enforce).

The model that has proven most successful in motivating contributions is the system of requiring proof of data contribution as a prerequisite to publication in the field of genetics. GenBank is probably the largest CDS in existence (in actuality it is a set of databases), containing more than 33 billion gene sequences from more than 140,000 different species (Benson et al. 2003). In the beginning of the GenBank project, the database hired its own staff to comb through journals and transfer published sequences into the GenBank database. This method was slow and error prone, but it worked acceptably well for several years. Still, the rapid acceleration of the field due to new sequencing techniques prompted GenBank to investigate ways to get researchers to submit data directly. In the late 1980s, GenBank began partnering with journals (Cinkosky et al. 1991) on a policy that required authors to deposit data in GenBank as a precondition of publication. Authors received an accession number on the submission of data that they could submit to the journals as proof of data deposit, and the journal could use this number to refer readers to the relevant data. This approach was beneficial to journals because it absolved them of having to print more and more "raw" sequence data and other data. Users also benefited because the electronic database provided a much more usable form of data access than copying sequences from printed pages. Today, most of the important journals in the field of genetics worldwide comply with this system, and require a GenBank accession number to accompany paper submissions wherever appropriate. The GenBank journal partnership model has also been adopted by other large CDSs such as the Protein Data Bank.

What is remarkable, and makes this system work, is that GenBank and the Protein Data Bank have received wide and consistent support from journals across several closely related fields to enforce this ban. Although game theorists might predict that some journals would forego this requirement to gain a competitive advantage over other journals, we have not heard of any such attempts. Currently, the system is so well established that public defection by individual journals would likely receive strong peer sanctioning from the scientific community.

The success of the journal accession number model does not eliminate the problem of how to motivate contributions to public databases. Some databases aggregate information that is extremely specialized, or too small to have been noticed and included into GenBank, the Protein Data Bank, or other larger databases. Some databases exist in areas of research outside those where all journals comply with the GenBank partnerships. And in perhaps the most interesting cases, some databases collect information that is more than a raw data dump, and instead require original analysis or synthesis.

In these last cases, the GenBank journal partnership model does not fit because the contribution is no longer an appendix to another work submitted elsewhere but is original work in itself, requiring a different sort of incentive model.

Rewards Formal rewards can also help motivate public goods contributions. The participants in social dilemma experiments contribute more when their likely individual payoff or marginal per capita return increases. Contribution can also be motivated by nonfinancial rewards, such as extra credit points (Ledyard 1995). Connolly and Thorn (1990) also showed that auction mechanisms where information providers post asking prices, information seekers post purchase bids, or both are posted together can increase sharing rates.

Direct financial rewards are not generally used to motivate contributions to CDSs. The closest parallels to a financial reward would be either funding contingency (discussed in the next section), or a situation where a contributor felt that documenting a public data contribution would yield an advantage for gaining a grant or promotion. In academia, however, there are parallel, nonfinancial reward systems that take the place of direct financial rewards. In particular, the journal system is a well-established part of the "academic reward" system. Success in publishing is tied to most other important rewards: hiring, promotion, tenure, and grant awards. Publications serve as tangible markers of success that represent less tangible contributions to the intellectual public good.

A challenge for CDSs is that data contributions are not yet well-recognized markers of professional success the way that publications are. Some projects are seeking to remedy this problem in unique ways. The GenBank publication-contingency model already discussed has been one successful way of linking data contribution to the existing reward system. Yet this model works best for data rather than analysis, and does not work as well when contributions require extensive annotation or analysis of data separate from publication. In this case, it makes more sense for CDS contributions themselves to be recognized and rewarded as "publications," rather than mere appendixes to publications.

The Alliance for Cellular Signaling (AfCS) had this in mind when it forged a partnership with the Nature Publishing Group to cosponsor the AfCS's "Molecule Pages" database.[2] The Molecule Pages are intended to be a set of over five thousand data reviews covering every molecule known to be involved in cellular signaling. The entire set of five thousand or more would require an investment of time and expertise far beyond what the paid staff of the AfCS could supply. Each "page" contribution requires considerable time—equivalent to writing a review article—and specialized expertise. But these pages were not review articles; they were highly structured database entries, and thus did not fit within existing review journals. The Nature partnership was an attempt to make these valued contributions into a type of publication. The Molecule Pages would go through a peer-review process organized by the highly respected journal *Nature*, and would be published online by the Nature Publishing Group rather than by the AfCS. This model of trying to make CDS contributions into publication-like accomplishments in their own right is an interesting model that may be used increasingly in the future.

Funding Contingencies   A third economic approach used to motivate contributions in other areas is to make research funding in some way contingent on contribution. To the best of my knowledge, this is not a model that fits with any existing public goods laboratory research. In a loose form, this system is already in place in the biological research community. The National Institutes of Health (NIH 2003) requires the investigators it funds to release data on request to other researchers and publish findings in a timely fashion. As a result, data such as gene sequences usually make their way into GenBank consistently and quickly. But as noted earlier, there are other more specialized or labor-intensive kinds of data that do not fit the GenBank model.

The PharmacoGenetics Knowledge Base is a CDS that has taken a new approach to funder-mandated data contribution. Pharmacogenetics is the study of how the same drugs affect different people, based on individual genetics or other factors. The PharmacoGenetics Knowledge Base is an attempt to aggregate emerging knowledge about drug/genetic interactions in one place. The NIH has given grants to thirteen labs to do research in this area. Unlike other programs, the NIH program officer convenes monthly teleconferences to exchange information among the thirteen labs. Project principal investigators also get together face-to-face twice a year to exchange information about their projects and report on findings. In this way, the program officer hopes to create a more cohesive set of projects and develop the PharmacoGenetics Knowledge Base as an important data resource. An arrangement is also in place with the *Pharmaceutical Review* to publish a selection of the most innovative database entries in a yearly synopsis. This collaboration represents an interesting use of a program officer's influence to manage and incentivize contributions to a public database.

Social/Organizational Solutions

The second major category of solutions to the social dilemma of CDS contributions is social/organizational solutions. Some research investigations in psychology and communication studies have examined the role of social identity and communication modality on cooperation. Experimental work in this area has focused more on theoretical issues than on understanding real-world solutions. The best sources of data on how CDSs might solve the everyday problem of motivating contributions are the SOC collaboratory database and the survey we conducted of CDSs.

Table 14.6

Which of these have been the most effective means of soliciting contributions—that is, which would you recommend to a database similar to yours? (mention all that apply)

Personal contact (e.g., e-mailing a known expert or colleague)	64%
Database Web site	55%
Professional channels—conferences or journals	41%
Links from other Web sites	16%
Prior agreements from funding contracts	7%

Communication   One of the best ways to increase cooperation in a social dilemma is to allow the participants to communicate with each other. Ledyard (1995) reported findings from multiple studies that showed that levels of cooperation increase from an expected baseline around 50 percent to levels varying from 70 to 90 percent when the study participants are allowed to communicate with each other. Communication can reverse the effect that cooperation tends to deteriorate over time: with repeated chances to communicate, cooperation gets stronger instead of weaker. The media matters somewhat, in that richer communication media tend to both increase cooperation more quickly and make it more resistant to defection as compared to leaner media (Bos et al. 2002).

While it seems to be clear that communication can motivate contributions, little is known about what kinds of communication are particularly effective. It does seem to be important that group discussion be on task (Dawes, McTavish, and Shaklee 1977), but there does not seem to be one particular communication tactic that is more successful than others. Threats of defection, promises of cooperation, arguments for the common good, and group identity building are all common approaches, and each can be effective.

Communication is also judged to be critical to the success of CDSs, as shown by the respondents' answers to survey questions in table 14.6. Three categories were endorsed with a high frequency: personal contact, the database Web site, and professional channels. Personal contact will be discussed in the next section.

We were somewhat surprised to see "the database Web site" get a strong endorsement. Of course, we knew that most of our sample did solicit contributions at the project's Web site—in many cases, that was how the database came to be in our sample. But we did not expect this to be rated as a highly effective means of reaching potential contributors. Generally one does not come across one of these specialized genetics database by accident, or by simply browsing the Web. Researchers presumably visit these sites to extract data for specific purposes. Solicitations on the Web site itself would seem to have one purpose: to try to recruit users to become contributors. In social dilemma terms, the Web site solicitation is a prompt to people benefiting from the public good that they should also contribute to it. The majority (55 percent) of database administrators believed this to be one of their most effective methods of obtaining data.

It is worth noting that the solicitations on the Web sites themselves were factual and understated. We did not find any Web sites that gave impassioned sales pitches about the value of the database, the importance of contributions, or that framed the problem as a social dilemma. This contrasts sharply with the tactics of many public goods resources such as public television fund-raising campaigns. The latter type of appeal might not be compatible with the scientific culture, or could be seen as a mark of unprofessionalism by managers of these resources. Alternately, perhaps it has not occurred to CDS managers to be more overt in their solicitations. This is an issue that deserves further investigation.

We expected "links from other Web sites" to be a crucial mechanism for solicitation, but it was not. This is in contrast to commercial Web sites, which often rely on banner ads, and e-community resources (blogs, discussion groups, etc.), and depend heavily on referrals. We do not know whether scientific databases do not rely on these mechanisms because they are judged to be ineffective or because they simply have not pursued this avenue.

Social Connections Butler and his colleagues (2007) found that social connections correlated with participation rates in online communities. Likewise in our survey, personal contact was rated as the most effective means of soliciting data contributions and was endorsed by 64 percent of the respondents. This is consistent with other research in the sociology of science, which has emphasized the significance of interpersonal connections among scientists (so-called "invisible colleges," after Price and Beaver 1966). Personal social networks among scientists are known to be critical to the transfer of ideas, hiring decisions, and funding priorities, so it is not surprising to find that these networks would continue to play a key role in CDSs.

Little research in the area of social dilemmas has examined the importance of personal connections. This is likely due to the fact that it would require experiments with preexisting social groups, which makes the recruitment and control of confounding variables difficult. There has been much research on the impact of social identity, which is the degree to which individuals perceive themselves as belonging to the same group. Many investigations on in-group/out-group classification have shown that small cues can create a sense of shared group membership, which leads individuals to be more generous in their actions and charitable in their opinions of each other (Brown 2000). Mark Van Vugt and Claire Hart (2004) found that when individuals have a strong sense of group membership, they are less likely to defect from a collaborating group, even when presented with a higher-payoff option. Similarly, Steven Karau and Jason Hart (1998) found that group cohesiveness decreased social loafing in a task that required group effort. Finally, communication has been closely linked to a sense of group membership (Moore et al. 1999). There may be a difference between one-to-one social network ties and the generalized sense of identity studied by these researchers; further research on these differences is warranted.

The best example of a CDS where shared identity seems to have been important is ZFIN, which was discussed previously. ZFIN is an online clearinghouse of resources for the zebrafish research community. The ZFIN collaboratory is a Web-accessible site containing a large, interrelated database of information on zebrafish genetics and anatomy, a bibliography, and practical research information such as a directory of individuals and companies.

According to the project managers, ZFIN has benefited from the close-knit nature of the zebrafish research community. Most early members of the community had a connection to George Streisinger at the University of Oregon. Streisinger pioneered the use of zebrafish as a model organism, and set a tone of generosity and collaboration for the community. ZFIN has tried to maintain Streisinger's example. One way in which ZFIN has attempted to do this is through the use of participatory design (Doerry et al. 1997).[3] ZFIN has enjoyed continued exponential growth since its inception, and at this writing counted over three thousand individual users, which probably represents most of this specialized field.

The importance of group identity also came across in another item in the CDS managers' survey, with the results shown in table 14.7. Again, personal connection is judged to be a significant motivator, endorsed by 61 percent of the respondents. Even more strongly endorsed were "a sense of obligation to the scientific community"

Table 14.7
What would you guess are the important motivations for outside contributors to your database? (check all that apply)

Desire to contribute to a valued resource	83%
Sense of obligation to scientific community	81%
Sense of professional accomplishment	62%
Personal connection to researchers running the database	61%
It is an alternative means of attaining professional credit recognition	51%
Desire to stake first claim to an area of study	50%
It is an alternative means of professional scholarly publication	39%
It is required by a journal or publisher	36%
It is required by a funding source	19%

and "a desire to contribute to a valued resource." These results indicate that there is probably more to contributors' motivation than simply doing an interpersonal favor or fulfilling an obligation to friends. The primary aim of scientist-contributors to CDSs, at least according to database managers, is to further the science itself and contribute to the community. The items in this survey do not attempt to tease apart an obligation to the science and a commitment to the social community. This topic is worthy of future study.

Survey items that matched more closely with a well-structured reward system, such as a journal/publisher requirement and a means of gaining alternate professional credit, were also deemed important motivators, although further down the list. This should be interpreted with caution, because our survey sample excluded GenBank and other databases that operated under formalized partnerships. The community spirit reflected in this item, therefore, could be an artifact of the smaller, more specialized databases we sampled.

Future Direction: Governance

Our investigations into contributor motivations to CDSs have begun to focus on the area of governance. Our interactions with managers of successful collaboratories, such as the Cochrane Collaboration (Dickersin et al. 2002), have shown that the relationship between participants and projects tends to be complex. In particular, CDS projects such as Cochrane tend to have sets of committees and working groups that plan, solicit, and review contributions in particular areas. Many participants also have roles as committee members or leaders, and are involved in ways that go far beyond contributions of data. It seems likely that these complex webs of roles and relationships help sustain and motivate ongoing contribution.

The literature on social dilemmas has little to say about how different governance structures may affect voluntary contributions. Researchers have explored some simple authority models (Ledyard 1995) and member-sanctioning models, as already discussed in Ostrom, Walker and Gardner 1992, but they have not delved into the variety and detail of governance models enough to provide much useful advice for database managers. This should be a focal area of future research.

Conclusion

There is an interesting match between the extensive body of experimental work on public goods research dilemmas and the real-world challenges of CDSs. Public goods research predicts that rewards, sanctions, communication opportunities, and social connections will all tend to improve contribution rates. In our study of CDSs, we saw each of these approaches used to a different extent. The highly successful partnership of academic journals in biology with databases such as GenBank and the Protein Data Bank ties rewards and sanctions together. In order to be published in peer-reviewed journals, which are the gatekeepers of the academic rewards system, authors must deposit raw data into these databases, or risk sanction (withholding publication). This partnership seems to have largely solved the problem of motivating contribution for two crucial classes of data: gene sequences and molecular structures.

Some other types of annotated data slip through the cracks of this system, however, because of the specialized nature of analysis required to process data for public consumption. We surveyed managers of voluntary contribution databases and found that their best recruitment efforts rely on other means. Social networks are judged to be important, as predicted by both public goods and e-communities researchers. These social connections can be one-to-one personal connections, but also could be feelings of personal connectedness to a community or a sense of mission.

There is a class of motivational methods that has seldom been tried in real-world collaboratories: market designs that allow some sort of currency to be traded in exchange for data, and permit information suppliers and producers to set "prices" according to the perceived value of the information (e.g., Connolly, Thorn, and Heminger 1992). In publicly funded CDSs, this currency could not be real money because researchers would not normally be allowed to sell information produced under a federal grant. But other currencies with recognition or exchange value could be imagined. The journal publication system provides one such currency, and the idea of a publication is being extended in a digital world in partnerships, such as the AfCS's Molecule Pages database, whose entries are published by the Nature Publishing Group. Many other types of currency might better incentivize the kinds of scientific contribution needed in the future.

There is also a large class of governance structures that has not been replicated or tested in laboratory settings. Collaboratory owners often puzzle over how to optimally structure organization charts, committees, ad hoc working groups, and advisory boards, and they struggle with the task of writing bylaws governing their interplay. Laboratory work in public goods does not help CDSs to make these managerial decisions, but they could in the future. As CDSs and other types of collaboratories continue to grow in prevalence and significance, hopefully the range of managerial tactics will also be better understood.

Notes

1. A single session on a Web site may include the viewing of multiple pages, so page view and "session" counts are separate measures of site traffic.

2. For additional information about the AfCS and the Molecule Pages, see chapter 11 (this volume).

3. Participatory design is a method that tries to involve potential users in all parts of the design process, not just requirements gathering and evaluation.

References

Bagnoli, M., and M. McKee. 1991. Voluntary contribution games: Efficient private provision of public goods. *Economic Inquiry* 29:351–366.

Baxevanis, A. D. 2002. The Molecular Biology Database Collection: 2002 update. *Nucleic Acids Research* 30:1–12.

Benson, D. A., I. Karsch-Mizrachi, D. J. Lipman, J. Ostell, and D. L. Wheeler. 2003. GenBank: Update. *Nucleic Acids Research* 31:23–27.

Berman, H. M., J. Westbrook, Z. Feng, G. Gilliland, T. N. Bhat, H. Weissig et al. 2000. The Protein Data Bank. *Nucleic Acids Research* 28:235–242.

Bos, N. D., J. S. Olson, D. Gergle, G. M. Olson, and Z. Wright. 2002. Effects of four computer-mediated channels on trust development. In *Proceedings of CHI 2002*, 135–140. New York: ACM Press.

Brown, R. 2000. Social identity theory: Past achievements, current problems, and future challenges. *European Journal of Social Psychology* 30:745–778.

Butler, B., L. Sproull, S. Kiesler, and R. Kraut. 2007. Community effort in online groups: Who does the work and why? In *Leadership at a distance: Research in technologically-supported work*, ed. S. Weisband and L. Atwater. Mahwah, NJ: Lawrence Erlbaum.

Chompalov, I., J. Genuth, and W. Shrum. 2002. The organization of scientific collaborations. *Research Policy* 31 (5): 749–767.

Cinkosky, M. J., J. W. Fickett, P. Gilna, and C. Burks. 1991. Electronic data publishing and GenBank. *Science* 252 (5010): 1273–1277.

Cohen, J. 1995. Share and share alike isn't always the rule in science. *Science* 268 (5218): 1715–1718.

Connolly, T., and B. K. Thorn. 1990. Discretionary databases: Theory, data, and implications. In *Organizations and communication technology*, ed. J. Fulk and C. Steinfeld, 219–233. Newbury Park, CA: Sage.

Connolly, T., B. K. Thorn, and A. Heminger. 1992. *Social dilemmas: Theoretical issues and research findings*. Oxford: Pergamon.

Dawes, R., J. McTavish, and H. Shaklee. 1977. Behavior, communication, and assumptions about other people's behavior in a commons dilemma situation. *Journal of Personality and Social Psychology* 35 (1): 1–11.

Dickersin, K., E. Manheimer, S. Wieland, K. A. Rovinson, C. LeFebvre, and C. McDonald. 2002. Development of the Cochrane collaboration's central register of controlled clinical trials. *Evaluation and the Health Professions* 25:39–63.

Doerry, E., S. Douglas, A. E. Kirkpatrick, and M. Westerfield. 1997. Participatory design for widely-distributed scientific communities. In *Proceedings of the 3rd conference on human factors and the Web*. Available at ⟨http://zfin.org/zf_info/dbase/PAPERS/Web97/web97-final.html⟩ (accessed April 24, 2007).

Fulk, J., R. Heino, A. J. Flanagin, P. Monge, and F. Bar. 2004. A test of the individual action model for organizational information commons. *Organization Science* 15 (5): 569–585.

Hardin, G. 1968. The tragedy of the commons. *Science* 162:1243–1248. Available at ⟨http://dieoff .org/page95.htm⟩ (accessed April 24, 2007).

Karau, S. J., and J. W. Hart. 1998. Group cohesiveness and social loafing: Effects of a social interaction manipulation on individual motivation within groups. *Group Dynamics: Theory, Research, and Practice* 2 (3): 185–191.

Ledyard, J. O. 1995. Public goods: A survey of experimental research. In *Handbook of experimental economics*, ed. J. H. Kegel and A. E. Roth, 111–194. Princeton, NJ: Princeton University Press.

Moore, D. A., T. R. Kurtzberg, L. L. Thompson, and M. W. Morris. 1999. Long and short routes to success in electronically mediated negotiations: Group affiliations and good vibrations. *Organizational Behavior and Human Decision Processes* 77 (1): 22–43.

National Institutes of Health (NIH). 2003. *Final NIH statement on sharing research data*. February 26. Available at ⟨http://grants2.nih.gov/grants/guide/notice-files/NOT-OD-03-032.html⟩ (accessed April 24, 2007).

Olson, M., and D. Porter. 1994. An experimental examination into the design of decentralized methods to solve the assignment problem with and without money. *Economic Theory* 4:11–40.

Ostrom, E., J. Walker, and R. Gardner. 1992. Covenants with and without a sword: Self-governance is possible. *American Political Science Review* 86 (2): 404–417.

Price, D. J. De S., and Beaver, D. 1966. Collaboration in an invisible college. *The American Psychologist* 21 (11): 1011–1018.

Schatz, B. 1991. Building an electronic community system. *Journal of Management Information Systems* 8 (3): 87–101.

Sprague, J., L. Bayraktaroglu, D. Clements, T. Conlin, D. Fashena, K. Frazer et al. 2006. The Zebrafish Information Network: The zebrafish model organism database. *Nucleic Acids Research* 34 (database issue): D581–D585.

Van Vugt, M., and C. M. Hart. 2004. Social identity as social glue: The origins of group loyalty. *Journal of Personality and Social Psychology* 86 (4): 585–598.

Weedman, J. 1998. The structure of incentive: Design and client roles in application-oriented research. *Science, Technology, and Human Values* 23 (3): 315–345.

Appendix 14.A: Survey Instrument

Relevant questions from Survey of Community Data System Administrators

Item	Responses
Which of these types of information are collected in your database? (select all that apply)	
Genomic Databases	18
Comparative Genomics	9
Gene Expression	12
Gene Identification and Structure	10
Genetic and Physical Maps	8
Intermolecular Interactions	4
Metabolic Pathways and Cellular Regulation	5
Mutation Databases	11
Pathology	3
Protein Databases	18
Protein Sequence Motifs	11
Proteome Resources	5
Retrieval Systems and Database Structure	5
RNA Sequences	10
Structure	10
Transgenics	3
Other (please specify)	15
Total Respondents	46
Which of these best characterizes the information in your database? (select all that apply)	
Data pulled from other databases	25
New data from various laboratories	30
Annotations of existing data	27
New, original analyses of data	17
Visualizations or other value-added analyses of data	24
Bibliographic information	26
Total Respondents	45
(skipped this question)	3
Who is sponsoring this database financially?	
Total Respondents	43

How dependent is your project on outside contributions?

Not open to outside contributions	0
Outside contributions are a useful supplement to the dataset put together by core project personnel	24
Outside contributions comprise a large component of the dataset, but less than half of the total data	5
Outside contributions are an essential part of the current dataset, comprising more than half of the published information.	16
Total Respondents	45

What is the nature of most of the outside contributions included in your database? (Check more than one if appropriate)

Suggestions about new published information that we should add to the dataset	23
Corrections/omissions related to mistakes in the dataset	26
Annotations on data already in the database	14
New data from other scientists' labs	27
New analyses (results) from other scientists' labs	13
Suggestions for new functionalities for the database	17
Other (please specify)	8
Total Respondents	45

How are contribution solicited? (check all that apply)

Through the database website	40
Through links from other websites	5
Through professional channels—conferences or journals	26
Through personal contact (e.g. emailing a known expert or colleague)	31
Through prior agreements from funding contracts	4
Other (please specify)	8
Total Respondents	45

Which of these have been the most effective means of soliciting contributions? i.e. which would you recommend to a databases similar to yours? (mention all that apply)

the database website	24
links from other websites	7
professional channels—conferences or journals	18
personal contact (e.g. emailing a known expert or colleague)	28
prior agreements from funding contracts	3
Other comments	5
Total Respondents	44
(skipped this question)	4

What would you guess are the important motivations for outside contributors to your database? (please rate each according to how important you think it is)?

	Very important	Important	Somewhat important	Not very important	Not at all important
Is required by a funding source	4	2	2	6	20
Is required by a journal or publisher	10	3	2	5	17
Desire to stake first claim to an area of study	6	8	7	8	10
Desire to contribute to a valued resource	11	14	9	4	2
Sense of obligation to scientific community	4	17	13	4	3
Personal connection to researchers running the database	7	11	7	7	7
It is an alternative means of attaining professional credit recognition	2	9	10	6	11
Is is an alternative means of professional scholarly publication	3	8	5	9	11
Sense of professional accomplishment	1	10	15	8	5
Total Respondents					43

How many outside researchers have contributed information to your database so far? (Please estimate if the exact number is unknown.)

<10	10
10–20	7
21–100	12
100+	10
Other (please specify)	6
Total Respondents	45

Does your database have any partnerships with journals in your field whereby the journal will 'co-publish' database contents? (If yes please describe)

Total Respondents	28

Have you ever been asked to write a letter documenting submission or recommending submitters to your database? (If yes please elaborate)

Total Respondents	30

When this project began did you expect the amount and quality of outside contributions to be more less or about what you have gotten?

Expected more	17
Expected less	6
Expected about what we have gotten	15
Had no expectations	7
Other (please specify)	0
Total Respondents	45

Are contribution reviewed or edited before they are added to the database? If yes please describe.

Total Respondents	39

What percentage of contributions require additional clarifications/ communications between database staff and contributors? (your estimate)?

Less than 10%	20
11–25%	5
More than 25%	14
Other (please specify)	4
Total Respondents	43

Do you offer any special protections for contributors who want to protect intellectual property?

Delayed publication of data	18
Partial/degraded publication of data	2
Anonymized publication	1
Please describe:	11
Total Respondents	28

Is this resource useful for one specific community or are there several disparate groups of potential users? (Please describe)

Total Respondents	42

How large is the community of people who could use this resource? (your estimate)

<200 worldwide	4
200–1000	14
1000–10,000	17
10,000+	9
Total Respondents	44

Are the users of your database the same community of scientists who produce the information or a different community?

Mostly the same community	18
Mostly separate community	1
Overlapping	24
Don't know	1
Total Respondents	44

What is your guess as to how many users are also contributors?

Less than 1%	20
2–10%	12
11–25%	6
more than 25%	4
Total Respondents	42

If your database has user registration how many registered users are there?

Total Respondents	17

If your database has analyzed web logs how much usage do you have?

Page views per month	26
Unique users per month	18
Peak month users (e.g. after updating)	9
Total Respondents	28

Do you share or synchronize information with other databases? (if yes please describe)

Total Respondents	38

Have you designed your database to accommodate users who would perform large-scale analyses on this data? (e.g. by allowing full-database downloading or supporting particular formatting.)

Total Respondents	41

Do you think that the information in your database is useful mostly as individual data points or as an aggregated dataset?

Individual data points	4
As an aggregated dataset	5
Both	35
Please describe:	0
Total Respondents	44

V Earth and Environmental Sciences

15 Ecology Transformed: The National Center for Ecological Analysis and Synthesis and the Changing Patterns of Ecological Research

Edward J. Hackett, John N. Parker, David Conz, Diana Rhoten, and Andrew Parker

Ecologists not only study how plants and animals are adapted to environments. They themselves must adapt to new demands as societies evolve and continually transform the environment.
—Sharon Kingsland, *The Evolution of American Ecology, 1890–2000*

On May 12, 2005, the director of the National Center for Ecological Analysis and Synthesis (NCEAS) announced to all the staff that

last week we received an e-mail from ISI [Thomson Institute for Scientific Information] stating that NCEAS had moved into the top 1 percent of all cited institutions in the world in the area of ecology and the environment (institutions are those units in an authors address, usually at the level of a university). That is, of the approximately 39,000 institutions that were represented in the addresses of cited papers, NCEAS is ranked 338th in total citations.... NCEAS is ranked 389th in number of papers, but 22nd in citations/papers, out of approximately 39,000 institutions. This seems like a striking piece of information, and a strong reflection on all of the scientists who have worked at NCEAS and their scholarly production.

This chapter describes the origins of NCEAS, and analyzes the network patterns and social processes of research that take place at the center. We argue that NCEAS is an exceptionally successful organizational adaptation to changes in the culture and conduct of ecological research. Ecology is a field science that has developed a symbiotic relationship between places in the field where inquiry is conducted and the knowledge derived and published from those inquiries. Sentient and tacit knowledge acquired through field research are essential for data analysis and interpretation (Henke 2001; Kohler 2002; Roth and Bowen 1999, 2001), and the distinctive features of the field site where research is done, combined with the scientist's immersion in the place, lend credence to the published results. The epistemic qualities of publications, in turn, confer distinction on field sites, and such names as Hubbard Brook, Harvard Forest, and Walden Pond echo through the literature. But NCEAS does not gather primary data, and apart from postdoctoral and sabbatical fellows, who are themselves transients, the small resident staff at NCEAS spend more time providing technical support of computers and analytic software than doing scientific research.

Changes in scientific knowledge and research technologies, a growing concern for interdisciplinary explanation, and stronger and more rapid connections between science and its applications have altered the environment for ecological research and placed new demands on the science of ecology. NCEAS was formed, we contend, as an organizational adaptation to this changing environment. In the course of a decade, NCEAS has become a place where scientists and environmental decision makers from diverse disciplines as well as institutions apply analysis and modeling tools to data sets drawn from geographically scattered sites with which they have only limited personal experience. NCEAS has catalyzed distinctive forms of research collaboration and produced high-impact science from its home in an office building in downtown Santa Barbara, California, ten miles from the university campus and farther still from the diverse sites where ecological fieldwork is done.

Precisely because it hosts work so different in substance and process from conventional research in ecology, NCEAS offers a strategic site for studying adaptive change in the organization, conduct, and content of science. Its history reveals how science and policy interact to create a place and pattern of research that shape how knowledge is produced (Feldman et al. 2005). NCEAS is a new form of scientific organization that bridges geographic and disciplinary distance, and catalyzes interactions among disciplines as well as across the social worlds of academe, policy, and practice. It fosters new patterns of collaboration that produce a distinctive form of knowledge. In this chapter we trace the varied intellectual, social, and policy currents that combined to create and shape this research organization, situating the account within a discussion of structural change in science. We examine patterns of collaboration, and analyze the process of collaboration and engagement with data that the center has pioneered.

Data and Methods

Our study of NCEAS began in 1998 and continued through 2005. We used a variety of methods that included interviewing administrators, resident scientists, and working group members; examining documents, publications, and citation data; observing working groups; and administering a brief questionnaire. Sociometric surveys were administered to a sample of working group members in 2002, and one of us was in residence as a participant observer in 2004–2005. Bibliometric data were gathered using scientists' self-reports and name searches through the Science Citation Index.

We spent more than 140 hours in ethnographic observation of working groups, and hundreds more observing informal interaction in the groups and conducting interviews. We observed working group interactions during the entire course of each working group session, arriving at NCEAS each morning before the scientists got to work, and leaving only after all work had been completed that day. We took detailed notes of group behavior as it occurred, adding further detail from recollection during the evening. We attached substantive codes to our notes, then gathered related material across working groups to produce a thematic understanding of group process. The interviews were transcribed, and excerpts were organized by topic. In the course of this chapter observations are summarized, interviews are quoted, surveys are tabulated, historical documents are excerpted, bibliometrics are analyzed, and networks are depicted.

We have been deeply engaged with our research subject throughout the project. Material from our study was used in two official, evaluative site visits (in 1999 and 2002), discussed on several occasions with the NCEAS director, and summarized at length within the center's (successful) renewal proposal.

The Origins of NCEAS

NCEAS was founded in May 1995 through a cooperative agreement between the National Science Foundation (NSF) and the University of California, with the state of California contributing additional support. The center's creation crystallized an emergent understanding among ecologists that their research was changing in fundamental ways:

• The *process* of ecological research was becoming more collaborative, involving a diversity of other disciplines, and engaging issues of policy, practice, and resource management
• The *scale* of ecological analysis was increasing from disjointed plots of several square meters to integrative analyses that pool data across sites and scales to make inferences about broader temporal and spatial processes
• *Research technologies* were making more frequent use of archival data, quantitative analytic techniques, and computer models, sometimes conducted asynchronously from remote locations
• *Knowledge and theory* were changing in ways reflected in the characteristics of specific publications (including their coauthorship, integrative aims, and appearance in higher-visibility journals), and in the knowledge about overarching ecological processes that would emerge from such publications

The proximal events that gave rise to NCEAS began with a one-page memo dated July 16, 1991, in which O. J. Reichman, a program officer at NSF, asserts that "ecological research problems are inherently multidisciplinary, requiring the efforts of biologists, engineers, social scientists and policymakers for their solution. Hence, there is a need for sites where a longer-term, multidisciplinary analysis of environmental problems can be undertaken." The memo refers to calls for such a center issued in the previous two or three years by the Association of Ecosystem Research Centers (AERC), the Long Term Ecological Research Network Action Plan workshop, and the Ecological Society of America (ESA); it closes by proposing five design criteria and an approximate annual budget for the center. About a year later, the ESA and the AERC convened a workshop of some fifty persons in Albuquerque, New Mexico, to outline the "scientific objectives, structure, and implementation" of a "National Center for Ecological Synthesis." Their joint report, issued on February 8, 1993, observes that "knowledge of ecological systems is growing at an accelerating rate. Progress is lagging in synthetic research to consolidate this knowledge base into general patterns and principles that advance the science and are useful for environmental decision making.... Without such synthetic studies, it will be impossible for ecology to become the predictive science required by current and future environmental problems" (ESA and AERC 1993, n.p.). A design study for the center followed in July 1993, which informed the announcement by NSF of a special competition for center proposals.

Responses occurred on several levels, and involved extensive discussions among funding agency officials, representatives of scientific societies, and scientists about the center's rationale, mission, and design. Various committees and working groups proposed alternative designs for the center along with divergent routes to the selection of its site; NSF chose to have an open competition for a single center. The substantive impetus for NCEAS—the need for "ecologists to look outward rather than inward to integrate extensive information across disciplines, scales, and systems" (ESA and AERC 1993, n.p.) remains an ongoing source of change in the content as well as conduct of ecological science that is sustained, accelerated, and perhaps modified by the center. Finally, NCEAS arose from a strategic convergence of interests. Again in the words of the ESA and AERC document (1993, n.p.): "Synthesis is needed to advance basic science, organize ecological information for decision makers concerned with pressing national issues, and make cost-effective use of the nation's extant and accumulating database."

The proximal events that created NCEAS are situated within deeper intellectual currents. The concept of "ecosystem"—developed by Raymond Lindeman in 1941–1942, and central to Eugene Odum's *Fundamentals of Ecology* (1953)—transformed ecology into an abstract and quantitative discipline that needed increasingly sophisticated mathematical models (Golley 1993). This need was further fueled by a series of large-scale data-gathering efforts, beginning with the International Geophysical Year (1957–1958), and continuing through the International Biological Program (1967–1974) and the International Geosphere-Biosphere Program (1990) (Golley 1993, 109–140; Kwa 1987, 2005). Within the United States, the institutionalization of long-term ecological data gathering began with a series of workshops convened in 1977–1979 in Woods Hole, Massachusetts. These laid the groundwork for six pilot Long Term Ecological Research projects, funded by NSF in 1980, now grown to twenty-six sites (chapter 16, this volume). Collectively, the Long Term Ecological Research projects commit ecologists to apply advanced methods to standardized data in order to study phenomena at larger spatial and temporal scales.

NCEAS Research and Organization

NCEAS supports three kinds of researchers: center fellows, postdoctoral fellows, and working groups. Center fellows are visiting scientists who reside at the center for three to twelve months. Postdoctoral fellows spend one to three years at NCEAS, working exclusively on their own research projects. They have no assigned mentor, although they have extensive contact with the six hundred scientists who visit NCEAS each year. They are also distinctly successful, publishing in the top scientific journals, including *Science* and *Nature*, securing coveted academic jobs, and winning research awards in their fields. Working groups, which are the focus of this analysis, bring approximately six to twenty people to the center for several-day intervals of intensive collaborative research. The groups are diverse in composition, often including senior and junior scientists in various disciplines and specialties as well as resource managers, government officials, and experts in simulation and analysis. A group typically meets several times, in different configurations, over a period of two or three years.

The research performed at NCEAS differs in several ways from the traditional field-based science of ecology. Most studies in ecology have concentrated on small spatial and temporal scales, while the focus at NCEAS is larger scale, often analyzing data covering substantial swaths of time and space. Where traditional empirical work in ecology involves hands-on spells of fieldwork, NCEAS scientists are frequently unfamiliar with the study sites from which their data were gathered. Advanced statistical and mathematical modeling techniques replace transects and trips to the field. Table 15.1 summarizes this comparison.

Place matters in science, and it matters greatly in ecology (Galison 1998; Gieryn 2002, 2006; Henke 2001; Henke and Gieryn 2007; Kohler 2002; Latour 1987). NCEAS

Table 15.1
Traditional collaboration model versus NCEAS working group model

Traditional ecological collaboration	NCEAS working groups
1. Field (contextualized)	1. NCEAS (decontextualized)
2. Small scale	2. Unlimited areas of study
3. Short term	3. Long term
4. Primary data	4. Secondary data
5. Site-specific team	5. Trans-site group
6. Single discipline	6. Multiple disciplines
7. Single institution	7. Multiple institutions
8. Academic setting	8. Nonacademic setting
9. Research	9. Research and practice

is an unusual place for ecological work because it removes scientists and data from their local contexts and usual university environments, and puts them on a neutral turf, creating a sense of strangeness and uncertainty that stimulates originality. The center has become a crossroads for scientists doing ecological research, broadly defined, and those involved in related policy and resource management. One participant called it "a bookmobile of people's minds. New people are always coming through with new ideas." Diversity has its challenges, some as mundane as basic communication. One working group was impeded because the term "risk averse" has quite different meanings for ecologists and economists, and what appeared to be substantive disagreements turned out to be a matter of definitional differences that repeated e-mail exchanges did not uncover (compare to Galison 1998). Sometimes there are problems with unspoken language. For example, when paleoecologists meet with contemporary ecologists, those whose work concerns deposits in the fossil record gesture and draw from bottom to top to signify the passage of time, while for contemporary ecologists time flows from left to right.

NCEAS is not only a new place to do ecological research, quite apart from the traditional field, library, or academic office. It is also an exemplar of a new form of research organization that depends, as collaboratories do, on new information technologies and in turn produces new forms of knowledge. Since 1990 observers of science have heralded this transformation in the organization of research, but there has been little agreement about the origins, nature, and significance of the change, and little empirical study of its appearance and effects.[1] In a critical summary of literature regarding this transformation in the social organization of research, Peter Weingart (1997, 593) distilled five characteristic properties of new patterns of knowledge production:

1. Knowledge is produced in a variety of new contexts that may be outside the university, ephemeral, or virtual (including research networks and collaboratories).
2. Knowledge is produced with an eye to its potential uses and users, not solely to increase our fundamental understanding of nature.
3. Research is transdisciplinary in its conduct and transmission, and is often embodied in the researchers rather than transmitted through the traditional pathways of publication.
4. The quality of research is evaluated by a heterogeneous collection of reviewers who apply economic, political, and social considerations in addition to the usual standards of scientific and intellectual merit.
5. Research expenditures are justified in social and political terms: knowledge is no longer an end in itself or a means to an end that may only later be discovered. Instead, research is an investment justified by its public benefits.

NCEAS organization and research display several of these characteristics. The work is performed off campus, and blends face-to-face and computer-mediated interaction. Members of user communities (policymakers and resource managers) are included in the research process, and the intended audiences for research transcend disciplines and the usual bounds of academic collaboration. NCEAS researchers are quite varied: some 3,400 scientists have worked at NCEAS, representing 49 countries, 531 different academic organizations, 428 nonacademic organizations (such as government agencies, companies, and nongovernmental organizations), and more than 360 scientific societies. About a quarter of NCEAS working groups focus at least in part on issues of environmental policy, resource management, conservation, or applications—such as disease ecology, ecological economics, and the like. Practical aims of the research, such as creating a marine reserve, designing a fisheries management plan, or devising an economic incentive scheme, are entwined with the academic aims of scholarly publication. By mid-2005, NCEAS has produced more than a thousand publications, including forty-one in *Science*, twenty-six in *Nature*, and twenty-one in the *Proceedings of the National Academy of Sciences*.

In addition to its significance as a form of scientific organization, the working group arrangements created within NCEAS occupy a distinctive place in the development of scientific collaborations. Derek Price (1986, 77, 79) observed that scientific collaboration "has been increasing steadily and ever more rapidly since the beginning of the [twentieth] century"—a change he judged to be "one of the most violent transitions that can be measured in recent trends of scientific manpower." While Price understood the diversity of arrangements embraced by the term collaboration, others narrowed the term to mean coauthorship in order to facilitate empirical research (e.g., Meadows 1974). But recent scholarship recognizes that collaboration describes a variety of working relationships, and arises for reasons that may include combining complementary skills, enhancing credibility, and building a real or illusory community to secure resources (Katz and Martin 1997; Maienschein 1993). Studies of collaboration performance show that distance matters (Olson and Olson 2000), trust may not (Shrum, Chompalov, and Genuth 2001), research technologies do (Hackett et al. 2004), and communications technologies help (Walsh and Maloney 2003), but tensions endure (Hackett 2005).

Empirical studies also underscore the importance of face-to-face interaction for effective communication and problem solving (Olson and Olson 2000; Rhoten 2003), and a sociological theory of intellectual creativity proposes that "cultural capital" (the abilities and reputations of scientists in a group) combined with "emotional energy, which gives them confidence, enthusiasm, and strength," leads to intellectual and scientific creativity (Collins 1998; 2000, 159). NCEAS is a collaborative hybrid, blending sophisticated information and data management technologies with intermittent but intense face-to-face interaction, thereby creating a critical mass of cultural capital and emotional energy. The informal social interactions and rituals that extend beyond the working day—"science at the bar," if you will—also generate and sustain emotional energy as well as group solidarity. One group would not begin work unless bowls of

M&M'S were available; others had favorite restaurants and signature drinks. Such rituals of social interaction generate the emotional energy that forms rich and durable social bonds, and that catalyze and facilitate productive group behaviors (Durkheim [1893] 1997; Collins 1998).

Within this new organizational form arise new patterns and processes of collaboration. We close this section on organization with a network depiction of collaborative patterns within the center, and then in the next section we employ observational data to examine aspects of the collaborative process.

Figure 15.1 depicts the networks of close collaborations formed among scientists who participated in NCEAS working groups during 2002.[2] A "close" collaboration is a

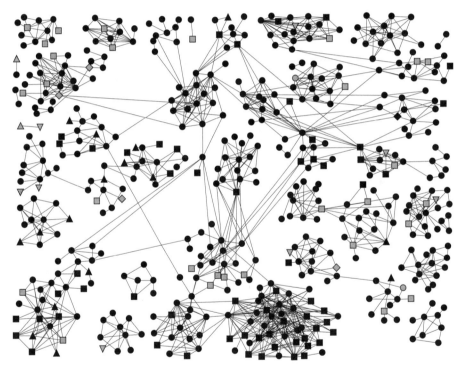

Science field: ◆ = engineering; ■ = physical sciences; ● = life sciences; ▲ = social sciences; ◇ = computation and math sciences;
                ▢ = environmental sciences; ◉ = environmental social sciences; △ = information sciences; ▽ = unknown

Figure 15.1
Network diagram of field affiliations and "close" collaborations of researchers *within* working groups at NCEAS (Rhoten 2003). Close collaborations refer to formal "knowledge producing" relationships "with someone you count among your closest professional and/or intellectual collaborators ... [and] with whom you develop and prepare papers, articles, presentations." (Note: Links *between* working groups indicate researchers who were members of multiple groups.)

formal, knowledge-producing relationship with someone you count among your closest professional and/or intellectual collaborators. Each node represents a single scientist; colors and shapes indicate the field of science with which one identifies. Groups
are clearly interdisciplinary in composition. The linkages among the thirty-eight working groups are formed by individual scientists who are members of more than one
group. The groups vary in the extent to which their members have close collaborative
ties with each other, with measures of network density (the actual number of ties
divided by the possible number of ties) from 60 percent down to a low of below 10 percent, and averaging 20 percent. This density is similar to that of research groups at other
interdisciplinary centers—a remarkable fact considering the ephemeral nature of
NCEAS groups (Rhoten 2003). If we add to the network collegial ties—those that entail
sharing information, ideas, or data without necessarily leading to an intellectual product—then the mean density for NCEAS groups exceeds 50 percent (see figure 15.2),

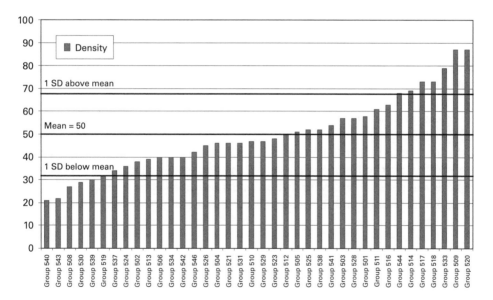

Figure 15.2

Collaboration density histogram

Density metrics of "close" and "collegial" collaborations of researchers *within* working groups at
NCEAS (Rhoten 2003). Close collaborations are defined as in the caption for figure 15.1. Collegial
collaborations denote informal "information sharing" relationships "with someone whom you
talk and share information, data and ideas casually but do not necessarily produce papers, articles,
presentations." In comparison with studies of other research groups, the mean density score of
50 percent is above average. The low number of groups below one standard deviation of the mean
indicates that in almost all cases, strong close and collegial collaborative research networks have
been established in each working group.

which is above the average for other research centers (Rhoten 2003). Taken together, these network data show that on average, NCEAS groups are disciplinarily diverse and rich in interaction.

A second survey completed by 91 out of 131 (69 percent) of NCEAS group members in summer 1999 offers evidence that participation has considerable influence on scientists' work habits and patterns of thought. Virtually all respondents agreed that integrative work is essential for the development of ecology (with 97 percent agreeing and 76 percent strongly agreeing), and that the synthesis of ideas across a field of science is crucial to further knowledge (with 93 percent agreeing and 75 percent strongly agreeing). Only 2 percent felt that persons at their career stage should specialize or that sharing ideas would be risky. Majorities of respondents indicated that the experience would make them more collaborative (74 percent), more likely to read outside their specialty (71 percent), and more integrative in their use of data (62 percent), explanatory models (59 percent), and theory (57 percent).

In sum, NCEAS represents a new form of scientific organization that has given rise to new patterns of collaboration that are unusually diverse, intense, durable, emotionally charged, and productive. Such distinctive social arrangements, in turn, shape the conduct of research along with the quality, impact, and character of the knowledge that is produced.

The Process of Collaboration

In the four sections that follow, we offer field observation and analysis of four key aspects of research collaboration at NCEAS: the challenges of obtaining relevant data from afar and developing trust in them; skepticism and emotional energy; the genesis of a scientific finding; and serendipity. Each of these is an essential element of the research process, anchored in the science studies literature, yet each appears in a distinctive way at NCEAS.

Uncertainty and the Challenges of Data Far Afield

Ecological field research is a precarious process in itself, and moving ecological data away from the field and apart from the tacit knowledge of the primary data gatherers jeopardizes understanding, analysis, and writing (Roth and Bowen 1999, 2001). Scientists reduce uncertainty by transforming field data into "immutable mobiles" that maintain important characteristics of the field, such as where the data were gathered, while being transported from the field into the lab and the office (Latour 1987, 227; 1999, 24–79). Collection boxes and rigorous note-taking systems are examples of techniques that support immutability and mobility by anchoring samples and artifacts to their points of origin in the field as they travel into labs for measurement, computers for analysis, tables for evidence, publications for communication, and databases for sharing. Metadata—data that describe data—is the current term of art for the stuff that builds this chain of evidence.

Our observations of ecological research at NCEAS show that data are more mutable and less mobile than the term immutable mobile would imply, and that there are steep challenges to providing sufficient metadata to remove uncertainty from archived observations. Even when data reside in a repository, they may be evaluated, trimmed, and shaped before use, and this process entails both the technical reconstruction of data and the social construction of trust in those data. In this process, data are *mutable* and *immobile*: they remain in place, and are transformed through the actions of researchers who evaluate, manipulate, and reform them through calculation, peer review, and virtual "travel" to the field to confirm or refine an observation.

For example, a working group was examining the relationship between biodiversity and primary productivity, using data collected by several autonomous groups working at a variety of ecological sites. The existing literature suggested a unimodal or triangular relationship between primary productivity and biodiversity (Gross et al. 2000). This working group was attempting to determine if this relationship applied to a more diverse set of species and biomes.

During the first day, a group of graduate students presented an analysis of the relationship between primary productivity and species richness in a desert biome. Their analysis revealed the expected unimodal relationship, but some members questioned the graduate students about outliers with extremely high biomass values. The graduate students explained that those were yucca plants that have high biomass when flowering every third year. Asked to verify that these were valid data points—real flowering yucca, not data-recording errors—they admitted that they could not. Nonetheless, they maintained that this was a plausible biomass for flowering yucca (about 70 kg, which is a large biomass in a desert) and that including the yucca data was essential for accuracy. Still skeptical, one of the principal investigators proposed discarding the data. The grads resisted, so the senior scientists insisted that the students verify their data. Searches of the Internet and the NCEAS library provided no confirming evidence about the correct biomass of yucca.

Returning to the meeting room, they were again challenged and again instructed to remove data from the four yuccas. The graduate students maintained that the biomass values were correct and must be included, or the analysis would be invalid. The group was committed to working by consensus, so members looked for compromises to break the impasse. Some suggested dividing the yucca biomass by three, since the high biomass results from triennial flowering. Others were prepared to accept this compromise, but one graduate student objected that many desert plants have flowering cycles longer than a year, so adjusting the four yuccas by their flowering cycle while not similarly adjusting other plants would introduce bias. Consensus moved toward accepting the data as reported; the discussion ebbed and flowed, and two principal investigators were inclined to divide the yucca biomass by three. Common sense, expedience, commitment, seniority, authority, and varied commitments to group harmony were at play in shaping these data.

One graduate student held his ground, however, refusing compromise, so a senior scientist called the field site to ascertain how the data were collected and how they should be treated. Field technicians confirmed the weight of flowering yucca, indicating that the reported biomass values, nearly excluded from the data as outliers or errors, were valid. The principal investigators also learned that these yuccas flower annually, not triennially.

Virtual travel to the field, in the form of a phone call, became the dispositive event in a vigorous and open process of evaluative peer review. This instant data evaluation is not uncommon in science (see Holton 1978), but it stands out for its collective character, occurrence at a distance from the field site, and likely persistence as environmental sciences increasingly rely on combining disparate data sets. Increasingly detailed metadata, including who collected them as well as how they were gathered, processed, and otherwise treated before entry into the data set, are intended to resolve such disputes in the future. But detailed studies of ecological fieldwork and the challenges of replication in science raise doubts about the likelihood of acquiring completely satisfactory metadata (Collins 1985; Roth and Bowen 1999, 2001).

Skepticism, Criticism, and Review on the Fly

In addition to the selection and evaluation of data, NCEAS working groups employ peer review in real time ("on the fly") to choose research directions for the group, demonstrate expertise, select the data and analytic techniques to be used, and evaluate the results. They assume a skeptical attitude toward the contributions of other members, scientists who are not present, and the stuff of research such as data sets, data manipulation techniques, theoretical orientations, and scientific terms (Owen-Smith 2001). Doing so not only sharpens the substance and process of research, it also builds confidence and trust within the group.

Expressions of skepticism and criticism, peer review on the fly, and the emotional energy generated and deployed in the process are illustrated in the following vignette of a single hour of a working group meeting. The exchange begins with a scientist, "A," summarizing a paper that showed that body size was not an inherited characteristic among small mammals. In the course of her presentation, she acknowledged that various versions of the paper drew sharp criticisms that forced the authors to reevaluate their findings, and that the paper was better for doing so. She also admitted that the paper's findings raised more questions than they answered. In all, she made relatively mild claims, and was somewhat flexible about their interpretation. Here is the discussion, with elements of peer review on the fly in ***bold italics*** and our interpretative commentary in brackets.

Referring to A's discussion, B mentioned a paper he did on birds. They had a problem because they did not look at **enough decimal places** [measure with enough precision]. Maybe this is A's problem?

A talks about a small mammal she studied and **rejects** B's suggestion.

B **asks** if she is differentiating between ten and eleven grams; and says it could be a matter of [too few] **significant figures**.

A **rejects** M's proposal, and says more about heritability among small mammals, then makes a connection to heritability of traits in giraffes. . . .

B then says it **might be geographic**.

A [holding up her pen] says, "I'm going to **stab** you with this!"

B says he is **just doing his job**.

[To this point it is parry and thrust, with A holding her ground. When emotion rises, B depersonalizes the exchange by invoking the "job." What follows is sharper and involves more participants.] A continues to discuss the specifics of this paper and a related analysis, reasserting the **claim that body size is not inherited** among small mammals.

C asks about **error in the calculation**.

A says it **doesn't matter**.

C pushes the issue, saying there might be **error in sampling** . . .

B notes that **standard errors go up** as body size increases. . . .

A replies that they have **tried this** . . . look in the appendix [to the paper] and see very clearly that **what he is suggesting is not the case**.

B says there **might be another statistical artifact**. . . .

A says, "We're **focusing on the wrong thing** . . . look at this." . . .

[For A criticism has derailed the discussion, so she tries to put it back on track.]

D **says loudly**, "**But you can't** . . . [do that, claim that]! This is the **argument** that I had with [a name]!" He **slams his fist**. "**This doesn't have any basis!**"

E says, "You **need to look at the phylogenetics** of the group."

A says defensively, "**It depends** on what you are looking at."

E says, also defensively, "That's fine! **I gave you all this data**."

A replies that she "**didn't know where E had got this data**, so she **didn't use** it."

E says that he "**got the data** from the — — — project."

D says, "He **did the calculations wrong!**"

[In an hour, six scientists made more than fifty evaluative remarks (peer reviewing), responses to evaluative comments, or third-party (bystander) interventions to reinforce a critique, blunt its effect, or reinforce a defense. Some comments exhibit strong emotion, and are sharply skeptical about the work presented and the work referenced. This rate of exchange speeds the collaboration, and the emotional energy displayed strengthens the commitment of group members to one another and the project.]

The Genesis of a Scientific Fact: "Holy %$#$#!"

Choosing and evaluating data, reviewing on the fly and exercising skepticism, and creating credibility, trust, and emotional energy are steps along the pathway to producing new and publishable findings. In the following discourse, observe how the interplay of skepticism and persistence generates new findings. Again, we offer edited field notes with commentary in brackets.

G gives a talk about allometric relations among plant clades, using a data set he has compiled that comprises 1,150 studies of 900 species. He finds a lawlike relationship between two key variables, fitted by an exponential model with a key parameter that equals about −0.75 (+/− random error) in data distributions as old as the Paleolithic era and as recent as a contemporary forest.

D asks to see a graph again, gets up and retrieves one of his own graphs, and compares the two. D's graph contains virtually all species except plants, and G's contains only plants. Both graphs show the same relationship between temperature and mass, and D proposes that these two properties of an organism allow you to calculate its metabolic rate, from which one can then calculate ontogenetic growth and population growth "based on first principles."

That idea hangs in the air as the group takes a break.

E presents results based on a data set that compiles life span, population density, extinction rate, metabolic rate, and other variables for three thousand flying mammals. She shows several graphs relating body size to other variables and exhibiting similarly patterned relationships for various mammal species.

G asks a question about how much energy is put into offspring each year.

D answers that mothers do not grow much after birth.

G says that it would be possible to put his plant data on this graph, too.

The group laughs at the idea of putting plants and mammals on the same graph.

[A daunting exercise of organized skepticism. Is it peer review in a single breath or does it instead represent uneasiness in the presence of a good idea? In either case, it is emotional energy and evidence of group solidarity: they are comfortable enough with one another to laugh.]

D asks to see another relationship, and they talk about technical details, which D and H talk about a bit.

H asks a question, and E answers him.

G says again that they can combine their data on plants and bats, and look at the relationships. Some of the group seems to *think this a goofy idea*, but G is serious. The discussion moves on, and then the group breaks for lunch. After lunch small groups are talking and working, while others are away and arriving late.

At 3:30, F suddenly yells "Holy %$#$#!" She says that [the relationship of body size to metabolism for] plants and animals that are plotted together on the same graph are similar in their relationship. She is very excited, and calls I and B over to look. She says she wants them to make sure that the relationship is correct before she tells anyone else. F carefully checks the data and how they have been manipulated. She says that plants behave like really big animals. B tells her [jokingly?] not to show this to D [who earlier spoke of first principles and such].

At 3:35, D and G enter the room. F tells them that [in terms of the relationship being studied] trees act like really big mammals.

G looks at the graph and says, "Oh, my God!"

D says, "YEAH!"

F says, "Isn't this amazing?"

D obviously believes the graph and is visibly excited.

[Extensive, buoyant emotional energy will hold some skepticism at bay and power the detailed analyses necessary to turn a finding into a publication.]

F says that right before she plotted the graph, she said to herself, "There is no way...."

She and G talk for a moment about the way she manipulated the data.

G repeats that in the graphs, trees look like big mammals. He also notes that there are no whales in the data.

D suggests putting sequoias in the data set.

F, still excited, exclaims, "That's really neat!"

D says that he was convinced that this had to be true. Smiling, he bellows, "Laws of nature, by God!"

F says, "So annual growth for trees and animals are the same!"

G tells F to look at the population density relationship for plants and animals now. She says that this is what she is doing.

D says, very excitedly, "This is ... HA HA HA!!"

B says he wouldn't have believed it if he hadn't seen it with his own eyes.

It is now 3:38. The group spends the balance of the day and much of the next one questioning, developing, and expanding this finding.

Persistence and skepticism are in dynamic balance, each appearing repeatedly but neither dominating. As Jason Owen-Smith (2001) has noted, skepticism tends to be expressed by senior scientists toward junior scientists (and in the preceding example, by men toward women). In the latter stages of the exchange recounted above, notice that the analysts are skeptical but suspend disbelief long enough to analyze the data, then reassert their skepticism to motivate a search for additional supportive evidence from convergent indicators (population density relationships) and at the limits of the size distribution (from other species, such as whales and sequoias). The success of the group depends on oscillation among speculation in words and analyses, the pursuit and presentation of creative ideas, and the rapid yet rigorous review of emerging results. Emotions are high, and passion is audible and visible, and these qualities hold the group together and carry it along.

Serendipity

New forms of research organization shape the patterns and processes in predictable ways, as described above, and also create a context within the organization but outside the group for serendipitous interactions that may yield strong as well as surprising findings (Merton and Barber 2004). The odds of serendipitous discovery are increased by the fast flow of scientists through the center, their high spatial density and rich interaction, their focused yet flexible research agendas, and minimal distractions. While serendipity is, by definition, an unexpected occurrence, characteristics of the organization may make such encounters (in the words of NCEAS director Jim Reichman) "anticipated but unpredictable." Here is an example of serendipity, with **bold type** calling attention to key elements of the encounter.

A scientist participating in a working group had heard about a center fellow who had an excellent reputation for modeling metabolic rates in animals. The working group member sought him out to talk about

a particular project that I have been working on—large bellied parrots. To give you some background, there are 200 individuals remaining in this species. They migrate from Tasmania to mainland Australia and winter there. They were once distributed over many tens of thousands of miles from Sydney to Adelaide. There were tens of thousands of these birds up until the middle of this century. In 1980, when they did the most recent census, there were 200. The recovery team has been speculating about the reasons for [the decline] for many years and has implemented many strategies, including a captive-breeding program.... We haven't had very clear answers [for the decline of this bird population]. We have detailed individual population models, and we have more than a decade of careful demographic observations, and we have a great deal of behavioral data ... [but] the only plausible explanation was that there had been so much of a loss of habitat on the fringes of the places that they seemed to live that there was insufficient seed to support them.

I talked to [this center fellow] about this for about an hour and he asked, to my way of thinking, **all kinds of oblique questions.** He asked things about their body size and how exposed their habitat was and what the wind speed was in winter and what was the temperature of the coldest month, and how big were their offspring and did their offspring migrate—questions that we needed the answers to but we thought had no relevance to anything. He **interrogated me for ages** and at the end he used an American expression and said, "I'm going to **throw a curve ball** at you, there's **one thing wrong with this picture.** It seems to me that these things are carrying a toxicological load. I would guess just from **doing the arithmetic in my head,** I would guess that these things are suffering under a nutrient-stress problem and that they are combating a toxicant." He asked if there were visible expressions of contaminants, if there were deformed beaks and whether there were closely related species that had the same problem and all sorts of **interesting questions that we had the answers to but hadn't keyed in to.** He said, "**The thing that's wrong here** is that there is no sewage works," and **this made my skin crawl** because the thing that I see when I come in from Tasmania and land in Victoria is a giant sewage plant, and I never bothered to mention it to him. It was one of those things where you think, "Wow!"

There's **no way that I would ever have run into this researcher.** I've **never read his papers** although he's published in journals in toxicology, [and] there **wasn't sufficient common ground** for us to assume that we would have been of any value to one another. It was an **entirely fortuitous** meeting—we had to be in this place at this time.

There are systematic aspects to serendipity, which are shared with the working groups and are predictable consequences of this form of scientific organization. The scientists are proximal, engaged, and emotionally charged; they differ in expertise and are previously unacquainted; they are removed from the field and familiar surroundings. They abstract key elements from the field data by virtue of imagination, recollection, and theory-based inference; it is as if distance matters by adding relief: what matters stands out from what doesn't, and removed in space and time from the setting some things (the sewage works, for example) are perceived more clearly than they might be in situ. The encounter is sharply focused and covers considerable scientific territory in short order; the scientific outcome is an emergent property of the setting, interaction pattern, and scientific engagement.

Summary and Conclusion

In a decade, NCEAS has become such a successful place for ecology that some say they cannot imagine the field without the center. Born of a transformation in the conduct of ecological research, it has contributed to that transformation in the form of hundreds of publications with high citation rates, new scientists trained in a novel (mentor-free) postdoctoral program, thousands of participants from diverse institutions connected and emerged through bonds of face-to-face collaboration, a new style of ecological science that spans field sites and supports more integrative theorizing, data archives and the means to use them (metadata, analysis and retrieval tools, and a culture of data sharing), and changes in scientists' orientation (attitudes and values) toward collaboration (particularly collaboration across disciplines and with practical aims). Taken together, these innovations constitute a new ensemble of research technologies that opens spheres of inquiry, creating new ways to address the central questions of a discipline and posing entirely new questions (Hackett et al. 2004).

NCEAS is a new form of research organization that shapes science as well as the practice of research in ecology and related fields. Collaborations catalyzed by NCEAS combine spells of intensive, face-to-face interaction that generate emotional energy with work that is asynchronous and spatially distributed. A new ensemble of technologies for doing ecological research is evolving as an adaptation to change in the environment of ecological research—one that applies broadly synthetic theories and computer-based tools for data management, modeling, and analysis to data sets that are aggregated from various published and unpublished sources, and evaluated in real time for quality and consistency. Data travel to NCEAS in the form of immutable mobiles that retain unshakable reference to their origins in the field. But on arrival they become mutable—recall the yucca—and immobile. The data are situated in one place, subject to scrutiny, evaluation, selection, reformation, and recombination. This phenomenon is not unique to ecology: terabyte-scale data sets of physics, astronomy, and some earth sciences are probably sessile over their lifetimes, given the computational resources required to store and manipulate them, yet necessarily mutable to accommodate changing research needs and measurement standards.

Scientists emerge from these intense and often successful research interactions with strongly favorable orientations toward research collaboration, serendipitous connections with others, and rich, varied networks of potential future collaborators. NCEAS not only changes the character or quality of research, and the training and interactions of researchers, it also changes the velocity of research through concentrated effort, virtual travel to the field, peer review on the fly, intense exchanges of ideas, emotional energy, and serendipity. NCEAS lends credibility to analyses of ecological data because the data are pooled over place and time, allowing the use of more sophisticated analytic and modeling techniques. Finally, NCEAS facilitates a form of interstitial science that creatively combines questions, concepts, data, and concerns from disparate fields and realms of practice (e.g., policy or resource management).

For a field science, it is ironic that a downtown office building has become a center of calculation and collaboration, where the distance from the field and the nearness to other scientists have become resources for scientific performance. The number and diversity of scientists passing through the center along with the quality and intensity of their interactions combine not only to create original science, new policies, and enduring collaborative networks but also to transform the culture of collaboration in the discipline and bestow credibility on the place itself.

Acknowledgments

This chapter was prepared for a working session of the Science of Collaboratories project in June 2005. A previous version was presented at the International Society for the History, Philosophy, and Social Studies of Biology in Vienna, Austria, in July 2003.

The work reported here was supported by grants from the NSF (SBE 98-96330 to Hackett, and BCS 01-29573 to Rhoten), and from the National Center for Ecological Analysis and Synthesis in Santa Barbara, California (DEB 94-21535). Much of the writing was done while Hackett was a center fellow at NCEAS (DEB 00-72909), and Rhoten was funded by REC 03-55353.

This research would not have been possible without the cheerful and unbounded support of Jim Reichman, the NCEAS staff, and the hundreds of scientists who took time from their research visits to answer our questions, complete our surveys, explain things to us, and simply allow us to spend time with them. We thank Nancy Grimm for suggesting NCEAS as a research site, and Jonathon Bashford for helpful analyses and discussions. We are also grateful to Bill Michener, David Ribes, Jim Reichman, and Leah Gerber for their detailed and insightful comments on previous versions of this chapter.

Notes

1. For studies on new modes of knowledge production, see also Michael Gibbons, Camille Limoges, Helga Nowotny, Simon Schwartzman, Peter Scott, and Martin Trow, *The New Production of Knowledge: The Dynamics of Science and Research in Contemporary Societies* (London: Sage, 1994); Helga Nowotny, Peter Scott, and Michael Gibbons, *Re-thinking Science: Knowledge and the Public in an Age of Uncertainty* (Cambridge, UK: Polity Press, 2001). Discussions of postnormal or postaca-

demic science include Silvio Funtowicz and Jerome Ravetz, "Science for the Post-normal Age," *Futures* 25, no. 7 (1993): 739–755; John Ziman, *Prometheus Bound: Science in a Dynamic Steady State* (Cambridge: Cambridge University Press, 1994). Issues of academic capitalism are addressed in Edward Hackett, "Science as a Vocation in the 1990s: The Changing Organizational Culture of Academic Science," *Journal of Higher Education* 61, no. 3 (1990): 241–279; Sheila Slaughter and Larry Leslie, *Academic Capitalism: Politics, Policies, and the Entrepreneurial University* (Baltimore, MD: Johns Hopkins University Press, 1997).

2. Based on self-reported survey data collected by the authors.

References

Collins, H. M. 1985. *Changing order: Replication and induction in scientific practice.* Beverly Hills, CA: Sage Publications.

Collins, R. 1998. *The sociology of philosophies.* Cambridge, MA: Harvard University Press.

Collins, R. 2000. The sociology of philosophies: A precis. *Philosophy of the Social Sciences* 30 (2): 157–201.

Durkheim, E. [1893] 1997. *The division of labor in society.* New York: Free Press.

Ecological Society of America (ESA) and Association of Ecosystem Research Centers (AERC). 1993. *National Center for Ecological Synthesis: Scientific objectives, structure, and implementation.* Report from a workshop held in Albuquerque, New Mexico, February. Available at ⟨http://www.nceas .ucsb.edu/nceas-web/center/NCES_AlbuquerqueNM_1992.pdf⟩ (accessed April 17, 1007).

Feldman, M., D. Guston, S. Hilgartner, R. Hollander, and S. Slaughter, eds. 2005. *Research policy as an agent of change: Workshop report.* NSF 05–209. Arlington, VA: National Science Foundation.

Galison, P. 1998. *Image and logic.* Chicago: University of Chicago Press.

Gieryn, T. 2002. Three truth-spots. *Journal of the History of the Behavioral Sciences* 38 (2): 113–132.

Gieryn, T. 2006. City as truth-spot: Laboratories and field-sites in urban studies. *Social Studies of Science* 36 (1): 5–38.

Golley, F. 1993. *A history of the ecosystem concept in ecology.* New Haven, CT: Yale University Press.

Gross, K. L., M. R. Willig, L. Gough, R. Inouye, and S. B. Cox. 2000. Patterns of species diversity and productivity at different spatial scales in herbaceous plant communities. *Oikos* 89:417–427.

Hackett, E. 2005. Essential tensions: Identity, control, and risk in research. *Social Studies of Science* 35 (5): 787–826.

Hackett, E., D. Conz, J. Parker, J. Bashford, and S. DeLay. 2004. Tokamaks and turbulence: Research ensembles, policy, and technoscientific work. *Research Policy* 33 (5): 747–767.

Henke, C. 2001. Making a place for science: The field trial. *Social Studies of Science* 30 (4): 483–511.

Henke, C., and T. Gieryn. 2007. Sites of scientific practice: The enduring importance of place. In *The handbook of science and technology studies*, ed. E. J. Hackett, O. Amsterdamska, M. Lynch, and J. Wajcman, 353–376. 3rd ed. Cambridge, MA: MIT Press.

Holton, G. 1978. Subelectrons, presuppositions, and the Millikan–Ehrenhaft dispute. *Historical Studies in the Physical Sciences* 9:161–224.

Katz, J., and B. Martin. 1997. What is research collaboration? *Research Policy* 26:1–18.

Kingsland, S. 2005. *The evolution of American ecology, 1890–2000*. Baltimore, MD: Johns Hopkins University Press.

Kohler, R. 2002. *Landscapes and labscapes*. Chicago: University of Chicago Press.

Kwa, C. 1987. Representations of nature mediating between ecology and science policy: The case of the International Biological Program. *Social Studies of Science* 17 (3): 413–442.

Kwa, C. 2005. Local ecologies and global science. *Social Studies of Science* 35 (6): 923–950.

Latour, B. 1987. *Science in action*. Cambridge, MA: Harvard University Press.

Latour, B. 1999. *Pandora's hope*. Cambridge, MA: Harvard University Press.

Maienschein, J. 1993. Why collaborate? *Journal of the History of Biology* 26 (2): 167–183.

Meadows, A. 1974. *Communication in science*. London: Butterworth.

Merton, R., and E. Barber. 2004. *The travels and adventures of serendipity*. Princeton, NJ: Princeton University Press.

Olson, J., and G. Olson. 2000. Distance matters. *Human-Computer Interaction* 15:139–178.

Owen-Smith, J. 2001. Managing laboratory work through skepticism: Processes of evaluation and control. *American Sociological Review* 66:427–452.

Price, D. 1986. *Little science, big science . . . and beyond*. New York: Columbia University Press. (Orig. pub. 1963.)

Rhoten, D. 2003. *A multi-method analysis of social and technical conditions for interdisciplinary collaboration*. Final report to the National Science Foundation, BCS-0129573. San Francisco: Hybrid Vigor Institute.

Roth, W., and G. Bowen. 1999. Digitizing lizards: The topology of "vision" in ecological fieldwork. *Social Studies of Science* 29 (5): 719–764.

Roth, W., and G. Bowen. 2001. Creative solutions and fibbing results: Enculturation in field ecology. *Social Studies of Science* 31 (4): 533–556.

Shrum, W., I. Chompalov, and J. Genuth. 2001. Trust, conflict, and performance in scientific collaborations. *Social Studies of Science* 31 (5): 681–730.

Walsh, J. P., and N. G. Maloney. 2003. *Problems in scientific collaboration: Does email hinder or help?* Manuscript, Tokyo University and University of Illinois at Chicago. Available at ⟨http://tigger.uic.edu/%7Ejwalsh/WalshMaloneyAAAS.pdf⟩ (accessed April 21, 2007).

Weingart, P. 1997. From "finalization" to "mode 2": Old wine in new bottles? *Social Science Information* 36 (4): 591–613.

16   The Evolution of Collaboration in Ecology: Lessons from the U.S. Long-Term Ecological Research Program

William K. Michener and Robert B. Waide

Scientific collaboration may be defined as working jointly with others in a research endeavor. Given this context, collaboration is an activity that has evolved in fits and starts in the ecological sciences. The historical research tradition and much of the existing literature in ecology, dating back to the seminal text *Fundamentals of Ecology* (Odum 1953), illustrates a paucity of significant collaborative efforts. In particular, most ecology citations have involved a relatively small number of coauthors—usually one to a few individuals who completed their short-term (i.e., one to three years) study looking at ecological patterns and processes in a relatively small area (i.e., square meter[s]) (Brown and Roughgarden 1990; Karieva and Anderson 1988). One of the early and notable exceptions to this generalization was the International Biological Program, which originated in the mid- to late 1960s, and involved large teams of scientists (mostly ecologists) working together in particular ecosystems (Golley 1993). The National Science Foundation's (NSF) Biocomplexity in the Environment program provides a more recent example (Michener et al. 2001) of a collaborative environmental research project involving numerous scientists from many disciplines.

The International Biological Program and Biocomplexity in the Environment clearly represent significant efforts that have nudged the community in the direction of increased collaboration—both within ecology, in the case of International Biological Program, and across ecology and other disciplines, in the case of Biocomplexity in the Environment. Even more illustrative of the history of collaboration in ecology is to examine how collaboration has evolved in a like-minded community of ecological scientists such as those engaged in the Long Term Ecological Research (LTER) program—a "network" of sites and scientists that have been engaged primarily in site-based science since 1981. The objectives of this chapter are to examine collaboration in the LTER Network, summarize the lessons that can be gleaned from this twenty-five-year-old program, and discuss the future of collaboration in relation to planned environmental observatories like the National Ecological Observatory Network (NEON).

LTER

Many environmental problems are extremely complex, requiring concerted multidecadal study. In recognition of this fact, the NSF created the LTER program in 1981—a program designed to foster long-term understanding of key ecological patterns and processes, such as the factors governing primary and secondary production (Hobbie et al. 2003). The initial network of six sites (with less than a hundred scientists) had grown by 2005 to twenty-six sites comprising more than eighteen hundred scientists and educators. These sites encompass a variety of climates and ecosystems in the conterminous United States, Alaska, Puerto Rico, and French Polynesia, and in Antarctica. Today, the LTER is viewed as a major scientific success story for the following reasons:

- By 2004, the number of LTER publications exceeded fourteen thousand
- Hundreds of students have received their graduate degrees working at LTER sites
- The Schoolyard LTER program annually reaches tens of thousands of K–12 students
- Significant scientific challenges such as understanding the dynamics of Hantavirus, a potentially fatal pulmonary disease transmitted by infected deer mice, have been resolved by LTER scientists (e.g., Yates et al. 2002)
- Over three thousand long-term databases have been developed and are accessible online as a national resource
- Similar national networks now exist in thirty countries, forming a global network of sites focusing on long-term ecological processes

The scope and culture of the LTER scientific community has undergone significant transformation since 1981. Research programs at the six initial LTER sites represented a loose confederation of mostly single-investigator projects, and little attention was given to data sharing, facilitating cross-site collaborations, or network-level science across all sites. The scientists populating the research staff at LTER sites typically represented the core ecological disciplines with the exception of a small number of statisticians and climatologists.

By 2006, the LTER had largely transformed itself into a fundamentally collaborative network. Most site-based science projects now employ interactive teams of ecologists as well as scientists from many other disciplines, including geographers, economists, and other social scientists. Two of the LTER sites are located in urban environments (Baltimore and Phoenix). Two other sites (North Temperate Lakes and Coweeta Hydrologic Laboratory) receive additional funding to broaden their research focus by including social scientists. LTER research increasingly involves scientists from beyond the LTER Network, including international scientists. The current LTER literature includes peer-reviewed articles from a large number of multidisciplinary, cross-site, and network-level research projects. The network has pioneered standards for data collection (e.g., Robertson et al. 1999) and data management (e.g., Michener and Brunt 2000). An open-door data-sharing policy was adopted in 1997.

Such radical changes did not occur overnight but instead represented an evolutionary and a generational shift in the LTER scientific enterprise. It is impossible to identify any one specific catalyst of this change, and it is likely that several interrelated mechanisms have contributed to increasing collaboration in the LTER. These mechanisms can be roughly categorized as funding agency incentives, increased networkwide communication, and enhanced coordination and standardization.

Funding Agency Incentives

The LTER's executive leadership is responsible for overseeing the direction of the overall program, and for proposing and, where possible, implementing processes that enable and enhance collaboration among the scientists and educators involved in the enterprise. A successful example was the development of a networkwide data-access policy that was adopted by the LTER Coordinating Committee and established as policy for the entire LTER Network in April 2005; the data-access policy ensures the online availability of LTER data and information products, including accurate and complete metadata, in a timely manner, and specifies the conditions for data use.[1] In many cases, however, consensus may not be reached easily or in a timely fashion, and proposed solutions may require financial support above and beyond what is included in site budgets. In several instances, the funding agency (i.e., the NSF) has played a pivotal role by establishing appropriate incentives.

Incentives for increasing collaboration have included supplemental funding opportunities that: provided high-speed Internet access (T1) to those LTER field sites that lacked such capacity, thereby enhancing communication among the investigators associated with a particular site as well as scientists throughout the network; supported cross-site collaborative research across two or more LTER sites; supported periodic All Scientists Meetings, which have provided a focus for collaboration; expanded the scope of LTER research to other countries; and funded an LTER Network Office to facilitate collaboration and coordination as well as support the array of related Network Office activities, training sessions, and meetings that are summarized below.

Several incentives that are also designed to increase collaboration have been incorporated into periodic requests for proposals for new LTER sites as well as the routine review of existing LTER sites. These include: requirements for individual sites to actively participate in networkwide activities; reviews of site contributions to the network; and reviews of the extent to which sites share data and information, and make them easily accessible and understandable (e.g., via high-quality metadata).

Increased Networkwide Communication

Several communication mechanisms have substantially increased collaboration within the LTER Network. The LTER Network News provides an important venue for sharing information throughout the network. The newsletter is published twice a year in both electronic and printed versions, and includes periodic updates of activities taking place at individual LTER sites, new publications, research and education opportunities, highlights of newsworthy LTER research findings, and a calendar and announcements of upcoming events. The LTER book series that details the science at individual LTER sites (e.g., Bowman and Seastedt 2001) along with a series of minisymposia that are held annually have enhanced communication within the LTER Network and between LTER and other organizations and funding agencies as well as among individual scientists, educators, and students. Increasingly, the LTER Web portal provides LTER scientists and the public with centralized access to LTER data and results, personnel and site characteristics databases, and news and information about the LTER sites as well as their science and education programs.[2]

The previously listed communication mechanisms allow individuals to identify opportunities, facilitate collaborative research (e.g., enabling scientists to discover salient data resources), and communicate the results of collaborations to others. Nevertheless, they represent somewhat more passive approaches to facilitating collaboration. In contrast, two different types of face-to-face meetings have been extremely successful for initiating and supporting collaborative efforts. First, a series of LTER All Scientists Meetings have been held whereby a large proportion of the scientists and graduate students from all LTER sites meet in a single location for several days. Poster sessions, plenary talks, and dozens of thematic breakout sessions are held, and there are many opportunities for one-on-one and small group interactions. Many cross-site, cross-network, and multi-investigator projects have emerged from these meetings. Meeting evaluations and surveys of the participants have been overwhelmingly positive, and the energy generated during the meetings engenders many successful proposals and collaborations. Second, the LTER Network Office supports a modest number of peer-reviewed small group activities (primarily travel and per diem costs), usually as a follow-up to the All Scientists Meetings. These group activities are product focused—that is, they bring small groups together for one or a small number of meetings to synthesize information in relation to a problem, complete a complex set of analyses, and complete one or more peer-reviewed publications or books.

Enhanced Coordination and Standardization

Opportunities for LTER scientists and information managers to enhance coordination as well as develop and adopt standardized methods have significantly facilitated scientific collaboration. Technological solutions and training opportunities have both led to improved coordination among sites. For example, a significant networkwide investment in improving LTER communications and networking infrastructure (i.e., upgrades in networking bandwidth) greatly facilitated intersite communication and coordination. Training and technology transfer have become integral to the LTER science enterprise, leading to better network coordination and enhanced collaboration.

For instance, annual meetings of the LTER information managers were inaugurated in the mid-1980s to coordinate cyberinfrastructure development and informatics activities among LTER sites. Both formal and informal training opportunities, such as in the use of new software tools like metadata management programs, rapidly became a part of the annual information managers meeting. Likewise, other independent one-time courses were established for training scientists and technical staff in the use of geographic information systems software, differential high-precision Global Positioning System technologies, and other new or underutilized technologies. These training efforts were not only important for technology transfer and improving coordination across the network but also for establishing personal trust and a sense of camaraderie among LTER personnel.

Historically, research methods including instrumentation, sampling approaches, data formats, and analytic protocols were unique to individual LTER sites, and in many cases, varied from scientist to scientist within a site. Such variability in methodologies exacerbated the difficulties that are encountered in collaborative work and synthetic science. As these difficulties were more frequently encountered, the LTER community reacted with a series of efforts to identify and establish standards.

Early in its existence, the LTER program employed scientists from across the network in developing a set of common standards for meteorologic measurements (Greenland 1986), and more recent activities have focused on establishing standards for methods to measure soils (Robertson et al. 1999) and primary productivity (Fahey and Knapp 2007). In several instances, it was determined by the LTER community in conjunction with the NSF and via focused workshops that the identification of standard approaches was not enough, and funding was required to acquire common technologies for all LTER sites—creating a de facto standard. Examples include: the identification and purchase of geographic information system software that resulted in standardizing spatio-analytic capabilities in the LTER Network; and the purchase of high-resolution Global Positioning System units that could be shared among the LTER sites to precisely geolocate points in the field and permanent plot boundaries. Such supplemental funding opportunities were responsible for greatly accelerating the networkwide adoption of state-of-the-art technologies. The establishment of such standards and equipment specifications made it possible for LTER scientists to more easily share and adopt common approaches, and collaborate on cross-site studies.

Evolving a Culture of Collaboration: Lessons Learned

The LTER program has grown and evolved over its twenty-five-year history, and collaboration is now fundamental to its function. Here, we present nine lessons about how best to facilitate collaboration based on our experiences from the LTER scientific and education enterprise.

Establish or Identify a Common Vision and Common Objectives

Despite agreement on a set of core research areas from the initiation of the LTER Network, networkwide collaboration has been hampered by the absence of specific networkwide research questions. The stimulation of collaborative research and synthesis has required that the LTER Network develop a common mission statement and research agenda. The LTER program is currently engaged in an intensive planning effort to develop a series of common scientific goals that will guide LTER research over the next decades. This planning activity is designed to complement existing investigations by providing a common focus and funding for cross-site, interdisciplinary research. The planning activity is a watershed event in that it underscores the recognition by the LTER community that a common vision and research agenda are prerequisites to the development of the next level of networkwide collaboration. It is anticipated that the plan will provide natural incentives for additional collaboration and standardization across the network, both of which will enable new research and synthesis efforts.

Provide Support for Face-to-Face Communication

The LTER scientific enterprise has been observed to advance in leaps that are stimulated by face-to-face interactions and interspersed with periods of steady productivity. This lesson is clear from the pattern of activities surrounding the LTER All Scientists Meetings. Modern communication technologies (e.g., tele- and videoconferencing or wiki pages) can help sustain the momentum engendered by face-to-face meetings, but usually are not sufficient for initiating such momentum. In addition, most ecologists do not have access to the most advanced grid and collaboration technologies, and are unaccustomed to their regular use.

Technology can provide mechanisms for facilitating communication, but must be augmented with effective plans for stimulating face-to-face interactions—that is, reducing the distance in collaboration (Olson and Olson 2000). For example, in 1996 the LTER Network developed a science theme addressing the relationship between biodiversity and ecosystem function. The initiation of this effort was assisted by an award from the National Center for Ecological Analysis and Synthesis (NCEAS) (chapter 15, this volume) providing for several meetings of the principals involved, which led to several synthetic publications (e.g., Waide et al. 1999; Willig, Dodson, and Gough 2001). The subsequent adoption of this research theme in research proposals on ecological informatics resulted in a proliferation of research and education initiatives focused on the topic of biodiversity-productivity relationships (Andelman et al. 2004). Although all of these efforts used state-of-the-art communication technologies, they all required routine face-to-face interactions to achieve success.

In the modern world of Internet, e-mail, and text messages, communication would not seem to be a problem. Yet all of these forms of communication are substitutes for conversation, and sometimes they are poor ones. By its nature, face-to-face conversation carries many more modes of information transfer than any electronic medium. At the same time, the rate of information transfer through conversation is probably more efficient than electronic communication. This is not to say that we should avoid e-mail but rather that we should select the optimum mix of communication methods to achieve our goals. When communication needs to be two-way (e.g., when complex topics are on the table or during brainstorming sessions), face-to-face meetings or real-time video- or teleconferences are most effective. When communication is one-way (e.g., progress reporting), e-mail may be the right approach. The productivity of conferences, whether live or digital, can be influenced by many factors, not the least of which is group size. The rules governing productive interactions should be understood and employed to optimize information transfer, and thus productivity. By making a suite of possible modes of interaction (e-mail, tele- and videoconferences, Web and wiki pages, and face-to-face meetings) easily available to LTER scientists, the LTER Network Office provides communication options to meet each need.

Invest in Developing and Adopting Standards

Common questions engender common approaches, so the most cost-effective technique to encourage standards is to develop questions jointly before the standards are adopted. Cultural issues are critical, as most scientists are trained to think for themselves and are skeptical of solutions devised by others. Therefore, it is imperative that the development of standards be well justified, and that the process for developing standards be transparent and engage scientists.

Support Cyberinfrastructure and Information Management

The efficiency of the scientific enterprise depends on the establishment of a cyberinfrastructure that meets the needs of scientists. Yet cyberinfrastructure itself has needs, and human capital must be increased to meet these needs. Scientists must be trained to make efficient use of cyberinfrastructure, but the gains in efficiency that new technology provides should not be offset by increased demands on scientists to interface with technology. The development of a trained cadre of technical personnel in support of science must be one of the goals of an improved cyberinfrastructure. The LTER Network addresses these issues in several ways. A committee comprised of scientists, information managers, and technologists (the Network Information System Advisory Committee) focuses on cyberinfrastructure challenges, including the recruitment and training of personnel. In addition, technical assistance and training is provided to LTER sites through the LTER Network Office.

Data provide the fodder for cyberinfrastructure tools, and adequate support for the acquisition and management of data is critical for improving collaboration. Much effort is wasted in trying to use data that have been improperly or inadequately documented or managed. The maximization of the value and repeated use of data should be one of the goals for any collaborative research, and may require a significant up-front investment in planning, cyberinfrastructure, and personnel. The development and adoption of a metadata standard by the LTER Network (Ecological Metadata Language) has been one step toward achieving this goal (Andelman et al. 2004).

Be Flexible and Engage Stakeholders in the Process

There is a natural tendency for people (especially scientists) to distrust any result or conclusion that they themselves have not had a hand in reaching. At the same time, not all issues can be addressed with equal input from all stakeholders, and hence there is a need for delegation to committees or subgroups. The interaction between any such subgroup and the community of stakeholders must be governed by mutually agreed on procedures, which include clear and open communication of the process, equal opportunity for participation, consensus building, responsiveness to stakeholders, efficiency, and accountability (Bovaird and Löffler 2003; Graham, Amos, and Plumptre 2003). If these procedures are adopted, long-lasting and stable institutions result. The ongoing LTER planning activity has been structured around this set of procedures, which is designed to maximize input and the communication of process.

Recognize the Value of Incentives and Oversight

Collaboration should not be forced on people, but at the same time, all scientists who take public funds for their research have a responsibility to share the results of their labor. Scientists are strongly driven by the desire to achieve, and thus collaboration often emanates from the bottom up. Nevertheless, the integration of individual research results into a larger-scale framework may not be a high priority for individuals, and as such may require encouragement. The form of that encouragement should be as benign as possible, but occasionally the need for top-down decision making manifests itself, and those decisions must sometimes be enforced for the good of the community. If the procedures listed in the previous section are followed, cooperation should be easier to achieve. The LTER planning activity provides a good example of the kind of conundrum that exists in developing collaboration. The scientific capital of the LTER Network exists in its sites and scientists, and research ideas flow from the bottom up. The scale of certain research endeavors, however, requires some degree of top-down organization. Balancing these two approaches requires both incentives and oversight, which are key elements of the planning activity.

Look beyond Your Normal Comfort Zone for Ideas and Collaborators

Parochialism endangers collaboration and promotes divisiveness. One way to avoid this problem is to consciously break down disciplinary or geographic boundaries that may channel research ideas. The time to identify competing ideas is at the formative stage of a research program, not after all the money has been spent. With that in mind, collaborators should be selected to promote intellectual diversity. The comfort that is obtained from working with the same set of colleagues over and over may lead to isolation. Many LTER sites address this issue by including collaborators from other sites in their research team. For example, during the early planning for the Luquillo LTER program, scientists from the Andrews, Coweeta, and Harvard Forest sites were added to a research team that consisted mainly of tropical ecologists. These scientists provided a breadth of focus that contributed significantly to the success of the Luquillo LTER program.

Learn from Your Predecessors

Many collaborative programs are built slowly over time, and useful knowledge about optimum approaches to networking may reside with the initial collaborators. Significant effort should be spent in understanding the reasons why institutions have developed the way they have before deciding to modify or rebuild them. Collaboration should improve efficiency, but only if we trust the knowledge accumulated by our predecessors. The LTER planning activity includes a specific effort to understand and evaluate the governance structure of the LTER program with the goal of achieving a more efficient and effective operation. A governance working group includes non-LTER experts as well as long-term participants in the LTER along with more recent recruits to the program.

Leverage

There will never be enough time or resources to accomplish everything that an individual or organization desires to achieve. Collaboration allows more power to be brought to bear on a problem when resources can be leveraged. The optimum leveraging of resources requires a degree of planning and coordination that goes beyond that involved in an individual research project. The end result of that planning, though, can be a much richer set of skills, expertise, and resources to achieve collective goals. To the extent that individual and collective goals overlap, leveraging can be a powerful tool to achieving one's aims. Examples of this principle abound in the LTER Network, and large, long-term experiments that leverage the participation of multiple investigators exist at most LTER sites.

An Exemplar: LTER Collaboration in Cyberinfrastructure Development

A major focus for collaboration between the LTER and other science enterprises has been in developing cyberinfrastructure—an effort that requires building partnerships as well as leveraging resources and expertise across an array of institutions. Two recent examples are the Knowledge Network for Biocomplexity and the Science Environment for Ecological Knowledge (SEEK)—large information technology research projects supported by the NSF.[3] The Knowledge Network for Biocomplexity is an intellectual consortium comprising NCEAS (chapter 15, this volume), the LTER, and the San Diego Supercomputer Center. The goal of this consortium is to integrate the distributed and heterogeneous information sources required for the development and testing of theory in ecology as well as its sister fields into a standards-based, open-architecture, knowledge network. The network provides access to integrated data products drawn from distributed data repositories for analysis with advanced tools for exploring complex data sets.

SEEK evolved from the Knowledge Network for Biocomplexity effort and represents one of the major research efforts by the Partnership for Biodiversity Informatics—a collaboration among LTER and non-LTER ecologists, computer scientists, and informatics experts. It addresses challenges associated with the accessibility and integration of extremely heterogeneous (spatially, temporally, and thematically) data in ecology. Such heterogeneity in data as well as in models and analytic techniques poses a significant challenge when attempting the synthetic analyses that are the essential ingredients of successful scientific collaborations.

The LTER engagement in the SEEK collaboration illustrates many of the lessons described above. First, in establishing the Partnership for Biodiversity Informatics, the LTER and the other partners looked well beyond their normal comfort zones in identifying collaborators, and in choosing the research topics that would be the focus of the collaborative research. The partnership encompasses computer scientists (one-third), applied informatics experts (one-third), and biologists (one-third), with half of those from the ecological sciences and the other half from the biodiversity sciences). The research topics represented an equivalent mix of basic science that appealed to the computer scientists and applied science that appealed to the biologists and informatics specialists. Second, the project effectively leverages and builds on prior research that has taken place at one or more of the institutions, such as Ecological Metadata Language, which was developed by the University of California (at San Diego and Santa Barbara) and the LTER Network Office. Third, effective communication was recognized at the outset as being central to the success of SEEK. The mechanisms that were established for SEEK include: monthly reports that summarize the progress made by all SEEK members; biweekly conference calls among the members of the SEEK executive committee; semiannual face-to-face meetings of all the SEEK developers and scientists; and daily communication, mediated by a project coordinator, among all the developers via "chat" and Voice over Internet Protocol (VOiP) tools.

The Future

As mentioned above, the LTER has evolved from a loose confederation of six individual sites funded in 1981 to a fundamentally collaborative scientific enterprise consisting of twenty-six sites, more than eighteen hundred scientists and educators, and a Network Office. The hallmark of the LTER has been and will continue to be its focus on high-quality, long-term, site-based research. Ecology and the related environmental sciences (e.g., oceanography and hydrology) are increasingly shifting attention to the questions that affect us at the regional, national, and global scales. For example, NEON is being designed as the first regional- to continental-scale research platform that will enable scientists to address grand challenge ecological and environmental science questions (National Research Council 2001, 2003), at both the appropriate spatial and temporal scales of resolution and the relevant scales of biological organization. NEON represents a paradigm shift in our scientific enterprise—requiring a leap into "big science" (i.e., massive capital investments and large numbers of scientists), and demanding new collaborations along with the broad engagement of the scientific, educational, and engineering communities. NEON will transform how we do science as well as the sociology of our science. The NEON science enterprise will be based on an open-door policy of rapid access to data. An open-access policy can provide scientists and decision makers with the data they need to address complex environmental questions. This paradigm shift means that we must continue to evolve as a scientific community—developing new cross-disciplinary partnerships, using NEON to leverage funds and support for research, education, and infrastructure, and finding better ways to communicate the importance of NEON and the findings thereof to the scientific community and the public.

We anticipate that the future success of NEON and the continued success of the LTER will depend in part on how well we as scientists are able to establish and foster cross-disciplinary collaborations to tackle key challenges. Based on the experiences from the LTER, we expect that the success of future collaborations will partly result from:

- Identifying objective(s) that are shared by the potential collaborators
- Establishing effective modes of regular communication and, most important, supporting routine face-to-face meetings
- Investing time in assessing and identifying the methods that will facilitate the collaboration, such as the standard procedures that will be employed

The lessons that we have learned in the past, however, may be inadequate for addressing the environmental challenges that lay ahead. For instance, NEON will require an unprecedented scale of collaboration that may be enabled through technical solutions. Yet developing a new class of collaboration technology in itself requires extensive collaboration among software developers, domain scientists, and information technologists. Despite the implied level of investment in time, money, and people to support such collaborations, the potential benefits are likely to be far-reaching. Much of the cyberinfrastructure needed by ecologists for the LTER and NEON, for example—that is, the cyberinfrastructure necessary for data access, curation, and preservation (Arzberger et al. 2004; Krishtalka and Humphrey 2000)—can also benefit scientists and educators from throughout academia as well as state and federal agencies. The high costs of advanced computing and communications will dictate that collaborations evolve and leverage resources in order to further support the ecological science enterprise.

Realizing the potential of scientific collaborations being planned for the LTER and NEON also requires continuing changes in professional and career reward structures. It is not unusual to see high-energy physics publications that have dozens to a hundred or more coauthors (chapter 8, this volume), with leaders tracking the contributions of each individual. As ecologists increasingly shift focus to the continental scale and issues that cross many disciplinary boundaries, similar changes in professional recognition may be expected. Clearly, an increasingly interdisciplinary mind-set will be necessary to understand the complex feedbacks between the physical environment, ecosystems, and society (Andelman et al. 2004). A key consideration as scientific collaboration continues to evolve within ecology will be how to foster collaboration so that it does not come at the expense of individual initiative, creativity, and credit.

Acknowledgments

This work is supported in part by NSF grants ITR 0225674, EF 0225665, and DBI 0129792, DARPA N00014-03-1-0900, and the Andrew Mellon Foundation.

Notes

1. For the LTER Network data-access policy, data-access requirements, and general data use agreement, see ⟨http://www.lternet.edu/data/netpolicy.html⟩.

2. The LTER Web site can be found at ⟨http://www.lternet.edu⟩.

3. More information on SEEK is available at ⟨http://seek.ecoinformatics.org⟩.

References

Andelman, S. J., C. M. Bowles, M. R. Willig, and R. B. Waide. 2004. Understanding environmental complexity through a distributed knowledge network. *BioScience* 54:243–249.

Arzberger, P., P. Schroeder, A. Beaulieu, G. Bowker, K. Casey, L. Laaksonen et al. 2004. An international framework to promote access to data. *Science* 303:1777–1778.

Bovaird, T., and E. Löffler. 2003. Evaluating the quality of public governance: Indicators, models, and methodologies. *International Review of Administrative Services* 69:313–328.

Bowman, W. D., and T. R. Seastedt, eds. 2001. *Structure and function of an alpine ecosystem: Niwot Ridge, Colorado.* New York: Oxford University Press.

Brown, J. H., and J. Roughgarden. 1990. Ecology for a changing earth. *Bulletin of the Ecological Society of America* 71:173–188.

Fahey, T. J., and A. K. Knapp, eds. 2007. *Principles and standards for measuring primary production.* New York: Oxford University Press.

Golley, F. B. 1993. *A history of the ecosystem concept in ecology.* New Haven, CT: Yale University Press.

Graham, J., B. Amos, and T. Plumptre. 2003. *Principles for good governance in the 21st century.* Policy brief no. 15. Ottawa: Institute on Governance.

Greenland, D. 1986. Standardized meteorological measurements for long-term ecological research sites. Available at ⟨http://intranet.lternet.edu/committees/climate/standard86.html⟩ (accessed April 17, 2007).

Hobbie, J. E., S. R. Carpenter, N. B. Grimm, J. R. Gosz, and T. R. Seastedt. 2003. The US Long Term Ecological Research Program. *BioScience* 53 (1): 21–32.

Karieva, P., and M. Anderson. 1988. Spatial aspects of species interactions: The wedding of models and experiments. In *Community ecology,* ed. A. Hastings, 35–50. New York: Springer Verlag.

Krishtalka, L., and P. S. Humphrey. 2000. Can natural history museums capture the future? *BioScience* 50:611–617.

Michener, W. K., T. J. Baerwald, P. Firth, M. A. Palmer, J. L. Rosenberger, E. A. Sandlin et al. 2001. Defining and unraveling biocomplexity. *BioScience* 51:1018–1023.

Michener, W. K., and J. W. Brunt, eds. 2000. *Ecological data: Design, management, and processing.* Methods in ecology series. Oxford: Blackwell Science.

National Research Council. 2001. *Grand challenges in environmental sciences.* Washington, DC: National Academies Press.

National Research Council. 2003. *NEON: Addressing the nation's environmental challenges.* Washington, DC: National Academies Press.

Odum, E. P. 1953. *Fundamentals of ecology.* Philadelphia: W. B. Saunders Company.

Olson, J., and G. Olson. 2000. Distance matters. *Human-Computer Interaction* 15:139–178.

Robertson, G. P., C. S. Bledsoe, D. C. Coleman, and P. Sollins, eds. 1999. *Standard soil methods for long-term ecological research.* New York: Oxford University Press.

Waide, R. B., M. R. Willig, C. F. Steiner, G. Mittelbach, L. Gough, S. I. Dodson et al. 1999. The relationship between primary productivity and species richness. *Annual Review of Ecology and Systematics* 30:257–300.

Willig, M. R., S. I. Dodson, and L. Gough. 2001. What is the observed relationship between species richness and productivity? *Ecology* 82:2381–2396.

Yates, T. L., J. N. Mills, C. A. Parmenter, T. G. Ksiazek, R. R. Parmenter, J. R. Vande Castle et al. 2002. The ecology and evolutionary history of an emergent disease: Hantavirus Pulmonary Syndrome. *BioScience* 52:989–998.

17 Organizing for Multidisciplinary Collaboration: The Case of the Geosciences Network

David Ribes and Geoffrey C. Bowker

Within the sciences, infrastructure has come to mean much more than "tubes and wires." Contemporary infrastructure-building projects for the sciences—often dubbed cyberinfrastructure—seek to develop the communication capacity to collaborate across distances and institutional barriers (Star and Ruhleder, 1994), work across the technical differences endemic to specialized disciplinary work, and manage the increasingly large and heterogeneous archives of scientific data (Bowker 2000). The goal of infrastructure building today is to encourage multiple configurations of collaboration and enable novel interdisciplinary research ties. Fostering such ties is no easy task. Developing collaborative ventures stretches well beyond the confines of the "technical" to addressing problems centrally defined as "sociological," such as forming communities, communicating across disciplinary boundaries, or meeting the needs of diverse career reward systems.

In this chapter, we focus on the work of multidisciplinary participants as they went about planning and building the Geosciences Network (GEON). GEON, a cyberinfrastructure project, seeks to produce a repertoire of high-end information technologies for the broader earth sciences:

The ultimate goal of GEON is to establish a new informatics-based paradigm in the geosciences, to provide a holistic understanding of the Earth's dynamic systems, thereby transforming the science. (GEON, 2002, 3)

GEON is intended to be an "umbrella infrastructure" for the geosciences, bringing together tools for collaboration and data that will serve the heterogeneous disciplines that study the earth. In organizing to produce this umbrella infrastructure, the participants drew together a wide range of earth and computer science experts representing multiple institutions across the United States. The network has twelve principal investigators (PIs) roughly split between those studying the earth and those studying computation, thereby presenting difficulties for collaboration. This is the first and most obvious disciplinary boundary to be crossed: computer and earth sciences. Yet there is also a second, often less prominently discussed, set of disciplinary boundaries: the earth science members of GEON are themselves subdivided by their expertise, which includes paleobotany, geophysics, and other specialties; the disciplines of the earth sciences vary by method and focus.

Both axes of collaboration must be rendered explicit in order to understand the work of developing infrastructure within the model of cyberinfrastructure: first, collaboration is across the domains (domain/domain), and second, collaboration is between computer and domain scientists (computer science/domain).[1] Both axes require work to overcome communication and organizational barriers. In this chapter, we trace three temporal phases as GEON participants sought to cross *both disciplinary axes of difference*; we capture and articulate the tactics and strategies as they went about building an umbrella infrastructure bringing together the heterogeneous earth and computer sciences.

GEON is a project in motion. At the time of this writing, GEON remains at the prototype stage. Thus, we do not focus on the end-product infrastructure; instead we analyze the practical processes in building the infrastructure (Bowker and Star 1999)—this is to date typical for such studies, since few specifically cyberinfrastructure projects have built up an extensive user base. The plan for the chapter is as follows. We first outline the two axes of collaboration, noting the particular difficulties that arise at each. We then explore the tactics and strategies adopted by the GEON participants to address working within the geosciences, and collaborating across earth and computer sciences. We focus on three phases in the project's early development. Our empirical analysis begins "before" GEON—that is, during its proposal-writing stage. It is here that the participants negotiated a vision for multidisciplinary collaboration; in the case of GEON, we found that key notions for the project were articulated such as a "balance" between computer and earth sciences research. Second, we focus on the initial meetings of GEON: the "kickoff" and "all-hands." While in the proposal participants put forward a multidisciplinary vision for the earth sciences, actually building that collaboration was a practical activity. The initial meetings set aside considerable time to begin forming a "GEON community," as earth and computer scientists alike learned of their disciplinarily grounded differences. Finally, we focus on the empirical "test beds" that served to coordinate work across disciplinary boundaries. The test beds are of scientific interest to the multiple constituencies participating in this cyberinfrastructure venture: Over time, geologists in multiple domains have developed extensive knowledge about these areas; and from the perspective of computer science it is the data sets themselves that are of interest.

Notes on Method

From its formal inception in 2002 we were invited to participate in the GEON project as "social informatics researchers." The PIs of the team had themselves identified future complications for working across computer science/domain and domain/domain boundaries: they recognized that communication across forms of expertise could be a bottleneck in the collaborative venture. The focus of this chapter reflects this interest on the part of the GEON participants. We characterize our research stance in this project as "social dimensions feedback" (Ribes and Baker 2007), in which our primary role as observers was coupled with occasional requests to communicate feedback and research findings. Our investigations have resulted in various opportunities to consult with GEON participants, the host institution (the San Diego Supercomputer Center) and the broader geoscience community.

The research was driven by grounded theory methodology (Clarke 2005; Star 1999): *iterations* of data collection were combined with *testing* against substantively generated theory as well as *constant comparisons* with historical and contemporary studies of infrastructure (Ribes and Finholt 2007). Between 2002 and 2005 we conducted ethnographic data collection, attending the meetings, workshops, and conferences organized within GEON. Such events were audio recorded, annotated, and selectively transcribed; archives were maintained using the qualitative analysis software suite NVivo. Furthermore, we were granted unconditional access to the various GEON e-mail Listservs, providing a voluminous and finely detailed stream of data. In the later years of data collection, the ethnographic research was supplemented by interviewing GEON participants, key members of the National Science Foundation (NSF), and representatives of the earth science institutions (such as the U.S. Geological Survey).

Two Axes of Collaboration

We should not treat "multidisciplinary collaboration" as a homogeneous entity. The configuration of each collaboration is specific. Influences on the character of collaboration include the particular representation of domain participants, the length of the engagement, or the purposes for working together. We focus on two critical axes of collaboration in infrastructure-building projects: multidisciplinary relations in GEON are *across the geosciences (domain/domain)* and *with computer scientists (computer science/ domain)*. Both of these present unique difficulties.

Within the classification of collaboratories (chapter 3, this volume), GEON can most usefully be understood as a *community infrastructure project*. These are projects whose goals are to develop resources to support scientific work in a particular domain, such as the earth sciences in the case of GEON. Chapter 3 (this volume) identifies three typical organizational difficulties encountered by such endeavors: aligning the research goals of domain scientists and information technologists; determining the best form of management; and producing career rewards and pathways for scientists who help build infrastructure for others to use. Here we are concerned with the first tension—

the tendency of goals to diverge in multidisciplinary teams. We examine the mechanisms that GEON participants have employed to navigate the difficulties noted in chapter 3:

Whose research agenda will be paramount? In partnerships between disciplinary experts and computer scientists, there is often conflict between pursuing the most technologically advanced solutions (which are of research interest to the computer scientists) and more immediately practical solutions.

In addition to the key difficulty identified above—collaboration across computer science/domain boundaries—we also point to the work of collaborating "within" the domain—that is, across the diversity of earth sciences. For many participants, one or both experiences of collaboration are novel. In this section, we characterize the difficulties across each boundary in turn: domain/domain followed by computer science/domain.

Domain/Domain: Toward an Umbrella for the Geosciences

Scientifically and organizationally, the geosciences span an enormous range of disciplinary configurations. The umbrella term geosciences is deceptively unifying; to say that "geoscientists study the earth," does not capture the heterogeneity of the natural phenomena and methods that fall under the term. The participants themselves identify over twelve disciplinary specializations within GEON; for instance, these include geophysics, paleobotany, seismology, and petrology. The criteria for knowledge formation and epistemological grounding differs across the geosciences by their history, traditions, and methods of inquiry (Rudwick 1976). Nature does not provide a coordinating framework for science: the methods, language, and concepts of the diverse earth sciences are a matter of culture, learned practice, and social organization (Knorr-Cetina 1999). Below we outline three kinds of disciplinary differences within the earth sciences: social organization, the willingness to share data, and the structure of data.

First, organizationally many of GEON's earth science participants are located in administrative units of different types. For example, self-identified geoscientists may be housed in geology, physics, or biology departments. This can also mean, for instance, that they have varying degrees of access to computing resources and services, such as whether a research team has information managers or other technical support staff. Such organizational differences make it challenging to build a cyberinfrastructure for the geosciences because the participants do not begin on the same footing for access to technical services or even with a shared familiarity with computing technologies. While a geophysicist may have an entire technical staff, a metamorphic petrologist may never have worked with software more specialized than a spreadsheet. These differences are organizational in that they stand in for the division of labor: Who is responsible for taking care of data? Is taking care of data a dedicated task of a specialized information manager, or does it compete with the needs of a professor to teach, conduct research, and write articles? Do scientists working for the U.S. Geological Survey have different data practices and research agendas than those based in a university?

Second, scientists have varying traditions for the curation and sharing of their data. A scientist may feel possessive of their data, hoping to draw out future insights, or they may feel uncertain of the quality and thus unwilling to share it with their peers (Borgman 2007; Campbell et al. 2002; Ceci 1988). The extent to which a particular group is prepared to exchange its data varies substantially by discipline. For example, field scientists such as paleobotanists and metamorphic petrologists collect relatively small data sets at particular geographic sites. The intense personal involvement with the research site and the data collection may lead to the unwillingness to contribute such data to a large anonymous repository. They may also feel that the data are incomprehensible or meaningless if not tied to local knowledge about a specific site. On the other hand, instrument-intensive scientists such as geophysicists have established traditions for using large arrays of remote instrumentation, and the discipline has been at the advancing edge of computer science for forty years, from the first analog computers to the first expert system (Bowker 1994). Publicly funded instrumentation often comes with stipulations to release data to the broader community of researchers after a fixed time. Similarly, seismologists have a long tradition of sharing data across both territories and nations: it is in the nature of their data that it does not respect geographic boundaries. Over time, geophysicists and seismologists have developed "cultures" that assume particular data-sharing practices. These varying traditions for data collection, curation, and sharing can seem morally weighted—"the right thing to do"—to the participants. In deciding the policies for an umbrella data repository, at times these varying traditions may even become the object of explicit conflict.

Third, the form and size of databases vary by disciplinary tradition and method. For instance, in mapping topology geologists have begun to use Light Distance and Ranging (LiDAR) scans of the surface of the earth. GEON has developed tools and resources to help geoscientists scale up their data technologies for such approaches. Such techniques generate billions of data points in a "LiDAR point cloud," which today are hosted in an IBM DB2 spatial database running on the DataStar terascale computer at the San Diego Supercomputer Center. In contrast, paleobotanists conduct observations in the field, and collect, classify, and organize samples at a smaller scale. Recently, paleobotanists have used electron microscopy, but most data are not available digitally; thus even "within" paleobotany, data structures will vary broadly. Each method, each disciplinary tradition, and often even each research team will have idiosyncratic methods for transforming the data they collect into databases. Generating tools for working across such diverse data structures is one specific goal of GEON.

Collaboration across the geosciences is an organizational, social, and technical problem requiring an alignment between the practical methods of diverse disciplines, the institutions in which science is practiced, and the standards that arrange data. To the extent that GEON encompasses heterogeneous earth sciences, the participants have had to articulate and negotiate such differences in building an umbrella for the earth sciences.

Domain/Computer Science: Novel Information Technology for the Earth Sciences

This brings us to our second axis of collaboration. Building information infrastructure requires domain scientists to work closely with computer scientists. Many of GEON's earth science participants had little or no experience working with computer scientists, and they were unfamiliar with the technical details of information systems or data interoperability.

Computer and earth scientists describe themselves as having different goals, based on reward systems within each research tradition. From the perspective of domain practitioners, computer scientists are disinterested in the practical results of their research or design work. They are said to sit on one side of the "brick wall," designing programs intended for domain use without much consideration for specific application needs, functionality, or accessibility (Suchman 1994). They are able to advance in their own field by publishing their technical innovations in journals, pointing to grants awarded and "demo" programs that stand as surrogates for successful development regardless of practical uptake. Meanwhile, these applications move seamlessly from vaporware to ghostware. Within computer science, the claim goes, little attention is paid to the life cycle of the application in the domain: Has the program been adopted? Does it meet the requirements of the users? Even less consideration is given to providing technical assistance or long-term support for operability (Weedman 1998).

A parallel claim is often set forth about domain scientists: they are rewarded for advances in earth science, but have few incentives to produce and maintain community resources. For example, designing algorithms or visualization packages have generally not been counted toward tenure case decisions. When developing computing resources they instead focus on the development of information technology tools that will serve their particular needs to investigate a scientific research question. What is traditionally rewarded within a scientific community are "science results"—broadly understood as new domain knowledge, or as is frequently stated in GEON, "something new about the Rockies"—rather than the production of long-term information infrastructure.

Within GEON, the problem of reward is often expressed in terms of the future careers of geoscience graduate students participating in the project. These students may have invested much time in creating tools for scientific research, but it is difficult to convey the significance of the contribution to the geoscience community focused on new knowledge. The result may be a graduate student with a record of experience that is strong within "geoinformatics," but that may appear weak to a traditional geoscience hiring committee.

The aggregate of these two trajectories—information technology's indifference to the domain, and domain scientists' individualist tendencies—amounts to a crucial problem with computer science/domain collaborations. If we want infrastructure to be a long-term, multiuse platform accessible to a community of the targeted users (Bowker and Star 1999; Star and Ruhleder 1994), the computer scientist must be configured to care about science implementation success as measured from *within* the domain, and each scientist must be motivated to care about creating infrastructure resources for a broader scientific community. Building technology that is usable in practice must matter to a computer scientist, and designing technology for a broader community must matter to an earth scientist.

Across the domain/domain and computer science/domain divides, GEON participants have had the task of creating an umbrella infrastructure for the earth sciences. Each of the next three sections identifies phases in the development of GEON, and how in each phase the participants worked to cross both boundaries. We begin before GEON, as the participants articulated a vision of collaboration in the proposal. We then outline the initial meetings, as the members sought to find means for communication across disciplinary boundaries. Finally, we explore the work around GEON's test beds, which helped to coordinate activity across both sets of boundaries.

Making a Vision: Writing the GEON Proposal

In this section, we trace the work of GEON's PIs as they sought to create a vision of multidisciplinary collaboration that balanced computer and domain science research. As the twelve PIs of the grant wrote the proposal, they were continuously aware of a *community opinion* that placed doubts on GEON as a *contribution* to the computer or earth sciences. In many senses, this was a formative controversy that occurred prior to the funding of GEON. The controversy has shaped the goals and methods of the project (Collins 1981; Scott, Richards, and Martin 1990). As in other fields, domain scientists have often felt—whatever assurances were given to the contrary—that money spent on computing resources was money not being spent on science. The balance between computer science and domain remains an ongoing concern for the GEON participants, but this concern was first articulated in the multiple iterations of writing the grant proposal.

The controversy was drawn along and across disciplinary lines: Is research in GEON geoscience? An exercise in computer science? Both? Or perhaps neither? The lines of debate can be summarized into two prevalent disciplinary arguments:

▪ GEON is not engaged in computer science research but merely in the application of information technology to geoscience problems and research

• GEON is not engaged in geoscience research but in experimenting with information technologies not yet sufficiently developed to contribute to practical earth science questions

To understand how this debate emerged, we must first turn to the history of the funding program for GEON.

Beginning from early planning meetings in 2000, the GEON PIs decided that the vision of the proposal would be to place the research goals of computer and domain science on equal footing. This goal was in marked contrast to more traditional "science-centered" or "technology-driven" projects. Computer scientists would not be "mere technicians," and geoscientists would not be sites for testing novel IT. In the practice of composing the proposal, the PIs found the task of satisfying both groups more daunting than initially envisioned; yet doing so was encouraged by the structure of the funding itself.

GEON was funded under the NSF's Information Technology Research (ITR) program, in which basic research remained a central goal. The requests for proposals issued as part of the ITR program specifically demanded new, experimental, and high-risk research. In order to justify GEON as an ITR project, the proposal writers had to demonstrate that the project would address important geoscience questions in addition to those of producing infrastructure. Because a part of its funds would come from computer science and the other part from the earth sciences, GEON would also have a double responsibility. As noted by one of the PIs, GEON would have to satisfy two sets of scientific criteria: "The RFP [request for proposals] from ITR was very clear, they want something risky, experimental, from the IT side, but we wanted GEO to fund us, too, and that meant they had to feel like we were doing something about geology, or for the earth science community."

GEON PIs described the difficulty as a tension between research and development (Lawrence 2006). Scientific infrastructure is meant to offer a relatively stable and transparent base for research. If GEON was to be a platform for geoscience, it would have to be accessible to the "average earth scientist"—supporting everyday work and making data accessible in a straightforward manner. Yet would such a stable set of technologies meet the criteria of computer science research that focuses on novel capacities? On the other hand, if the proposal placed too great an emphasis on the contemporary research questions of computer science, geoscientists would see it as experimental rather than stable.

In such a scenario, what would a balance between computer science and domain research look like? It was not possible to answer this question in advance; rather, it was carefully crafted and negotiated over two iterations of the proposal-writing process.

The first GEON proposal was explicitly declined by NSF on the grounds of a poor balance between computer science/domain research. One of the GEON PIs stated that reviewers noted that the first proposal leaned too far in the direction of computer science research: "We threw in a lot of computer science and digital libraries kinds of research, and we also threw in a whole lot of earth science. We thought we were covering our bases, but they [the review panel] thought we were stretching ourselves thin."[2] Why should the NSF Directorate for Geoscience fund information technology research when its mandate is clearly to generate new knowledge about the earth? Within computer science a similar, if muted, debate played out over whether the infrastructure building was a contribution to knowledge of computing. If GEON relied on relatively established hardware and software technologies, then it came closer to an implementation project rather than computer science research. In this case, why should the Directorate for Computer and Information Science and Engineering fund this project?

The second ITR proposal had to demonstrate stronger geoscience contributions without going too far in the other direction and causing disinterest from its computer science constituency. Participants' most noteworthy response to the first proposal's rejection was to tie information technology research to specific sites of geological science; these came to be known as the mid-Atlantic and the Rocky mountain *test beds*. The test beds were chosen because they were important sites for geoscientific research and had been studied for over a century. Further, each test bed had well-documented science questions drawn from the various disciplines making up GEON (domain/domain balance), and had multiple data sets in each area. For example, data integration and visualization in the mid-Atlantic can serve to help bring together data, evidence, and scientists in current controversies in seismology involving continental growth through accretion: "To assess this mechanism of continental growth, the models must be constrained by multidisciplinary observational data sets within the region that will be assembled by the GEON geoscience team" (Keller 2003, n.p.). Here we can see the identification of a problem set, the communities that are participating in a theoretical debate, and at least a suggestion of the formal models and data sets that would be required for technical integration. The test beds could help to bring all three elements together.

The test beds were a highly successful addition to the second GEON proposal. The PIs have noted that the reviewers responded well to them. More important for the GEON participants, the test beds served to "balance" the vision of collaboration for the project, giving the computer scientists specific data sets to work with, and the earth scientists particular geographic regions to focus their research.

Through the negotiation process, GEON became imbued with this particular vision of the computer science/domain collaborative construction of infrastructure. This vision was articulated in its grant proposal through the allotment of funds, the distribution of responsibility, and the promises for "deliverables" in the form of computer and earth sciences knowledge. Such a vision was carefully articulated among participants. Thus, more than simply serving to secure funding for the project, the proposal writing was a constitutive process for participants. Over the years, members have regularly returned to the proposal as a resource for articulating the GEON collaborative vision.

Proposal to Collaboration: From a Shared Vision to a Community of Practice

Above we described the crafting of a shared vision of multidisciplinary collaboration through proposal writing. Still, a proposed *plan* on paper was not the *activity* of working together. While having the proposal funded was the formal inception, the next step was moving from a paper GEON to a practical organization. As with writing the proposal, the practice of multidisciplinary collaboration was an accomplishment. In this section we focus on the *meetings of GEON* as the sites for organizing from a funded proposal to a practical collaboration. Such gatherings served to foster the shared understandings that are the keystones of multidisciplinary collaboration; Jean Lave and Etienne Wenger (Lave and Wenger 1991) draw attention to mutual learning in such groups and call these communities of practice.

Lave and Wenger (1991) have discussed communities of practice as a useful unit of analysis for understanding how heterogeneous groups come together to perform complex tasks. In particular, they focus on the process of social learning that occurs when people who have a common interest in some subject or problem collaborate over an extended period to share ideas, find solutions, and build innovations. Contrary to received understandings, community should not be considered a common starting point for organized action but the reverse: community is the *product* of shared activity, collectively negotiated meanings and purposes, and trajectories of shared learning. Above we have already described the *differences* in the research methods and goals of the GEON participants, primarily characterized by the boundaries computer science/domain and domain/domain; in practical collaborative work, the concept of a community of practice emphasizes how members come to work across those boundaries.

The first GEON meeting was the kickoff, and it was structured to help the participants begin communicating across their disciplinary specializations. Through such gatherings and over time, the participants articulated an understanding of the collective challenges facing GEON. While the PIs had collaborated in writing the proposal, the kickoff meeting had more ambitious goals: it brought together the research teams of the PIs, and provided an opportunity for individual participants to communicate their research questions and collectively debate the understanding of "what GEON is to be."

The kickoff meeting served to introduce the information technology team and its planned technologies to the geoscientists. In turn, the geoscientists presented their science questions and some initial descriptions of the kinds of data necessary to achieve their goals (see figure 17.1).

The great majority of the time at this meeting was spent as individual scientists (earth and computer alike) presented their research to the larger team. So, for example, a geoscientist described the mechanisms for pluton formation—an igneous rock body formed at great depth and intruding among others. A computer scientist described

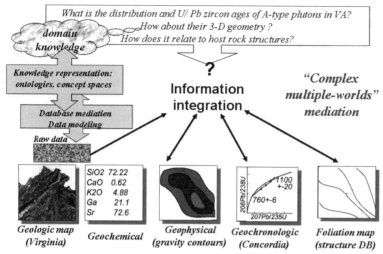

Figure 17.1
Elaborate slide shows are composed to share technical knowledge with the heterogeneous experts of GEON; this slide captures the notion of data integration

ontologies—an information technology for representing concepts as semantic relations. Each presentation was followed by a discussion period, allowing the participants to ask for clarification or draw links across their research. Along with computer science and geoscience introductions, this meeting also served to begin coordinating research goals among earth scientists: Would GEON's lithology ontologies draw from the already-established British rock classification? How could LiDAR data-cleaning techniques be used for applications mapping the topology of drainage basins? The participants discussed the diverse research conducted by GEON earth scientists and considered the ways in which individual research goals could be aligned with those of the larger project.

In a received understanding of community, members coming from similar formal positions and backgrounds already hold common beliefs. In contrast, the notion of a community of practice emphasizes the *production* of a community identity through shared learning experiences and explicit discussions of common purpose. From this perspective, communities are not so much about extant homogeneity as about generating a common orientation for members. A key feature of the kickoff meetings was the inclusion of a broader array of participants from the geosciences than the PIs. A community infrastructure involves a wider set of participants than those we have identified as "computer science and domain." Such activities always draw on technical and administrative resources that are often later forgotten in accounts of scientific and technological activity, but that are seminal in building successful infrastructure.

The kickoff meeting and subsequent annual meetings encompassed graduate students, information managers, ancillary research staff, and the project administrators. We can only identify these as GEON community members after the fact. They began from highly heterogeneous starting points: scientists/professors, graduate students, technicians, and information managers—all of whom had to be successfully integrated into building up and maintaining a functioning cyberinfrastructure. As was typical for such collaborations, the set of personnel was ever shifting—and the boundaries between participating, lurking, and ignoring were fluid. For example, information managers are the curators of geoscience data, specifically tasked with the responsibility of preserving databases and helping with access. The diversity of speakers at GEON meetings assisted in bringing such "long-term" concerns to the table in matters of planning and design. Including heterogeneous participants during the process of design means they can stand-in for the diversity of downstream users in GEON's future as a functioning infrastructure. Through the learning environment created in the initial meetings, these heterogeneous participants *became* a community despite their initial differences.

From a narrow instrumentalist perspective of "doing research" or even "building infrastructure," we could say that "nothing gets done" in such meetings; however, presentations on scientific and technical specializations came to shape a common foundation for the heterogeneous participants. They built up common knowledge and vocabularies for the multiple participating disciplines. As the tasks shifted from introductions to practical collaborations, the participants were able to begin from a set of basic understandings about the research questions constituting GEON's base of expertise. This kind of exchange proved doubly valuable in the long term for future relations between computer science and domain. Specifically, computer scientists came to have a much deeper understanding of how the domain functions, the kinds of work that geoscientists do, and the way they produce knowledge.

Collaboration to Work: Coordinating Activity across Disciplinary Boundaries

We have covered the development of a shared vision for collaboration and the emergence of a community of practice. What remains for multidisciplinary activity is the organization of the work itself. At the core of GEON is the production of novel technological resources for the domain in the form of information tools that will support geoscientific work.

A key goal in the GEON project is achieving interoperability. Interoperating the geosciences means producing computer-mediated linkages between the multiplicity of data sets and the computing resources in the earth sciences. This has included, for example, creating schemas that permit queries for simultaneously searching multiple databases. By making heterogeneous data sets interoperable two prospects emerge: transforming everyday work in the geoscience fields to answer questions that cannot be approached by one discipline alone, and acting as proof that information technology can be used to facilitate interdisciplinary synthesis. In this section we ask: How are such technologies collaboratively designed while meeting the disciplinary requirements of earth scientists (new knowledge about the earth) and computer scientists (new knowledge about computation)? There are, of course, multiple approaches adopted by GEON participants; here we return to the test beds in order to examine how these served to coordinate activity across disciplinary boundaries.

To elaborate this example we draw on the concept of "boundary objects." Susan Leigh Star and James Greisemer (1989) described boundary objects as sustaining multiple meanings for heterogeneous members while also meeting the informational requirements of all. The notion helps to explain the collaboration of expert groups, such as scientists, without relying on the assumption that they need to establish a consensus of purpose or technical meaning among themselves. This is a good way to understand how the test beds serve to coordinate work in GEON across two sets of disciplinary boundaries: computer science/domain and domain/domain. For earth scientists the test beds were sites of empirical research in many subfields, while for computer scientists the test beds collected data sets in multiple formats; in sustaining different meanings for these participants, the test beds also coordinated activity *within* the geosciences and *across* to computer science.

As noted, the test beds are two geographic regions in the United States: the mid-Atlantic and the Rocky Mountains (see figure 17.2). They were added to GEON during the second round of proposal writing with the specific intention of grounding applications of information technology to sites of empirical geoscience research. In the earth science the test beds are sites of investigation for many subfields, and thus they meet the requirements for disciplinary diversity. For instance, the Rocky Mountains are a prime site for orogenic processes—or mountain building—between the stable interior of North America and the plate margin of the West Coast; it is also the site of multiple fossil deposits; and a rich stratigraphic record has been captured, over the millennia, as intraplate stresses have superimposed basins. Geologically, then, the Rocky Mountain test bed is a site of contemporary and historical inquiry for seismologists, geophysicists, and paleobotanists alike. While varying in their specific interests and methods, many earth scientists could come together to conduct their research within this test bed: the Rocky Mountain was an umbrella (domain/domain) for various empirical concerns.

Conversely, for the database specialists of GEON, the Rocky Mountain test bed provided multiple complex data sets. In their decades of research, seismologists, geophysicists, and paleobotanists have built up collections of data about the area; for them it

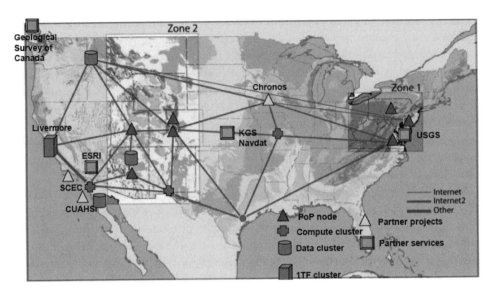

Figure 17.2
GEON partners and the two test beds: Rocky Mountain on the left, and mid-Atlantic on the right

was the geologic formations that were of interest, while for GEON's computer scientists it was the databases themselves. The varying schemas and semantics of these data collections offered compelling research scenarios for the information technology team. It challenged them to devise approaches to create semantic and logical interoperability across heterogeneous databases. A GEON user can search multiple integrated data formats, including shapefiles, relational databases, WMS maps, Excel files, geoTIFFs, ASCII files, and netCDF files. In addition, users can search across multiple databases. For example, GEON hosts the PaleoIntegration project, which enables interoperability among several global fossil and sedimentary rock data sets (Rees 2007).

The test beds provided organizational cues for producing an alignment between particular scientific questions and information technologies. Through them, information technology applications were driven by geoscience questions; in GEON they called this the "science driver model." Computer science developments became grounded through science drivers and the specificities of domain information structures rather than abstracted understandings of an imagined geoscience. For example, in the kickoff meeting described earlier, earth scientists dedicated an afternoon to discussing the data sets that would be required for addressing the question, "What is the nature of interactions among Paleozoic, Laramide, and late Cenozoic basins?" The participants identified six distinct databases that the information technologists could use to focus their integration work. This first step of outlining science questions along with their corresponding databases was followed by iterative discussions as the geoscientists came to specify their questions in greater detail and the information technologists came to understand the databases at a finer granularity.

Thus, test beds and the science driver model of development, served as devices for managing the distribution of resources. As we have noted, GEON's computer scientists are high-end researchers rather than technical support workers. Yet even though information technology was highlighted in the GEON proposal, there was also an acknowledgment that in building infrastructure, low-level technical support work would also be necessary. Much of the basic work of integrating databases, for instance, was not cutting-edge research for computer scientists. In other words, this work was considered technical support rather than the generation of new, publishable knowledge. Working to integrate data from the test beds afforded compelling research questions, but it also demanded a certain amount of basic implementation.

The GEON proposal necessarily acknowledged some low-level service provision by the information technology team: "While not viewed as IT research, format and schema incompatibility issues will be addressed specifically for the test bed–related databases." (GEON, 2002, 5). As described above, for information technology participants, there was a thin but important line between providing the support necessary for the research and slipping into a service capacity. Domain scientists who have extensive experience working with information technology, including sophisticated technology for data collection or the management of databases, often consider information technology as a technological substratum to be delegated to a specialized staff. GEON's philosophy, however, was of an equal partnership between computer and earth scientists.

With the increasing involvement and complexity of information systems in scientific work this relationship is changing, and in community infrastructure-building projects, the relationship must necessarily be reconfigured. But old habits die hard. The particular work and content of these technicians often remains invisible to scientists (Shapin 1989); scientists may pass on "to do" lists for the technicians rather than engage in a close collaboration. On many occasions in the early period of GEON's development, the geoscientists requested particular "low-end" services from the information technology team such as building Web sites. This resulted in high-priced and high-end computer science researchers who specialize in, for instance, semantic mapping, creating low-end front-ends for Web service databases. The outcome was unsatisfying to all the participants: computer scientists had no interest in writing Web pages and so produced mediocre outputs, while geoscientists became dissatisfied with the technical team's inability to provide quality service.

The problem was of poorly aligned expectations. The management of information technology resources for GEON was the site of several skirmishes around the understanding of the nature of the project. For some of the earth science GEON members, the information technology team appeared as a source for bountiful high-tech service, such as Web pages, user interfaces, and data set cleanup. Many of these requests by the geoscientists were communicated directly to the information technology team of GEON, rather than through the information technology PIs. As the larger goals and organizational vision of GEON solidified, it became clear that such projects fell outside the bounds of GEON's work. And yet how does one withhold information technology resources from a participant's work without causing strife? This resulted in tensions about the role of the information technology team within GEON, perceptions of efficacy, and the reopening of further debates about GEON's mandate.

Once again a return to the GEON vision of dual computer and geoscience research goals was necessary. In order to do so, structures and routines to manage the distribution of information technology were established. In this case an organizational "protective boundary" was built around the information technology resources. In the second and third years of GEON (2003 and 2004), as specific science goals solidified around the two original test beds, these became focal points for resource distribution. Decisions about what did or did not count as a relevant test bed development of information technology resources were delegated to two earth science PIs. Requests for any development efforts on the part of the geosciences participants went through one of the two test bed representatives, who in turn made executive decisions about the importance of the request relative to the timeline, the significance to the project, and the labor required, and then passed on those requests deemed necessary to the information technology team. In order to gain traction, visions of science-driven information technology development had to be grounded in practical arrangements.

The test beds sustained scientific meanings for all the participants: they are comprised of rich fossil sites for paleobotany; they are complex stratigraphic formations for seismology; and they are data integration problems for computer science. By simultaneously meeting the research needs of diverse groups, the test beds can be described as boundary objects, facilitating coordination across disciplinary interests without necessitating a "translation" or erasing of difference. As Star and Greisemer (1989, 388) observed in their studies of multidisciplinary collaboration, "We find that scientific work neither loses its internal diversity nor is consequently retarded by lack of consensus." They describe cooperative work in such settings as operating in an "ecology," by which they mean that one group's views need not necessarily be devalued relative to the other: it is not that computer science is in the service of geoscience but rather that both parties seek to address contemporary research problems. The concept of boundary objects allows us to understand the coordination of heterogeneous scientific work in such a manner as to serve multiple sustained interests. As we have seen, boundary objects do not "foreclose conflict" but rather provide practical and material points of shared orientation, affording mechanisms for the navigation of disagreement.

Conclusion

It is paradoxical that most cyberinfrastructure projects have relatively short time horizons, while all the evidence is that the work of building infrastructure is inevitably long and complex. It is an open question how long it takes genuinely new questions to emerge from a new information infrastructure. According to previous research on the productivity paradox in computing (i.e., productivity goes down when computers are introduced into the workplace and may require decades to reverse this trend), we might expect changes to require at least fifteen to twenty years (David 1989). Projects such as GEON, however, mark a clearly innovative trajectory that recognizes the centrality of community-building work; the PIs have evolved some of the organizational strategies that will be necessary to achieve this end as well as move beyond narrow conceptions of "tubes and wires" infrastructure. The next phase of GEON, sometimes called GEON2, aims to populate the databases, polish the interfaces, and people the community of researchers.

The work of community building is time-consuming in itself. In writing the proposal a vision was set, forming a basis for a community of practice; this took months of work. In ambitious multidisciplinary endeavors, such as infrastructure building, our findings suggest that time and resources must be appropriately allocated to carefully plan crossings of domain/domain and computer science/domain boundaries.

In this chapter, we have traced three moments in fostering such multidisciplinary collaborations. This process began before the project through proposal writing. We have argued that proposal writing was a form of collaborative work that established the criteria, organization, and distribution of labor for future activity in the project. Over the years of GEON, the participants regularly came back to the proposal in moments of identity crisis. Whenever it appeared that efforts were leaning too heavily in either the direction of earth or computer science, the proposal served as a reference point for a computer science/domain balance by which to return focus to "learning something new about the Rockies" or "doing some serious computer science."

Moving from the vision articulated in the proposal to the action and organization of a large-scale infrastructure project was the next step. The GEON meetings offered a venue as the participants within geology and across to computer science shared their research agendas and topics. It is difficult to measure or formally evaluate progress achieved in such early meetings. We contend that the shared learning experiences in meetings, of demonstrating diverse research agendas, topics, and methods, later proved invaluable to long-term multidisciplinary collaborations. Efforts to make accessible and relatively transparent the technical specializations—*among* domain scientists and *with* computer scientists—were seminal to the more practical work of building infrastructure.

Building scientific infrastructure involves a kind of collaboration that must foster deep understanding. This is as true across domain and computer science as it is within the domains. It is the information technologies themselves that presented many of the unforeseen complications in building GEON. While within the theoretical computer science literature many of the base technologies of GEON were considered resolved (see for example Sheth 1999), there remained a significant gap between theoretical resolution and enacting production quality systems (Fountain 2001). These technologies simultaneously presented a source of complication and communicative difficulty between information technology and domain, and occasions for aligning understandings through discourse. In projects where there are multiple competing interests, as in the case of GEON, which is earth and computer science research, sites such as the test beds serve in the common coordination of work. We have labeled such coordination sites boundary objects for their ability to simultaneously preserve multiple meetings and satisfy the informational requirements of competing interest groups. It is often assumed that collaboration requires consensus; the concept of boundary objects and the processual nature of a community of practice in GEON reminds us that this is not necessarily the case. Rather, collaboration across disciplinary difference can be a matter of generating shared orientation (or community identity) through common tasks or projects.

Acknowledgments

We would like to thank Karen Baker, Chaitan Baru, Steve Epstein, Florence Millerand, and the editors of this volume for their comments on drafts of this chapter. This material is based on work supported by the NSF under grants #04-33369 ("Interoperability Strategies for Scientific Cyberinfrastructure: A Comparative Study"), #0525985 ("The Standardized Revolution of Science: Building Cyberinfrastructure for the Geosciences"), and #0225673 ("GEON"). Any opinions, findings, and conclusions or recommendations expressed in this material are those of the authors, and do not necessarily reflect the views of the NSF.

Notes

1. The term domain is a coinage from within computer science and information technology circles to refer, somewhat generically, to fields of application—in this case, the earth sciences. We adopt this actor's category with some ambivalence, as on occasion earth scientists themselves have chafed at the term. Additionally, we use the terms earth science and geoscience interchangeably, as do the participants, to refer to the various fields that GEON seeks to bring under its umbrella infrastructure.

2. Actual proposal reviews are considered confidential material at the NSF. The data on "why" the first proposal was not funded is based on secondhand accounts.

References

Borgman, C. L. 2007. *Scholarship in the digital age: Information, infrastructure, and the Internet.* Cambridge, MA: MIT Press.

Bowker, G. C. 1994. *Science on the run: Information management and industrial geophysics at Schlumberger, 1920–1940.* Cambridge, MA: MIT Press.

Bowker, G. C. 2000. Biodiversity datadiversity. *Social Studies of Science* 30 (5): 643–683.

Bowker, G. C., and S. L. Star. 1999. *Sorting things out: Classification and its consequences.* Cambridge, MA: MIT Press.

Campbell, E. G., B. R. Clarridge, M. Gokhale, L. Birenbaum, S. Hilgartner, N. A. Holtzman et al. 2002. Data withholding in academic genetics: Evidence from a national survey. *JAMA* 287 (4): 473–480.

Ceci, S. 1988. Scientists' attitudes toward data sharing. *Science, Technology, and Human Values* 13 (1–2): 45–52.

Clarke, A. 2005. *Situational analysis: Grounded theory after the postmodern turn.* Thousand Oaks, CA: Sage Publications.

Collins, H. M., ed. 1981. Knowledge and controversy: Studies of modern natural science. Special issue, *Social Studies of Science* 11 (1).

David, P. A. 1989. Computer and dynamo: The modern productivity paradox in a not-too-distant mirror. Discussion paper series no. 172. Stanford, CA: Stanford University, Center for Economic Policy Research.

Fountain, J. E. 2001. *Building the virtual state: Information technology and institutional change.* Washington, DC: Brookings Institution Press.

Keller, G. R. 2003. GEON (GEOScience Network): A first step in creating cyberinfrastructure for the geosciences. *Electronic Seismologist* (July–August). Available at ⟨http://www.seismosoc.org/publications/SRL/SRL_74/srl_74-4_es.html⟩ (accessed June 19, 1007).

Knorr Cetina, K. 1999. *Epistemic cultures: How the sciences make knowledge.* Cambridge, MA: Harvard University Press.

Lave, J., and E. Wenger. 1991. Situated learning: Legitimate peripheral participation. New York: Cambridge University Press.

Lawrence, K. A. 2006. Walking the tightrope: The balancing acts of a large e-research project. *Computer Supported Cooperative Work* 15 (4): 385–411.

Rees, A. 2007. Phanerozoic earth and life: The PaleoIntegration Project. Paper presented at geoinformatics 2007 conference, San Diego, California, May. Available at ⟨http://gsa.confex.com/gsa/2007GE/finalprogram/abstract_121912.htm⟩ (accessed June 19, 2007).

Ribes, D., and K. S. Baker. 2007. Modes of social science engagement in community infrastructure design. In *Proceedings of the third communities and technology conference,* ed. C. Steinfield, B. Pentland, M. Ackerman, and N. Contractor, 107–130. New York: Springer.

Ribes, D., K. S. Baker, F. Miller, and G. C. Bowker. 2005. Comparative Interoperability Project: Configurations of community, technology, organization. In *Proceedings of the fifth ACM/IEEE-CS joint conference on digital libraries*, 65–66. New York: ACM Press.

Ribes, D., and T. A. Finholt. 2007. Tensions across the scales: Planning infrastructure for the long term. In *Proceedings of the 2007 International ACM SIGGROUP Conference on Supporting Group Work*, 229–238. New York: ACM Press.

Rudwick, M. 1976. The emergence of a visual language for geological science, 1760–1840. *History of Science* 14:149–195.

Scott, P., E. Richards, and B. Martin. 1990. Captives of controversy: The myth of the neutral social researcher in contemporary scientific controversies. *Science, Technology, and Human Values* 15:474–494.

Shapin, S. 1989. The invisible technician. *American Scientist* 77:554–563.

Sheth, A. P. 1999. Changing focus on interoperability in information systems: From system, syntax, structure to semantics. In *Interoperating geographic information systems*, ed. M. F. Goodchild, M. J. Egenhofer, R. Fegeas, and C. Kottman, 165–180. Boston: Kluwer Academic Publishers.

Star, S. L. 1999. The ethnography of infrastructure. *American Behavioral Scientist* 43:377–391.

Star, S. L., and J. R. Griesemer. 1989. Institutional ecology, "translations," and boundary objects: Amateurs and professionals in Berkeley's Museum of Vertebrate Zoology, 1907–39. *Social Studies of Science* 19:387–420.

Star, S. L., and K. Ruhleder. 1994. Steps toward an ecology of infrastructure: Complex problems in design and access for large-scale collaborative systems. In *Proceedings CSCW 1994*, 253–264. New York: ACM Press.

Suchman, L. 1994. Working relations of technology production and use. *Computer Supported Cooperative Work* 2 (1–2): 21–39.

Weedman, J. 1998. The structure of incentive: Design and client roles in application-oriented research. *Science, Technology, and Human Values* 23 (3): 315–345.

18 NEESgrid: Lessons Learned for Future Cyberinfrastructure Development

B. F. Spencer Jr., Randal Butler, Kathleen Ricker, Doru Marcusiu, Thomas A. Finholt, Ian Foster, Carl Kesselman, and Jeremy P. Birnholtz

This chapter describes the experiences and lessons learned from the NEESgrid project, an interdisciplinary effort to develop and deploy cyberinfrastructure for the National Science Foundation's (NSF) George E. Brown Jr. Network for Earthquake Engineering Simulation (NEES). Cyberinfrastructure is a concept used to describe the combination of computers, networks, services, and applications that scientists and engineers increasingly rely on to conduct their research (Atkins et al. 2003). In the NEES case, the cyberinfrastructure activity focused on a $10 million cooperative agreement over the period 2001–2004 to build NEESgrid. NEESgrid was envisioned to be a collaboratory for earthquake engineering, where a collaboratory uses cyberinfrastructure to join resources (e.g., instruments), people, and data via computer-supported systems (Finholt 2002, 2003).

Earthquake engineering is the field of civil engineering concerned with the performance of built environments under seismic loading. Benjamin Sims (1999) provides an excellent detailed overview of the practice in the earthquake engineering field. Briefly, earthquake engineering has three broad modes of inquiry described as structural, geotechnical, and field experimental. The majority of earthquake engineering researchers portray themselves as doing structural research. Primary methods of conducting structural research include physical simulation, such as the testing of scale structures and components on hydraulically actuated shake tables or reaction walls (e.g., see the pictures of equipment at the University of Nevada at Reno and the University of Minnesota in figure 18.1), and numerical simulation, such as computational simulations of structures. Geotechnical research is concerned with the performance of soil, sand, and clay under seismic loading. The primary methods of conducting geotechnical research also include physical simulation, such as sample buckets of soil spun in giant centrifuges (e.g., see the picture of the centrifuge at the University of California at Davis in figure 18.1), and numerical simulations, such as computational models of liquefaction. Finally, field experimental researchers can be oriented to structural questions, tested by instrumenting and shaking actual buildings, and geotechnical questions, tested by analyzing vibrations generated by large "shakers" mounted on

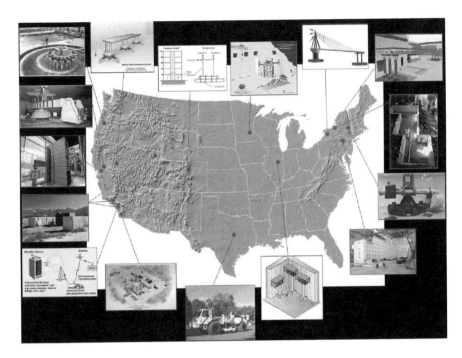

Figure 18.1
Location and capabilities of the sixteen NEES equipment sites

trucks (e.g., see the picture of the University of Texas truck in figure 18.1). The NEES program also included tsunami researchers, not typically grouped with earthquake engineering, but sharing similar orientations, such as the use of physical and numerical simulations to study phenomena (e.g., see the picture of the wave basin at Oregon State University in figure 18.1). Prior to NEES, most earthquake engineering research was organized around small faculty lab groups, consisting of a professor, one or two PhD students, and two to three master's degree students.

Beyond the cyberinfrastructure component, the NEES program also consisted of two additional critical elements. First, $66 million went to construct sixteen new earthquake engineering research laboratories at fifteen universities. Figure 18.1 shows the location and capabilities of these new labs (including shake tables and strong walls for structural tests, centrifuges for geotechnical tests, wave basins for tsunami tests, and various types of field equipment). Second, $3 million went to design and launch the NEES Consortium Inc., or the nonprofit entity that the NSF would fund over the period 2004–2014 to maintain and operate the NEES systems. As of October 1, 2004, the operational control of NEES passed to the NEES Consortium, and the grand opening ceremony for NEES was held on November 15, 2004.

The authors of this chapter were the focal figures in the evolution of NEESgrid, including the project director (Bill Spencer), the associate project director (Randy Butler), the manager of software distribution (Doru Marcusiu), the coprincipal investigators in charge of the grid technology and middleware (Ian Foster and Carl Kesselman), and the coprincipal investigator in charge of collaboration technology, requirements assessment, and usability evaluation (Tom Finholt). This chapter is distilled from a longer "lessons learned" document submitted by this group to the program managers of NEES at the NSF (Spencer et al. 2006). The sections that follow capture our experience in the development of NEESgrid over the period 2001–2005. In the first section, we describe the importance of forming and maintaining focus on specific goals as a way of integrating the often-unwieldy collection of collaborators that comes together around cyberinfrastructure projects (e.g., domain scientists—in this case earthquake engineers, technologists, and funding sponsors). The next section emphasizes the significance of and strategies for achieving a partnership between cyberinfrastructure users and developers. The third section describes the value of project management methods and tools, and the reluctance of academically oriented developers and researchers to embrace project management techniques. The fourth section illustrates where communication gaps arise in cyberinfrastructure projects, and how these gaps can be addressed. Following that, the next section elaborates on the role that a clearly understood software process plays in coordinating activity. And the final section summarizes our NEESgrid experience and extrapolates to other large-scale cyberinfrastructure projects.

You Must Have a Target and Know How to Reach It

"It's not the plan that's important, it's the planning," suggests an often-repeated observation about large-scale projects. While a well-constructed project execution plan is valuable, the planning process itself is one of the most crucial aspects of the development of cyberinfrastructure. It is during the planning process that effective communication and management strategies are developed, and it is also during the planning process that the real issues—what a community wants, what the development team can provide, and what the obstacles are—are identified. Therefore, we believe that at the beginning of a cyberinfrastructure project, the technologists and the users need to jointly establish as well as document what the overall goals of the project will be, including what needs to be accomplished, what can be accomplished, and how the work will be organized and completed.

Our experience with NEESgrid suggests that determining the overall goals requires just as much consideration as planning for project execution. In particular, the overall goals need to be defined clearly and in terms relevant to cyberinfrastructure development. For example, in the NEESgrid case, the overall goals were frequently stated in terms of broad aspirations shared by earthquake engineers (e.g., "make structures safer")—but not in terms of more specific goals useful in focusing cyberinfrastructure development. During the course of NEESgrid's development, then, there was often a lack of precisely stated project goals. One consequence of this imprecision was that the sponsor, the community, and the developers made frequent shifts in direction, which turned out to be costly in terms of both time and energy. Late in the NEESgrid effort, we introduced a way to explicitly track development goals via a projectwide "requirements traceability matrix" (RTM, discussed in greater detail below). Because the RTM described the relationship between community needs and development tasks, it was a great tool to keep the users and the technologists aligned on common goals.

Pilot and prototype projects provide an additional way to increase alignment between the users and the technologists. Specifically, pilot efforts clarify what will work and what the community will need without committing large amounts of resources. Further, pilot projects have the benefit of demonstrating progress and are useful in attracting participation by community members. We believe that NEESgrid would have benefited significantly from an earlier development of prototypes, in terms of both building community confidence in the NEESgrid team and producing a clearer project execution plan. As it happened, more than halfway through the project NEESgrid did develop two highly successful prototypes: the Multi-Site Online Simulation Testbed (MOST) and a smaller-scale version dubbed "Mini-MOST." MOST was a joint project between two NEES sites (the University of Illinois at Urbana-Champaign and the University of Colorado), the NEESgrid team, and the National Center for Supercomputing Applications (NCSA) to simulate the response of a two-bay frame structure to an earthquake via physical and computational models. The two external physical supports of the structural frame were at the University of Illinois at Urbana-Champaign and the University of Colorado, while the central, inner support was represented virtually via software running at NCSA. Despite its late appearance, MOST gave users a tangible example of what NEESgrid could do for them. Similarly, Mini-MOST provided a realistic preview of NEESgrid capabilities through portable, tabletop devices, which although much smaller than the equipment used in MOST, still exercised the same NEESgrid components. As a result, Mini-MOST offered a low-cost approach for both demonstrating NEESgrid and training future users. For example, in 2004 student teams at the Colorado School of Mines, the University of Southern California, and Keio University used the Mini-MOST setup to successfully conduct the first multisite simulation test to incorporate a structural control device.

Prototype and pilot projects are significantly easier when they can be accomplished using existing applications and services. For example, NEESgrid took advantage of many already-available suites of services and applications such as: Globus, developed at the Argonne National Laboratory and the University of Southern California (Foster and Kesselman 1999), to provide grid support; CHEF (now called Sakai),[1] developed at the University of Michigan, to provide collaborative tools that proved extremely user-friendly; OpenSees, a powerful computational framework for developing earthquake simulation applications; and Data Turbine, a commercial product developed by the New Hampshire engineering firm Creare that allows users to scroll back through live data streams. Existing software, whether open source or commercial, must still be integrated, and this integration can present its own set of complications. A cost-benefit analysis of all alternative solutions in terms of both development and longer-term maintenance should be conducted. If integrating the software requires too much time, or its requirements end up drastically limiting the functionality originally promised to the users, it may not be worthwhile. Finally, a key factor to address when looking at such software is whether it will receive long-term support.

Users and Technologists Need Each Other to Succeed

Beyond planning, an additional critical principle of cyberinfrastructure development is that there needs to be a full partnership between a user community and cyberinfrastructure technologists. As noted in the *Report of the National Science Foundation Blue-Ribbon Advisory Panel Report on Cyberinfrastructure* (Atkins et al. 2003), a balance must be struck between the concerns of technology developers (e.g., novelty and uniqueness) and the concerns of user communities (e.g., reliability and usability). We believe this balance is best achieved through "user-centered design." In particular, technologists must respond to user requirements, and engage users in determining system capabilities and functions. Integrating notions of user-centered design into cyberinfrastructure development can be problematic, however, because cyberinfrastructure is often far removed from the everyday experience of most domain researchers. Therefore, we feel it is important that individuals who have credibility within a user community, typically through membership, and can communicate a compelling cyberinfrastructure vision should lead cyberinfrastructure projects. Specifically, in the case of communities that do not have a deep familiarity with cyberinfrastructure, someone who is well respected within the community can be a more effective advocate for technology than a technologist, who may be viewed as an outsider (Birnholtz and Finholt 2007). For example, members of a community need to feel that the leader of a cyberinfrastructure project shares their priorities, speaks their language, and has the same things to gain or lose by adopting a proposed technology. The knowledge of how a given user community functions must also be matched with the ability to effectively bridge between the community and technologists. A domain expert, for instance, can best identify priorities among competing demands within a community and also keep technologists focused on these priorities. As a user community comes to better understand a project and its potential, its members may start to view the project's visions and goals differently. A certain amount of change and adjustment is to be expected.

Yet a domain scientist who is intimate with the development process can help negotiate these possible shifts in requirements so that other members of the user community understand the consequences of changing goals midcourse.

Having a technologically savvy expert from the earthquake engineering community in charge of NEESgrid helped both the earthquake engineers and the developers reach a working middle ground on a number of issues, such as the spiral development model, which we discuss in more detail later in this chapter (Boehm 1995). The strength of spiral development is that it controls risk, such as locking in software technology too early, by converging iteratively on designs and deployed systems. A weakness of the spiral approach, though, particularly from the perspective of earthquake engineers trying to build NEES equipment sites, was that often technologists could not provide immediate and precise answers (e.g., what model of digital video camera to install) because the underlying NEESgrid system was still in flux. The NEESgrid team used two approaches to help alleviate the concerns of the NEES equipment sites stemming from features of the spiral model. First, the NEESgrid director pushed for more quality control and testing than the technologists would have normally used during development. This approach greatly increased the confidence of the earthquake engineering community in the overall reliability of the NEESgrid software and helped the earthquake engineers understand when functionality was scheduled to arrive—even when it didn't exist yet. Second, the deputy director of NEESgrid was a technology expert who marshaled opinions and ideas from the various technical subleads (chief architect, usability team, project manager, data architect, packaging, and operations), and then contributed this feedback into decision making about the NEESgrid project. This feedback also helped make project progress and future trajectories more visible to the earthquake engineering community.

Effective Project Management Is Essential at All Levels

Leadership is only one element of success in cyberinfrastructure development. Specifically, the large scale of cyberinfrastructure efforts, such as NEESgrid, means that project leaders must have effective ways of communicating tasks to project participants and also for assessing task performance. To meet these goals, NEESgrid adopted a formal project management structure. At the highest level were the project director (representing the domain community), the deputy director (representing the technologists), and the project manager, who oversaw the day-to-day project execution. Interacting constantly—daily, or even several times a day—this group made decisions based on both their own experience and the input of the entire management team, consisting of leaders of all the major project areas. The entire management team, which met on a weekly basis throughout the length of the project, coordinated activities across the

Project	Contact	Status May 12	Current status
Experiment-based deployment	Doru/Sridhar	*Yellow*	*Yellow*
Education/training	David	GREEN	GREEN
Mini-MOST outreach	Shirley	GREEN	GREEN
Acceptance planning/testing	Lee/Sridhar	*Yellow*	GREEN
Data turbine	Laura/Chuck	RED	*Yellow*
Computational simulation component	Greg/Tomasz	*Yellow*	*Yellow*
PNNL e-notebook	Jim	GREEN	GREEN
Data models	Kincho/JP	GREEN	GREEN
Experiment-based development @ Uminn	Chuck	*Yellow*	*Yellow*
Experiment-based development @ Fast-MOST	Sridhar/Laura	GREEN	GREEN
Data infrastructure	Joe/Randy	*Yellow*	GREEN
Packaging/releases	Doru	GREEN	*Yellow*
Documentation	Cristina	GREEN	*Yellow*
Transitioning	Bill	GREEN	*Yellow*
Operations	Doru	GREEN	GREEN

Figure 18.2
Use of a three-level coding scheme kept weekly project meetings short and effective

entire project. For example, the weekly meetings were occasions for the technical leads to identify emergent needs and request additional resources.

In NEESgrid, project management was made much more coherent through the effective use of particular tools and methods. For example, we used a Gantt chart to track deliverables and provide a visual index of task completion. The Gantt chart was also useful in communicating progress to the NSF sponsors and the larger earthquake engineering community. Figure 18.2 shows an effective mechanism we used to organize conversation within the weekly management team calls. The participants coded issues in advance according to a three-level scheme (green = OK, yellow = progress slowed, and red = progress stalled). During the call, each area lead was given three minutes to review their issues, where the coding scheme allowed the leads and the team to focus immediately on problem areas (e.g., yellow or red issues).

Finally, to ensure that development activity remained aligned with user needs, we used the RTM (Finholt, Horn, and Thomé 2003). The RTM provided a formal representation of user requirements lined up against project development activity. For example, the NEESgrid RTM listed requirements down rows and development activity across columns. Empty cells in the RTM corresponded to areas where either a requirement was not being met, or the development activity wasn't matched to a driving need. In addition to monitoring the NEESgrid project, the RTM also helped communicate expectations to the earthquake engineering community as well as insulate the NEES-grid technologists from the uncontrolled proliferation of features and capabilities.

Communication Is Crucial

A major challenge in achieving cooperation within a cyberinfrastructure development project is bridging communication gaps between technologists and domain users, among technologists, and between the cyberinfrastructure team and outside groups—particularly when these groups are often geographically distributed (Cummings and Kiesler 2003; chapter 5, this volume; Connaughton and Daly 2005).

Technologists and Users
In terms of technologists and users, each community possesses its own expertise, and more significant, its own work culture and language, often with little overlap. Therefore, clear channels of communication must be established. Because the technologist and user communities can be extremely diverse groups in terms of needs, roles, and skills, it is important early on to identify leaders and representatives on both sides who are able to answer questions and articulate concerns knowledgeably (i.e., to translate ideas from outside to the home community). Within NEES, differences between the users, the technologists, and the sponsors led to several kinds of confusion.

One source of confusion in the early development of NEESgrid was that the technologists and the users often approached the same problem from conflicting perspectives (Hofstede 1991). For example, the technologists typically value generality of design, while the users will settle for more customized solutions that address urgent needs. The NEESgrid collaboration experienced initial tension as a result of conflict between these two disparate design approaches (akin to a "first contact" gone awry; see Ruby 2001). The technologists frequently erred on the side of universal solutions, assuming it was easier to anticipate future needs with the correct preliminary design versus extensive and expensive rework at a later point. By contrast, the earthquake engineers were impatient with strategies that appeared to introduce unnecessary complexity in the name of interoperability (e.g., community authorization services) at the expense of solving specific and crucial user problems (e.g., data collection and storage). The differences in design approach were often compounded by misunderstandings due to the absence of a common terminology and simple miscommunication. For example, software developers are usually more skilled at manipulating code than they are at interacting with others. As a result, in NEESgrid, technologists often underestimated how members of the user community received their statements. A common miscommunication, as an illustration, involved confusion over theoretical versus practical feasibility. That is, when technologists would say, "Yes, that can be done," this was generally a statement that a feature or service was theoretically possible, but it was interpreted by the users to mean that a given feature or service would be delivered within the resources and constraints of the NEESgrid project. An important management function in NEESgrid was the recognition of theoretical speculation and subsequent intervention to avoid disappointment (i.e., when apparently promised features failed to materialize because the technologists were just "thinking out loud").

An additional source of confusion in the early evolution of NEESgrid reflected different conceptions of the customers or end users for NEESgrid. For example, rather than a simple, monolithic community of users, NEES consisted of several subgroups. One class of users reflected the concerns of the equipment site providers, who are responsible for the operation, maintenance, and support of experimental facilities. The primary needs of the site providers include safe and secure systems for remote control and the observation of equipment as well as reliable data capture and archive technology. System administrators constituted another class of users, primarily concerned with computer hardware requirements, upgrades, and maintenance as well as software issues such as maintaining and supporting both the system software and the NEESgrid software. Another user class included local researchers, concerned with the interfaces between the NEESgrid software and their sensors and instruments. Remote researchers represented a new kind of user, concerned with the capacity of NEESgrid systems to support the operation and viewing of experiments conducted at distant locations. Sponsors, such as the NSF program officers, needed to see that NEESgrid activity was satisfying high-level goals, such as broadening participation in earthquake engineering through use of the NEESgrid software. And finally, application developers themselves represented a key user community. For instance, in order to develop software to control a distributed experiment among multiple sites, application developers needed a more detailed understanding of what the NEESgrid components were, how they worked, and why they were necessary.

A final source of confusion observed between technologists and users in NEES involved differences in the clarity of goals. Technologists, for example, had the advantage of understanding, for the most part, how NEESgrid should function and the potential benefits NEESgrid might deliver (e.g., federated data, shared instrumentation, and remote collaboration). By contrast, the earthquake engineers had a body of tools and practices that already worked for them, and therefore were more skeptical about the promised virtues of NEESgrid. The conception of NEESgrid as a "system integration" project particularly compelled members of the NEESgrid team to approach the earthquake engineers with a set of existing solutions in mind, without fully considering whether the use of these solutions represented net gains for the earthquake engineers. The NEESgrid user community, as a result, was understandably resistant as they were confronted with applications and services developed mostly to meet needs in other communities (e.g., high-energy physics), with little or no accommodation for the special demands of earthquake engineering research. An important mechanism for stimulating a greater sense of ownership of the NEESgrid technology by earthquake engineers was the use of small prototype projects to increase the familiarity of the users with potentially valuable aspects of NEESgrid. In general, providing users with concrete examples of what a system will be able to do is essential to increasing acceptance and adoption. Demonstrations of system functionality also strengthen relationships between the users and the technologists, and offer an opportunity for the users to give feedback and help shape the final product to a much greater extent. Several such demonstrations took place throughout the development of NEESgrid, including: the remote observation of tests conducted on three shake tables at the University of Nevada at Reno in late 2002; MOST in July 2003, combining physical experiments at the University of Colorado at Boulder and the University of Illinois at Urbana-Champaign with numerical simulation at the NCSA; and the 2004 NEESgrid Reference Implementation, which consisted of two miniaturized versions of MOST that sites could use to test their NEESgrid installations (see figure 18.3).

NEESgrid would have benefited from more and earlier demonstration projects, including simple measures such as "mock-ups" of screen views representing typical research activity using the completed NEESgrid software. NEESgrid would have benefited from more workshops, where users could gain hands-on experience with emerging NEESgrid technology. During NEESgrid, we did conduct a few training workshops prior

Figure 18.3
The NEESgrid Reference Implementation used to demonstrate and test the NEESgrid software

to the final software release, and these were valuable for orienting prospective system administrators as well as revealing deficiencies in performance and documentation.

Among Technologists

In terms of communication and coordination among the technologists on the NEES-grid project, challenges arose from the diverse and distributed composition of the team, reflecting experts in: grid systems (e.g., Globus at the Argonne National Laboratory and the University of Southern California); grid operations and middleware (e.g., the NCSA); computational simulation (e.g., the NCSA, the University of California at Berkeley, and Mississippi State University); teleoperation and observation (e.g., the Argonne National Laboratory); and collaboration tools (e.g., the University of Michigan). In particular, all of these groups had experience developing their specific NEES-grid components, but did not have experience working together to integrate the separate technologies. Achieving successful integration was both a product of leadership, such as keeping everyone aware of their contribution to the delivery of the overall NEESgrid system, and project management discipline, such as adherence to project deadlines. One important way NEESgrid developers succeeded in sticking to the deadlines for final releases was to hold weeklong, collocated development sessions that we called "integration weeks" (Teasley et al. 2000; Teasley et al. 2002).

Each integration week had as its target the production of a well-tested release that met certain criteria established in advance. For NEESgrid, the software and documentation were tested in the Mini-MOST test bed as a way to validate the release. This sort of real testing meant that just getting the software to compile was not good enough; it also had to work under operational conditions. In addition, we had a set of well-defined acceptance tests that were developed in collaboration with the earthquake engineering community. The technologists utilized these acceptance tests during each integration week as a way to test modules (unit tests) and the entire system (workflow tests) more fully. The integration week sessions allowed the NEESgrid team to immerse itself in the project without distractions. All members of the team would gather in one place to finish a release, with the goals to be met by the release clearly in mind. Integration weeks were structured. Each morning and evening, the team would meet to talk about what had been achieved, what the next objectives would be, and whether the priorities needed to be readjusted. As an important side benefit, the weeklong immersion strengthened relationships among the technologists, and promoted a team approach to resolving problems and making progress toward project goals.

Between the Cyberinfrastructure Team and Outside Groups

While good communication within a cyberinfrastructure project team is crucial, it is also important to maintain strong ties with external groups and organizations. In the case of NEESgrid, the project director also coordinated formal communication between the project and the principal investigators at the equipment sites, the NEES Consortium development team (responsible for creating the nonprofit corporation expected to operate and maintain NEES from 2004 through 2014), and the NSF. The executive advisory board, an independent entity comprising prominent domain scientists and technology experts, became a key way for the NEESgrid team to relate to outside groups. The board's composition ensured that both the interests of the earthquake engineering and the cyberinfrastructure communities were well represented. The executive advisory board met twice a year to: review and make recommendations on NEESgrid technical directions, strategies, and project management; recommend strategies for improving communications with the community and the NSF; and advise the project director as needed on overall administrative issues. An executive advisory board with sufficient depth and breadth in both the cyberinfrastructure and domain fields can be a valuable asset to the management team of a cyberinfrastructure project, providing honest assessments of the team's progress while advocating to sponsors and the community on behalf of the project. For this to occur, however, the board members have to be as committed to the project as the project team itself. And just as significant, there needs to be close, regular, and trusting interaction between the board and the project management team. The executive advisory board is also advantageous to the extent that the tools and applications known by board members can be transferred to the project being advised.

Perhaps the most critical external relationship managed by a cyberinfrastructure project is the relationship with the funding sponsors. A close, positive relationship with a sponsor, for example, provides strong impetus to move a project forward and offer direction. To build this kind of relationship, sponsors need to see evidence of progress, and they need access to information about the project's status. Genuine partnership in this context can be challenging, and it is sometimes hard to distinguish advice from micromanagement. The funding agency representative who wants a good working relationship makes frequent site visits, takes tours, and is intimately familiar with everything the project does; at the same time, the representative does not get buried in details but maintains an effective high-level relationship. A final observation is that cyberinfrastructure projects are often more than stand-alone entities and can be important models that are of interest to other communities. In the case of NEESgrid, technologists were dealing with earthquake engineers, but discovered that the project was being watched with interest by other communities, such as environmental scientists, seismologists, and oceanographers, who saw NEES and NEESgrid as the first of many such collaboratories to be built. The members of a cyberinfrastructure development team should think carefully about how their project is viewed by other communities, and how they can leave a lasting, positive impression.

The Importance of a Software Development Process

The software development approach adopted by the NEESgrid team provided a crucial source of coherence and direction. We decided to use a spiral development strategy characterized by incremental and iterative releases of services and applications. The spiral model worked well on several levels. First, technologies essential to cyberinfrastructure undergo constant evolution. Through iterative releases we were able to deliver functionality early while preserving the capacity to substitute newer versions of components in later software releases. Second, feedback from early releases was used to fine-tune subsequent releases, ensuring a better fit to user needs. In practice, the spiral model had several distinct phases: experiment-based development (2001–2003), experiment-based deployment (2003–2004), and communitywide deployment (2004–2005).

In the first phase of development, the NEESgrid team focused on a small set of "early adopter" equipment sites. Real-world earthquake experiments and workflows at these sites were identified, and then used as targets for integrated development. Specifically, as systems evolved they were immediately tested in field settings, providing valuable early feedback to the developers about the performance and functionality of systems. The close relationship between the developers and the equipment site personnel meant that feedback was often rapid, resulting in an accelerated evolution of the NEESgrid software. A canonical instance of this approach was the effort with the University of Nevada at Reno to implement data collection, distribution, and viewing mechanisms for use with its three shake tables. For example, because of this close collaboration, the NEESgrid team was able to demonstrate a fully integrated data-taking and viewing system, in use with a live experiment, within the first year of the project. The MOST experiment, described earlier, was the culmination of the "experiment-based development" that marked the first phase of NEESgrid activity. Through intensive support and guidance from the NEESgrid team, earthquake engineering researchers at the University of Illinois at Urbana-Champaign and the University of Colorado were able to conduct the world's first distributed experiment, using the NEESgrid software to simultaneously control physical simulations in Urbana and Boulder, while also combining these with numerically simulated structural elements.

In the second phase of development, the NEESgrid team focused on deploying early production versions of NEESgrid in support of a wider array of earthquake engineering experiments. In contrast to the first phase, marked by the active involvement of NEESgrid personnel in supporting the use of NEESgrid systems by the experimenters, in this second phase a production version of NEESgrid was released. The equipment sites went through the exercise of installing the NEESgrid system and attempting to run it themselves. For each site, the NEESgrid team carefully tracked the following: whether the NEESgrid system was successfully installed; whether the installed software worked as specified; and how the site users reacted to the software. These data produced important improvements in the building and packaging of the NEESgrid software, and also resulted in enhanced documentation. For example, work with the tsunami basin facility at Oregon State University was an instance of the "experiment-based deployment" activity that characterized the second phase of NEESgrid development. The Oregon State University researchers used a NEESgrid installation to capture, store, and replay video recordings of simulated tsunamis. In the Oregon State University and other instances, the experiences of the equipment site personnel were recorded in reports made available to the wider earthquake engineering community via the NEESgrid Web site.

The final phase of development focused on the delivery of NEESgrid software that met specific acceptance criteria identified cooperatively by the NEESgrid team and the earthquake engineering community. Specifically, acceptance was demonstrated by successfully passing two kinds of tests. First, the NEESgrid team had to show that the released components functioned properly in isolation. A typical component test, for instance, might involve successful authentication via a single sign-on procedure. Second, the NEESgrid team had to show that the released components worked together to accomplish sequences of actions or workflows—for example, that a user could authenticate, identify a data source, capture a data stream, store the stream, and subsequently retrieve the data for later viewing. In both cases, component and workflow tests were conducted live in front of representatives from the NEESgrid team and the earthquake engineering community. The test results were documented and made available to the public. This testing program assured that the NEESgrid code met production-level quality standards, as opposed to the looser standards sometimes applied to "research" code. This quality assurance was a crucial element in building confidence in NEESgrid, and convincing sites and users to adopt the software.

Conclusion

We believe the experience with NEES, during the period 2001–2004, offers a set of general lessons that can be applied to other collaborative, multisite, multidisciplinary cyberinfrastructure projects. In the first place, projects must account for the role that significant differences in professional culture will play in the development of cyberinfrastructure. These cultural gaps mean that even when information is communicated in seemingly objective ways common to project management (i.e., reports, requirements documents, etc.), there is a strong possibility for differing interpretations by the diverse groups involved in a cyberinfrastructure project. In some cases, this "cultural dissonance" was detrimental to the progress of NEESgrid. This suggests that in carrying out projects that involve communities that come from different professional cultures, it is important to identify and accommodate cultural variation.

Second, strong leadership is essential in both bridging cultural divides and fostering trust between groups. In the NEESgrid case, the selection of a project director from the earthquake engineering community served two critical functions. First, the project director was able to leverage strong relationships with key players in all groups to act as a translator and broker between the groups, thereby ensuring that communicated information did not contribute to the cycles of misinterpretation identified above. That is, effective leadership helped the participating groups to constructively utilize shared information rather than continue to view this information as evidence of deficiencies on the part of the other groups. Second, the project director increased the representativeness of the project leadership team by simultaneously being a part of the earthquake engineering and development teams. This gave the earthquake engineers the important sense that their needs and interests were being taken into consideration by the cyberinfrastructure developers, and for the same reason, afforded increased legitimacy to the development team in the eyes of the earthquake engineers.

Finally, progress in cyberinfrastructure projects demands periodic deliverables that can be demonstrated under authentic use conditions. These demonstrations help to focus development and keep developers oriented to high-priority user requirements. From the users' side, the demonstrations offer tangible evidence that the development project is meeting their needs and provides a preview of future functionality. In particular, within the context of NEESgrid, two distinctive types of demonstration activity proved particularly valuable: experiment-based development (where users and developers focused development around driving problems from actual earthquake engineering experiments), and experiment-based deployment (where the adoption of NEESgrid was motivated by specific plans to utilize NEESgrid systems to conduct experimental tests). Apart from demonstrations, users can benefit from "objects to think with" such as mock-ups and use case scenarios.

This chapter highlights sources of previously undocumented risk in cyberinfrastructure development projects. We have also suggested a number of proven steps, derived from our experience in NEESgrid, that can be used to mitigate these risks (e.g., the failure to deliver usable systems, delays in delivery, or cost overruns). As cyberinfrastructure development becomes more prevalent, it will become increasingly important to both continue research on the challenges of cyberinfrastructure projects and apply the findings of this research to improve future projects.

Acknowledgments

This work received support from the George E. Brown Jr. NEES program of the NSF under award number CMS-0117853, the NSF Middleware Initiative, and the NSF's NCSA CORE award. We gratefully acknowledge the extensive and, in many cases, continuing contributions of numerous colleagues, which space does not allow us to list by name. We particularly recognize the generosity of Jerry Hajjar, Charles Severance, and Joy Pauschke for taking the time to read and comment on the NSF report that was the basis for this chapter.

Note

1. Further information about the Sakai project is available at ⟨http://www.sakaiproject.org⟩.

References

Atkins, D. E., K. Droegemeier, S. Feldman, H. Garcia-Molina, M. L. Klein, D. G. Messerschmitt et al. 2003. *Revolutionizing science and engineering through cyberinfrastructure: Report of the National Science Foundation Blue-Ribbon Advisory Panel on Cyberinfrastructure.* Arlington, VA: National Science Foundation.

Birnholtz, J. P., and T. A. Finholt. 2007. Cultural challenges to leadership in cyberinfrastructure development. In *Leadership at a distance: Research in technologically-supported work*, ed. P. Weisband, 195–208. Mahwah, NJ: Lawrence Erlbaum.

Boehm, B. W. 1995. A spiral model of software development and enhancement. In *Human computer interaction: Toward the year 2000*, ed. R. M. Baecker, J. Grudin, W. A. S. Buxton, and S. Greenberg, 281–292. San Francisco: Morgan Kaufman.

Connaughton, S. L., and J. A. Daly. 2005. Leadership in the new millennium: Communicating beyond temporal, spatial, and geographic boundaries. *Communication Yearbook* 29:187–213.

Cummings, J., and S. Kiesler. 2003. *KDI initiative: Multidisciplinary scientific collaborations.* Arlington, VA: National Science Foundation.

Finholt, T. A. 2002. Collaboratories. *Annual Review of Information Science and Technology* 36:73–107.

Finholt, T. A. 2003. Collaboratories as a new form of scientific organization. *Economics of Innovation and New Technologies* 12 (1): 5–25.

Finholt, T. A., D. Horn, and S. Thomé. 2003. *NEESgrid requirements traceability matrix.* Technical report NEESgrid 2003–13. Available at ⟨http://it.nees.org/documentation/pdf/TR_2003_13.pdf⟩ (accessed June 20, 2007).

Foster, I., and C. Kesselman. 1999. *The grid: Blueprint for a new computing infrastructure.* San Francisco: Morgan Kaufmann.

Hofstede, G. 1991. *Cultures and organizations: Software of the mind.* London: McGraw-Hill.

Ruby, R. 2001. *Unknown shore: The lost history of England's arctic colony.* New York: Henry Holt and Company.

Sims, B. 1999. Concrete practices: Testing in an earthquake-engineering laboratory. *Social Studies of Science* 29 (4): 483–518.

Spencer, B. F., R. Butler, K. Ricker, D. Marcusiu, T. A. Finholt, I. Foster, and C. Kesselman. 2006. *Cyberenvironment project management: Lessons learned.* Available at ⟨http://www.nsf.gov/od/oci/CPMLL.pdf⟩ (accessed June 20, 2007).

Teasley, S. D., L. Covi, M. S. Krishnan, and J. S. Olson. 2000. How does radical collocation help a team succeed? In *Proceedings of the 2000 ACM conference on computer-supported cooperative work,* 339–346. New York: ACM Press.

Teasley, S. D., L. Covi, M. S. Krishnan, and J. S. Olson. 2002. Rapid software development through team collocation. *Transactions on Software Engineering* 28 (7): 671–683.

VI   The Developing World

19 International AIDS Research Collaboratories: The HIV Pathogenesis Program

Matthew Bietz, Marsha Naidoo, and Gary M. Olson

The HIV/AIDS epidemic is one of the major health crises of our time. Nearly forty million people are currently living with HIV, and roughly 2.8 million individuals died from the disease in 2005. Sub-Saharan Africa has been hit especially hard. Approximately two-thirds of infected persons (and three-quarters of infected women) live in sub-Saharan Africa. Furthermore, although southern Africa contains only 2 percent of the world's population, it accounts for one-third of all AIDS deaths (UNAIDS 2006).

Solving a health crisis of this nature must involve collaborative, global efforts since the areas of the world most affected by AIDS are also the least likely to have the expertise needed to combat it. Strategies focused at the local level are also important because HIV infection occurs in several strains, and a treatment or vaccine for one strain may not provide protection against another. The strain most prevalent in Africa, for example, is different from the strain seen in the United States and Europe. The strain specificity of vaccines requires that Africa develop its own vaccine for the African strain(s) of HIV. Additionally, because of differences in culture, the standard of living, and the medical infrastructure, treatment programs developed in other parts of the world may not be effective in southern Africa, even if the drugs work. It is not sufficient for Africa to simply import treatments created in the United States or Europe.

In recognition of the needs described above, a number of international programs have been formed to help combat this major health issue. In this chapter, we present a case study of one such international HIV/AIDS research collaboration. Specifically, we discuss our efforts to study and support the communication needs of the dispersed participants of the HIV Pathogenesis Program (HPP), a collaboration between South Africa, the United Kingdom, and the United States. In addition, we present the lessons we learned as a result of our work with this project as we believe they are applicable in other contexts. We begin the chapter with a description of our involvement in the HPP, including the methods we used to study the work practices and needs of the scientists involved in the project. Next, we provide an overview of the HPP, especially as it relates to the project's need for social and technical infrastructure to support collaboration. The main portion of the chapter looks at the implementation of a technology to support real-time distributed laboratory meetings, and we explore some of the factors that led to its successful adoption. We end by contemplating the role this technology played in the HPP's continuing success.

Studying Collaboration

We have been involved in studying several AIDS research projects, both within the United States and internationally. Of these various projects, we have studied the HPP in the greatest depth and for the longest period of time.

During this project, we worked closely with the scientists involved in the HPP to accomplish two goals. First, we attempted to gain a better understanding of their science and its practice, and their specific communication and technology needs. Second, based on our analyses of these data, we recommended and introduced a particular collaborative technology that we felt would help support the work of the HPP, and we tracked the extent and character of its use. Our approach was from the tradition of participatory action research (McTaggart 1991). For example, we collaborated with the participants to identify communication and technology needs. We worked with them to identify and correct any problems as they arose. Until the HPP hired someone to provide training and support for the technology, we also supplied that service. Thus, in conducting this research, we straddled a line between being outside observers and participants. Our own involvement was a key factor in shaping how the HIV researchers chose, implemented, and used collaboration technologies. As such, our goal in this chapter is to not only report on the HPP but also reflect on our own participation.

After some initial exploratory discussions in 2001, we began working with the HPP in early 2002, and continued our formal involvement through early 2004. During this time, we made extended visits to the South African and U.S. sites; we conducted interviews with the participants; we observed the scientists and staff at work; and we administered surveys to gather data about the scientists' technology and collaboration readiness. Late in 2002 we added a full-time coordinator in South Africa to assist with the deployment of technology as well as the monitoring and support of technology usage. Throughout the study period, we have been regularly involved at the sites, both as observers and assisting with the technological development. Table 19.1 summarizes our data collection activities and the time during which they occurred.

The HPP History

The Partners AIDS Research Center, located in Boston, Massachusetts, is one of the world's foremost AIDS research laboratories. Bruce Walker, the center's director, has been a driving force behind the HPP. The HPP was not the first project in Africa for

Table 19.1
The HPP data collection

Activity	Notes
Interviews	• Subject's work practice and daily routine, current technology use, and attitudes toward information technology
	• Baseline interviews in early 2002, repeated in late 2003
	• Several follow-up and special-purpose interviews from mid-2002 through late 2004
Observations and site visits	• Observe work practices, communication, and coordination behavior
	• Observation in laboratory, meetings (face-to-face and online), and clinical sites in both the United States and Africa
	• Formal observation periods and ongoing day-to-day interaction with scientists
Log analysis	• Characterize patterns of use of Centra conferencing software
	• Data from August 2003 through June 2005
Other data	• Project documents, including grant applications, publications, and procedural documents
	• Interviews (formal and informal) with external collaborators and other scientists who were in some way connected to this project
	• Attended annual meetings and conferences related to the project

Walker's laboratory. In the late 1980s, he began working in Africa with a project that collected samples at hospitals in Senegal and flew them back to the United States for analysis. In a later project, a postdoctoral researcher was sent to Uganda to begin laying the groundwork for vaccine trials by building an immunology laboratory and staffing it with people from Uganda.

In the late 1990s, Walker's lab wanted to study HIV/AIDS in children, but it turned out that pursuing that interest required going outside the United States. As Walker explained to us in 2004, "We had gotten more interested in studying pediatric HIV infection. We had been studying it, and with the advent of AZT for mothers at the time of pregnancy, and better diagnostic testing here in the U.S., the numbers of pediatric HIV infection cases in the U.S. dropped dramatically. So we couldn't actually even do the studies here."

After investigating several potential research sites, the lab started working with researchers at the University of Natal in Durban, South Africa, in 1999. At first, there was no sense that this would turn into a large, ongoing project. One postdoc was sent to South Africa to manage the project out of a "closet in the old part of the building." Initially the project was expected to operate like the earlier one in Senegal, where blood samples were collected in Africa and shipped to the United States for processing. This vision soon changed, as Walker again told us: "We realized that there were good people there that we could basically do some laboratory studies. We started those studies. And then realized that there was a way that we could potentially become even more involved if we could build more infrastructure." When we had our initial contact with Walker's project in 2001, the participants were in the process of formalizing their collaboration as the HPP. In addition to Walker and the original postdoc (who was by this time based in the United Kingdom), three more U.S.-based researchers and some junior staff were involved in the project. The South African research group was led by a leading pediatric HIV researcher from the University of Natal (now the University of KwaZulu-Natal). The lab was staffed by a research program director (who essentially managed all day-to-day activity in the lab), an administrative assistant, and six student researchers (who did most of the hands-on work in the laboratory).

The South African project site initially occupied a small lab suite at the university's Nelson Mandela School of Medicine. The space consisted of a cramped and ill-equipped single-room laboratory, a small office for the researchers, and a separate office in another part of the building for the lab manager. Blood samples came to the laboratory from two clinics that were treating HIV-positive mothers and children.

In the early days of the collaboration, cross-site interaction was accomplished primarily through travel. The collaboration was often described using an "exchange" metaphor: scientists from the United States and the United Kingdom would provide the expertise, while the laboratory in South Africa would supply the data. Each of the researchers would make a two-week trip to South Africa three times per year. The visits were staggered so that a U.S./UK-based researcher would be on-site for two out of every four weeks. The researchers described these visits as intense, nonstop activity for the entire duration. They would spend their time teaching new laboratory assays or techniques, troubleshooting problems, discussing data, and mentoring students.

The information technology infrastructure for the HPP during this initial phase was extremely limited.[1] Most of the laboratory staff shared a single computer (which had been rescued from the trash), and high-priority tasks like data analysis or paper writing took precedence over using the computer for communication with the other sites. The network connections were too slow and unreliable for even the most basic Web browsing, let alone more bandwidth-intensive tasks. All three rooms in the laboratory shared a single phone line.

The low level of technology readiness (see chapter 4, this volume) was not just a factor within this project but rather a wider issue within South Africa as a whole. Few people had computers at home, and even fewer had network access. Bandwidth was scarce and expensive. Telecommunications were controlled by a state-run monopoly, which tended to offer poor service. In interviews and observations, it became clear that the lab staff were painfully aware of the bandwidth limitations. They would plan their work around the periods when the network was most likely to be available, even sometimes coming in to work before dawn just to get online.

Similarly, there was little social infrastructure available to support the use of technology in the labs. The South African laboratory received a minimal level of support from the university's information technology department. The staff had no in-house technical support to install and maintain their computers. None of the staff had received any formal computer training. While the U.S. and UK sites had access to better computers and ample bandwidth, support was still supplied by an external department, few of the staff had formal computer training, and there was little awareness of the potential of new collaboration technologies.

When we began working with these groups, their technology use was limited to office programs (word processing, spreadsheets, and presentation tools), e-mail, Internet access, and specialized packages for controlling and receiving data from laboratory instruments. None of the participants were using stand-alone or networked databases, data or videoconferencing, or other advanced collaboration tools. Their lack of familiarity with collaborative and communication applications meant that the group was facing a large learning curve.

Access to data was also a problem. Data were stored in spreadsheets, which would be printed on a regular basis and shipped to the other sites. If data were required more quickly, however, a more complicated process was used. First, the scientists requesting the data would try to be as specific as possible about what was needed to minimize the amount of data being sent. Then, files would be sent both as e-mail attachments and faxes. The e-mail provided higher fidelity, but often would be delayed or fail to go through if the files were too large. Yet the phone lines were of a poor enough quality that a fax would frequently disconnect, or come out blurry and have to be resent multiple times.

Similarly, the South African scientists were especially frustrated by their lack of access to scientific articles. Their university's library did not subscribe to many publications in print, let alone in electronic format. Even when the library did subscribe, print copies would often not appear in the library until months after they had been published. The scientists were able to access abstracts online, but when they needed documents or articles, they would have to request that their U.S. counterparts fax them.

The lack of communication among project sites was a recognized issue. While the lab manager in South Africa would typically have a daily phone conversation with the principal investigators at the other sites, it was too expensive for other lab staff to make international calls. Even e-mails were infrequent and would typically be sent only when there was a specific question that required an answer. Except during the site visits, junior scientists in the African lab did not have direct access to the scientists from the other sites.

As a result, the Durban lab did not have immediate access to the U.S./UK scientists' help for two out of every four weeks, and because they had different areas of expertise, it might be three months before a particular problem or idea could be discussed in person. Maintaining closer contact with the U.S. and UK labs between site visits was a pressing need.

In terms of the dimensions of collaboration success discussed in chapter 4 (this volume; see also Olson and Olson 2000), the HPP was generally high on collaboration readiness, but quite low on technical readiness. The collaboration was proceeding despite the enormous geographic distances among the three sites. But the financial and human costs were high. The large amounts of travel and the expensive phone conferences were a drain on the project's resources.

Additionally, the project was beginning to experience more problems that threatened the ability to successfully conduct research. Some attempts to use new lab procedures in the South African laboratory had failed when none of the U.S./UK scientists were on-site. Tensions were arising across sites due to misunderstandings and the difficulty of communicating. Interestingly, other challenges were related to the project's growing success. For instance, data sharing became a larger issue as the lab began to generate data more rapidly. Another example of a challenge caused by success was the project's growth. In summer 2002, the laboratory moved into a newly remodeled and expanded space, and shortly thereafter began planning for another move into an entirely new building dedicated to HIV/AIDS research. More people were being hired. New funding streams, new projects, and new collaborators increased both the size and complexity of the collaboration.

Many of the complications that the HPP experienced resulted from the difficulties in working across national, organizational, cultural, and other boundaries. While one could imagine these problems in almost any collaborative project, they are more likely to happen, and tend to be more complicated and more difficult to resolve, in long-distance international collaborations (Armstrong and Cole 2002). In the rest of this chapter, we will discuss our attempt to address some of these problems through the implementation of a real-time collaboration platform.

Enabling Real-time Communication

One of the needs that we identified early in our involvement with the HPP was for more real-time communication. As explained above, the participants at all of the sites expressed frustration with the difficulty of communicating when they were not visiting each others' sites.

In traditional laboratories, the weekly meeting is a crucial time for exploring any problems that had come up during the week, giving individuals the chance to present results or ideas to the rest of the lab members for comment, and making sure that everyone is "on the same page." Regular seminars and journal clubs provide opportunities for lab members to present their research and learn about what others in the field are working on. These structured events allow for the coordination of activities as well as the development of a lab's shared knowledge and identity. But at the HPP, these opportunities existed only within and not across sites.

On the basis of our visits to project sites during 2002, we recommended that the HPP use Centra Symposium to support virtual lab meetings. This product has been used successfully for long-distance collaboration and teaching, including real-time classes between the United States and South Africa (Cogburn and Levinson 2003). Like WebEx, Microsoft LiveMeeting, and similar packages, Centra has a large suite of tools to support real-time conferencing. What set Centra apart, however, was that both the voiceover Internet protocol (VoIP) and the data conferencing were optimized for low-bandwidth networks.

Preparing the HPP for Centra-supported meetings required implementing technologies and procedures at many levels. Through a combination of infrastructure

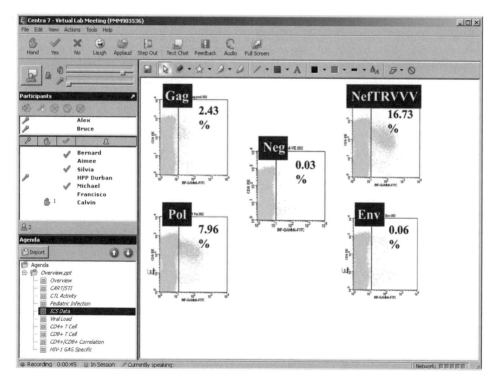

Figure 19.1
Centra screen shot

development, external support, and internal enthusiasm, the project successfully adopted the technology over a period of two years.

In planning the Centra implementation, we saw three significant challenges to address: an insufficient network infrastructure, incompatibilities among the operating systems, and the absence of human infrastructure to support the technology use. The most pressing of these was the lack of network bandwidth in southern Africa. The participants in the United States and United Kingdom had ample network capacity as well as excellent reliability, both at work and home. The South African participants, on the other hand, had a limited and unreliable connection to the Internet. The problem existed at several levels, ranging from overcrowded national backbones and international connections to a lack of capacity within the University of Natal itself.

During the period of our involvement, the speed and availability of network connections increased immensely in South African universities. The scientists no longer had to come to work early in the morning or stay late at night just to be able to download data files or documents. Nevertheless, these improvements were not sufficient for real-time conferencing. Universities were gobbling up bandwidth as fast as it was made available, and network reliability remained an issue.

In the end, by going outside the university, the bandwidth problem was solved (or at least brought to a workable level). While the laboratory would use the university-provided network for all of its regular Internet use, the project contracted with a commercial Internet service provider to supply a separate broadband connection for real-time conferencing applications.[2] The new connection still only offered enough bandwidth for a single computer to connect to the server. Centra is designed around a one-person-per-computer model, but a typical meeting would include anywhere from three to fifteen people at the South African site. We worked around this limitation by displaying Centra on a large screen in a conference room and passing around a microphone when someone wanted to speak.

We faced another challenge with incompatibilities among the operating systems in use by the project participants. The South African site used Microsoft Windows–based personal computers exclusively, the UK site used only Apple Macintosh computers, and the U.S. site was mixed. Centra would only run on Windows, and the budget could not provide for new computers for all of the Mac users. We attempted to find a technological work-around, but in the end, the UK and U.S. sites purchased a small number of Windows-based computers that the Mac users could use for Centra meetings.

A final hurdle with Centra was related to the human infrastructure necessary to support its use. As mentioned previously, when we first began working with the HPP, there was little human support for its use of technology. In both the United States and South Africa, support was provided by centralized computing services. The support that was available was geared toward the computers (mostly for installation and maintenance) rather than the people who used them. Most of the researchers had not received any formal computer training.

As part of our involvement with the HPP, we offered both technical and social support for the use of Centra. In our early site visits, our work involved not only observing how the group used technology but also supplying computer training and advice. As we worked toward implementing Centra, we installed software, trained users, did troubleshooting when problems arose, and managed the Centra server.

But we soon found that our own distance from the project was also a problem in the technology implementation. We were located at the University of Michigan, and we experienced many of the same distance-related frustrations that the HIV researchers felt. As a result, there was a long ramp-up period before successful implementation: our first on-site contact with the HPP was in February 2002, but the first Centra meetings did not occur until August 2003. The lack of progress was frustrating not only for us but also for the HPP. As one South African lab member explained to us in 2004,

[My expectations of Centra] were very low. Yeah. Very low. And I think it was fueled by the frustrations of the project and not getting going. There were kind of promises as to what Centra could do, largely from the show and tell ... at the beginning. And so, there were these high expectations, and then, I suppose partly because of the [lack of] availability of local staff to do the training, and those that had some training but didn't put their training into practice, then they got frustrated. So there was initially a negative view, whether Michigan could deliver and whether Centra could deliver.

Implementing a better support structure was clearly a priority. In late 2002, the HPP hired a staff member who could support the technology. We also hired a South African coordinator to support our research. "I think [having someone on site] made a huge difference," noted another South African lab member. "Because, also you know, to try and contact [Matt] overseas, although he obviously was very willing but, you know, you don't have somebody on the spot."

In the end, however, one of the most powerful forces pushing the implementation was the enthusiasm of the U.S.-based project director, especially after his initial skepticism. In a 2004 interview, Walker told us that

it was explained to me, and I thought, you know, there's no way. This can't work. This can't really work the way they say it does. So we actually went ahead and we set this whole [ISDN] videoconferencing thing at the HPP.... And I think it was in a conversation with you where basically, I had still never really tried Centra.... And you basically said, well, Marsha's in South Africa right now, why don't we just do it right now. And within a couple minutes, sitting in my computer here, I was talking to Marsha in South Africa. And I was just blown away. Literally blown away. Even despite the fact that you told me so much about it, I couldn't believe it when I actually saw it.

After this, Walker became almost evangelistic about Centra and has advocated for its use at every available opportunity, not only for this project, but also several other projects with which he is involved.

As Walker points out, Centra was not the only real-time conferencing system available to the project. In 1998, the South African Department of Health published the "National Telemedicine Project Strategy," which called for the widespread adoption of telemedicine systems. ISDN-based videoconferencing is a major component of this program. Through this program, many doctors and medical researchers became aware of videoconferencing, and the popularity of this technology in medical circles boomed across South Africa. At about the same time that we were beginning to implement Centra, the HPP installed a high-quality ISDN system in the conference room of its new lab building. In the same interview, Walker went on to compare the two systems:

So we immediately started to think about [Centra] as a way to do things. And in fact, it wasn't more than a few weeks later after we'd done a couple of [Centra test] sessions with South Africa, that we were actually on our regular weekly [ISDN] videoconference call, which was problematic because we could get Oxford on, but not Boston at the same time. And they were reviewing data, and the quality was so poor with the videoconferencing that they actually said, well actually why don't we try to show the slides by Centra, and do the videoconferencing to talk. So they fired up Centra in the same room, and basically realized that the [ISDN] videoconferencing was totally obsolete for what we were doing. We have never used that videoconference since, even though it's the state-of-the-art videoconferencing material, we only use the Centra stuff. And we use it all the time.

There are some key differences between these two technologies and their use that help to explain the different outcomes. First, Centra is better suited to the work of the scientists. Most of their meetings and cross-site communications involve discussing data, which are poorly supported in their videoconferencing system. Second, their videoconferencing system does not support multipoint conferences, and yet the collaboration involves three sites. Centra, on the other hand, can support many sites in the same meeting. Finally, the ISDN videoconferencing system is extremely expensive to use. Our initial interviews with project members suggest that one factor limiting the number of telephone conference call meetings between sites was the cost, yet ISDN calls were at least twice as expensive as a phone call. In contrast, Centra, which operates over the Internet, carries no per-minute usage charges.

We discovered that in supporting the group's use of the technology, we were also encouraging behavior that may have improved their meeting process. For example, Centra works best when PowerPoint slides are loaded in advance (especially for large meetings or presentations). Meetings on Centra therefore often had an agenda and presentation planned out in advance—something that was not the norm for other project meetings. Similarly, the need to reserve meeting time on the shared server led to earlier and more formal scheduling of contact between the sites.

From Adoption to Use

Once Centra's usefulness had been demonstrated, it quickly became the de facto choice for weekly lab meetings. We also observed that the scientists began using the software for more than lab meetings. Smaller groups used it to meet and discuss sub-projects. It has been used for one-to-one meetings to discuss both scientific and administrative issues. South African students in the project met with mentors based in the United States and United Kingdom using Centra. When students were preparing to give presentations at the International AIDS Conference, they first gave a practice talk in a virtual lab meeting. Colleagues and collaborators from other South African universities have connected for research seminars. Centra is now being used to train clinicians who are participating in the rollout of antiretroviral therapies in the KwaZulu-Natal province of South Africa.

Several steps were taken to ensure that the technology would continue to be useful for the HPP after the authors' involvement ended.[3] As part of the implementation process, we trained most of the project participants on Centra, and they are now comfortable enough with the software that they do not typically need technical assistance at meetings. In addition, the HPP added a staff member in South Africa who took on responsibility for supporting the project's technology, educational development, and collaboration.

We stopped providing support for the project at the end of 2004, although we do continue to track how the HPP is using the technology. Server log analysis shows that the project went from two to three meetings per week in the first few months of use to a sustained level of five to eight meetings per week after two years. Additionally, during our involvement, we provided Centra free to the project through a research server at the University of Michigan. In 2005, the HPP began purchasing the software as a service directly from Centra and is paying for its use from its own budgets.

Many of the participants have expressed that they still wish they had more opportunities for face-to-face interaction with their remote colleagues. But we feel that the use of real-time collaboration software has helped reduce the communication vacuum that used to exist between principal investigator site visits.

The Impact

In late 2004, we asked Walker if he had ever expected the project to grow and thrive, and he responded, "No. No. This was a total side project. And I had anticipated that we would do a little bit of work. But never, never ever conceived that it would become the size that it's become. Or taken the attention of mine that it's grown to take. . . . I would say I'm spending 50 percent of my time right now related to the projects in South Africa."

The HPP is not only big but also successful. The project has directly led to an increased capacity to treat and study HIV and AIDS in the KwaZulu-Natal region of South Africa. A number of historically disadvantaged students have been given the opportunity to work with some of the world's best biomedical researchers and present their work at conferences all over the globe. The project has produced numerous publications, many with South African first authors, published via first-rate conferences and in journals (for example, Kiepiela et al. 2004).

Given a large, complex project like the HPP, it is difficult to make definitive claims about the impact of a technology intervention on the overall project success. Still, we do see evidence that the technology itself was successful. Interviews with the project participants suggest that the scientists believe Centra was useful and an important communications tool. The software was used to not only support virtual meetings but also other communications, including never-before-possible real-time interaction between students and their distant mentors. The technology continued to be used within the project after the authors' involvement ended, and was in fact adopted for other projects. For example, HIV/AIDS doctors in South Africa are now using Centra to have clinical conferences with doctors in the United States, and some of the HPP scientists have adopted the same conferencing system for their other projects in China, South America, and other parts of the world.

The HPP offers an example of successful distributed science, and the successful adoption of collaboration technologies to support that science. From its beginnings as a small project with little cross-site interaction, it became a vibrant and productive project at the leading edge of HIV/AIDS research that has successfully integrated new collaboration technologies into its day-to-day work.

Notes

1. We take a broad view of infrastructure, which includes both the technical and social structures to support collaboration; see G. M. Olson and J. S. Olson, "Distance Matters," *Human Computer Interaction* 15, nos. 2–3 (2000): 139–178.

2. The rollout of broadband DSL connections in South Africa beginning in 2003 made this a practical alternative to the university's system.

3. Moving interventions from ad hoc or experimental status into infrastructure is at the heart of attempts at "sustainable" development. A common complaint about development projects is that if the infrastructure is not locally sustainable, higher-level activities will not be able to continue after the outsiders' support ends.

References

Armstrong, D. J., and P. Cole. 2002. Managing distances and differences in geographically distributed work groups. In *Distributed work*, ed. P. J. Hinds and S. Kiesler, 167–186. Cambridge, MA: MIT Press.

Cogburn, D. L., and N. S. Levinson. 2003. US-Africa virtual collaboration in globalization studies: Success factors for complex, cross-national learning teams. *International Studies Perspectives* 4 (2): 34–51.

Kiepiela, P., A. J. Leslie, I. Honeyborne, D. Ramduth, C. Thobakgale, S. Chetty et al. 2004. Dominant influence of HLA-B in mediating the potential co-evolution of HIV and HLA. *Nature* 432 (7018): 769–775.

McTaggart, R. 1991. Principles for participatory action research. *Adult Education Quarterly* 41 (3): 168–187.

Olson, G. M., and J. S. Olson. 2000. Distance matters. *Human Computer Interaction* 15 (2–3): 139–178.

UNAIDS. 2006. *2006 Report on the global AIDS epidemic.* Geneva, Switzerland: UNAIDS.

20　How Collaboratories Affect Scientists from Developing Countries

Airong Luo and Judith S. Olson

Collaboratories transform geographically bounded laboratories into virtual organizations with the hope of advancing science in two ways: by increasing the number of participants and the diversity of approaches. One way to broaden participation is to reach out to scientists in developing countries. Studies show that scientists from developing countries remain behind the scientists from developed countries because of access to resources, colleagues, and so on (Gibbs 1997; May 1997). Collaboratories *promise* a solution by allowing easy access to data and instruments remotely, and allowing collegial exchange through both formal meetings and informal exchange via e-mail and Listservs (Finholt 2002).

It is not clear whether this promise has become a reality. We have been investigating the factors in collaboratories that help and hinder scientists from developing countries in becoming a part of the "invisible college" of high-performing scientists. In what follows, we first review what is known about productivity in science, how scientists in developing countries suffer on a number of these dimensions, and how collaboratories promise to provide advantages to overcome some of the barriers. We then describe our data collection methods and report on our findings.

Productivity in Science

The productivity of individual scientists is affected by their social and organizational contexts (Fox 1991). Productivity in science is driven by access to resources and knowledge gained from colleagues. Access to knowledge from colleagues consists of both knowledge of scientific practice and other knowledge about the field. Since scientists build on and extend other people's work, and the validity of scientific work needs to be evaluated by other scientists, collegial communication plays an especially important role in scientists' lives. Collegial communication helps scientists clarify the relevance of terms, identify suitable topics, receive more timely feedback, share research methods, and obtain social and emotional support (Garvey and Griffiths 1967; Hagstrom 1965, 1971; Pelz 1956; Pelz and Andrews 1976; Kraut et al. 1990).

When people are working on the same project, they have several advantages having to do with collegial communication. They know each other (who to talk to for what), have common ground (a vocabulary and methods known to both), and have an implicit obligation to pay attention to each other and respond. When people are copresent, these informal exchanges take place in the hallway, a cafeteria, or other meeting places (Kraut et al. 1993). The mere physical presence of another person creates an obligation for people to engage (Kiesler and Cummings 2002; Kraut, Egido, and Galegher 1988). When people are distant from each other yet part of the same community of scholars, however, they, too, feel an obligation to pay attention to each other and respond (Constant, Sproull, and Kiesler 1996).

How Scientists in Developing Countries Are Disadvantaged

In addition to the literature about science in developing countries, we borrow here from the literature on the differences in productivity in prestigious and less prestigious institutions in the United States, since most (but not all) institutions in developing countries are less prestigious than those in developed countries.

Institutions with higher prestige have more productive individuals partly because more resources are available (Allison and Stewart 1974; Crane 1965; Fox 1991; Hargens and Hagstrom 1967; Zuckerman 1988). These resources include laboratory facilities, computers, library holdings, graduate student skills, and time available for research. Harriet Zuckerman (1988) found that about 0.3 percent of the universities were granted 21 percent of the funds available to U.S. colleges and universities in 1979–1980, with the next 0.7 percent receiving an additional 43 percent, leaving the remaining 99 percent of the institutions to share the remaining 36 percent. Developing countries generally spend much less than 1 percent of their gross domestic product on scientific research, whereas developed countries spend between 2 and 3 percent (UNESCO 2005). Scientists in some developing countries have neither advanced laboratory equipment nor the skilled permanent personnel to operate and maintain it (chapter 19, this volume; Gaillard 1991).

Scientists from developing countries have been seen as isolated on both informational and interpersonal dimensions (Davidson, Sooryamoorthy, and Shrum 2002). The opportunities for scientists from developing countries to access timely scientific information have been seriously limited, although as more scientific information is on the Internet, this gap may be closing. Scientists in developing countries are also isolated interpersonally. They usually have smaller research communities and tend to be dispersed over long distances. Infrastructure problems with transportation and communication hinder scientists in developing areas from engaging in regular collegial communication as well as benefiting from the intellectual stimulation that accompanies contact. Jacques Gaillard (1991) found that scientists in developing countries interact only with colleagues in the same institute, or even often in the same department or research unit.

How Collaboratories Promise to Provide Advantages

Collaboratories provide remote access to instruments and data. For example, the Protein Data Bank is a centralized resource where investigators deposit 3-D macromolecular structures. The Protein Data Bank was developed first among a consortium of institutions in the United States, now with mirror sites in Europe and Asia. It contains over twelve thousand structures, and is accessed sixty thousand to a hundred thousand times a day (Arzberger and Finholt 2002). Such collaboratories make it possible for scientists in developing countries to access the data they could not get previously.[1] Another collaboratory, TB Structural Genomics Consortium, provides centralized facilities that carry out routine tasks such as protein production, crystallization, and X-ray data collection for its members from 134 labs in 79 institutions in 15 countries.

Collaboratories usually require their members to adopt the same technology, the same data format, and the same workflow across different sites. Standardization promises to help scientists learn from each other (Nentwich 2003), and adopt and implement more advanced technologies and management practices.

Many collaboratories also offer forums for both formal and informal communication. In addition, by being designated as members of the collaboratory, scientists from developing countries become known as having some legitimacy, and consequently other members have an implicit obligation to pay attention to them. Collaboratories help scientists stay informed about who is doing similar research, and with whom they can communicate and collaborate.

Potential Barriers to Realizing the Promise

Despite the new opportunities for scientific collaboration afforded by collaboratories, we know that distance still matters (Olson and Olson 2000). Although data and instruments are online, access requires advanced computer systems and network infrastructure. Data sharing calls for great computer capacity to process large quantities of data. Unfortunately, the digital divide exists in developing countries at least as much as it does in the United States. Greater benefits from the Internet accrue to people with higher social and economic status, and whose resources empower them to adopt the Internet sooner as well as more productively than their less well-off neighbors (DiMaggio et al. 2001). A 2003 report compared network access for three regions: the European Economic Area, the ten countries that joined the European Union in May 2004, and a number of other countries neighboring the European Union (Williams et al. 2003).

The core capacity of research networks in the second group of countries was one-fifth of the first, and one-twenty-fifth in the third. This implies that only those researchers in countries that have a high-capacity research network will be able to take full advantage of collaboratories. Those without will suffer further research exclusion.

Although networks increase the possibility for scientists to reach a larger group of like-minded researchers, it cannot guarantee that communication will take place or be effective. Communication via text is less rich than face-to-face interactions, and even communication over video is not as good as face-to-face. The obligation to respond to someone is far greater in face-to-face communication than in e-mail or discussion forums on the Internet. In addition, the probability of cultural miscommunication is much higher in text-based conversations than face-to-face discussions because of the lack of immediate feedback about how a message was received (Olson and Olson 2000). Dispersion has a number of other effects (O'Leary and Cummings 2007). Spatial distance reduces the probability of spontaneous communication (Burke et al. 1999; Dennis et al. 1988; Saunders, Van Slyke, and Vogel 2004). And when the people attempting to communicate are many time zones apart, problem solving has to take place asynchronously rather than in real time (Grinter, Herbsleb, and Perry 1999; Herbsleb et al. 2000; Malone and Crowston 1994). When people are isolated from collaborators, they have a decreased awareness of what others are doing (Armstrong and Cole 2002; Dennis 1996; Tan et al. 1998). And when the participants are amassed primarily in one area (as in the developed countries), the remote participants are likely to feel less empowered and more influenced by the majority (Allmendinger and Hackman 1995; Kabanoff 1991; Mannix 1993), thereby reducing the potential creativity that comes from diversity.

The potential barriers to realizing the promise are substantial. Yet we do not know how they play out in real scientific collaborations, which is why we instituted this study.

Data Collection

From the nearly two hundred collaboratories identified by the Science of Collaboratories project (see the introduction to this volume), we found seven that had participants from developing countries (see table 20.1). We interviewed thirty-three scientists from China, Korea, New Zealand, South Africa, Morocco, and Taiwan. We also interviewed nine U.S. scientists and one European scientist who participate in the same collaboratories as the scientists from developing countries. Airong Luo, who speaks fluent English, Korean, and Chinese, conducted the interviews. She translated the interviews into English, conveying the meaning of the conversation, but not necessarily word-by-word literal translation. Thus, the passages in quotes used for evidence are true to their meaning but are not direct quotes. All the collaboratories we studied were distrib-

Table 20.1

The collaboratories studied

Collabo-ratory	Field	Distribution of collaborators	Number of participants interviewed
A	Biomedical science	1 lab in the United States and three labs in China	1 from the United States and 6 from China
B	Biomedical science	30 labs in 6 countries	3 from China
C	Biomedical science	55 labs from 12 countries	3 from Korea, 1 from the United States, and 1 from China
D	Molecular biology	About 246 participants	1 each from the United States, Korea, Taiwan, and South Africa
E	Molecular biology	134 labs in 15 countries	1 each from the United States, Korea, New Zealand, and India
F	High-energy physics	167 institutions in 37 countries	3 from the United States, 5 from China, and 2 from Morocco
G	High-energy physics	181 institutions in 38 nations	1 from Europe, 4 from Korea, 1 from the United States, and 3 from China

uted research centers, providing access to data, instruments, and colleagues (chapter 3, this volume).

In order to check whether these sciences in the developing world were indeed non-world-class ones (e.g., China does world-class seismology research; Wagner et al. 2001), we examined the relative impact of publications in the past ten years in the fields we studied. They were all below the world average.[2]

We interviewed the participants on how they became involved in the collaboratory, the benefits they experienced, and the barriers to its use. They described their collaborative work, the frequency of communication, and the technologies they used for communication. We also examined the Web content, such as Web forums and meeting minutes provided on the Web sites of the collaboratory projects. In addition, we reviewed documents such as annual reports.

The Results

Collaboratories enable scientists from developing countries to access resources and communicate with scientists from developed countries. However, the ways in which scinetists achieve this are governed by many sociotechnical and cultural factors. Because of distance, the size and dispersion of collaboratories, funding situations, and their local communication infrastructure, scientists from developing countries encounter more barriers than do their collaborators in the developed world.

Resources

As discussed above, one of the potential advantages of collaboratories is that they enable scientists to access instruments they would not be able to afford. As Dr. B from New Zealand in Collaboratory E said: "One of the biggest benefits of the collaboratory is to help us reach the facilities in the United States. The person who runs the beamline collects the data for us and processes them, and sends them back." Similarly, a Korean scientist in another collaboratory told the story that when he was going to look for funding to build facilities for Korean scientists in his field, he found that there was such a collaboratory in the United States already and that he could use the facilities remotely. In two of the collaboratories we studied, the scientists can send their samples to the United States to have their data analyzed by instruments there. In exchange, their results are made public after the original scientists have had them for a certain time.

Collaboratories D and E require their members to deposit data into their databases. They share their recent work and unpublished data so others can obtain information about current work in a timely way. They help avoid scientists duplicating each other's work. Scientists even share when and how their experiment was done, what kinds of materials were used, and so on. Dr. S. from Collaboratory E reported: "[When conducting experiments], you have to try a lot of different procedures. Someone finds out that some procedures were better than other procedures. . . . if you have some information from other people about what is the shortest way and which can take the least time, that is very useful information. So we can share experiences."

Communication

Many collaboratories hold annual meetings, where participants can get to know each other and present their research findings. Participants value the personal contact they have with other scientists at these meetings. When asked how conferences help, Dr. B from New Zealand commented: "Talking to other investigators . . . often helps to clear any problems, any questions. It's just the personal contact that is very valuable. Although I already knew some of the people before [the collaboratory] was formed, there were many more who became part of it since then. And I got to know them from a number of conferences." Similarly, Dr. L. from Korea said: "Only after you meet people, you can have a feeling about what kind of people they are. You can know whether you want to collaborate with them and how to collaborate with them. We meet people at conferences." Unfortunately, not all the scientists from developing countries have the money to travel, and most of the annual meetings and conferences are in the United States or Europe.

In some collaboratories, all presentations from the conferences are posted online, so people who could not attend have a chance to know what was presented. Dr. N., a Chinese high-energy physicist in Collaboratory F, reported that he could seldom go to the conferences because of budget and visa problems, but he "read" most of the presentations. This point was echoed by his colleague, Ms. Y., who said that their collaborators in the United States posted the documents that describe their working process online, and since they were latecomers to the project, she would go to the Web site to find answers to her questions.

In a number of collaboratories, the most significant success is having the scientists from developing countries learn the procedures. Dr. J., a Chinese AIDS research in Collaboratory A, mentioned that he had not realized that his work was not of high quality until he collaborated with his partners in the United States. He learned quality control procedures. Similarly, in Collaboratory G, Dr. C., a Chinese high-energy physicist, remarked:

We were very impressed by the way our American collaborators conduct their mass-production quality control. For every chamber, they have a book [of guidelines for mass-production quality control], which describes the detailed regulation for each process, from how to prepare the parts to testing and cleaning the parts. For each step, people who are in charge should sign the documents so that it will be easy to assign responsibility if problems occur.... I learned the management process and brought it back to our lab in China.... Later, scientists and engineers from other labs in our institute visited our lab and borrowed our experiences.

Some analysis techniques involve tacit knowledge requiring time to learn, and are learned by watching others do the analyses. For example, in one collaboratory, AIDS researchers need to learn to use what is called an Elispot method. Scientists judge what spot size denotes a positive reaction. As a Chinese doctoral student, Mr. H. remarked that "when we first used this Elispot reader, we were not sure whether we were making the right judgments. Then I was sent to the lab in the United States where scientists are more experienced in this technology and worked with them for about one month. I conducted experiments there and I observed how they made judgments for the test results. Then I became more confident."

Working side by side with scientists from developed countries also affected scientists' motivations. Dr. W., an AIDS researcher in China, said that the U.S. scientists' motivations were to obtain recognition by the scientific community, encouraging them to do their best work. Dr. W. noted that in China, the scientists focused more on being recognized in their own institution, to be promoted. Dr. W.'s colleague, Dr. Q, told a story of one of his U.S. colleagues: "Once one of our American colleagues came to our lab to help us with an experiment. We arranged sightseeing for her during the last day of her stay here. Two days before she went back, the experiment was finished. The result was satisfying, but she wanted it to be better. So she gave up the sightseeing opportunity and continued with the experiment until we got better results."

Many collaboratories do communicate in other ways than face-to-face. Some collaboratories use videoconferencing systems for communication and talking about visual aspects of the data. Unfortunately, like support for travel, many developing country scientists cannot afford expensive videoconferencing systems, and thus lose out in participating in the conversation. An AIDS researcher from China stated:

Currently when we have a teleconference, we can only discuss the data. But we can't view the data and discuss the data at the same time. When we discuss the data, we only do oral interpretation. I think this is the largest deficiency. In the process of research, if you can't view the data, and only listen to people describing them and express your opinion, it will be too limited. It will depend on whether the describer can describe correctly and whether people who try to understand can understand correctly.

Many collaboratories encourage informal communication through instant messenger and Web forums, and yet they are seldom used. The fact that they are in widely different time zones discourages the use of instant messaging. Tele- and videoconferencing are used for more formal and scheduled communication, such as discussing research plans. Some who did not use the Web forums claimed that they were not well designed and intuitive. In addition, distance communication tends not to be effective unless people have some personal contacts before. For example, a participant from Taiwan and Korea in Collaboratory D reported that they seldom contacted other collaboratory members. Rather, they saw the only benefit of the collaboratory being the data analysis service. A participant from the United States, in contrast, was in contact with other members, but only those he met personally at the annual conference.

Some collaboratories require scientists to communicate their activity and research methods through the databases. Unfortunately, "out of sight, out of mind," scientists forget to comply. Without reminders, they do not pay attention to the needs of the scientists in the developing countries. On the other hand, in one collaboratory, since the Chinese scientists can attend at most two of the four annual conferences due to their limited travel funding, and can seldom participate in videoconferences due to the time difference and poor communication infrastructure, the U.S. and European scientists often feel they do not know what is going on in China.

Other Barriers to Success for Collaboratory Scientists from Developing Countries
Some local restrictions hinder the productivity of scientists in developing countries. For example, some collaboratories require the exchanges of reagents of blood samples. In the United States, there is a sophisticated social system to support the transporting and exporting of reagents or other materials. Research universities in the United States

usually have a service that helps scientists do this. But in developing countries such as China, the scientists have to do this kind of work themselves. For instance, scientists often need to contact an airline directly and seek its help.

The Chinese government also imposes strict restrictions on exporting materials related to biological research. The scientists have to apply to different levels of government offices to obtain permission to export blood samples to the United States. Dr. J., the AIDS researcher in Collaboratory A, reported that it took seven months to export the blood samples that their U.S. partners needed. For the U.S. scientists, it took three days.

Conclusions and Implications

Being a member of a collaboratory from the developing country does provide benefits. The primary advantage is having access to data and instruments. Although there is some communication, it is much more formal than informal. Videoconferences are used for scheduled meetings; some people participate in Web forums, but not as many as one would hope. The scientists in developed countries forget to post their activities, and do not implicitly pay attention to the remote scientists. Informal communication takes place much more frequently at face-to-face conferences, although the formal presentations are put online for those who could not travel. Learning new procedures and tacit knowledge happens again face-to-face with scientists from developing countries traveling to the laboratories in the developed countries. The barriers to productivity appear to be less about infrastructure (e.g., networking and processing capacity) than about cost. There is less spontaneous communication, it is less rich, and there is less awareness of what is going on in remote locations. It is easy to see why these scientists might feel less empowered.

It appears that the full value from the collaboratories will come only when there is sufficient money for travel to conferences and long laboratory visits. We can hope for technology solutions (e.g., high-resolution video/data displays or easy-to-use Web forums), but most of the progress is likely to be in social systems—having funding agencies understand the importance of face-to-face encounters to supplement the data sharing and remote instrument use, and incentive systems to encourage the entry of more informal information in the shared database.

Notes

1. In the taxonomy developed by the Science of Collaboratories project, the Protein Data Bank is classified as a community data system; see chapter 3 (this volume).

2. See ⟨http://www.in-cites.com⟩.

References

Allison, P. D., and J. A. Stewart. 1974. Productivity differences among scientists: Evidence for accumulative advantage. *American Sociological Review* 39 (4): 596–606.

Allmendinger, J., and J. R. Hackman. 1995. The more the better? A four-nation study of the inclusion of women in symphony orchestras. *Social Forces* 74 (2): 423–460.

Armstrong, D. J., and P. Cole. 2002. Managing distances and differences in geographically distributed work groups. In *Distributed work*, ed. P. Hinds and S. Kiesler, 167–212. Cambridge, MA: MIT Press.

Arzberger, P., and T. A. Finholt. 2002. *Data and collaboratories in the biomedical community: Report of a panel of experts meeting held September 16–18, 2002 in Ballston, VA*. Washington, DC: National Institutes of Health. Available at ⟨http://nbcr.sdsc.edu/Collaboratories/CollaboratoryFinal2.doc⟩ (accessed June 22, 2007).

Burke, K., K. Aytes, L. Chidambaram, and J. J. Johnson. 1999. A study of partially distributed work groups: The impact of media, location, and time on perceptions and performance. *Small Group Research* 30 (4): 453–490.

Constant, D., L. Sproull, and S. Kiesler. 1996. The kindness of strangers: The usefulness of electronic weak ties for technical advice. *Organization Science* 7 (2): 119–135.

Crane, D. 1965. Scientists at major and minor universities: A study of productivity and recognition. *American Sociological Review* 30 (5): 699–714.

Davidson, T., R. Sooryamoorthy, and W. Shrum. 2002. Kerala connections: Will the Internet affect science in developing areas? In *The Internet in everyday life*, ed. B. Wellman and C. Haythornthwaite, 496–519. Oxford: Blackwell.

Dennis, A. R. 1996. Information exchange and use in group decision making: You can lead a group to information, but you can't make it think. *MIS Quarterly* 20 (4): 433–457.

Dennis, A. R., J. F. George, L. M. Jessup, J. F. Nunamaker, and D. R. Vogel. 1988. Information technology to support electronic meetings. *MIS Quarterly* 12 (4): 591–624.

DiMaggio, P., E. Hargittai, W. R. Neuman, and J. P. Robinson. 2001. Social implications of the Internet. *Annual Review of Sociology* 27:307–336.

Finholt, T. A. 2002. Collaboratories. *Annual Review of Information Science and Technology* 36:73–107.

Fox, M. F. 1991. Research productivity and the environmental context. In *Research and higher education*, ed. T. G. Whiston and R. L. Geiger, 103–111. Buckingham, UK: SRHE and Open University Press.

Gaillard, J. 1991. *Scientists in the third world*. Lexington: University Press of Kentucky.

Garvey, W. D., and B. C. Griffith. 1967. Scientific communication as a social system. *Science* 157 (3792): 1011–1016.

Gibbs, W. W. 1997. Lost science in the third world. *Scientific American* 273 (2): 76–83.

Grinter, R. E., J. D. Herbsleb, and D. E. Perry. 1999. The geography of coordination: Dealing with distance in R&D work. In *Proceedings of the international ACM SIGGROUP conference on supporting group work*, 306–315. New York: ACM Press.

Hagstrom, W. O. 1965. *The scientific community*. New York: Basic Books.

Hagstrom, W. O. 1971. Inputs, outputs, and the prestige of university science departments. *Sociology of Education* 44 (4): 375–397.

Hargens, L. L., and W. O. Hagstrom. 1967. Sponsored and contest mobility of American academic scientists. *Sociology of Education* 40 (1): 24–38.

Herbsleb, J. D., A. Mockus, T. A. Finholt, and R. E. Grinter. 2000. Distance, dependencies, and delay in global collaboration. In *Proceedings of the 2000 ACM conference on computer-supported cooperative work*, 319–328. New York: ACM Press.

Kabanoff, B. 1991. Equity, equality, power, and conflict. *Academy of Management Review* 16 (2): 416–441.

Kiesler, S., and J. Cummings. 2002. Proximity and distance in work groups. In *Distributed work*, ed. P. J. Hinds and S. Kiesler, 57–80. Cambridge, MA: MIT Press.

Kraut, R., C. Egido, and J. Galegher. 1988. Patterns of contact and communication in scientific research collaboration. In *Proceedings of the 1988 ACM conference on computer-supported cooperative work*, 1–12. New York: ACM Press.

Kraut, R., R. S. Fish, R. W. Root, and B. Chalfonte. 1990. Informal communication in organizations: Form, function, and technology. In *People's reactions to technology in factories, offices, and aerospace*, ed. S. Oskamp and S. Spacapan, 145–199. Beverly Hills, CA: Sage Publications.

Kraut, R., R. S. Fish, R. W. Root, and B. Chalfonte. 1993. Informal communication in organizations: Form, function, and technology. In *Readings in groupware and computer-supported cooperative work: Assisting human-human collaboration*, ed. R. Baecker, 287–314. San Mateo, CA: Morgan Kaufmann.

Malone, T. W., and K. Crowston. 1994. The interdisciplinary study of coordination. *ACM Computing Surveys* 26 (1): 87–119.

Mannix, E. A. 1993. Organizations as resource dilemmas: The effects of power balance on coalition formation in small groups. *Organizational Behavior and Human Decision Processes* 55 (1): 1–22.

May, R. M. 1997. The scientific wealth of nations. *Science* 275 (5301): 793–796.

Nentwich, M. 2003. *Cyberscience: Research in the age of the Internet*. Vienna: Austrian Academy of Science.

O'Leary, M. B., and J. N. Cummings. 2007. The spatial, temporal, and configurational characteristics of geographic dispersion in teams. *MIS Quarterly* 31 (3): 1–19.

Olson, G. M., and J. S. Olson. 2000. Distance matters. *Human-Computer Interaction* 15:139–178.

Pelz, D. C. 1956. Some social factors related to performance in research organization. *Administrative Science Quarterly* 1 (3): 310–325.

Pelz, D. C., and F. M. Andrews. 1976. *Scientists in organizations: Productive climates for research and development*. Ann Arbor, MI: Institute for Social Research.

Saunders, C., C. Van Slyke, and D. R. Vogel. 2004. My time or yours? Managing time visions in global virtual teams. *Academy of Management Executive* 18 (1): 19–31.

Tan, B. C. Y., K. Wei, R. T. Watson, D. L. Clapper, and E. R. McLean. 1998. Computer-mediated communication and majority influence: Assessing the impact in an individualistic and a collectivistic culture. *Management Science* 44 (9): 1263–1278.

United Nations Educational, Scientific, and Cultural Organization (UNESCO). 2005. UNESCO science report 2005. Paris: UNESCO Publishing.

Wagner, C. S., I. Brahmakulam, B. Jackson, A. Wong, and T. Yoda. 2001. *Science and technology collaboration: Building capacity in developing countries*. Santa Monica, CA: Rand.

Williams, D., M. Bonač, I. Butterworth, D. Davies, S. Jaume-Rajaonia, T. Mayer et al. 2003. Summary report on the SERENATE studies: Study into European research and education networking as targeted by eEurope. Information society technologies, IST-2001-34925). SERENATE Consortium. Available at ⟨http://www.serenate.org/publications/d21-serenate.pdf⟩ (accessed June 22, 2007).

Zuckerman, H. 1988. The sociology of science. In *Handbook of sociology*, ed. J. S. Neil, 511–574. Newbury Park, CA: Sage.

Conclusion

Final Thoughts: Is There a Science of Collaboratories?

Nathan Bos, Gary M. Olson, and Ann Zimmerman

The project whose work led to this book was optimistically named. The Science of Collaboratories (SOC) was a goal rather than a reality in 2000, when the project began. That is still the case, although we believe that goal is significantly closer to being realized.

Two chapters in this book are most directly targeted at building a science: "From Shared Databases to Communities of Practice: A Taxonomy of Collaboratories" (chapter 3) and "A Theory of Remote Scientific Collaboration" (chapter 4). Chapter 3 is an attempt to classify the diversity of projects being attempted in long-distance science. Classification is an activity that most emerging fields need to engage in early in their development. The goal of the work presented in this chapter was to take a bottom-up approach. The coauthors resisted creating a classification too soon, and rejected the "easy" categorization of collaboratories by discipline (e.g., biological sciences or physics) or the collaborative technology used (e.g., videoconferencing or application sharing). By focusing instead on goals, challenges, and the types of information and resources shared, the coauthors took steps to form a truly cross-disciplinary understanding of the collaboratory phenomena.

Chapter 4 takes the theory building a step further by laying the groundwork for causal models that might help to predict collaboratory success. The theory of remote scientific collaboration hypothesizes relationships between predictors of success (the nature of the work; common ground; collaboration readiness; management, planning, and decision making; and technology readiness) and an expansive list of success measures that was generated at an early SOC workshop (see introduction, this volume). Starting with this framework should make it easier for future contributors to design both empirical investigations (e.g., testing any subset of the hypothesized links between factors and success metrics) and theoretical expansions (e.g., challenging or modifying the lists of factors and success metrics).

These two chapters are not the only ones that contribute to a science of collaboratories, however. Every chapter in this book was chosen because it brings the study of long-distance scientific collaboration closer to being a science by identifying issues, vocabulary, metrics, and conceptual frameworks, and most important, building up the cumulative case knowledge of the field. It is still true, though, that these pieces are not yet drawn together into a well-established and coherent field of study.

In this concluding chapter, we describe the way toward a true science of collaboratories. We will first explore the disciplinary roots of this proposed new science. Five disciplinary areas will be discussed, and their contributions to an emerging science of collaboratories will be weighed. These areas are: computer science, science and technology studies (STS), management science, the field of information, and behavioral economics. Of course, even these labels are gross oversimplifications; figure C.1 attempts to lay out subdisciplines in a slightly more comprehensive way. Nevertheless, this rough attempt to trace disciplinary origins has value in understanding the way forward. In the final sections of this chapter, we will look at the recent cyberinfrastructure initiative and other emerging trends.

Adventures in Cross-Disciplinary Research

In the effort to create a science of collaboratories, we are not starting from scratch; there are numerous existing disciplinary traditions from which to draw. Figure C.1 shows a set of influences, and tries to represent their contribution by their proximity,

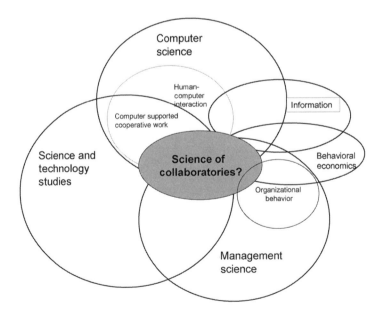

Figure C.1
Disciplinary influences on the SOC

size, and the degree of overlap. We will discuss how this emerging science is drawing from its home discipline of computer science, two other major influences—STS and management science—and last but not least, the broad and evolving field of information as well as the area of behavioral economics.

No author or chapter can be easily pigeonholed into a particular domain—each contributor has worked in multiple disciplinary areas and draws on various theoretical frameworks to inform their work. Yet each has influences, some of which are more readily apparent than others. We may better understand the disciplinary roots of a proposed science of collaboratories by analyzing some of these influences.

Computer Science and the Science of Collaboratories

The impetus and funding for the study of collaboratories per se has come primarily from computer science. Many early projects calling themselves collaboratories involved computer scientists and were funded by the National Science Foundation's (NSF) Computer and Information Science and Engineering (CISE) Directorate or the Department of Energy's Collaboratories 2000 program. The SOC project was also supported by the NSF-CISE through the Information Technology Research program.

A focus on emerging technology has been a strong point of collaboratory research to date. Within this book, chapter 6 ("A National User Facility That Fits on Your Desk") may best exemplify this perspective. This chapter details the technology challenges of designing a complete collaboration tool kit, including what were then bleeding-edge technologies such as screen sharing and videoconferencing, while still providing for basic needs such as security and access control. Chapter 6 identifies issues that remain core problems for technology development in this area; these challenges are enumerated later in this section as computer science research questions.

The experiences described in chapter 6 also show why a science of collaboratories must look beyond computer science, as the Environmental Molecular Sciences Laboratory's work quickly took it into nontechnical problems related to promoting user acceptance and the adoption of technology, providing long-term support for its use, and accommodating inevitable technological change. Within the computer science tradition, there are some nontechnical traditions to draw from, such as research in human-computer interaction with its focus on user-centered design, and computer-supported cooperative work with its emphasis on developing technology to support groups as well as individual users. Yet neither of these subdisciplines by themselves offers a comprehensive theoretical framework or a large enough community of researchers to address the range of issues facing collaboratories.

It is also important to ask about the advantages and limitations of investigating the science of collaboratories from the perspective of computer science alone. A science of collaboratories must respond rapidly to changes in computer science infrastructure in order to stay relevant. In the area of large-scale science, the previous decades have seen the focus shift to and from technologies related to information retrieval, metadata and ontologies, digital libraries, interface design, middleware, grid technologies, and security, to name just a few. Each of these areas has social and behavioral issues associated with it. It takes a commitment from researchers to keep up with the changing technological landscape, and a trained eye to be able to distinguish what is truly useful and worth the investment of time to explore or adopt. Good relationships between computer scientists, technologists, domain scientists, funding agencies, and others are a key part of technology development and diffusion, as many chapters in this volume make clear.

The rapidly changing nature of computer science research presents a problem for a science of collaboratories. The constant turnover of new technologies creates new research opportunities, but it also makes it difficult to pursue a coherent study of related issues. By the time those seeking to form a collaboratory have identified the most salient questions related to, for example, remote instrument sharing, the focus of the field (and the associated funding) may have moved on to another topic. To be considered a science, a science of collaboratories must develop a coherent research agenda along with a set of core problems and approaches that go beyond the latest technological trends. Thus, researchers interested in collaboratories must draw from ideas and concepts outside the discipline of computer science. That said, the following computer science–related research questions and topics are ones that we identified as crucial to the further development of a science of collaboratories; there are certain to be others as well.

- *Design* What kind of user-centered design methods are appropriate for collaboratories? There has been a move from studies of how software works for individual or small groups of users, to a focus on how entire systems work for large, distributed groups (e.g., Star 1999; Zimmerman and Nardi 2006). The latter is particularly relevant for the design of middleware and grid technologies.

- *Adoption* What adoption/diffusion issues are unique to scientific communities? Chapter 13's discussion of the role of participant leaders is relevant to this question. Other explorations in this volume that provide insights into this question include chapters 6, 16, and 19.

- *Commercial versus custom software* Should the development of collaboratory technologies focus on specialized tools designed for particular disciplines or on general-purpose tools that can be reused? Similarly, what is the role of commercial off-the-shelf software versus researcher-developed tools?

- *The digital divide* International collaboratories will continue to struggle with integrating the technology "haves" and "have-nots." This topic is treated in chapters 19 and 20. The further globalization of science seems inevitable. As science grows in scale and cost, it may become an economic necessity for large-scale collaboratories to tap intellectual resources in countries with less infrastructure.

• *Cyberinfrastructure*   This is a new broad-based initiative to ensure that scientists and engineers will have the most advanced as well as appropriate information and communication technologies available to support their work. We describe these efforts in more detail later in this conclusion.

Management Science

The trend in collaboratory research has been toward larger-scale efforts. This development necessitates a new research focus on the complex and unique management issues of distributed scientific collaborations that involve potentially thousands of people. There is, however, little tradition in the management literature on the study of scientific organizations. When several authors in this volume proposed a symposium to the Academy of Management a few years ago, the submission did not fit into any special-interest group, nor was there a conference track where the symposium could be easily placed. Still, we did find positive and open-minded reviewers, suggesting that that field is ready to grow in the area of the study of scientific organizations. And by necessity, a science of collaboratories must dramatically increase its base of knowledge related to management and governance.

It will not be enough to simply take existing management theory, developed mostly to understand for-profit organizations, and apply it to scientific collaborations. Scientific communities have different purposes and ways of organizing themselves than do corporations (or government or nonprofit organizations, for that matter). A new management literature needs to be written to address scientific collaborations. A central goal of this book has been to build up the case knowledge on the management of collaboratories, particularly those that have persisted over time and have had a measure of success in sustaining participation. We wanted this volume to contain a wealth of information about the structure, organization, management practices, and challenges of a wide range of collaborations, and we believe we have succeeded in achieving that goal. The following chapters, in addition to the ones mentioned below, are among those that include substantive discussions of various management and coordination issues: "A Theory of Remote Scientific Collaboration" (chapter 4), "The National Virtual Observatory" (chapter 7), "High-Energy Physics: The Large Hadron Collider Collaborations" (chapter 8), "Organizing for Multidisciplinary Collaboration: The Case of the Geosciences Network" (chapter 17), and "NEESgrid: Lessons Learned for Future Cyberinfrastructure Development" (chapter 18).

As the editors, we encouraged the chapter authors to compare and contrast the governance practices they implemented or observed in collaboratories with other models such as those from the corporate or academic worlds. For example, Cummings and

Kiesler found that good management was a key to success for geographically distributed collaborations. Rogers and Onken noted that at least one of the glue grant projects, in some respects, "functions like a small biotech company." Other projects, such as the three biomedical collaboratories described by Teasley, Schleyer, Hemphill, and Cook, modeled their practices after collocated academic centers and employed collaboration technologies to facilitate distributed operations. Their comparative analysis is unique, and valuable in identifying the barriers and enablers that affected the adoption of technology within each center. Michener and Waide described the Long Term Ecological Research program, which extended the idea of a center to include a network of centers, supporting both within-site and cross-site activities. And other projects, such as the Biomedical Informatics Research Network—explored by Olson, Ellisman, James, Grethe, and Puetz—developed organizational forms that are even more loosely associated, yet are managing to take on some highly coordinated activities.

Our foray into the management of collaboratories has, by design, raised more questions than answers. Below, we highlight research questions and topics related to management that deserve further attention.

- *Size and scaling* Should the governance structure of a small collaboratory look radically different than that of a larger one? Should large-scale projects start out at their intended size (and funding levels), or begin small and grow? At what break points should different governance models be implemented?
- *Roles and responsibilities* What are the roles of a collaboratory leader? What roles should be left for internal or external advisory boards? What roles are best served by representative committees of scientists? How involved should funding agency personnel be in management and governance? These types of decisions have sometimes been taken seriously as the craft knowledge of academic leaders, but they have rarely been studied as research topics in their own right.
- *Matching governance to project goals and phases* As Michael Rogers pointed out, governance decisions made by different glue grant projects reflect different project goals.[1] For example, the Alliance for Cellular Signaling designed a tightly coordinated network of laboratories, rather than a looser affiliation, because it required a completely standardized data set. In contrast, the Inflammation and Host Response to Injury project focused on face-to-face meetings rather than videoconferencing because it needed to build trust between surgeons (see chapter 11, this volume). Is there a more comprehensive theory or perhaps a pattern language that can guide this matching? In addition, Rogers expects that governance should change across project phases. A management structure that worked well for the data collection and resource generation phase, may not work for the data analysis or application phases.
- *Incentives and motivation* What organizational features make independent scientists more willing to participate and sustain their participation in large-scale collaborative efforts? Insights into this question could also be informed by behavioral economics,

which is discussed further below. The management literature, however, has a somewhat broader view of motivation, and can draw on prior research on human resource management and organizational behavior to understand the organizational practices that tend to motivate different behaviors. In addition, researchers are different from other types of employees. This is reflected in various chapters of the book, such as in chapter 14's analysis of incentives for data sharing, and chapter 16's discussion of carrot-and-stick management. Chapter 8 describes a potentially crippling disincentive in high-energy physics collaborations, which occurs when younger scholars avoid large, long-term projects for fear that publishable results will not be produced in time to help them obtain jobs. These science-specific incentive and motivation issues have received almost no scrutiny in the management literature, but they would benefit greatly from that perspective.

• *Evaluation*   Closely tied to both management and motivation is the issue of evaluation. No matter what values are espoused in mission statements, over time those factors that are measurable tend to become more highly valued. The few established tools we have, such as publication rates and citation patterns, are inadequate to the job of measuring the variety of relevant outcomes. One important role of researchers will be to develop as well as validate new measures that will allow collaboratories to document and, ideally, quantify their successes in many categories. In this volume, chapter 11 looks at approaches employed by the National Institutes of Health to evaluate entire programs. Chapter 10 provides a fine-grained assessment of a particular collaboratory system. And chapter 4 lays out an agenda for a range of research in the area.

Science and Technology Studies (STS)

STS, sometimes also called the sociology of science or the history and philosophy of science, is an established field of study on the practices of scientists. Some of the classic works in these areas are: Thomas Kuhn's *The Structure of Scientific Revolutions* (1962), which demonstrated that the process of science was not just a slow aggregation of impartial facts but instead underwent paradigm shifts; Bruno Latour and Steve Woolgar's *Laboratory Life* (1979) pioneered the ethnographic study of scientific practice in context and laid out the analytic frameworks that are still used today; and Everett Rogers's *Diffusion of Innovation* (1962), now in its fifth edition (2003), helped establish the importance of social networks in the spread of new practices.

More recently, Thomas Hughes's study of the U.S. electric network (1983, 1989) spawned a research program in large sociotechnical systems. And even closer to the content of this book, historian Peter Galison's *Image and Logic* (1997) traced the rise of "big physics," as that community came to manage large-scale collaboration, remote instrumentation, data sharing, and even changes to the very concept of an experiment. As a multidisciplinary field positioned at the intersection of sociology, history, and the philosophy of science and technology, STS scholars have addressed many of the core issues described in this book.

In many ways, STS and management overlap in their choice of topics. Yet one way of understanding the unique approach of each is in its purpose. Management scholars have typically been interested in evaluation, prediction, and prescription, taking human organizations to be designed objects that must be actively managed. In contrast, STS scholars have tended to focus on thick descriptions that historically contextualize scientific phenomena—understanding knowledge production as a social activity—along with the sociopolitical consequences of science and technology. Researchers in STS frequently take a detached, analytic viewpoint, using methods from anthropology and history to explore the practice, organization, and institutions of science as extant phenomena. Management science and STS are most productively viewed as complementary rather than competing.

One analytic perspective that has proved fruitful in STS is to decompose organizations and practices into separate dimensions of space, time, artifacts (physical objects), and information. This viewpoint has influenced the field of management science and computer-supported cooperative work. For example, the often-reproduced matrix by Geraldine DeSanctis and R. Brent Gallupe (1987) shows time and space as separate dimensions.

Within this volume, the chapter titled "Ecology Transformed: The National Center for Ecological Analysis and Synthesis and the Changing Patterns of Ecological Research" (chapter 15) exemplifies the STS approach. This chapter is similar in topic to a number of others in this volume, but it is discernibly different in its disciplinary frame. The reader may find it particularly interesting to compare chapter 15 to chapter 16, which describes another successful and ongoing project in ecology, the Long Term Ecological Research Network. Chapter 16 takes the perspective of managers, and is organized under headings that a manager could easily parse and apply to other projects. Chapter 15, by contrast, is intended primarily to add to prior work in STS. It brings in Latour's (1987, 1999) concept of an "immutable mobile" to make an argument that knowledge may be less immutable over distance than previously assumed. Consistent with the tradition of using ethnomethodology, chapter 15 is also interested in the microprocess of how knowledge is coconstructed by participants. A large section of the chapter is devoted to a detailed description of the incidents surrounding one particular finding.

In spite of the rich contributions from STS, below we enumerate topics and questions for future investigation that are relevant to collaboratories.

• *Boundary objects* Boundary objects enable collaboration without consensus; they facilitate work across differences in research goals or disciplinary diversity. Are collaboratories inventing new kinds of boundary objects? Collaboratories frequently involve attempts to bridge gaps of institution, discipline, or national culture, and sometimes all of these at once. STS researchers often focus on the role of specific boundary-spanning objects in such attempts (e.g., Star and Griesemer 1989). Many of the infrastructure artifacts described in this book, such as the BIRN Smart Atlas and BIRN-in-a-Box (chapter 12) and the Geoscience Network's test beds (chapter 17), could be seen as boundary objects, and analyzed as such.

• *Management of space and time*   What is the role of face-to-face meetings and permanent collocation in fostering long-distance collaboration? Long-distance collaborations almost always involve some face-to-face contact, via travel, meetings, or sabbaticals and other forms of longer-term exchange. Among other contributions in this book, chapters 13, 15, 16, and 20 stress the usefulness of such contact. Travel is expensive, however, and so must be used judiciously. Previous STS studies of laboratory space may yield new insights into long-distance collaboration as well. Managing and sustaining collaborations over increasingly long spans of time is also a topic relevant to collaboratories, as illustrated in chapters 8 and 16. Chapter 20 looks at these issues as they involve scientists from the developing world, for whom collaboratories, despite their great promise, have not yet provided a way to fully integrate their participation into projects of interest to them.

• *Collaboratories in society*   STS researchers have long been interested in the interaction between scientific communities and the general public (see Star and Griesemer 1989; Irwin 2002). Many collaboratories are much more open to the outside than was previously typical in scientific projects, and some even invite direct contributions from non-professionals. Examples of these open collaboratories are discussed in chapter 3 under the heading of community contribution systems.

Other Perspectives

Two emerging disciplines are having an influence on the study of collaboratories: the study of information, and a more behaviorally oriented approach to economics.

Information

Schools of information are being rapidly formed at U.S. universities and elsewhere.[2] The SOC project, for example, was administered from within the University of Michigan's School of Information. Schools of information are sometimes created from scratch (such as the program at Pennsylvania State University), and other times they evolve from an existing program, such as a school of library science (e.g., at the University of Michigan and Syracuse University) or a computer science department (e.g., at the University of California, Irvine).

What unique perspectives do such schools bring to the study of collaboratories? As mentioned, STS researchers have often tried to understand scientific activity by decomposing phenomena along the dimensions of time, space, and objects. George Furnas, a

Table C.1
Collaboratory types by resource and activity

	Tools (instruments)	Information (data)	Knowledge (new findings)
Aggregating across distance (loose coupling, often asynchronously)	Shared instrument	Community data system	Virtual learning community, virtual community of practice
Cocreating across distance (requires tighter coupling, often synchronously)	Infrastructure	Open community contribution system	Distributed research center

Source: (Bos et al., this volume)

faculty member at the University of Michigan's School of Information, proposed an information-centric addition to this list at an early SOC workshop. He asked whether collaboratory activities could be divided into tiers based on the kind of information they generated—ranging from data, to information, to knowledge, to wisdom (following Ackoff 1989). This line of thinking prompted a great deal of discussion during and after the workshop. One attempt at applying this analysis made its way into this volume in chapter 3. In table C.1, collaboratory types are classified on two dimensions: the type of intellectual activity, and the type of information being processed. In this table, the Ackoff (1989) hierarchy is collapsed, data and information are grouped together, and knowledge also includes wisdom. We added a third column, "Tools," because so many collaboratories are focused on their development, although in some cases these are not physical tools but conceptual ones such as data standards.

Another contribution of the science of information may be the integration as well as application of ideas from the fields of library science and archival studies. Collaboratory participants often initially underestimate the difficulty of managing data and information, as pointed out a number of times in this book (e.g., chapters 7, 11, and 16). Library science and archival studies emphasize the development of metadata, indexing schemes, access standards, and good archiving practices, and are welcome additions to the science of collaboratories; they will be essential to the success of future collaboratories. These themes have surfaced in the NSF's initiatives in cyberinfrastructure, which are discussed further below.

Some research topics and questions for the information domain are articulated below.

• *Level of information* Do differences in the information-processing tasks of collaboratories map onto differences in organizational structure or management practices? An initial hypothesis might be that collaboratories primarily concerned with tools or information can be more tightly structured, relying on formal communications and including more contracted deliverables, while collaboratories involved with knowledge creation must be more flexibly structured to allow for innovation.

• *Long-term information management*   What are the best archiving practices for a collaboratory? How can a high-tech project plan for inevitable advances in storage, processing, and data standards? How can information be preserved as technologies change?

• *Metadata*   Organizing collections of data and information so they can be accessed and used later requires effective indexing, or metadata. Numerous collaboratory projects face this issue, particularly those that focus on creating extremely large or federated databases (e.g., chapter 1, this volume; chapter 7, this volume).

Behavioral Economics

The tools and concepts of economics are more and more frequently being applied to behavioral problems, and a science of collaboratories can benefit from this as well. A paper by Kan Takeuchi and his colleagues (2007) is an example of utilizing economic theory to design methods to allocate time on the large, expensive shake tables used in an earthquake engineering collaboratory. Allocating scarce resources is a common problem in collaboratories, and this line of research may find more general applications (e.g., chapter 18, this volume).

Another line of research that borrows from economics is the study of how incentives affect collaboration. Progress is being made in understanding how other types of online communities should be designed to maximize participation (e.g., Girgensohn and Lee 2002; Ludford et al. 2004; Preece and Maloney-Krichmar 2005). Chapter 14 in this volume on motivating contributions to community data systems uses literature from game theory and economic behavior to understand contributor motivation in collaboratories.

The field of economics also tends to be interested in government-level policymaking, which a science of collaboratories must consider. One interesting topic of investigation would be to assess the impact of the U.S. Bayh-Dole Act (1980). This act is widely credited with spurring technology transfer by allowing universities to profit from inventions supported by federal government–funded research. Its impacts, however, are not yet fully known or understood (Thursby and Thursby 2003), and there is concern in the collaboratory realm that the Bayh-Dole Act has made universities more protective of intellectual property and less open in forging multiuniversity collaborations. Some of the topics and questions for investigation within behavioral economics are listed below.

• *Resource allocation*   How should scarce resources, such as large shared instruments, be allocated? Are there algorithms that can allocate resources more efficiently or fairly than human committees are currently doing?

• *Internal competition*   How should collaboratories allocate internal resources, (e.g., funds and personnel) to maximize effectiveness? What kinds of internal competition should be encouraged, and what kinds would undermine cooperation?

• *Science policy*   How can science policymakers most effectively distribute their funds and structure their programs? What are the comparative rates of return from small versus large, or national versus international, collaboratories?

• *Intellectual property law*   How do national and international intellectual property laws help or hinder collaboratories? What changes would spur innovation as well as promote sharing?

Cyberinfrastructure: The Next Big Push

In the past few years, particularly in the United States, the term cyberinfrastructure has come into common use. In chapter 18 on NEESgrid, the coauthors note that cyberinfrastructure is used to join resources (e.g., instruments), people, and data via computer-supported systems. Much of the impetus for cyberinfrastructure came from a report published by the NSF in 2003 (Atkins et al. 2003). This document laid out a vision of how science and engineering could be done in the future, taking advantage of the advances in information and communication technologies. The report called on the NSF to create an overarching program that would facilitate the development of cyberinfrastructure.

In 2004, such an office came into being, initially within the CISE Directorate. The program was reorganized in 2005 as the Office of Cyberinfrastructure and moved to the Office of the Director. This gave it organizationally a status that spanned all of the NSF. In 2006, Dan Atkins, lead author of the 2003 NSF report, became the head of the Office of Cyberinfrastructure.

The vision of cyberinfrastructure presented in the NSF report was broad. It covered not only high-end computing and networking but the full range of tools needed to accelerate progress in science. Figure C.2 shows more specifically what kinds of capabilities were proposed as cyberinfrastructure functions.

Recently, the NSF's Cyberinfrastructure Council (2007) published a report titled *Cyberinfrastructure Vision for 21st Century Discovery*. This report lays out the primary priorities for the Office of Cyberinfrastructure in the coming years. There are four areas of emphasis:

• *High-performance computing*   Many areas of science require high- end computing resources—in the terascale or petascale range—for the modeling, simulation, and analysis of huge data sets (see, e.g., chapter 1, this volume). In cooperation with other government agencies, universities, and industry, the NSF has taken the lead in creating and sustaining such computing resources, including the provision of appropriate software and tools to make such resources as widely useful as possible.

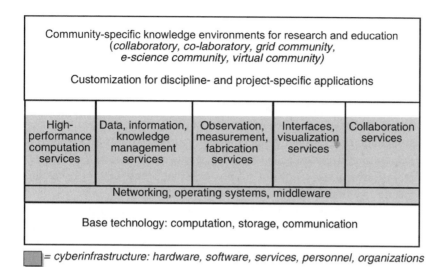

Community-specific knowledge environments for research and education
(*collaboratory, co-laboratory, grid community,
e-science community, virtual community*)

Customization for discipline- and project-specific applications

High-performance computation services	Data, information, knowledge management services	Observation, measurement, fabrication services	Interfaces, visualization services	Collaboration services

Networking, operating systems, middleware

Base technology: computation, storage, communication

= *cyberinfrastructure: hardware, software, services, personnel, organizations*

Figure C.2

Integrated cyberinfrastructure services to enable new knowledge environments for research and education (figure from Atkins et al. 2003, 13)

- *Data, data analysis, and visualization*   As indicated by the surveys cited in the Atkins report, data are probably the most central element of scientific and engineering research. We are witnessing an explosion in the amount of data in all areas, as new sensing and networks make possible the collection and aggregation of large data sets. We have seen examples of this throughout the cases in this volume (in, e.g., chapters 1, 7, and 8). The NSF cyberinfrastructure initiatives hope to ensure that the large repositories that result will be well documented, easily shareable, and well preserved. Along the same lines, tools to support the access, analysis, and display of data must be developed as needed for the various areas of science.

- *Virtual organizations for distributed communities*   Virtual organizations offer flexible, secure, and coordinated resource sharing among dynamic collections of individuals, institutions, and resources (Foster, Kesselman, and Tuecke 2001), and are at the heart of the collaboratory vision discussed in this book (see, e.g., chapters 1 and 2, this volume). For the many reasons we have illustrated here, such organizations can be effective, but they are also hard to create and maintain. We believe that the research reported in this volume goes a long way toward identifying those factors that can help facilitate successful virtual organizations.

- *Learning and workforce development*   The elements of cyberinfrastructure that enhance research can also enhance learning. Opportunities for mentoring and experience-based learning can abound in the kinds of virtual organizations enabled by cyberinfrastructure. This can have positive affects for education at all levels. In addition, specific focus needs to be given to the development of expertise in cyberinfrastructure so that cyberinfrastructure-enabled science can flourish in the future.

The Next Generation of Collaboratories

This volume is best seen as a report on the state of the art of collaboratories in the early twenty-first century. We have come a long way from the visionary statements of William A. Wulf (1989) and the National Research Council (1993). The issues involved in creating and maintaining successful collaboratories are much more subtle and complex than these early visions realized. To put it simply, experience has shown us that success involves much more than the technology.

So where are we going? It is important to see the emergence of collaboratories as an evolutionary stage. Much scientific research has been collaborative for a long time, and certainly there were technologies to support such collaboration long before the Internet. So the emergence of collaboratories for scientific research is a continuation of long-standing trends. What is perhaps new is the greater richness and variety of options for supporting scientific collaboration. There are numerous possibilities for person-to-person communication, data are easier to aggregate and share, and remote access to scientific instruments has improved. In sum, as political, scientific, and social demands make collaboration more and more necessary, there is concomitantly better technology to support it.

In this volume we have surveyed a broad range of examples of collaboratories past and present. These efforts now span all areas of science, and indeed they are beginning to penetrate the humanities, too. Project Guttenberg's Distributed Proofreaders is an instance from this realm (Newby and Franks 2003). But as we have also seen, merely embarking on a collaboratory effort is no guarantee of success. A host of factors, reviewed most succinctly in chapter 4 (this volume), can affect the success or failure of a collaboratory. As chapter 4 made clear, these are familiar issues for any socially organized activity, but the introduction of geographic dispersion as an added element complicates the situation. Geographically dispersed collaborations are difficult to carry out successfully, and such efforts must pay even more attention to sociotechnical influences. We hope that by making these factors explicit and illustrating them with concrete examples, we can enable greater success for collaboratories in the future. In the past two decades we have been self-conscious about collaboratories. But as the elements of such organizations transition to common infrastructure, we may take such organizations for granted in the future.

We close this volume by considering the question, What next? In our view, there are several trends that will affect how collaboratories emerge in the coming decades.

▪ *The technology infrastructure* The simplest projection to make is that the technology available to support collaboratories will continue to evolve. There is every indication that tomorrow's scientists will enjoy a steady increase in computational power, available memory and storage, networking bandwidth, and network security.

• *Social technologies*   One of the biggest growth areas in the past few years has been social technologies, including blogs, wikis, recommender systems, instant messaging, awareness systems, and folksonomies, which offer new opportunities for collaboratories. Further, even traditional technologies like videoconferencing are giving much more attention to what we might call "social ergonomics," which include things such as gaze direction, eye contact, and other features (Nguyen and Canny 2005). For instance, 3-D audio for audio conferencing is being explored (Gardner 1998; Lumbreras and Sánchez 1999; Leung and Chen 2003). The point to be made here is that as technology develops, more attention is being given to the crucial social and ergonomic issues that may make these technologies more useful for human collaborations.

• *Cohort changes*   When Jonathan Grudin and Leysia Palen (1995) updated Grudin's (1994) quite negative assessment of collaborative technologies, one thing they observed was that the population of users was changing. People using the new technologies had different experiences and were more comfortable with many of the aspects of collaborative tools. We believe the same situation will occur with regard to collaboratories. Many of today's senior scientists grew up in a different world, without all the tools that have now become common. In our own work we have seen more resistance among senior scientists to using new tools, but the younger scientists emerging now have a different history. Instant messaging, blogs, voice-over Internet protocol, and many other technologies are taken for granted by a new generation of researchers. As these young scientists move into positions of influence, the adoption patterns of collaboration tools will certainly change, although not always in ways that we can anticipate.

• *Consolidation of knowledge about successful collaboratories*   As evidenced by the reports in this book, we are learning what it takes to succeed in a collaboratory. As investigators themselves and their funding agencies become more familiar with these lessons, different standards will be imposed on projects. Findings such as those reported in this volume will influence which projects get supported, and how they evolve. The more these results are widely shared, the more success we will see. But we need to be careful here. There are many areas where we know what to do to succeed, but where the knowledge and lessons are not followed. We cannot be passive about such matters. If the experiences and knowledge reported in this volume (and elsewhere) can help to shape future projects, however, this book will have succeeded in its goal.

Notes

1. Personal communication with the authors, June 10, 2007.

2. For example, the I-School Project consists of academic units interested in the relationship between information, technology, and people. See ⟨http://www.ischools.org/oc/⟩.

References

Ackoff, R .L. 1989. From data to wisdom. *Journal of Applied Systems Analysis* 16:3–9.

Atkins, D. E., K. Droegemeier, S. Feldman, H. Garcia-Molina, M. L. Klein, D. G. Messerschmitt et al. 2003. *Revolutionizing science and engineering through cyberinfrastructure: Report of the National Science Foundation Blue-Ribbon Advisory Panel on Cyberinfrastructure*. Arlington, VA: National Science Foundation.

Bayh-Dole Act. 1980. Public law 96–517.

DeSanctis, G., and B. Gallupe. 1987. A foundation for the study of group decision support systems. *Management Science* 33 (5): 589–609.

Foster, I., C. Kesselman, and S. Tuecke. 2001. The anatomy of the grid: Enabling scalable virtual organizations. *International Journal of High Performance Computing Applications* 15 (3): 200–222.

Galison, P. L. 1997. *Image and logic: A material culture of microphysics*. Chicago: University of Chicago Press.

Gardner, W. G. 1998. 3-D audio using loudspeakers. Boston: Kluwer Academic.

Girgensohn, A., and A. Lee. 2002. Making Web sites be places for social interaction. In *Proceedings of the 2002 conference on computer-supported cooperative work*, 136–145. New York: ACM Press.

Grudin, J. 1994. Groupware and social dynamics: Eight challenges for developers. *Communications of the ACM* 37 (1): 93–104.

Grudin, J., and L. Palen. 1995. Why groupware succeeds: Discretion or mandate. In *Proceedings of the fourth European conference on computer-supported cooperative work*, ed. H. Marmolin, Y. Sundblad, and K. Schmidt, 263–278. Boston: Kluwer Academic.

Hughes, T. P. 1983. *Networks of power: Electrification in Western society, 1880–1930*. Baltimore, MD: Johns Hopkins University Press.

Hughes, T. P. 1989. The evolution of large technological systems. In *The social construction of technical systems*, ed. W. E. Bijker, T. P. Hughes, and T. J. Pinch, 51–82. Cambridge, MA: MIT Press.

Irwin, A. 2002. The politics of talk: Coming to terms with the "new" scientific governance. *Social Studies of Science* 32:235–296.

Kuhn, T. S. 1962. *The structure of scientific revolutions*. Chicago: University of Chicago Press.

Latour, B. 1987. *Science in action*. Cambridge, MA: Harvard University Press.

Latour, B. 1999. *Pandora's hope*. Cambridge, MA: Harvard University Press.

Latour, B., and S. Woolgar. 1979. *Laboratory life: The social construction of scientific facts*. Beverly Hills, CA: Sage Publications.

Leung, W. H., and T. Chen. 2003. A multi-user 3-D virtual environment with interactive collaboration and shared whiteboard technologies. *Journal of Multimedia Tools and Applications* 20 (1): 7–23.

Ludford, P. J., D. Cosely, D. Frankowski, and L. Terveen. 2004. Think different: Increasing online community participation using uniqueness and group dissimilarity. In *Proceedings of the SIGCHI conference on human factors in computing systems*, 631–638. New York: ACM Press.

Lumbreras, M., and J. Sánchez. 1999. Interactive 3D sound hyperstories for blind children. In *Proceedings of the SIGCHI conference on human factors in computing systems*, 318–325. New York: ACM Press.

National Research Council, Committee on a National Collaboratory. 1993. *National collaboratories: Applying information technology for scientific research*. Washington, DC: National Academies Press.

National Science Foundation (NSF), Cyberinfrastructure Council. 2007. *Cyberinfrastructure vision for 21st century discovery*. Arlington, VA: National Science Foundation. Available at ⟨http://www .nsf.gov/pubs/2007/nsf0728/index.jsp⟩ (accessed July 6, 2007).

Newby, G. B., and C. Franks. 2003. Distributed proofreading. In *Proceedings of the 3rd ACM/IEEE-CS joint conference on digital libraries*, 361–363. Washington, DC: IEEE Computer Society.

Nguyen, D., and J. Canny. 2005. Multiview: Spatially faithful video conferencing. In *Proceedings of the SIGCHI conference on human factors in computing systems*, 799–808. New York: ACM Press.

Preece, J., and D. Maloney-Krichmar. 2005. Online communities: Design, theory, and practice. *Journal of Computer-Mediated Communication* 10 (4): article 1. Available at ⟨http://jcmc.indiana .edu/vol10/issue4/preece.html⟩ (accessed July 6, 2007).

Rogers, E. M. 1962. *Diffusion of innovations*. New York: Free Press of Glencoe.

Rogers, E. M. 2003. *Diffusion of innovations*. 5th ed. New York: Free Press.

Star, S. L. 1999. The ethnography of infrastructure. *American Behavioral Scientist* 43 (3): 377–391.

Star, S. L., and J. R. Griesemer. 1989. Institutional ecology, "translations," and boundary objects: Amateurs and professionals in Berkeley's Museum of Vertebrate Zoology, 1907–39. *Social Studies of Science* 19:387–420.

Takeuchi, K., J. Lin, Y. Chen, and T. Finholt. 2007. Shake it up baby: Scheduling with package auctions. *Proceedings of the ACM Conference on Electronic Commerce* 8:113.

Thursby, J. G., and C. Thursby. 2003. University licensing and the Bayh-Dole Act. *Science* 301 (5636): 1052.

Wulf, W. A. 1989. The national collaboratory: A white paper. In *Towards a national collaboratory: Report of an invitational workshop at the Rockefeller University, March 17–18, 1989*, ed. J. Lederberg and K. Uncaphar, appendix A. Washington, DC: National Science Foundation, Directorate for Computer and Information Science Engineering.

Zimmerman, A., and B. A. Nardi. 2006. Whither or whether HCI: Requirements analysis for multi-sited, multi-user cyberinfrastructures. In *CHI '06 Extended Abstracts on Human Factors in Computing Systems*, 1601–1606. New York: ACM Press.

Contributors

Mark S. Ackerman
School of Information and
Computer Science and Engineering
University of Michigan
Ann Arbor, MI

Paul Avery
Department of Physics
University of Florida
Gainesville, FL

Matthew Bietz
School of Information
University of Michigan
Ann Arbor, MI

Jeremy P. Birnholtz
Department of Communication
Cornell University
Ithaca, NY

Nathan Bos
Applied Physics Laboratory
Johns Hopkins University
Laurel, MD

Geoffrey C. Bowker
Center for Science, Technology, and
Society
Santa Clara University
Santa Clara, CA

Randal Butler
National Center for Supercomputing
Applications
University of Illinois at Urbana-
Champaign
Urbana, IL

David Conz
School of Interdisciplinary Studies and
Center for Nanotechnology in Society
Arizona State University
Tempe, AZ

Eric Cook
School of Information
University of Michigan
Ann Arbor, MI

Daniel Cooney
Cooney Information Group, LLC
Ann Arbor, MI

Jonathon N. Cummings
Fuqua School of Business
Duke University
Durham, NC

Erik Dahl
MAYA Design, Inc.
Pittsburgh, PA

Mark Ellisman
Departments of Neurosciences and
Bioengineering
University of California at San Diego
La Jolla, CA

Ixchel Faniel
School of Information
University of Michigan
Ann Arbor, MI

Thomas A. Finholt
School of Information
University of Michigan
Ann Arbor, MI

Ian Foster
Department of Computer Science
University of Chicago
Chicago, IL

Jefffrey S. Grethe
Biomedical Informatics Research Network
University of California at San Diego
La Jolla, CA

Edward J. Hackett
School of Human Evolution and Social
Change
Arizona State University
Tempe, AZ

Robert J. Hanisch
Space Telescope Science Institute
Baltimore, MD

Libby Hemphill
School of Information
University of Michigan
Ann Arbor, MI

Tony Hey
Microsoft Corporation
Redmond, WA

Erik C. Hofer
School of Information
University of Michigan
Ann Arbor, MI

Mark James
Biomedical Informatics Research Network
University of California at San Diego
La Jolla, CA

Carl Kesselman
Information Sciences Institute
University of Southern California
Marina del Rey, CA

Sara Kiesler
Human-Computer Interaction Institute
School of Computer Science
Carnegie Mellon University
Pittsburgh, PA

Timothy L. Killeen
National Center for Atmospheric
Research
Boulder, CO

Airong Luo
School of Information
University of Michigan
Ann Arbor, MI

Kelly L. Maglaughlin
School of Information and Library
Science
University of North Carolina at Chapel
Hill
Chapel Hill, NC

Doru Marcusiu
National Center for Supercomputing
Applications
University of Illinois at Urbana-
Champaign
Urbana, IL

Shawn McKee
Department of Physics
University of Michigan
Ann Arbor, MI

William K. Michener
Long Term Ecological Research Network
Office
Department of Biology
University of New Mexico
Albuquerque, NM

James D. Myers
National Center for Supercomputing
Applications
University of Illinois at Urbana-
Champaign
Urbana, IL

Marsha Naidoo
ICAM: International Co-ordination and
Management
Pretoria, South Africa

Michael Nentwich
Institute of Technology Assessment
Austrian Academy of Sciences
Vienna, Austria

Gary M. Olson
School of Information
University of Michigan
Ann Arbor, MI

Judith S. Olson
School of Information
University of Michigan
Ann Arbor, MI

James Onken
Office of the Director
Office of Research Information Systems
National Institutes of Health
Bethesda, MD

Andrew Parker
Department of Sociology
Stanford University
Stanford, CA

John N. Parker
National Center for Ecological Analysis
and Synthesis
Santa Barbara, CA
Barrett Honors College
Arizona State University
Tempe, AZ

Mary Puetz
Information Management Consultant
Washington, DC

David Ribes
School of Information
University of Michigan
Ann Arbor, MI

Kathleen Ricker
National Center for Supercomputing
Applications
University of Illinois at Urbana-
Champaign
Urbana, IL

Diana Rhoten
Social Science Research Council
New York, NY

Michael E. Rogers
Pharmacology, Physiology, and Biological
Chemistry Division
National Institute of General Medical
Sciences
National Institutes of Health
Bethesda, MD

Titus Schleyer
University of Pittsburgh
School of Dental Medicine
Center for Dental Informatics
Pittsburgh, PA

Diane H. Sonnenwald
Swedish School of Information and
Library Science
Göteborg University and University
College of Borås
Borås, Sweden

B. F. Spencer Jr.
Department of Civil and Environmental
Engineering
University of Illinois at Urbana-
Champaign
Urbana, IL

Stephanie D. Teasley
School of Information
University of Michigan
Ann Arbor, MI

Anne Trefethen
Oxford e-Research Centre
Oxford, England

Robert B. Waide
Long Term Ecological Research Network
Office
Department of Biology
University of New Mexico
Albuquerque, NM

Mary C. Whitton
Department of Computer Science
University of North Carolina at Chapel
Hill
Chapel Hill, NC

William A. Wulf
Department of Computer Science
School of Engineering and Applied
Science
University of Virginia
Charlottesville, VA

Jason Yerkie
Corporate Executive Board
Washington, DC

Jude Yew
School of Information
University of Michigan
Ann Arbor, MI

Ann Zimmerman
School of Information
University of Michigan
Ann Arbor, MI

Index